Anglo-Saxon Studies 4

DYING AND DEATH IN LATER
ANGLO-SAXON ENGLAND

D1520055

Anglo-Saxon Studies

ISSN 1475-2468

General Editors

John Hines

Catherine Cubitt

'Anglo-Saxon Studies' aims to provide a forum for the best scholarship on the Anglo-Saxon peoples in the period from the end of Roman Britain to the Norman Conquest, including comparative studies involving adjacent populations and periods; both new research and major re-assessments of central topics are welcomed.

Books in the series may be based in any one of the principal disciplines of archaeology, art history, history, language and literature, and inter- or multi-disciplinary studies are encouraged.

Proposals or enquiries may be sent directly to the editors or the publisher at the addresses given below; all submissions will receive prompt and informed consideration.

Professor John Hines, School of History and Archaeology, Cardiff University, Colum Drive, Cardiff, Wales, UK CF10 3EU

Dr Catherine Cubitt, Centre for Medieval Studies, University of York, The King's Manor, York, England, UK YO1 7EP

Boydell & Brewer, PO Box 9, Woodbridge, Suffolk, England, UK IP12 3DF

Previously published volumes in the series
are listed at the back of this book

DYING AND DEATH IN LATER ANGLO-SAXON ENGLAND

Victoria Thompson

THE BOYDELL PRESS

First published 2004
The Boydell Press, Woodbridge
Reprinted in paperback and transferred to digital printing 2012

ISBN 978-1-84383-070-2 hardback
ISBN 978-1-84383-731-2 paperback

The Boydell Press is an imprint of Boydell & Brewer Ltd
PO Box 9, Woodbridge, Suffolk IP12 3DF, UK
and of Boydell & Brewer Inc.
668 Mount Hope Ave, Rochester, NY 14620-2731, USA
website: www.boydellandbrewer.com

A CIP catalogue record for this book is available
from the British Library

Library of Congress Catalog Card Number: 200302803

Papers used by Boydell & Brewer Ltd are natural, recycled products
Made from wood grown in sustainable forests

Printed and bound in Great Britain by
CPI Group (UK) Ltd, Croydon CR0 4YY

Contents

Illustrations

Acknowledgements

In writing this book I have incurred debts of many kinds, to friends and family as well as to those who have helped and guided me intellectually (and these categories are by no means mutually exclusive). I have been greatly assisted by the staff of the British Library, the Bodleian Library, and the faculty of the Centre for Medieval Studies at the University of York. I am more grateful than I can say for the emotional and intellectual support of Chris, Alison (and Matthew) Daniell, Edward James and Farah Mendlesohn, Katherine Lewis, Noel James, Joanna Huntington, Susie Holden, Lucy Hunter, Jessica Haydon and Sophie Holroyd. I am also indebted beyond measure to Helen Gittos, John Blair, Sarah Semple, Andrew Reynolds, Sam Turner, Howard Williams, Felicity Clark, Jane Hawkes, Kellie Meyer, Alice Cowen, Philip Shaw, Simon Trafford, Aleks Pluskowski and Nick Orchard for their patience in hearing me out and their unstinting generosity with their own ideas. Aleks Pluskowski was equally generous in illustrating the sculpture from Masham, Middleton and Newent. Ben Whitworth rescued me at the eleventh hour from much stylistic awkwardness. Thanks are due to the British Library and Dr Aleks Pluskowski for permission to reproduce images in this book. My deepest debts are to my father, my sisters and my brother, and above all my mother, to whom this book is dedicated.

SHEILA MARY THOMPSON (NÉE GUISE-MOORES)
18 JUNE 1927 – 26 MARCH 2002
Study to be like her

Abbreviations

ASE	*Anglo-Saxon England*
Assmann	B. Assmann (ed.), *Angelsächsiche Homilien und Heiligenleben* (reprinted Darmstadt, 1964)
BAR	British Archaeological Reports
BL	British Library
Bodl.	Bodleian Library
CASSS	*Corpus of Anglo-Saxon Stone Sculpture*
CBA	Council for British Archaeology
CCCC	Cambridge, Corpus Christi College
CCSL	Corpus Christianorum, Series Latina
CH Comm.	M. Godden (ed.), *Ælfric's Catholic Homilies: Introduction, Commentary and Glossary*, EETS SS 18 (Oxford, 2000)
CH I	P. Clemoes (ed.), *Ælfric's Catholic Homilies, the First Series, Text*, EETS SS 17 (Oxford, 1997)
CH II	M. Godden (ed.), *Ælfric's Catholic Homilies, the Second Series, Text*, EETS SS 5 (Oxford, 1979)
Councils	D. Whitelock, M. Brett and C. N. L. Brooke (eds), *Councils and Synods of Great Britain with Other Documents Relating to the English Church. Volume I. Part 1, 871–1066; Part 2, 1066–1204* (Oxford, 1981)
CSASE	Cambridge Studies in Anglo-Saxon England
EEMF	Early English Manuscripts in Facsimile
EETS	Early English Text Society
EHD	*English Historical Documents*
EHR	*English Historical Review*
HBS	Henry Bradshaw Society
HE	Bede, *Ecclesiastical History of the English People*, ed. B. Colgrave and R. A. B. Mynors (Oxford, 1969)
JBAA	*Journal of the British Archaeological Association*
JEGP	*Journal of English and Germanic Philology*
LS I	W. Skeat (ed.), *Ælfric's Lives of Saints*, Volume I, EETS 76 and 82 (reprinted in one volume, Cambridge, 1999)
LS II	W. Skeat (ed.), *Ælfric's Lives of Saints*, Volume II, EETS 94 and 114 (reprinted in one volume, Oxford, 1966)
Napier	A. S. Napier (ed.), *Wulfstan: Sammlung der ihm zugeschriebenen Homilien nebst Untersuchungen über ihre Echtheit* (Zürich, 1967)

NM	*Neuphilologische Mitteilungen*
OS	Ordinary Series
PL	*Patrologia Latina*, ed. J. P. Migne, 221 vols (Paris, 1844–64)
Raunds	A. Boddington, *Raunds Furnells: The Anglo-Saxon Church and Churchyard*, English Heritage Archaeological Report 7 (London, 1996)
RS	Rolls Series
S	P. H. Sawyer, *Anglo-Saxon Charters: An Annotated List and Bibliography*, Royal Historical Society Guides and Handbooks 8 (London, 1968)
SS	Supplementary Series
Supp.	J. C. Pope (ed.), *Homilies of Ælfric, A Supplementary Series*, 2 vols. EETS 259 and 260 (Oxford, 1967 and 1968)
TRHS	*Transactions of the Royal Historical Society*

Unless specified otherwise, all quotations of Anglo-Saxon poetry are taken from the relevant volume of *The Anglo-Saxon Poetic Records*, 6 vols, ed. G. Krapp and E. Dobbie (New York, 1931–53).

Introduction

In mid-June, 918, a woman's corpse was carried a hundred kilometres across the West Midlands, from her death-bed in Tamworth to her grave in Gloucester.[1] The body was that of Æthelflæd, Lady of the Mercians (*c*. 870–918), eldest child of Alfred the Great, but there is little more to be said with certainty about this funeral.[2] We do not know exactly how old she was, how she died or what kind of medical treatment she may have had, whether her body went by ox-cart or barge, whether she was embalmed or shrouded, carried in a coffin or on a bier. Nor can we say who attended her body on its last journey, who presided at her funeral, how elaborate that funeral was, what kind of grave awaited her or what monument stood over it. We do not know how those who mourned expressed their emotions, or how they commemorated her. Nonetheless, Æthelflæd is a good case study with which to begin this book. There are other questions which *can* be answered about her encounters throughout life with the dying, dead and buried, and we can make many more informed guesses. Also, paradoxically, the very fact that so many areas of ignorance can be pinpointed in this particular case demonstrates how much can be known, more generally, about high-status funerals in the last two centuries of Anglo-Saxon England. An analysis of Æthelflæd's experiences introduces many sources, questions and ideas, while never letting us forget how much has vanished and how, as Wormald puts it, 'as Anglo-Saxonists, we cultivate the borders of prehistory'.[3]

A close look at Æthelflæd may show up the shortcomings of many of our sources but it also illuminates their riches. The necessarily speculative study which opens this book not only looks at Æthelflæd's own burial, it also traces how her living experience was shaped by encounters with death, funerals, corpses, monuments, relics and intercessory prayer. No direct account provides the information

---

[1] *S.a.* 918 in S. Taylor (ed.), *The Anglo-Saxon Chronicle: A Collaborative Edition. Volume 4: MS B* (Cambridge, 1983); K. O'Keeffe (ed.), *The Anglo-Saxon Chronicle: A Collaborative Edition. Volume 5: MS C* (Cambridge, 2001); G. P. Cubbin (ed.), *The Anglo-Saxon Chronicle, A Collaborative Edition, Volume 6: MS D* (Cambridge, 1996).

[2] F. T. Wainwright, 'Æthelflæd, Lady of the Mercians', in H. P. R. Finberg (ed.), *Scandinavian England: Collected Papers by F. T. Wainwright* (Chichester, 1975), pp. 305–24; R. Abels, *Alfred the Great: War, Kingship and Culture in Anglo-Saxon England* (London and New York, 1998), pp. 121–2 and 230; S. Keynes, 'King Alfred and the Mercians', in M. Blackburn and D. N. Dumville (eds), *Kings, Currency and Alliances: History and Coinage of Southern England in the Ninth Century* (Woodbridge, 1998), pp. 1–45, 9–10.

[3] P. Wormald, *How Do We Know So Much about Anglo-Saxon Deerhurst?*, Deerhurst Lecture 1991 (The Friends of Deerhurst Church, 1992), p. 1.

sought here about Æthelflæd, and in this she is typical: no English layperson is visible in much more detail until we reach Edward (the Confessor) in 1066. But she may be approached obliquely through a wide range of material, and this methodology sets the tone for the book as a whole.

The sources may not allow an overview or a continuous narrative, but they do permit a picture gradually to be assembled through close readings of some of the texts, images, sites and objects produced during the period of around two and a half centuries nominally bounded by the reigns of Alfred (871–99) and William I (1066–87). This book thus employs a range of different approaches in the attempt to make sense of its elusive subject matter. The first chapter trawls through narrative, documentary, art-historical and archaeological evidence to reconstruct what can be known about Æthelflæd of Mercia. Chapter Two takes a step back and looks at the broader context of social and cultural developments in the last centuries of Anglo-Saxon England, how these in turn condition changing attitudes to dying, death and burial, what sources this society generated and how we may most usefully interrogate them. The four chapters which form the rest of the book follow a rough chronological order, structured around the time-lines of individual lifecycle and Christian history. Chapter Three looks at the ritual surrounding the death-bed, following priest and parishioner through sickness, dying and death to burial and on to Judgement. It also considers the centrality of confession and penance to these rites, asking what we can learn about pastoral care for the dying, and how lay rituals may have complemented those supplied by the clergy. Chapter Four concentrates on the understanding and protection of the body in health and sickness, on the death-bed and in the grave. Chapter Five also looks in detail at the grave and funerary monuments, focusing in particular on the rich and complex *wyrm* symbolism which is constantly invoked both textually and iconographically. Chapter Six, finally, has judgement as its main theme, both the Last Judgement and the ways in which this found its echoes on earth, in the law-courts and the burials of outcasts, and in the developing ideology of a complex Christian culture of burial.

Although the book focuses on the period from Alfred to William I, various factors make these chronological boundaries permeable, and the most important of these are the burial practices themselves, since customs which become widespread in our period have deep roots, and continue to flourish for generations.[4] 1066 is not the watershed of popular imagination, and some words, ideas and practices are pursued across the period of the Norman Conquest and even into the twelfth century. One of the most detailed descriptions of the death-bed comes in a late twelfth-century *Soul and Body* poem from Worcester.[5] Written in alliterative

[4] J. Barrow, 'Urban Cemetery Location in the High Middle Ages', in S. Bassett (ed.), *Death in Towns: Urban Responses to the Dying and the Dead, 1000–1100* (Leicester, 1992), pp. 78–100, 78–9; R. Shoesmith, *Excavations at Castle Green, Hereford*, CBA Research Report 36 (London, 1980), pp. 4–5; *Raunds*, p. 6.

[5] D. Moffat, *The Soul's Address to the Body: The Worcester Fragments* (East Lansing, 1987); R. Buchholz, *Die Fragmente der Reden der Seele an den Leichnam*, Erlanger Beitr(ge zur Englischen Philologie 6 (Erlangen and Leipzig, 1890).

verse and remarkably close to some pre-Conquest material, it certainly falls within our brief, although the ninth, tenth, and eleventh centuries remain the primary focus of attention.

This period saw great changes, including the development of a widely written vernacular, the ecclesiastical and educational reforms initiated by Alfred, the mid-tenth-century rise of Benedictine monasticism in the south, the proliferation of small, local churches set in consecrated churchyards, the growth of crowded market towns, the development of a landscape of manorial complexes and nucleated villages, the addition of Scandinavians, Hiberno-Norse and Anglo-Scandinavians to the cultural mix of these islands, the kings of Wessex becoming the kings of England, and the conquests first of Cnut then of William.[6] Although these changes did not occur simultaneously, or apply uniformly, they condition Anglo-Saxon practices and beliefs in various ways, they have important effects on our sources, and they must always be taken into account.

It is easier to describe the big picture, however, than it is to examine the experiences of individuals. The textual material tends to focus on the abstract and ideal at the expense of the personal and concrete, giving us a clear picture of how the literate wanted to die, but very little information on how they really did. In contrast, the archaeological data provided by skeletons and grave-cuts are hard to date to a specific generation, or assign to a particular social group. As a result of these inherently skewed sources of information, the responses of individual people to dying and death are elusive and easily overlooked. But, as Garrison says, 'even for those intent on constructing master narratives, the experience of individuals must have a role as a component of that project and a touchstone for evaluating its success'.[7] A close look at Æthelflæd goes some way to compensate for the cultural bias towards generalization, even if the bulk of this study has to conform to it.

In theory, a study of dying and death should be a way of looking at the whole of Anglo-Saxon culture, not merely its apex, since not all Anglo-Saxons were kings, abbots or ealdormen, but everybody died, and most people were buried. In practice, of course, most of the written evidence relates to high-ranking men, whether ecclesiastics or, less often, laymen. This is less true of the archaeology, where in the manorial church of Raunds Furnells we probably have a representative rural population, and major churches such as Winchester and

---

6 Alfredian reform: Abels, *Alfred the Great*, pp. 219–57. Monasteries and parish churches: J. Blair, 'Secular Minster Churches in Domesday Book', in P. Sawyer (ed.), *Domesday Book: A Reassessment* (London 1985), pp. 104–42; J. Blair and R. Sharpe (eds), *Pastoral Care before the Parish* (Leicester, 1992); J. Hill, 'Monastic Reform and the Secular Church: Ælfric's Pastoral Letters in Context', in C. Hicks (ed.), *England in the Eleventh Century: Proceedings of the 1990 Harlaxton Symposium* (Stamford, 1992), pp. 103–18. Towns: J. Campbell, *The Anglo-Saxon State* (Hambledon and London, 2000), pp. 188–92; A. Reynolds, *Later Anglo-Saxon England: Life and Landscape* (Stroud, 1999), pp. 159–80. Landscape: Reynolds, *Later Anglo-Saxon England*, pp. 111–57. Scandinavians and Anglo-Scandinavians: A. Rumble (ed.), *The Reign of Cnut, King of England, Denmark and Norway* (Leicester, 1994); D. Hadley, *The Northern Danelaw: Its Social Structure, c. 800–1100* (Leicester, 2000).

7 M. Garrison, 'The Study of Emotions in Early Medieval History: Some Starting Points', *Early Medieval Europe* 10:2 (2001), pp. 243–50, 243.

Exeter cathedrals had exclusive burial rights for many centuries, but even here the bias of excavation towards the great churches means that in graves as well as manuscripts we are often looking at the practices of the prosperous, well informed and well connected. Studying Æthelflæd's experiences allows us to ask whether she is acting differently from the men around her, but we are still within the tiny world of the powerful and rich, and an overview of the evidence suggests that this is largely inescapable.

Our sources include grave-cuts and their contents, rites for the sick, dying and dead, medical texts, commemorative masses and psalms, surviving churches and their churchyards, funerary sculpture and manuscript art, wills, charters and confraternity agreements, necrologies and obit lists, lawcodes and pastoral letters, chronicles, saints' lives, homilies and poetry. The wealthy generated most of this material or, by their sponsorship of the Church, fostered the environment which produced it. However, merely claiming that a gravestone, say, 'reflects status' will not tell us anything very useful about that particular stone. In order for status to be asserted, the stone needs to be an aspirational object which many other people would like but are not permitted or cannot afford to have; it must transmit a recognizable message, perhaps several messages. Thus, the art works, buildings, and rituals sponsored by the powerful would have been seen by many people less well-off, whose ambitions they also embodied, and in this sense they can inform us about the wider culture. Of course, this does not mean that the Anglo-Saxon population consisted only of the upwardly mobile, whose entire range of death-related desires was acted out for them by those kings, ealdormen and abbots. In the practices condemned by churchmen or banned by royal law, in anecdotes and metaphors, and even in some of the burials, we can catch glimpses of other cultural strata. Complex responses are also evident in the homilies, particularly the anonymous ones; although many of the death-related images in these texts are conventional *topoi* we can use them to unpick contemporary responses to these ideas, looking at how the homilists translate their sources or how they stray from them, which ideas they use, and in what combination.

Before 1066, language did not divide social classes as it was to after the Conquest, although there were many different dialects across England, with the Norse-influenced dialects of northern England developing very differently from those in the south. The speakers of different dialects of English could probably have understood one another, however, and Townend has recently argued convincingly that Old English and Old Norse were also mutually intelligible.[8] Within each community, aristocrats and peasants spoke much the same language, and although the Church reserved Latin for the most sacred liturgical moments almost every other religious text was available in English by the eleventh century. These texts included the Gospels, Psalms, Hexateuch, prayers, Creed, confessional formulae, the *regulae* of Benedict and Chrodegang, homilies and saints' lives, and much of this had also been reinvented as English poetry (including both Creed

---

[8]   M. Townend, *Language and History in Viking Age England: Linguistic Relationships between Speakers of Old Norse and Old English* (Turnhout, 2002).

and Paternoster). This looks like an intentional programme of accessibility rather than a makeshift second-best by a Church which had lost its grip on Latinity. It also means that there were no *linguistic* barriers to the circulation of complex ideas about death, burial and judgement.

The conceptual categories of pre-Conquest English do not always map on to those of the modern language, and, rather than accusing the Anglo-Saxons of imprecision because a word for sickbed (*legere*) can also mean grave, or a word for maggot (*wyrm*) can also mean scorpion, we must take these layers of meaning into account in analysing what the texts have to tell us. Late Anglo-Saxon England also provides a large enough corpus of vernacular writing to reveal the various ways in which a single Latin word might be translated, either by different writers or within one man's work, as when Ælfric translates Bede's *ligneo in locello* (wooden coffin) as *treowenre cyst* (wooden chest) but *locellum de marmore alba* (white marble coffin) as *marm-stane . . . þruh* (marble-stone sarcophagus).[9]

Vernacular poetry is another seam of great richness, dealing with many different kinds of dying and death, although it is not easy to correlate poetic accounts with social and cultural practice. The four main poetic manuscripts all date from the late tenth or early eleventh centuries, but it is probable that some, much, perhaps, of their content is generations older. Debating the original context of many of these poems is an inconclusive task, and here it is assumed that they tell us something useful about the sensibilities and practices of the age in which they were copied and preserved. The poems' boundaries with other kinds of text blur, both in form and content. Laments structured around the question *hwær cwom . . .* (what has become of . . .) occur in homilies as well as *The Wanderer*, one of the poems most frequently referred to in the following pages. Texts as disparate as the Paternoster and passages of the Anglo-Saxon Chronicles inhabit what Stanley calls 'the borderland of prose and verse';[10] and alliterative phrases are found in lawcodes, monumental inscriptions and vernacular rubrics to liturgical texts. The manuscripts, of course, make no distinction of layout between poetry and prose, and in the absence of an Anglo-Saxon *Ars Poetica* the difference is hard to categorize. As a result, editors differ in their readings: where the Anglo-Saxon Chronicles are concerned Plummer prints the 959 and 975 entries on Edgar as verse, whereas Whitelock terms them rhythmical, alliterative prose.[11] In the present study poetry is laid out continuously as it is in the manuscripts, rather than following the conventional but distracting modern practice of pairs of alliterating half-lines snaking down the middle of the page.

The sculpture is as rich and complex a source as the literature. For the period as a whole, the majority of the sculpture comes from the north of the country, and apparently from secular or parish churches, whereas most of the texts come from the south and are associated with churches linked to the Benedictine reform. There

---

[9] *HE* iv.19; *LS* I, XX, pp. 436–8.
[10] E. G. Stanley, 'The Judgement of the Damned', in M. Lapidge and H. Gneuss, *Learning and Literature in Anglo-Saxon England* (Cambridge, 1985), pp. 363–91, 390.
[11] C. Plummer (ed.), *Two of the Saxon Chronicles Parallel* (Oxford, 1892); D. Whitelock (ed.), *The Anglo-Saxon Chronicle, A Revised Translation* (London, 1961).

are obvious dangers in using one to read the other. However, there are a few texts that refer to monuments, such as the description in Æthelwulf's *De Abbatibus* of Abbot Sigwine being buried beside 'the tall cross that he had raised himself', or the aside in *De Obsessione Dunelmi* that casually mentions the marking of the site of Earl Aldred's murder by a stone cross.[12] (It is notable that in neither of these cases was the cross primarily intended as a grave-marker.) These stones are a treacherous source, with enormous problems of access, dating and interpretation, but they cannot be overlooked.[13] Even pieces whose images of human figures which look mildly comic to our ill-informed eyes represent effort, investment, and the desire to make a public and permanent statement, and they embody profound truths about how these people wanted to be remembered. No one denies that images such as the Winchester Quinity (Plate 1) are fine art: in a representative comment, Talbot Rice calls them 'lovely line-drawings'.[14] If the sculptural art of the north of England at the same period has not met with such universal approval, it may be that we need to emancipate our own aesthetic sense.[15]

Much of the material surveyed above was designed to inform its audience about the mysteries of dying and death. This rich archive reflects the paradoxical place of death in Christianity, a belief system which is fascinated by death yet denies its existence.[16] This wealth of sources also reflects the fact that, of all the challenges of loss and change with which human beings are confronted, death is the greatest, and is therefore the catalyst for a wide range of cultural responses, designed to console, to explain the inexplicable and to reassure survivors of their continued individual and communal existence.[17] Even within the single culture under consideration here, there are different, sometimes competing, interpretations of dying, death and the afterlife.[18] An officially approved doctrine of Purgatory was only to be formulated in the papacy of Innocent III (1198–1216), and the location of the soul before Doomsday, the value of intercessory prayer and the significance of the buried body were passionately debated in late Anglo-Saxon England. There were various understandings of the relationship of mind, soul,

---

[12] Æthelwulf, *De Abbatibus*, ed. A. Campbell (Oxford, 1967), lines 538–9, p. 43; T. Arnold, *Symeonis Monachi Opera Omnia* I (London, 1882), p. 219.

[13] R. Bailey, *England's Earliest Sculptors* (Toronto, 1996), pp. 3–22; P. C. Sidebottom, 'Schools of Anglo-Saxon Stone Sculpture in the North Midlands', unpublished Ph.D. thesis, University of Sheffield, 1994, pp. 1–26.

[14] D. Talbot Rice, *English Art, 871–1100* (Oxford, 1952), p. 217.

[15] M. Abusabib, *African Art: An Aesthetic Inquiry* (Uppsala, 1995), pp. 45–8.

[16] P. Binski, *Medieval Death: Ritual and Representation* (London, 1996), p. 214; S. Brandon, *The Judgment of the Dead: An Historical and Comparative Study of the Idea of the Post-Mortem Judgment in the Major Religions* (London, 1967), pp. 113–14; J. Le Goff, *The Birth of Purgatory* (Chicago, 1984), pp. 174–5.

[17] A. van Gennep, *The Rites of Passage* (London, 1960); V. Turner, *The Ritual Process: Structure and Anti-Structure* (London, 1969), especially chapter 3, 'Liminality and Communitas'; R. Hertz, 'A Contribution to the Study of the Collective Representation of Death', reprinted in R. Needham and C. Needham, *Death and the Right Hand* (New York, 1960), pp. 27–86; É. Durkheim, *The Elementary Forms of the Religious Life* (New York, 1965); C. Geertz, *The Interpretation of Cultures* (New York, 1973).

[18] A. J. Kabir, *Paradise, Death and Doomsday in Anglo-Saxon Literature*, CSASE 32 (Cambridge, 2001), pp. 1–3.

life, living body and corpse, by no means all compatible. Godden analyses a range of traditions about mind and soul, and uses vernacular poetry, particularly *The Seafarer* and *The Wanderer*, to argue that, outside the learned tradition, a difference was perceived between the *mod* (mind, thought, emotion), understood as part of the body, and the *sawl* or *gast*, which leaves the body at death.[19] Although Godden does not explore the implications of this for the understanding of the corpse, the idea of awareness embedded in the body haunts vernacular descriptions of the body in the grave. Similarly complex and contradictory theories are explored in other genres and media. Anglo-Saxon artists and writers strained at the boundaries of the possible to represent the almost unimaginable, and their awareness of this is reflected in their linguistic and iconographic creativity.[20]

As many Anglo-Saxon writers knew, the single word *deaþ* contains an encyclopaedia of meanings. It can happen at any time of life; some people go without warning while others have a drawn-out dying. Some die socially long before they do so physically, shunted to the sidings of their own lives, while others seem vital and influential long after their physical bodies have died. Memories of the dead, and sometimes also their physical remains, are manipulated by the survivors, who can now project their own desires and readings on to the vacated space. A death may represent the loss of all interest in life for the survivors, or offer them great opportunities, and sometimes it does both. The functions once performed by the dead person may be picked up by others, or fall into abeyance. In death's immediate aftermath, there are decisions to be made about whom to tell and how to tell them, how to dispose of the corpse and the degree of investment in the funeral and in long-term commemorative plans. Although we do not have much in the way of direct accounts of these decisions, their fossil traces are everywhere, even in the simplest grave or the most laconic entry of a death in the Anglo-Saxon Chronicles. To study death is, inevitably, to study life; the crises that death creates serve as a magnifying glass for a culture's deepest concerns. As Campbell observes of tenth-century society, 'concern for the right treatment of the dead was passionate'.[21] In asking questions about how England's inhabitants in these centuries buried their dead, how they remembered them, how they confronted the prospect of personal mortality, how they envisaged the body in the ground and imagined the fate of the soul, we go to this society's heart.

---

[19] M. Godden, 'Anglo-Saxons on the Mind', in Lapidge and Gneuss, *Learning and Literature in Anglo-Saxon England*, pp. 271–98.
[20] H. L. C. Tristram, 'Stock Descriptions of Heaven and Hell in Old English Prose and Poetry', *NM* 79 (1978), pp. 102–13; M. Schapiro, 'The Image of the Disappearing Christ: The Ascension in English Art around the Year 1000', *Gazette des Beaux-Arts* 23 (1943), pp. 135–52.
[21] J. Campbell, 'England, *c*. 991', in J. Cooper (ed.), *The Battle of Maldon: Fiction and Fact* (London, 1993), pp. 1–17, 2.

1

Æthelflæd, Lady of the Mercians

Æthelflæd was the daughter of Alfred, king of Wessex, and wife of Æthelred, ealdorman of Mercia. She was unusual in being a female politician and war-leader, but she was also representative of her class and gender, as aristocratic daughter, sister, wife and mother. She was extraordinary, in her ability to order the building of a minster-mausoleum, to fund intercessory masses and to translate saints' relics, but ordinary in that her investment in these bones, buildings and ceremonies typified the behaviour of great laymen and women in the decades around 900, not just in England but also in continental Europe.[1] With many powerful women, there is debate over the extent of their agency, and it is hard to know whether Æthelflæd was governing independently, or whether events and decisions were engineered by the men around her. If these questions cannot be answered for Elizabeth I, we are unlikely to be able to answer them for Æthelflæd nearly seven centuries earlier. The present discussion argues that Æthelflæd was acting on her own initiative, wielding authority rather than merely influence, particularly from 902 when the exiguous evidence suggests that she ruled alone.[2] She is presented as independent in the Mercian Register, annals later assimilated into the West Saxon chronicle tradition, but presumably produced by someone in her circle.[3] She thus inhabits an unusual space where gender and gender roles are concerned. She and her husband Æthelred are also hard to define in terms of status. From the Chronicles' perspective they were ealdorman and lady of the Mercians, but other sources, Mercian, Irish and even West Saxon, elevate them to the rank of king and queen, suggesting that they were perceived in different ways by different people at the same time.[4] This very oddity allows us to ask whether Æthelflæd's death-related activities are peculiarly female, royal, or both.

More generally speaking, responses to death may also be divided into the imaginative, the emotional and the practical, each of which structures the other two and is structured by them in turn. Emotional responses leave little trace (in itself a *caveat* that early medieval emotional landscapes may not correspond with our own). We know that Æthelflæd experienced the deaths of younger siblings, of

---

[1] M. McLaughlin, *Consorting with Saints: Prayer for the Dead in Early Medieval France* (Ithaca, NY, and London, 1994), pp. 126–8.

[2] Keynes, 'King Alfred and the Mercians', pp. 27–9 and 37.

[3] F. T. Wainwright, 'The Chronology of the "Mercian Register"', *EHR* 60 (1945), pp. 385–92; P. Stafford, *Unification and Conquest: A Political and Social History of England in the Tenth and Eleventh Centuries* (London, 1989), p. 8.

[4] Stafford, *Unification and Conquest*, p. 26; N. Cumberledge, 'Reading between the Lines: The Place of Mercia within an Expanding Wessex', *Midland History* 27 (2002), pp. 1–15, 3.

her father Alfred in 899 and her mother Ealhswith in 902, the deaths in battle of men who fought for her, and the death of her husband Æthelred in 911. She had one surviving daughter, Ælfwynn, who briefly succeeded her; William of Malmesbury claims that Ælfwynn's birth was so difficult that Æthelflæd chose not to have any more children.[5] About her response to most of these experiences we can say nothing, but there are two, very different, references that are worth dwelling on. The first of these, in Asser's *Life of King Alfred*, concerns the deaths of her siblings, the second, the Mercian Register, describes the deaths of men who fought for her.

The bitter death

In the first, the emotional reference is so elliptical as to be almost invisible. It needs to be embedded in evidence from other sources before it comes into focus, and even then it tells us not about Æthelflæd as an individual but about her culture. When Asser, Alfred's biographer, introduces the subject of the king's children, he lists those who lived to grow up, then adds *exceptis his, qui in infantia morte praeueniente praeoccupati sunt* (in addition those who were snatched away in infancy by an early death).[6] As Stevenson notes in his edition, this passage is followed by a lacuna, and the original text probably also specified how many of the children died young. Asser goes on to outline the survivors' early careers, but he says nothing more about the lost babies. There are very few parallels for this passage, beyond the reference in Bede's *Historia Ecclesiastica* to the deaths of two seventh-century royal infants, whose names and place of burial are given.[7] Otherwise, the death of a particular baby is almost never mentioned in Anglo-Saxon sources, although there are many general references to death in childhood, whose cumulative implication is that children were ascribed identity and value, certainly after baptism. None of this should be taken for granted; in many cultures a young baby is not considered fully human, and the child may not have a distinct identity for several years.[8]

Despite the rarity of explicit mentions, the loss of a baby would have been common. Reconstructing the demographics of Anglo-Saxon England is perpetually problematic but it has been suggested that child mortality was around thirty per cent.[9] Crawford argues for considerable investment in child-care on the basis of adult skeletons found with cleft palate, which prevents babies from suckling, meaning that to nurse them adequately requires great commitment from adults.[10] However, although many families experienced the death of young

[5] William of Malmesbury, *De Gestis Regum Anglorum*, 2 vols, ed. W. Stubbs, RS 90 (London, 1887 and 1889), p. 136.
[6] Stevenson, *Asser's Life of King Alfred*, ch. 75.
[7] *HE* ii.14.
[8] R. Cecil, 'An Insignificant Event? Literary and Anthropological Perspectives on Pregnancy Loss', in R. Cecil (ed.), *The Anthropology of Pregnancy Loss: Comparative Studies in Miscarriage, Stillbirth and Neo-Natal Death* (Oxford, 1996), pp. 1–14, 7.
[9] S. Rubin, *Medieval English Medicine* (New York, 1974), p. 50.
[10] S. Crawford, *Childhood in Anglo-Saxon England* (Stroud, 1999), pp. 94–5.

children, Alfred's is almost the only one for which we have direct information. High child mortality might logically suggest that parents felt less attachment to those children.[11] But humans are not logical, and certainly in the late medieval and early modern periods there was a wide range of recorded emotional responses to the deaths of children, with great care expended not only on those too young to be economically productive but also on those so ill or congenitally deformed that there was small likelihood they would ever be independent.[12] This is just as true of the early Middle Ages, as Crawford amply demonstrates.

Asser may not have known the names of these dead children of Alfred's and Ealhswith's, or perhaps, unlike Bede, he did not think it necessary to record them. Nor does he say anything about their funerals in the text as it survives. But his language argues against concluding from these omissions that their deaths did not matter. He juxtaposes two very similar verbs, *praeuenire* and *praeoccupare*, the repetition intensifying the idea that death has come too soon. The very fact that he records their deaths at all suggests that their brief existence was important, and further support for this comes a hundred years later, in one of the homilies of Ælfric, abbot of Eynsham. When death came into the world, it took on three different forms, he says:

> *Mors acerba, mors inmatura, mors naturalis. þæt is on Englisc, se bitera deað, se ungeripode deað, and gecyndelica. Se bitera deað is gecweden þe bið on cildum, and se ungeripoda deað, on geongum mannum, and se gecyndlica, þe becymð þam ealdum.*[13]

> Mors acerba, mors inmatura, mors naturalis. That is, in English, the bitter death, the unripe death and the natural death. The bitter death is so called which is among children, and the unripe death, among young people, and the natural, that which comes to the old.

Ælfric is basing his text on the seventh-century *Prognosticon Futuri Saeculi* of Julian of Toledo, one of the central texts governing early medieval understanding of Christian beliefs about death and the afterlife.[14] Ælfric was perfectly ready to rework his sources if they did not suit his purposes, but he does not do so here.[15] Julian and Ælfric not only differentiate between appropriate responses to the deaths of young and old, they also distinguish between the *unripe* death of the young, and the *bitter* death of children. To lose a child, they imply, had a particular

[11] L. Stone, *The Family, Sex and Marriage in England 1500–1800* (London, 1977), p. 81; C. Gittings, *Death, Burial and the Individual in Early Modern England* (London, 1984), pp. 81–2.
[12] B. Gottlieb, *The Family in the Western World, from the Black Death to the Industrial Revolution* (Oxford, 1993), pp. 132–8.
[13] *Supp.* I, XI, p. 420, lines 110–17.
[14] Julian of Toledo, *Prognosticon Futuri Saeculi*, PL 96, col. 462; E. Raynes, 'MS Boulogne-sur-Mer 63 and Ælfric', *Medium Ævum* 26 (1957), pp. 65–73; M. M. Gatch, *Preaching and Theology in Anglo-Saxon England: Ælfric and Wulfstan* (Toronto, 1977), pp. 129–46.
[15] M. Godden, 'Ælfric's Saints' Lives and the Problem of Miracles', *Leeds Studies in English* n.s. 16 (1985), pp. 83–100; A. J. Frantzen, *Before the Closet: Same-Sex Love from Beowulf to Angels in America* (Chicago, 1998), pp. 212–13; J. Hill, 'Ælfric, Authorial Identity and the Changing Text', in D. Scragg and P. Szarmach (eds), *The Editing of Old English* (Cambridge, 1994), pp. 177–89.

anguish about it. The only grave found within the tenth-century church at Raunds was that of an infant, and the infants in the tenth- to twelfth-century graveyard were interred with particular care.[16] Thus Asser's recognition, however fleeting, of the existence of these unnamed babies lifts the veil for a moment on a world of grief.

'Cut down at Derby's gate': the Lord–Retainer bond

The other passage contains a more explicitly emotional reference. The D text of the Anglo-Saxon Chronicle, *s.a.* 917, drawing on the Mercian Register, records that Æthelflæd took Derby, where *þær wæron eac ofslægene feower hyre þegna þe hire besorge wæron binnan þam gatan (there, also, four of the thegns who were dear to her were slain inside the gates).*[17] The Anglo-Saxon Chronicles are a problematic group of texts, not a monolithic whole but a kaleidoscope of shifting voices, modes and genres. Drawn up at different times and places and mostly surviving in later compilations and copies, the separate strands composing them are now hard to unpick. The Mercian Register covers 902–24 and gives the clearest picture of Æthelflæd's adult life, dominated by the never-ending battle to fortify Mercia.[18] Its main focus is the long list of defensive *burhs* that she built, against a background of ceaseless military and diplomatic activity. Many of her men must have been killed, at Derby and elsewhere, yet only these four merit a mention, and we only learn the place where they fell, and that they were *besorge* to Æthelflæd. Their names go unrecorded.

Besorge is an uncommon word. It has implications of care and anxiety as well as love and value, and this may be what prompted the chronicler to use it here instead of, say, the more common *leof. Besorge* came to Ælfric's mind when, in revising his homily for the second Sunday after Easter, he wanted to explain God's feelings for the human soul. He first quotes Isaiah 49:15 on the improbability of a mother forgetting her child, then adds Ðus *besorge synd eowre sawla gode, gif ge swa gesælige beoð þæt ge secað hine mid modes smeaungum and mid weorce fremminge* (Your souls are dear (*besorge*) to God in the same way, if you are so blessed that you seek him with meditative mind and effective deeds).[19] It would be rash to read very much into a single word, however unusual or apparently carefully chosen, but there may be a hint here that *besorge* has associations appropriate to describing a woman's care and authority. The Chronicle entry for 917 alerts us to the emotional complexities of the bond between a lord and his followers, and raises the possibility that its author was aware of how that relationship was affected by Æthelflæd's gender. We may also be catching a glimpse of a cultural tradition which enshrines sorrow as a woman's work, and

---

[16] *Raunds*, pp. 8 and 29–30.
[17] Cubbin, *MS D, s.a.* 917.
[18] P. Stafford, *Queens, Concubines and Dowagers: The King's Wife in the Early Middle Ages* (London, 1983), p. 118.
[19] *CH* I, Appendix B 3, p. 536, line 44.

perhaps we should add Æthelflæd to the long list of women whose grief is recorded in Anglo-Saxon vernacular literature.[20]

Chroniclers were not always so unforthcoming in recounting the details of the fallen; it is conceivable that in being incorporated into the main West Saxon Chronicle the Mercian Register was abbreviated. In contrast, the A and D Chronicles *s.a.* 903, which record a Fenland battle between the Danes and the West Saxons, go into considerable detail, worth quoting in full:

> *þær wearð Sigulf ealdormon ofslægen 7 Sigelm ealdormon 7 Eadwold cynges ðegen 7 Cenulf abbod 7 Sigebreht Sigulfes sunu 7 Eadwald Accan sunu 7 monige eac him, þeh ic ða geðungnestan nemde; 7 on ðara Deniscena healfe wearð ofslægen Eohric hira cyning 7 Æðelwald æðeling ðe hine to þæm unfriðe gespon, 7 Byrhtsige Beornoðes sunu æðelinges 7 Ysopa hold 7 Oscytel hold 7 swiðe monige eac him þe we nu genemnan ne magon; 7 þær wæs on gehwæðre hond micel wæl geslægen, 7 þara Deniscena þa wearð ma ofslægen, þeh hie wælstowe gewald ahton.*[21]

Ealdorman Sigulf was killed there and Ealdorman Sigelm, and Abbot Cenulf and Sigebreht son of Sigewulf and Eadwald son of Acca, and many besides, although I named the most distinguished; and on the Danish side their king Eohric was killed, and the ætheling Æthelwold, who had egged him on to break the peace, and Byrhtsige son of the ætheling Beornoð, and Ysopa the hold, and Oscytel the hold, and many others whom we cannot name here, and there was a great slaughter on both sides, and there were more killed on the Danish side, although they held the battlefield.

What both the 903 and the 917 passages from the Chronicles bring home is the small-scale and personal nature of this kind of warfare. The author of the 903 entry in the A and D Chronicles knows not only the names but the ranks and the relationships of the important dead on both sides. Many other Chronicle entries make it clear that these Anglo-Danish kings, æthelings, jarls and holds are familiar characters from the contemporary political scene, not unknown and demonized 'heathens'. Indeed, some of them were family: Æthelwold, listed above among the *Deniscena* dead, was Æthelflæd's first cousin.

St Oswald's Gloucester: cult centre and mausoleum

No record of any reaction from Æthelwold's family to his defection and death survive outside the laconic accounts of the Chronicles. Æthelflæd's imaginative and practical responses to certain other deaths, including the prospect of her own, are better documented, but they are hard to disentangle from each other and the division between practical and imaginative may be artificial: safeguarding one's well-being in the life to come is an intensely pragmatic activity. Both devotional and political reasons led her and her husband to found a new church in Gloucester for their burials. There were many factors governing the particular choices that they made, some going back into the past of the Mercian state and others intimately linked to the politics and society of their present.

---

[20] A. Renoir, 'A Reading Context for *The Wife's Lament*', in L. E. Nicholson and D. W. Frese (eds), *Anglo-Saxon Poetry: Essays in Appreciation* (Notre Dame and London, 1975), pp. 224–41.

[21] J. Bately (ed.), *The Anglo-Saxon Chronicle, A Collaborative Edition, Volume 3: MS. A* (Cambridge, 1986).

Æthelflæd and her husband Æthelred, ealdorman of Mercia from 883, ruled only the western half of the former kingdom. Mercia had been divided with the Vikings in 877, so that the former East Mercia had become a series of small polities, possibly based around the five boroughs of Lincoln, Nottingham, Stamford, Leicester and Derby. Charter evidence suggests indirectly that Æthelred may have been incapacitated by illness from *c.* 902, and when he died in an unrecorded location in 910/911, he was buried in Gloucester.[22] So perhaps from 902 and certainly from 911 Æthelflæd ruled Mercia on her own, working with her brother Edward, king of Wessex, to build up the defences of Mercia against the armies of the Danish north and east.[23] Mercia was still in many ways independent, a subordinated province in West Saxon eyes but still a kingdom to other onlookers, and perhaps to the Mercians themselves.[24] Even this brief account shows that Mercian and West Saxon relationships were complex, and much of this complexity is played out in the choice of Gloucester as a new cult centre and mausoleum for Mercia's rulers. By the time of her own death in 918, Æthelflæd had been investing in her church in Gloucester for about twenty years. Although there had been an old minster dedicated to St Peter since the seventh century, they built a new church, also initially in honour of St Peter. In 909, the relics of St Oswald, seventh-century king of Northumbria, were translated from Bardney (Lincolnshire) to the new church, which then added Oswald to its existing dedication to Peter. This new foundation is the church in which Æthelred was buried in around 911, and Æthelflæd herself seven years later. This long process of investment in one particular church and its cults shows ultimately why it was so important, in June 918, that her corpse be transported those hundred kilometres.

Gloucester had been founded by the Romans, and substantial Roman remains were probably still visible in the tenth century as the new church was largely built of recycled Roman stone. The church of St Mary de Lode suggests continuity from the Roman period, as a Roman house was succeeded first by a sub-Roman mausoleum or chapel, and then by the Anglo-Saxon church.[25] In the late seventh century the minster of St Peter was founded nearby by King Osric of the Hwicce.[26] By the Middle Saxon period, the Roman city had become little more than farms among ruins, grouped around St Peter's and St Mary's.[27] Nonetheless, as a Roman site, a place with a long Christian history and a royal centre, it was a place of great symbolic resonance. In the years around 900, Gloucester's fortunes were transformed. Æthelflæd and Æthelred rebuilt it as a fortified *burh*, with a mint and new streets: Thacker terms it Mercia's 'capital', while Heighway more

[22] A. Campbell, *The Chronicle of Æthelweard* (London, 1962), p. 53.
[23] Wainwright, 'Chronology of the "Mercian Register"', p. 388.
[24] Keynes, 'King Alfred and the Mercians', p. 2.
[25] C. Heighway, 'Saxon Gloucester', in J. Haslam (ed.), *Anglo-Saxon Towns in Southern England* (Chichester, 1984), pp. 359–83, 359–61.
[26] A. T. Thacker, 'Chester and Gloucester: Early Ecclesiastical Organisation in Two Mercian Burhs', *Northern History* 18 (1982), pp. 199–211, 207.
[27] Heighway, 'Saxon Gloucester', p. 365.

cautiously describes it as 'unique' in Mercia at this date.[28] Another reason for choosing Gloucester may have been the proximity of Bishop Werferth, the most learned English churchman of his generation, at Worcester, just thirty kilometres upriver.[29]

Æthelflæd and her husband ignored the existing churches and established a new foundation, housing secular canons, on a site between the river and the minster church of St Peter's, possibly as early as the 890s, as William of Malmesbury claims the building project was under way before King Alfred's death in 899.[30] The new church's dedication, also to St Peter, reflects his unrivalled popularity in Anglo-Saxon England.[31] Similar rebuilding was happening in Wessex, where Æthelflæd's brother Edward was transforming the cityscape of Winchester, building the New Minster immediately adjacent to the seventh-century cathedral where their father Alfred had been buried.[32] In 901, Alfred's body was moved from the Old to the New Minster, and this is where their mother Ealhswith was also buried in 902. Edward himself was to be buried there in 924, and Keynes suggests that Edward's intention was to create not only a royal church, but perhaps also 'a church for the new political order'.[33] Æthelflæd could have chosen to send her husband's corpse to join her natal family in the Wessex heartland, and announce plans to be buried there herself, but this would have been to emphasize Mercia's subordinate and provincial status. Instead Æthelred and Æthelflæd took a conscious decision not to fall in with West Saxon plans for the new royal mausoleum at Winchester. Another option might have been to invest in one of the ancient power-centres of Mercia, most obviously Winchcombe or Repton, mausolea of Mercian kings. But this would have been a reckless reassertion of Mercia as an independent kingdom. Gloucester provided a middle way, lying in the deep south of Mercia, close to the West Saxon border, thereby shifting Mercia's centre of balance towards its more powerful neighbour. Royal bodies mattered after death as well as in life, and a royal tomb remained a focal point, as is clear from the account in the Fonthill Letter in which an outlaw clears

---

[28] R. H. M. Dolley and C. E. Blunt, 'The Coinage of Alfred the Great', in R. H. M. Dolley (ed.), *Anglo-Saxon Coins* (London, 1961), pp. 77–94; Thacker, 'Chester and Gloucester', pp. 209–10; C. Heighway, 'Excavations at Gloucester, 4th Interim Report: St Oswald's Priory, Gloucester, 1975–6', *Antiquaries Journal* (1978), pp. 103–32, 123.

[29] C. Heighway, *The Golden Minster: The Anglo-Saxon Minster and Later Medieval Priory of St Oswald at Gloucester*, CBA Research Report 117 (York, 1999), pp. 7–10.

[30] William of Malmesbury, *De Gestis Pontificum Anglorum*, ed. N. Hamilton RS 52 (London, 1870), p. 293.

[31] J. Higgitt, 'The Iconography of St Peter in England, and St Cuthbert's Coffin', in G. Bonner, D. Rollason and C. Stancliffe (eds), *St Cuthbert, His Cult and Community to AD 1200* (Woodbridge, 1989), pp. 267–85; M. Clayton, *The Cult of the Virgin Mary in Anglo-Saxon England*, CSASE 2 (Cambridge 1990); V. Ortenberg, *The English Church and the Continent in the Tenth and Eleventh Centuries* (Oxford, 1992).

[32] F. E. Harmer, *Select English Historical Documents of the Ninth and Tenth Centuries* XVI (Cambridge, 1914), pp. 27–8.

[33] S. Keynes (ed.), *The Liber Vitae of the New Minster and Hyde Abbey Winchester, British Library Stowe 944, together with Leaves from British Library Cotton Vespasian A. viii and British Library Cotton Titus D xxvii*, EEMF 26 (Copenhagen, 1996), p. 17.

himself by going to Winchester and swearing an oath on Alfred's tomb.[34] Seizing the royal burial site at Wimborne was one of Æthelwold's first steps in his coup attempt of 900, and the translation of Æthelred II's brother Edward was an important part of the reconciliation of different factions at the later tenth-century court.[35] Decisions about the disposal of royal corpses were neither private nor merely symbolic.

The translation of St Oswald

Founding a new church in a revitalized town was only the first step. Next came the need for a suitable protector and advocate. The Chronicles record two different events *s.a.* 909. C says that 'in this year the body of St Oswald was brought from Bardney to Mercia' (although D has the same entry under 906); the A manuscript records a joint Mercian and West Saxon harrying of 'the north army' (while D files the same events under 910). It is tempting to conflate these two episodes, and imagine Oswald's bones being borne back as the spoils of the raiding party, perhaps even to see the rescue of the relics as the aim of the expedition.[36] That is not what the Chronicles say, however, and events must have been more complex; holy human remains with a guaranteed pedigree were a valuable commodity, and the bones could equally have been stolen by someone in Lincolnshire and sold to the Mercians, or given into their hands for safekeeping. Even if Oswald did come to Gloucester as loot, this could have interesting implications for the treatment of the relics in the forty years since Lincolnshire fell to the Danes.

Bardney is fourteen kilometres east of Lincoln, part of an ancient ritual landscape in the Witham valley.[37] Although the church may have suffered Viking attack a generation earlier, the 909 'liberation' of the relics suggests that the shrine and its attendant community had not been completely destroyed. In 1982 Sawyer argued on toponymic grounds that Bardney might have survived, as its estate does not seem to have been broken up, and he adduces the relic-gathering exercise of 909 as further evidence.[38] In 1998 he partially retracted this statement, arguing that the estate was 'more likely to have been kept intact by a powerful layman than by a church'.[39] However, this putative powerful layman, Englishman or Dane, may have been aware of the importance of Oswald's cult and have taken it on himself to be the protector of the bones. There is little archaeological

[34] *EHD* I, p. 503.

[35] B. Yorke, 'Anglo-Saxon Royal Burial: The Documentary Evidence', in T. Dickinson and E. James (eds), *Death and Burial* (York, 1992), pp. 41–6, 44.

[36] A. Thacker, 'Kings, Saints and Monasteries in Pre-Viking Mercia', *Midland History* 10 (1985), pp. 1–25, 18–19; A. Thacker, '*Membra Disjecta*: The Division of the Body and the Diffusion of the Cult', in C. Stancliffe and E. Cambridge (eds), *Oswald: Northumbrian King to European Saint* (Stamford, 1995), pp. 97–127; D. Rollason, *Saints and Relics in Anglo-Saxon England* (Leicester, 1989), p. 154.

[37] P. Everson and D. Stocker, 'The Straight and Narrow Way: Conversion of the Landscape in the Witham Valley', in M. Carver (ed.), *The Cross Goes North* (York, 2003), pp. 271–88.

[38] P. Sawyer, *Kings and Vikings: Scandinavia and Europe AD 700–1100* (London, 1982), p. 104.

[39] P. Sawyer, *Anglo-Saxon Lincolnshire* (Lincoln, 1998), pp. 98–9.

evidence from Bardney, but two pieces of carved stone suggest that ecclesiastical activity continued between the late ninth and late eleventh centuries.[40] Given Bardney's strong royal connexions and status as a sister house of Repton, it is plausible that channels of communication remained open.[41] The 'Danelaw boundary' was not exactly the Berlin Wall.

Oswald's relics had many attractions for Æthelred and Æthelflæd. He was a king who had died fighting pagans, a Northumbrian whose head and right arm were still in the Anglian north, at Bamburgh and Chester-le-Street, but who had also had a cult following in the lost lands of East Mercia. Nelson argues that Oswald may have been chosen because of real or perceived dynastic connexions between the Northumbrian royal house and Alfred's maternal ancestors.[42] The saint was a figurehead who could unite the far northern powers of Bamburgh and the community of St Cuthbert with the houses of Wessex and Mercia, against the Danes, their common enemy. Oswald's niece, Osthryth, had established the cult at Bardney in the late seventh century with her husband, an earlier Æthelred of Mercia, a coincidence of names which is unlikely to have been overlooked.[43] The new church in Gloucester, originally dedicated to St Peter, took on the name of the saint whose body it now housed, although it clearly also retained its association with St Peter. When Æthelflæd died in 918, *xii nihtan ær middan sumera binnan Tam weorþige* (twelve nights before midsummer at Tamworth), the Mercian Register recorded that she was buried *binnan Gleaw cestre on þam east portice sancte Petres cyrcean* (at Gloucester in the east *porticus* of St Peter's church).[44] Although only St Peter is named, she was presumably buried in close proximity to Oswald's shrine. These two saints, Prince of the Apostles and King of Northumbria, made for a formidable pair of intercessors. Æthelred and Æthelflæd are recorded as devotees of other English cults as well as Oswald's.[45] They donated a gold chalice to St Milburh's at Much Wenlock, and they have been suggested as the means by which St Alkmund was translated to Shrewsbury, St Werburg to Chester and St Guthlac to Hereford, but the primacy of Oswald is demonstrated by their choosing to be associated with him in perpetuity.[46]

The north wall of the nave of St Oswald's church is still standing, and the site of the church was excavated between 1967 and 1983. It was much smaller than the contemporary New Minster, Winchester, but elaborately decorated with carved stone door-jambs and door- and window-arches, and plastered inside and out. The small, rectangular, continuous nave and chancel had an apsidal west end, there was a *porticus* to the north, east and south, and doors stood opposite

---

[40] P. Everson and D. Stocker, *Lincolnshire*, CASSS V (Oxford, 1999), p. 75.
[41] Sawyer, *Anglo-Saxon Lincolnshire*, p. 65.
[42] J. Nelson, 'Reconstructing a Royal Family: Reflections on Alfred, from Asser, Chapter 2', in I. Wood and N. Lund, *People and Places in Northern Europe, 500–1600: Essays in Honour of Peter Hayes Sawyer* (Woodbridge, 1991), pp. 47–66, 53.
[43] *HE* iii.11.
[44] O'Keeffe, *MS C, s.a.* 918. William of Malmesbury refers to St Oswald's as the site of her tomb: Heighway, *Golden Minster*, p. 11.
[45] Cumberledge, 'Reading between the Lines', p. 5.
[46] Heighway, *Golden Minster*, p. 36.

each other in the north and south walls. St Oswald's was precocious by English standards (if old-fashioned by Carolingian ones) and unusually elaborate in the generation in which it was built.[47] Soon after the building of the church was completed a stone screen, plastered and painted with foliage and perhaps also angels, was added to mark off nave from chancel.[48] There was no sign of any grave-cut within the church before the late twelfth century, though graves clustered thickly about its walls.[49]

The first phase of the church was almost all built of large blocks of re-used Roman limestone, with unmortared foundations. Immediately to the east a free-standing building was constructed in a very different technique, at some time between *c*.900 and the early eleventh century. Although it had been almost entirely robbed out, enough remained to show that its massive walls rested on a rubble and mortar raft. Nothing of the original floor survived, but a stone and rubble platform was interpreted as the base for a pillar. This suggests that there may have been a structure at Gloucester like the surviving crypt at St Wystan's, Repton, where four barley-sugar pillars support the vaulted roof of a lower, underground chamber that probably predates the structure at St Oswald's.[50] Repton may evoke the spiral columns at the shrine of St Peter in Rome; Verkerk stresses the frequency with which medieval church builders drew on their experiences as pilgrims, using architectural and iconographical references to recreate sacred spaces.[51] St Oswald's may thus have referred both to Repton and to Rome in its architecture, invoking the burials of former kings of Mercia and the tomb of St Peter himself.

Heighway and Hare speculate that this free-standing building to the east may have housed either the tombs of Æthelred and Æthelflæd, or the shrine of St Oswald, or both. No burials were found here either; the tombs are therefore likely to have been above ground, perhaps in either an upper or a lower chamber, and given the absence of grave-cuts they could have been structured as box-shrines. Several richly carved gravestones from the first half of the tenth century were found at St Oswald's but there is no way of telling whose graves they marked. However, their decoration, which draws both on Carolingian acanthus motifs and insular decorative foliage styles, indicates that they came from an aesthetic environment which would have been familiar to Æthelflæd. The closest comparanda include the Alfred Jewel, probably made for her father, the gold embroideries donated to the shrine of St Cuthbert, which incorporate the name of

[47] R. Gem, 'Anglo-Saxon Architecture of the 10th and 11th Centuries', in J. Backhouse *et al.*, *The Golden Age of Anglo-Saxon Art* (London, 1984), pp. 139–42.
[48] Heighway, *Golden Minster*, pp. 7–8, 122–3, 170–3.
[49] Heighway and Hare, in Heighway, *Golden Minster*, pp. 11–12, 196.
[50] H. M. and J. Taylor, *Anglo-Saxon Architecture* (Cambridge, 1965) II, pp. 510–16; H. M. Taylor, 'Repton Reconsidered: A Study in Structural Criticism', in P. Clemoes and K. Hughes (eds), *England before the Conquest* (Cambridge, 1971), pp. 351–90.
[51] J. B. Ward-Perkins, 'The Shrine of St Peter and Its Twelve Spiral Columns', *Journal of Roman Studies* 12 (1952), pp. 21–33; Ortenberg, *The English Church and the Continent in the Tenth and Eleventh Centuries*, p. 184; D. H. Verkerk, 'Pilgrimage *ad Limina Apostolorum* in Rome: Irish Crosses and Early Christian Sarcophagi', in C. Hourihane (ed.), *From Ireland Coming: Irish Art from the Early Christian to the Late Gothic Period and Its European Context* (Princeton, 2001), pp. 9–26, 11.

her sister-in-law, and the border-pattern of a picture in which Athelstan, her nephew, presents a book to St Cuthbert.[52] The lush, stylized plant-life of these grave-slabs would have been an appropriate decorative mode with which to commemorate high-ranking members of her circle, and in them we catch a glimpse of the material richness of Æthelflæd's Mercia, which has otherwise almost completely vanished.[53] Differential weathering suggests that some gravestones stood inside and others in the open air: all the most elaborately carved fragments were probably indoors. Despite the investment they represent, these stones did not mark their owners' graves for more than around a hundred years at most, and five of the six have only survived broken up for building rubble in the foundations of walls constructed in the late tenth or early eleventh century. One interpretation of this re-use is that it represents a slighting of the inhabitants of the graves; another, perhaps more likely, is that their bones were removed to even more elaborate homes, either within St Oswald's or elsewhere.[54]

Liturgy in life and death: an agreement with Worcester

Nothing can be said of any liturgical accompaniment to Oswald's translation to Gloucester, or of the ritual surrounding Æthelred's and Æthelflæd's own burials. But these ceremonies are likely to have been elaborate; this is suggested by a charter (S 223), which records a bargain struck between Æthelflæd and her husband on the one hand, and Werferth and the cathedral community of Worcester on the other, at some point before 899.[55] The document records an arrangement for Æthelred and Æthelflæd to receive spiritual benefits in life and death in return for a financial investment, a type of agreement recorded in England from soon after 800.[56] The liturgical activity recorded here has a strong funerary focus, although Worcester was not the church in which they were to be buried. The agreement may predate the foundation of St Oswald's, in which case perhaps their first intention had been burial at St Peter's, Worcester, and only later did they decide to found a more personal institution at Gloucester. Alternatively, they may have been casting their net wide, establishing confraternal relationships with several churches rather than restricting themselves to one.

The document is notable for its affective language, emphasizing the personal connexion between the representatives of Church and State. It begins with an invocation of and prayer of thanks to the Trinity, for whose love, 'and for St Peter's and the church's at Worcester and also for Bishop Werferth's', the agreement has been drawn up.[57] It draws toward a close with renewed emphasis on the *estfullan mode* (dedicated spirit) which the rulers of Mercia are bringing to the contract.

---

[52] J. West, 'A Carved Slab Fragment from St Oswald's Priory, Gloucester', in F. H. Thompson (ed.), *Studies in Medieval Sculpture* (London, 1983), pp. 41–53.

[53] R. Cramp, *Studies in Anglo-Saxon Sculpture* (London, 1992), pp. 148–66.

[54] Heighway, *Golden Minster*, p. 67.

[55] S 223; Harmer, *Select English Historical Documents* XIII, pp. 22–3 and 54–5.

[56] J. Crick, 'Posthumous Obligation and Social Identity', in W. O. Frazer and A. Tyrrell (eds), *Social Identity in Early Medieval Britain* (Leicester, 2000), pp. 193–208.

[57] Harmer, *Select English Historical Documents* XIII, p. 22.

These phrases of love, friendship and gratitude evoke an intimate, emotional relationship embracing God, St Peter, Werferth, the Worcester community, Æthelflæd and Æthelred. Its repeated use of *heo willað* (they desire) and *heo cyðeð* (they declare) gives it the force of an oral performance, whether or not this is the language which was actually spoken. The document records Mercia's rulers redirecting income in exchange for their memory being kept eternally fresh.[58] It is precise about where the money is to come from, with Æthelred and Æthelflæd rerouting half the fines imposed upon the people of Worcester in market place and street, within the burh and without, *ðære cyrcean hlaford, Godes þances 7 Sce Petre* (to the lord of the church, for the grace of God and St Peter).[59] This money has a complex pedigree: the crimes of the citizens are helping to pay for the salvation of their rulers, and the more the citizens fight, cheat, steal and vandalize, the better off the cathedral will be.

The exactitude with which these taxes, fines and market-rights are discussed is echoed in the terms of the liturgical provision supplied by the cathedral community, specifying that the couple are to obtain one dedicated psalm at three daily offices and a mass and thirty psalms every Saturday, that the daily psalm is to change from *De Profundis* to *Laudate Dominum* at their deaths, but the arrangement is to endure in perpetuity.[60] This is a lavish amount of spiritual attention. For purposes of comparison, consider the arrangement that Charles the Bald came to with the canons of St Martin, Tours, in 867, to have one of the Penitential Psalms added to each of the daily offices on his behalf. McLaughlin describes this as a privilege that 'religious houses did not grant . . . readily, even to kings', but there is no hint in the text that Worcester found this burdensome.[61] Rather, the agreement is represented as loving and reciprocal. The chaos of the world outside the cathedral, with its haggling, its sharp practice and violence, is implicitly contrasted with the timeless liturgical space inside the church, where the same psalms are to be repeated every week *on ecnysse* (for ever).

The phrase at the beginning of the charter, 'all the good things that He has given us', puts this exchange in the context of gift and counter-gift: Mercia's rulers are returning to God some of the riches with which He has earlier blessed them.[62] This phrase reveals an acquaintance with a complex economy of prayer that had evolved over the previous centuries in tandem with the idea that the souls of the dead were still capable of accepting help from the living.[63] Votive masses, an eighth-century development, were perceived as an offering to God, linking heaven and earth, living and dead, in a perpetual cycle.[64] The idea of masses

---

[58] *Ibid.*, p. 23.
[59] *Ibid.*
[60] *Ibid.*
[61] McLaughlin, *Consorting with Saints*, p. 162.
[62] B. H. Rosenwein, *Negotiating Space: Power, Restraint, and Privileges of Immunity in Early Medieval Europe* (Manchester, 1999), p. 23.
[63] Kabir, *Paradise, Death and Doomsday*, pp. 47–8, citing Augustine, Gregory's *Dialogues*, Bede's *Vision of Dryhthelm* and Ælfric.
[64] F. Paxton, *Christianizing Death: The Creation of a Ritual Process in Early Medieval Europe* (New York, 1990), p. 68; McLaughlin, *Consorting with Saints*, pp. 212–13.

assisting the souls of the dead has its origins in late Antiquity; although it was a contentious idea for some time, endorsement for the idea is promulgated in the *Dialogues* ascribed to Gregory the Great, where the effectiveness of intercessory prayer is dramatized with vivid stories.[65] Bishop Werferth was intimately familiar with this text, having translated the *Dialogues* into English as part of Alfred's educational reform programme.[66] His translation endorses Gregory's theology absolutely and even expands on it in places.[67] Paxton calls the later ninth century 'a time of energetic creation and synthesis in ritual life', with every community reinterpreting its liturgical inheritance.[68] This agreement reveals something of the engine powering this energy, fuelled by worldly and heavenly ambitions, secular and spiritual powers.

The dialogues *and the dead*

Werferth's own understanding of the ritual and practice appropriate for the death-bed emerges in his translation of Gregory's *Dialogues*.[69] Like the *Prognosticon* of Julian of Toledo, this is one of the foundation texts for the early medieval understanding of the fate of the soul. Gregory uses miracle stories to illustrate articles of faith, recounting tale after tale of saintly figures who were his con-temporaries in sixth-century Italy to show that sanctity does not only manifest itself in the distant past. On the whole, Werferth's translation is faithful, but the process of translation is always a creative one, and a close look at his vocabulary tells us something of his assumptions about burial practice. Gregory's hagio-graphical episodes are packed with death-bed scenes, and he frequently refers to the washing and preparation of the corpse, often with a tag such as *ut mos est* (as is the custom). Werferth usually passes on Gregory's account without com-ment: *quem ex more lotum, vestimentis indutum, et sabano constrictum* (which according to custom [was] washed, dressed in clothes and confined with a sheet) becomes Werferth's typically faithful *hine thwogon 7 mid hrægle gegyredon 7 mid scytan bewundon swa hit þeaw wæs* (they washed him and dressed him with clothes and with a sheet wound him as was the custom).[70] Werferth does not comment on the distinction between *vestimentum* and *sabanus*, which he translates literally with *hrægl* (clothes) and *scyt* (sheet). Given his concern to explain the unfamiliar practice looked at next, this suggests that Werferth took

[65] The reliability of the ascription to Gregory has been called into question, and Dunn suggests that seventh-century Northumbria is a more plausible environment for the *Dialogues'* composition, although their author will be referred to here as 'Gregory'; M. Dunn, *The Emergence of Monasticism, from the Desert Fathers to the Early Middle Ages* (Oxford, 2000), pp. 130–7, 199–200.

[66] Stevenson, *Asser*, ch. 77.

[67] H. Hecht, *Bischofs Werferth von Worcester, Übersetzung der Dialoge Gregors des Grossen* (Leipzig, 1900), p. 342.

[68] Paxton, *Christianizing Death*, p. 207.

[69] Stevenson, *Asser*, ch. 77; D. Whitelock, 'The Prose of King Alfred's Reign', in E. G. Stanley (ed.), *Continuations and Beginnings: Studies in Old English Literature* (London, 1966), pp. 67–103, 67–8.

[70] *Dialogues*, Book 3, ch. 17, *PL* 77, col. 264.

it for granted, as Gregory had done, that corpses could go clothed as well as shrouded to the grave.

But Werferth found another story more challenging. On a trip to Constantinople, a man called Stephen appears to have died and his body is to be made ready for burial:

> *Cumque medicus atque pigmentarius ad aperiendum eum atque condidiendum esset quaesitus, et die eodem minime inventus, subsequente nocte corpus iacuit inhumatum.*[71]

> However, since a doctor and embalmer ('painter') to open him up and embalm him had been sought but not found that day, the corpse lay unburied the following night.

Werferth had an idea of the concept of anointing the corpse with spices, but failed to find an English noun to translate *pigmentarius* and so reworked the sentence to read 'the doctor . . . who knew how to work with spices'. Another difficulty was presented by *aperiendum eum atque condidiendum*, which becomes 'that he might anoint and bury him', implying that the opening of the body and 'pickling' to which the Latin refers were alien concepts. Did Werferth think that *aperiendum* referred to the opening up of the grave? Finally, Werferth interpolated a subordinate clause to distance himself from the practice he is describing, explaining 'because it was the custom in that land, that the bodies of good men should be anointed with costly ointments, before they were buried'. Thus, his version of the passage becomes:

> *þa sona wæs soht, hwær se læce wære, þe cuþe wyrtgemang wyrcan, þæt se mihte hine besmyrwian 7 bebyrwan, forþon hit þeaw wæs on þam landum, þæt man mid deorwyrþum smeringum godra manna lichaman smyreð, ær hi man bebyrge. þa þy dæge ne mihte nan læce beon funden, ac þy æfterfylgendan nihte þæt lic læg unbebyrged.*[72]

> Then at once it was sought where there might be a doctor who knew how to work with spices, so that he might anoint and bury him, because it was the custom in that land that the corpse of a good man be anointed with valuable ointment before he be buried. No doctor could be found that day, wherefore the following night the corpse lay unburied.

This suggests that the washing, clothing and shrouding of the corpse were familiar practices in Mercia around 900, at least in episcopal circles, a deduction supported by contemporary continental *ordines in agenda mortuorum*. Embalming, however, is another matter; Werferth firmly categorizes it as something foreign, perhaps even specifically Byzantine. This implies that even the use of externally applied substances such as myrrh and balsam to disguise rather than delay the onset of decay was unfamiliar. The more interventionist approach described by Gregory was wholly opaque to him. This apparent ignorance of embalming makes it that much more likely that Æthelflæd's own funeral cortege moved speedily from Tamworth to Gloucester in June 918. It also shows us a cultural world in which the decay of the human body was perceived as rapid and inevitable.

---

[71] *Dialogues*, Book 4, ch. 37, *PL* 77, col. 384.
[72] Hecht, *Bischofs Werferth von Worcester*, p. 318.

Eanbald and Eastmund: the rights of the dead

For these people, the spirits of the dead were very close. Prayers for the dead were not formulaic mouthings of abstract piety, but profound expressions of the realities by which people lived. The dead were vulnerable and they were owed due care from the living, who had an obligation to uphold their rights on their behalf. Furthermore 'the dead' were not anonymous hordes but known individuals, with faces, names, stories and evolving, reciprocal relationships with the living. This is exceptionally clear in another Worcester document, recording a complex law-suit heard by Æthelred and Æthelflæd, and written as if spoken by Werferth of Worcester in the first person (*Ic Werferð biscop cyðe*).[73]

It emerges that, over a century earlier, Bishop Milred had given an estate at Sodbury, Gloucestershire, to a man called Eanbald for the use of his family as long as the holder was in holy orders. If there were no suitable family member, then the land would revert to Worcester cathedral 'for the sake of all their souls'. Only two lifetimes later the family broke the terms of the agreement but held on to the property. Successive bishops sought to regain the estate, but no progress was made until Æthelred took power (*ne mihton to nanum rihte becuman ær Æðelred wæs Myrcna hlaford*). In a hearing before Æthelred, Eadnoth, the land's current occupier, swore to return the estate to Werferth or find a suitable family member to run it, but his entire kin severally replied that they would rather forfeit the estate than be ordained. The case therefore came back to court, and Æthelred and Æthelflæd pressed Werferth (*heo ealle to me wilnodon*) to agree that Eadnoth be allowed to hold the land in return for an annual fifteen shillings and the performance of penance (*him eac þone scrift healde*). The chief interest of this text for us lies in the description of the death of Eastmund, the second man to hold the Sodbury estate and presumably himself in holy orders:

> Ond he þa Eastmund ær his ende bebead on þæs lifgendan Godes noman þam men þe to þam lande fenge, þæt he þonne on þa ilcan wisan to genge þe Mired bisceop bebead; gif he þonne to þan gedyrstig wære þæt he þæt abræce, þæt he wiste hine scyldigne beforan Godes heahsetle æt þam miclan dome. þa æfter Eastmundes forðsiðe bereafode seo mægð þæs ilcan londes ge þa gastas þara forðgewitenra manna ge þone bisceop 7 þa ciricean æt Weogornaceastre.[74]

Then Eastmund, before his death, asked in the name of the living God that the man who inherited the land do so in the same way that Milred commanded; if he were so presumptuous as to break it, then he should know himself guilty before God's throne at the great judgement. Then, after Eastmund's death, the family stole that same estate both from the spirits of the dead men and from the bishop and the church at Worcester.

Not only have the family members flouted Eastmund's will (which is clearly also a written document: *Eastmundes erfegewrit* is among the evidence that Eadnoth gives to Werferth), and thereby defrauded the community at Worcester, they have also stolen from the spirits of the dead. This theft from the dead refers to the land itself, but only as an embodiment of something much more important,

[73] Harmer, *Select English Historical Documents* XV, pp. 25–7 and 57–9.
[74] *Ibid.*, p. 26.

the intangible benefits which would have accrued to the spirits of Eanbald and Eastmund if the land had remained in clerical hands, either the family's or the cathedral's, as intended. Had a member of the family stayed in holy orders, it would have been his job to pray for the souls of his kin; failing that, the reversion of the land to the cathedral would secure intercession *for heora ealra saule* (for all their souls). Eastmund puts the postulated theft of the estate in perspective by summoning up the image of *Godes heahsetle æt þam miclan dome* (God's throne at the great judgement). The ghosts of Eanbald and Eastmund will then be able to present their case directly to God, and, while they may have been robbed of their rights, the ghosts of the robbers will be denounced as *scyldig* (guilty) and confronted with damnation. Eastmund's reported speech here has the force of an anathema, or even a death-bed curse. The *gastas* of the dead men precede Werferth and his cathedral syntactically; they are just as physically present in the text, and perhaps even more vulnerable to damage and deceit. They have their rights, which the living have a duty to uphold. Eanbald and Eastmund are not saints, and can work no miracles from beyond the grave to force the living to their will, they are only the ordinary dead, and given that Bishop Milred died in about 775 and this court case is taking place in the 890s they are also likely to be the long dead. But they have not been forgotten, and the ordinary dead need to be understood for the extraordinary dead, like Oswald, to be put in context. We might also note the hint of flattery in the remark that 'there was no justice until Æthelred became lord of the Mercians', juxtaposed with the reference to 'the great judgement' at the end of time, implying that justice tempered with mercy was also the distinguishing feature of court cases heard by Æthelred and Æthelflæd. In their presence even the dead could get a fair hearing.

Æthelflæd's death and the political consequences

Æthelflæd's death on 9 June 918 transformed the political scene, and the fortunes of Mercia. In spring 918 she had received the submission of the men of Danish York, who needed her support against the encroaching Norse-Irish, a deal abandoned at her death, when her brother Edward immediately marched on Tamworth.[75] A few months later her only child, Ælfwynn, was 'deprived of all authority in Mercia and taken into Wessex'; nothing more is heard of this 'second Lady of the Mercians'.[76] Æthelflæd's death may also have created enough of a crisis in Northumbria to allow the take-over of York by the Dublin Norse. As a result, hostile Scandinavian factions persisted north of the Humber throughout the reigns of her brother Edward and her foster-son Athelstan, leading to the violent climax of the battle of *Brunanburh* in 937.

And what happened to Gloucester? Its prominence was very closely inter-twined with its connexion to Æthelflæd. Although Athelstan died there in 939,

[75] R. R. Darlington, P. McGurk and J. Bray, *The Chronicle of John of Worcester: Volume II, The Annals from 450–1066* (Oxford, 1995), p. 380.
[76] M. Bailey, 'Ælfwynn, Second Lady of the Mercians', in N. Higham and D. H. Hill (eds), *Edward the Elder, 899–924* (London, 2001), pp. 112–27, 122–5.

his body was taken to Malmesbury. After this, as Hare points out 'Gloucester is barely found in the itinerary of English kings',[77] and the tide of Benedictine reform seems never to have washed over the town's churches. It was not enough simply to establish and endow a church; in order for it to endure, it needed powerful patrons. Without the vested interest of the descendants of those original founders this was unlikely to happen, and Ælfwynn was either unable or unwilling to invest in her parents' church. The fate of St Oswald's indicates the dilemmas facing the wealthy in the tenth and eleventh centuries: whether to establish your own burial church, as Ealdorman Ælfgar and his daughters were to do in the tenth century at Stoke-by-Nayland in Suffolk, to concentrate on a major minster or monastery, or to spread your investment across several churches.[78] The will of Ælfgar's younger daughter, Ælfflæd, the widow of Byrhtnoth who was killed at Maldon in 991, reveals some of the risks of setting up proprietary churches; she uses gifts of land to create reciprocal obligations with friends and kinsman who will be the church's protectors, but to no ultimate avail.[79] By 1066 the lands Ælfflæd had left to Stoke were in a variety of different hands and there is no indication in Domesday Book that an important church had been there.[80]

Questions were raised earlier about whether Æthelflæd's behaviour could be seen as gender-specific in any way. Other than that tantalizing reference to her feelings at Derby, the conclusion must be no. She and her brother Edward acted in parallel, each founding new mausoleum churches in their respective revitalized urban centres of Winchester and Gloucester. Creating an appropriate environment for burial was a pious action suitable for both men and women. It is harder to answer the question of whether her actions should be seen as royal or aristocratic; as Blair remarks, 'the new aldermannic families of the eighth and ninth centuries founded minsters as naturally as kings had done in the seventh'.[81] Establishing proprietary churches became one of the defining activities of tenth-century aristocrats. Nonetheless, within her own generation, Æthelflæd was acting in a more royal than aristocratic fashion, living as she did in a period of hiatus between the old, pre-Viking, dispensation and the new.

This analysis has taken in a wide range of sources, and been forced by necessity to rely on incidental references and chance survivals. Our perception of Æthelflæd is entirely governed by these very limited sources, which present her in her public roles as warrior, patron, judge. We only catch glimpses of her extensive network of genuine and fictive kin relationships. Nothing will tell us who washed and dressed her body in Tamworth, and brought it to its final resting-place 'in the east *porticus* of St Peter's at Gloucester', or who, other than the clerics of St Oswald's, attended her funeral. Whoever these people were, their

---

[77] M. J. Hare, 'The Two Anglo-Saxon Minsters of Gloucester', Deerhurst Lecture 1992 (The Friends of Deerhurst Church, 1993), p. 8.

[78] D. Whitelock, *Anglo-Saxon Wills* (Cambridge, 1930), pp. 103–4 and 137.

[79] V. Thompson, 'Women, Power and Protection in Tenth and Eleventh-Century England', in N. Menuge (ed.), *Medieval Women and the Law* (Woodbridge, 2000), pp. 1–18.

[80] Whitelock, *Wills*, p. 105, n. 19.

[81] J. Blair, 'Minster Churches in the Landscape', in D. Hooke (ed.), *Anglo-Saxon Settlements* (Oxford, 1988), pp. 35–58, 40.

relationship with her is unlikely to have ended at death. The Worcester community, if they fulfilled their obligations, would have continued to remember her, singing *Laudate Dominum* three times a day and celebrating mass on Saturday to keep her *gemynde* (memory) fresh.

Æthelflæd's involvement with death and burial brings together many of the themes of this book. She lived in a world where the dead can be hurt as well as helped, where their rights can be aired in court, where their bodies are not fixed in a final resting place but can be moved from tomb to tomb, and this is not only true of saints but of her own father, and perhaps also of herself.[82] In building a church to house their tombs as well as some of the most prestigious primary relics in England, and entering into a confraternity agreement with cathedral canons, she and her husband exemplify a widespread ideal. Her devotion to St Peter is also characteristic. The recorded activities of Æthelflæd and her articulate, wealthy and powerful family represent the concerns of many of their contemporaries and fellow countrymen writ large. But this chapter remains a study of one unusual individual. Anglo-Saxon England contained many different cultures, and even for those who subscribed to the same broad beliefs and ideals about dying, death and the dead as Æthelflæd did, there were many different ways of expressing them, in a wide range of media. To get closer to understanding this multiplicity, we need to ask questions about the meaning of Christianity and paganism, the role of priests and monks, the ways in which ideas about Christianity might be conveyed to the laity, the role of the laity in constructing Anglo-Saxon Christianity, attitudes to the body that take sex, birth and disease into account as well as dying and death, and the degree to which visions of the afterlife structured and were structured by contemporary experiences.

---

[82] William of Malmesbury, *Pontificum*, p. 293.

2

Dying and Death in a Complicated World

DYING AND DEATH IN CONTEXT

Death, burial and christianity

Æthelflæd and her circle are recorded as model Christians in their attitudes to death, but our sources define many other inhabitants of these islands as imperfect Christians or not Christians at all. Before going any further, we need to look more closely at these words. This chapter will first consider the wider context of the different cultures of Anglo-Saxon England, and how their interaction in fields such as politics, belief, land-holding and ethnicity might affect people's responses to death. It then looks closely at Vercelli Homily IX, one of the most elaborate and considered attempts to define death in surviving Anglo-Saxon literature.

What precisely does it mean, to have a Christian burial? One answer, based on the most authoritative biblical and patristic sources, would be a simple matter of disposal. The corpse is irrelevant until reassembled at Doomsday, and the fate of the soul depends entirely on the actions performed in life.[1] 'Let the dead bury the dead', Christ says to a would-be follower who wishes to attend to his father's funeral (Luke 9:60). Different parts of this ideal have informed the ways that Christian societies have buried their dead at various times and places, but overall this précis is not remotely representative of early medieval Christian burial practice.[2] Complex ritual, visible structures, enduring commemoration and various ways of making graves are all prominent features of late Anglo-Saxon funerary culture. Every form of Christian practice is culturally embedded: even within the Gospel narratives Christ's own funeral comes with a stone tomb, grave-clothes, ointments and mourners. Burnell and James speak of 'different, competing or regionally demarcated christianising influences', suggesting that rival, even incompatible, interpretations of Christian practice and doctrine could and did co-exist, long before the Reformation.[3] Coffins, shrouds, sackcloth and ashes, ceremonies at the death-bed, funeral masses, rites of committal, *libri uitae*, and

---

[1] The *locus classicus* justifying votive masses and intercessory prayer is II Maccabees 12:43–5. Explicit refutation of the possibility of posthumous salvation comes in the parable of Dives and Lazarus (Luke 16:19–31) and also II Corinthians 5:10. J. A. Trumbower, *Rescue for the Dead: The Posthumous Salvation of Non-Christians in Early Christianity* (Oxford, 2001), pp. 33–55.

[2] G. Rowell, *The Liturgy of Christian Burial* (London, 1977), pp. 72–84.

[3] S. Burnell and E. James, 'The Archaeology of Conversion of the Continent: Some Observations and Comparisons with Anglo-Saxon England', in R. Gameson (ed.), *St Augustine and the Conversion of England* (Stroud, 1999), pp. 83–106, 84.

grave-markers or memorial stones are all historically conditioned developments, not inbuilt features of the Christian system. Late Anglo-Saxon burials do not exist in a vacuum; they define themselves both in terms of and against other funerary practices, past and present, desirable or unacceptable.

Where death is concerned, there are very few consistent elements in Christian mythology, and these can only be expressed in the broadest terms before cultural relativity starts creeping in:

- Death was not part of God's blueprint but came about through the weakness of Eve and Adam.
- Death is not the end for either the soul or the body, which will be reunited and finally damned or saved at the end of time.
- Christ died for the sins of humanity; while dead His spirit remained active and powerful, redeeming the souls of virtuous Old Testament figures.
- He bodily came back to life and was taken up to heaven.
- His death offers the opportunity of redemption to all human beings.

These structuring narratives organize and interpret the biological experiences of dying and death in a Christian culture, but they also generate many unresolved questions. The Bible is unclear as to whether one should imagine an individual judgement at death, a universal judgement at the end of time, or both, and where the soul might go during any interim period. Other questions centre around whether the corpse matters after the soul has left it, and whether bodily decay is a way of assessing the fate of the soul, whether the living can help the dead towards salvation and, if so, whether these activities should be directed at the body or the soul. These are vitally important questions, not merely for the theologians and legislators, but also for the bereaved, a category in which most people find themselves at some stage in their lives. They are also questions which (wisely, perhaps) the Church did not answer consistently, or in detail. Anglo-Saxon writers and artists seized on every part of this framework, exploiting patristic and apocryphal traditions to eke out the spare biblical accounts, and using their creative skills to embellish, re-interpret and occasionally invent satisfying narratives.

Burial in a changing landscape

By Alfred's accession in 871, the English kingdoms had been undergoing conversion to Christianity for over two and a half centuries. It is easy to assume that once the 'conversion' period ends (usually put at *c.* 750), the 'converted' period begins, but the achievement of a society consistently virtuous in thought, word and deed is an impossible goal, and Christianity itself is subject to continuous historically conditioned change. Many Christian writers and historians of Christianity define religion in terms of polarities which do not correspond to lived experience, which is one of endless renegotiation.[4] In the absence of rules

---

4   C. G. Brown, *The Death of Christian Britain: Understanding Secularisation, 1800–2000* (London and New York, 2001), pp. 11–15.

for burial, experimentation can be predicted as people fumble towards acceptable solutions, and such experimentation appears in late Anglo-Saxon cemeteries. Furthermore, a solution acceptable to Christians in one generation may appear inappropriate fifty or a hundred years later. Grave 511 from Repton (Derbyshire) suggests the complexities we are dealing with: here is a man who was buried in the late ninth century, next to an important church, in a grave which was aligned east–west, but he had a Thor's hammer amulet around his neck and his sword at his side. As Richards says, 'this was someone for whom the options were being kept open'.[5] Grave 93 from the cemetery underlying York Minster is another anomaly: here a man was buried lying east–west at some point in the tenth to eleventh centuries, one of only two oriented burials since, although this was undoubtedly a Christian cemetery, the prevailing orientation was north-east to south-west, following an earlier Roman alignment. His head was packed around with stones, uncommon at this site, and he was lying in a clinker-built construction which may have been part of a boat.[6]

The real surprise is finding so few other burials conducted along such inventive lines, given the numerous cultures of Anglo-Saxon England. In the generation before Æthelflæd's birth, Wessex, East Anglia, Northumbria and Mercia were still ruled by their own dynasties, although the last three kingdoms were soon to be transformed by the Danish invasions and settlement of the 860s and 870s. Although the newcomers had their own ideas about death and burial, these remain stubbornly resistant to being pinpointed in the landscape with very few exceptions, such as Repton and the nearby barrow field at Ingleby, and some thirty anomalous and widely distributed graves furnished in an apparently Scandinavian idiom.[7] Nor were the English themselves culturally uniform. Institutions of State and Church may have been very different across the English kingdoms, though the early to mid-ninth century is poorly documented. Outside Wessex, the administrative landscape of shire and hundred or wapentake was yet to emerge, and probably only took shape in the wake of the West Saxon conquest of the Anglo-Danish polities of East Mercia and East Anglia in the tenth century.[8] The division of the landscape in this way has implications for the development of parish churches and churchyards, as well as for the burials of executed criminals,

[5] J. D. Richards, 'Pagans and Christians at a Frontier: Viking Burial in the Danelaw', in Carver, *Cross Goes North*, pp. 383–95, 88.

[6] M. Carver (ed.), *Excavations at York Minster, Volume I: From Roman Fortress to Norman Cathedral. Part 1: The Site* (London, 1995), pp. 86–7 and *Part 2: The Finds*, pp. 500–5; cf. the ninth-century burial from Kiloran Bay, on Colonsay, where a man buried with a boat and a horse had two slabs scratched with crosses to mark the grave. H. Shetelig, 'Ship-Burials at Kiloran Bay, Colonsay, Scotland', *Saga-Book* 5 (1906–7), pp. 172–4.

[7] M. Biddle and B. Kjølbye-Biddle 'Repton and the 'Great Heathen Army', 873–4', in J. Graham-Campbell *et al.* (eds), *Vikings and the Danelaw: Select Papers from the Proceedings of the Thirteenth Viking Congress* (Oxford, 2001), pp. 45–96; J. D. Richards, 'Boundaries and Cult Centres: Viking Burial in Derbyshire', *ibid.*, pp. 97–104, and J. D. Richards *et al.*, 'The Viking Barrow Cemetery at Heath Wood, Ingleby, Derbyshire', *Medieval Archaeology* 39 (1995), pp. 1–50; J. Graham-Campbell, 'Pagan Scandinavian Burial in the Central and Southern Danelaw', in Graham-Campbell, *Vikings and the Danelaw*, pp. 105–24, and 'Pagans and Christians', *History Today* (Oct. 1986), pp. 24–8.

[8] F. Stenton, *Anglo-Saxon England* (3rd edn, Oxford, 1971), p. 293.

who, as Reynolds has shown, were buried in separate cemeteries located on precisely these administrative boundaries.[9] Lay and clerical jurisdiction came to overlap, on the page, in the courts and on the ground.

The ninth to eleventh centuries see a growth in small estates in many different areas, with changing settlement patterns and different kinds of land-holding. A process that seems to be happening in both Cornwall and the Yorkshire Wolds is likely to be a complex one. Turner suggests that while some Cornish carved stones, such as the hogback from Lanivet, are funerary, the 'Hiberno-Saxon' crosses are territorial statements by local churches and monasteries, defying secular encroachment.[10] Similar patterns of lordship, church foundation and monumentality are detectable in Dumfries and Galloway in the eighth to tenth centuries; Crowe uses the style of sculpture at Whithorn and related sites as evidence of cultural and social relationships, and he sees this culture as developing in an 'Anglian mode' but functioning within 'the wider Hiberno-Norse trading world'.[11] Hiberno-Saxon, Anglian, Hiberno-Norse: the vision of unity conjured up by the title of this book, with its glib reference to 'later Anglo-Saxon England', needs to be replaced by a Venn diagram of overlapping linguistic, iconographic, political and ideological fields. Anglo-Saxon society breaks down into many subgroups: male and female; adult and child; celibate and sexually active; criminal and law-abiding; rural and rapidly expanding urban; monastic, clerical and lay; educated and illiterate; Mercian, West Saxon, East Anglian and Northumbrian, as well as British and Anglo-Scandinavian; wealthy and poverty-stricken; aristocrat, thegn, ceorl and slave. Nor are these categories rigid; they shift, overlap and subdivide. A ceorl might become a thegn; a West Saxon prince became leader of the Danes of York; at least one slave became a priest.[12] Nonetheless, there were important unifying factors connecting the different cultural zones of England, paramount among which were Christianity and a mutually intelligible language, English (which was probably also intelligible to native speakers of Norse dialects).[13]

By the mid- to late ninth century, England's ecclesiastical landscape was dominated by minsters, a complex term encompassing a variety of organizations, some much older and wealthier than others, with differing degrees of regular life and parochial responsibility. This remained generally true of West Mercia and Wessex into the eleventh century.[14] In eastern England, however, a new spiritual

---

[9] A. Reynolds, 'Burials, Boundaries and Charters in Anglo-Saxon England: A Reassessment', in S. Lucy and A. Reynolds (eds), *Burial in Early Medieval England and Wales*, Society for Medieval Archaeology Monograph 18 (London, 2002), pp. 171–94.

[10] S. Turner, 'Making a Christian Landscape: Early Medieval Cornwall', in Carver, *Cross Goes North*, pp. 171–94, 186–8; J. D. Richards, 'Cottam: An Anglo-Scandinavian Settlement on the Yorkshire Wolds', *Archaeological Journal* 156 (1999), pp. 1–111, 86–100.

[11] C. Crowe, 'Early Medieval Parish Formation in Dumfries and Galloway', in Carver, *Cross Goes North*, pp. 195–206.

[12] D. Whitelock, *The Will of Æthelgifu: A Tenth Century Anglo-Saxon Manuscript* (Oxford, 1968), p. 8.

[13] M. Townend, 'Viking Age England as a Bilingual Society', in D. Hadley and J. D. Richards (eds), *Cultures in Contact: Scandinavian Settlement in England in the Ninth and Tenth Centuries* (Turnhout, 2000), pp. 89–105, 90; Townend, *Language and History in Viking Age England*.

[14] Blair, 'Minster Churches in the Landscape'.

territory of smaller churches was emerging, associated with the nascent institutions of manor and parish.[15] Thus in the tenth century one was more likely to live near a church in Yorkshire and Lincolnshire than in Hampshire or Dorset, though it does not necessarily follow that more people had access to any pastoral services that the church provided. Different types of church are distinguished for the first time in mid-tenth century legislation, in a context that implies the authorities are regulating an existing and already complex situation.[16] The lawcode VIII Æthelred (5.1) lists headminsters, middle-ranking churches, smaller churches with graveyards, and field-churches, and Morris points out that that category of 'smaller church with graveyard' could include 'churches in boroughs with special rights, churches owned by consortia of freemen, churches on bookland, and smaller manorial churches'.[17] Homilies, lawcodes and penitentials construct a rhetoric of inclusivity that assumes everyone had access to a church and was willing and able to confess and take communion at least annually. Reality was probably less tidy, but in the interplay of these texts and landscapes we catch a glimpse of real problems and attempted resolutions.

Textual evidence for burial practice in England before the mid-ninth century is patchy, depending on sources such as Bede's *Historia Ecclesiastica* (731) which concentrate on monasteries.[18] If, in the seventh to ninth centuries, church-associated burial was only extended to the wealthy and influential, then very few people other than the professional religious (themselves a small group) had access to it. This in turn indicates that burial away from a church is no indication of whether someone was a baptized and communicating Christian, a pagan, a heretic or a criminal. In the Middle Saxon period, for the great majority, factors such as place of residence, kinship or affinity probably governed the choice of place of burial, although a funeral mass in a church might well have preceded the actual committal to the earth. These hypotheses are borne out by archaeological evidence, which reveals a culture of comparatively unregulated burial practice.[19] Hamwic (Southampton, Hampshire) had nine cemeteries, all small and short-lived, in use between the early eighth and the late ninth centuries, some of which had several coffined burials, while others had none.[20] Artefacts such as necklaces, coins and knives suggest some people were buried in their clothes, but these come from the earlier graves. Only two of Hamwic's cemeteries, and very few nationally, show any sign of a structure that could have been a church or oratory, although, as Hadley warns, there are obvious dangers in arguing from negative evidence.[21] Scull also discusses Hamwic, as well as Ipswich, York (minimally)

---

[15] J. Barrow, 'Survival and Mutation: Ecclesiastical Institutions in the Danelaw in the Ninth and Tenth Centuries', in Hadley and Richards, *Cultures in Contact*, pp. 155–76, 166–8.

[16] II Edgar, 1: F. Liebermann, *Die Gesetze der Angelsachsen* I (Halle, 1903), p. 196.

[17] R. Morris, *The Church in British Archaeology*, CBA Research Report 47 (London, 1983), p. 64.

[18] Morris, *The Church in British Archaeology*, p. 50.

[19] M. Adams, 'Excavation of a Pre-Conquest Cemetery at Addingham, West Yorkshire', *Medieval Archaeology* 40 (1996), pp. 151–91.

[20] A. Morton, 'Burial in Middle Saxon Southampton', in Bassett, *Death in Towns*, pp. 68–77.

[21] D. M. Hadley, 'Burial Practices in Northern England in the Later Anglo-Saxon Period', in Lucy and Reynolds, *Burial in Early Medieval England and Wales*, pp. 209–28, 212.

and London, and highlights the complexity and diversity of burial at these, the best understood of the Middle Saxon trading sites.[22]

In the decades around 900, however, changes are taking place in the landscape, practice and ideology of burial. The earliest reference to soul-tax (*sawelsceatt*) comes from charters from the 870s, from Winchester and Worcester, suggesting at this stage only that the church is charging for the privilege of burial, although as the tenth century progresses it seems to develop into a compulsory burial fee as church-associated graves become normal rather than aspirational.[23] From the early tenth century references to 'heathen burials' begin to appear regularly as landmarks in the boundary clauses of reliable charters, and the idea that unhallowed burial is in itself punitive is first visible in legislation from the reign of Athelstan (924–39).[24] In the following generations the idea of holy ground takes on new force, explored in lawcodes, homilies and religious ceremonies.[25] In the late ninth century burial next to a church is still a privilege; by the late eleventh century it has become a regulated norm, in a bounded space made holy by formal ritual rather than informal association.

But there is no uniformity. Morris stresses regional differences in burial practice and cemetery location; variety is also visible in liturgical books of the period, which survive from the later tenth century onwards.[26] We might also adduce the astonishing range of form and iconography found in ninth- to eleventh-century grave furniture and structure, above and below ground, within and between cemeteries, and the small, problematic corpus of burials accompanied by grave-goods. Although at the time ideas about funerary norms may have seemed a matter of common sense and unquestioning practice, from our perspective they are rapidly changing and various in their incarnation. The very concept of 'Christian burial' is one of these rapidly changing ideas.

The question of christian identity

Abrams argues that in the early Middle Ages 'religion was as much about conduct (what you did, and where, and with whom) as about belief'; her point, about the communal nature of religion and its role in structuring group identity, is a valid one, but conduct and belief are not easily separable.[27] Lay religious practice may have been, as Fletcher calls it, 'a piety of performance' rather than one of conscience; certainly, the average thegn or reeve (if there were such a person) may not have pondered much on eschatological niceties, or even the ethical rights and

22 C. Scull, 'Burials at Emporia in England', in D. Hill and R. Cowie, *Wics: The Early Medieval Trading Centres of Northern Europe* (Sheffield, 2001), pp. 67–74, 73.
23 J. Blair, *The Church in Anglo-Saxon England* (Oxford, forthcoming).
24 Reynolds, 'Burials, Boundaries and Charters', p. 175.
25 H. Gittos, 'Creating the Sacred: Anglo-Saxon Rites for Consecrating Cemeteries', in Lucy and Reynolds, *Burial in Early Medieval England and Wales*, pp. 195–208.
26 Morris, *The Church in British Archaeology*, p. 62.
27 L. Abrams, 'Conversion and Assimilation', in Hadley and Richards, *Cultures in Contact*, pp. 135–54, 137–9.

wrongs of his daily conduct.[28] But the rules governing life do not always hold good in the face of death. At every death significant choices had to be made, and the people confronted with these challenges had a vast range of potential responses, in which belief and behaviour structured each other. By remembering how questions about death remained open in later Anglo-Saxon England, it becomes easier to understand these various practices as part of a great ongoing experiment. It bears repeating that there was no such thing as Christian burial, if by this we mean burial carried out in accordance with articulated ecclesiastical guidelines. This is the period in which the deposition of the body in the grave becomes the focus for elaborate Christian ritual and when the consecration of churchyards starts to be a liturgically formal ceremony, when particular churches assert rights over certain corpses while other corpses forfeit their claim to lie in hallowed ground, but there is no directive, ecclesiastical or lay, about the appearance, the structure or the furniture of the Christian grave. The inference is that every church took its own executive decisions, or allowed gild or family members to take them.

Kilbride complains that commentators on the spread of early medieval Christianity fail to specify the mechanisms of Christianization, which are clearly more complex than the teleological *post hoc* conversion narratives choose to suggest.[29] These mechanisms are also longer-lasting: tenth- and eleventh-century homilies and penitentials show that the Church understood that the struggle to 'Christianize' a society would not end until Doomsday. At the beginning of this chapter we asked what it meant to have a Christian burial; this cannot be answered without also looking at the question of how Christians defined themselves in life. Schreiter, writing about Roman Catholic missionary challenges in the twentieth century, defines cross-cultural Christian identity by five interlocking criteria. These are doctrinal and symbolic consistency, communal expression of prayer and sacrament, behavioural responses to the teaching of the Gospel, willingness to be assessed by other Christian communities, and readiness to contribute to the wider Church. This pentangular model is more complex than a simple dialectic of belief and behaviour, and has the advantages of setting the individual Christian and Christian community, such as a parish, in its wider ecclesiastical context. Although we rarely have the evidence to evaluate Anglo-Saxon performance in each of his fields, they remain a useful analytic tool.[30] Schreiter is writing from within the Church hierarchy, however, and his five criteria do not allow the laity an active role in the construction of Christian identity.

Brown compensates for this in his study of British Christianity in the nine-teenth and twentieth centuries. He argues that historians of Christianity have identified four religious modes, namely institutional, intellectual, functional (charitable and educational) and diffusive (outreach and mission). This ignores a fifth mode, 'discursive Christianity', which he defines as subscription to protocols

---

[28] R. Fletcher, *Bloodfeud: Murder and Revenge in Anglo-Saxon England* (London, 2002), p. 119.

[29] W. Kilbride, 'Why I Feel Cheated by the Term "Christianisation"', in A. Pluskowski (ed.), *Early Medieval Religion*, Archaeological Review from Cambridge 17:2 (2000), pp. 1–17, 12.

[30] R. J. Schreiter, *Constructing Local Theologies* (London, 1985), esp. ch. 6 and 7.

of 'rituals or customs of behaviour, economic activity, dress, speech and so on which are collectively promulgated as necessary for Christian identity'. These discourses may be produced officially by the clergy, or emerge from a community or family, or be private developments by individuals. His overall conclusion, that all other roles of religion are predicated on a discursive base, allows him to discuss modern social conventions such as 'Sunday best' or 'Sunday lunch', practices which the clergy never implemented or defined, and of which they sometimes disapproved, but which were nonetheless fundamental to lay Christian identity.[31] Given the absence of explicit instruction from the Church, late Anglo-Saxon burial may be just such a practice, constructed at the local level with degrees of priestly and lay involvement varying from community to community. The conceptual models of Schreiter and Brown, used in tandem, dissect the monolithic concept 'Christianity' into its constituent elements and show how they may be continuously reinvented as they intersect with different kinds of secular activity.

How to make a grave

This interaction is particularly important to bear in mind when considering the vexed issue of grave-goods. As Halsall points out, there is still a lingering desire among some historians and archaeologists to understand furnished burial as signalling non-Christian practices.[32] But clothed burial posed no problems for Werferth of Worcester: at what point along the spectrum does clothed burial segue into burial with grave-goods? Gräslund argues that while the eleventh-century graves from Gotland in Sweden are all furnished, only the pagans have food vessels, suggesting Christian burials are only accompanied by signals of rank, whereas pagan ones also have 'objects intended to be used in another life'.[33] But this definition only holds good for eleventh-century Gotland. Burnell and James draw attention to the Frankish burials from churches such as Cologne and St-Denis, containing vessels of all kinds, as well as offerings of food.[34] Ivison lists personal jewellery, a comb, a key, abbatial staffs of office, glass beads, crosses, coins and inscribed objects and vessels from the Byzantine and Frankish graves of tenth- to fourteenth-century Corinth.[35] Cuthbert, bishop of Lindisfarne, who died in 687, was buried with a wealth of personal items attested both archaeologically and textually. In a famous passage his corpse is described as 'wearing shoes to meet Christ in', which certainly makes them sound like 'objects to be used in another life', and precisely the same idea turns up again six centuries

---

[31] Brown, *The Death of Christian Britain*, pp. 115–69.
[32] G. Halsall, 'The Viking Presence in England? The Burial Evidence Reconsidered', in Hadley and Richards, *Cultures in Contact*, pp. 259–76.
[33] A.-S. Gräslund, 'The Conversion of Scandinavia – A Sudden Event or a Gradual Process?', in Pluskowski, *Early Medieval Religion*, pp. 83–98, 84.
[34] Burnell and James, 'Archaeology of Conversion', pp. 86–7; E. James, 'Burial and Status in the Early Medieval West', *TRHS* 5th ser. 39 (1989), pp. 23–40.
[35] E. Ivison, 'Death and Burial at Medieval Corinth (*c.* 960–1400)', in Dickinson and James, *Death and Burial*, pp. 117–21.

later, in the writing of Durandus of Mende.[36] There may well be an ideological distinction between 'graves containing status-markers' and 'graves containing objects for use in an after-life', but it is unlikely that this boundary corresponds to the division between people who defined themselves as 'Christian' or 'pagan'.

Ælfric stresses, in two separate homilies, that the resurrection body will not rise dressed in its shroud (*reaf*) but in spiritual garments, a point not made in his sources, and implying that he encountered people who believed they would indeed be wearing their burial shrouds in heaven.[37] The Norman bishop of Durham, William of St-Carileph (1081–96), was buried with his crosier, as were the thirteenth-century archbishops of York: is this a symbol of rank aimed at the onlookers at the funeral, or a means of asserting episcopal status at the Resurrection?[38] The records of the opening of Edward the Confessor's tomb in the twelfth century describe the regalia, jewels and fabrics with which he had been interred in 1066.[39] From Cuthbert to Edward, from the late seventh to the mid-eleventh centuries, there is not a single surviving intact and identifiable grave of a king or a bishop at any of the important churches they used as mausolea.[40] As a result, when isolated furnished burials are found, they are hard to place.[41] But our understanding of those ninth- to eleventh-century graves which *do* include weapons or jewellery might be very different if Æthelflæd's grave at Gloucester or the royal tombs at New Minster, Winchester, had survived into an era of antiquarian enquiry.

There is no intrinsic reason why grave-goods, however defined, should not have faded out and returned at various points over these centuries, for more complex reasons than the movement of the Viking armies in the 860s and 870s. In particular, the rise and fall of monasteries and concomitant ideals of austerity over the period need to be taken into consideration. There may be many different factors governing the presence or absence of furnished graves.[42] The seventh and eighth centuries produced several kings who retired into monasteries or to Rome, suggesting a widespread cult of renunciation in the face of death. But this royal habit stops in the ninth century, just as monasticism seems to be losing its drive.[43] Other forms of evidence also point to a complex process. Cubitt notes that the 'gradual failure' of evidence for church synods after 825 cannot be ascribed to Viking activity and she looks instead to changes in the relationship between

---

[36] B. Colgrave, *Two Lives of St Cuthbert* (Cambridge, 1985), p. 131; Rowell, *Liturgy of Christian Burial*, p. 65.

[37] *CH* I, XV, p. 303, lines 113–15; *Supp.* I, XI, pp. 433–4, lines 339–42.

[38] O. Owen, 'The Strange Beast that is the English Urnes Style', in Graham-Campbell, *Vikings and the Danelaw*, pp. 203–22, 206–7.

[39] F. Barlow, *The Life of King Edward who Rests at Westminster* (2nd edn, Oxford, 1992), Appendix 5, pp. 152–3.

[40] Yorke, 'Anglo-Saxon Royal Burial', p. 45.

[41] J. Graham-Campbell, 'Pagan Scandinavian Burial', Graham-Campbell, *Vikings and the Danelaw*, pp. 105–23.

[42] G. Halsall, 'Burial, Ritual, and Merovingian Society', in J. Hill and M. Swan (eds), *The Community, the Family, and the Saint: Patterns of Power in Early Medieval Europe* (Turnhout, 1998), pp. 325–38.

[43] C. Stancliffe, 'Kings who Opted Out', in P. Wormald *et al.* (eds), *Ideal and Reality in Frankish and Anglo-Saxon Society* (Oxford, 1983), pp. 154–76.

Wessex and Mercia, and the shifting balance of power from archbishop to king.[44] Barrow argues that the paucity of bishops in northern and eastern England from the late ninth to mid-tenth centuries may be the result of royal West Saxon rather than Viking machinations.[45] If seventh- to eighth-century lay burial without grave-goods originates in aristocratic imitation of monastic ideals, the ninth- and early tenth-century unfurnished graves, coming from an age with few or no monks to set the trend, may need another explanation. Indeed, graves from this period from York and Winchester contained cloth woven with gold, and one grave from the Old Minster, Winchester, had decorated silver garter tags as well, showing that some late Anglo-Saxons could be sumptuously clothed in death.[46] At least gold thread is archaeologically identifiable: clothes of wool, linen, or imported silk, however wonderfully embroidered, would completely disappear under most circumstances, and we must never forget how much we may have lost. Despite the excellent preservation of the timber at St Peter's, Barton-on-Humber, no textile remains of any kind were found in the graves.[47] Perhaps these people were buried naked, but more probably the textiles, whether clothes or shrouds, have just vanished.

Late Anglo-Saxon graves may generally have been unfurnished, but they had a wide range of forms. This is particularly clear at St Oswald's, Gloucester, since the site was first used as a cemetery in the late Roman period and then, after a long gap, continuously from around 900 till 1855, and the years from 900 to 1230 show more variety in burial practice than any other period. Here and nationwide Anglo-Saxon grave-diggers employed stones, charcoal, sand, chalk, mortar, tile, clay and other materials to distinguish the grave-cut from the surrounding soil. This range of underground form is not limited to one part of the country, nor to one type of cemetery, nor apparently to one social class, and it probably cannot be ascribed to a single cause. The variety is such that, although most burials continue to lie supine, with their heads to the west, with few or no identifiable objects added to the graves, there is no such thing as a typical late Anglo-Saxon grave. Surviving canon law shows no interest in the subject. If the Church did not articulate a rejection of grave-goods, then who did?

'Christian' and 'pagan'

The silence of canon laws on the minutiae of burial practice is all the more striking given their detail on other issues of which their authors did disapprove,

---

[44] C. Cubitt, *Anglo-Saxon Church Councils, c. 650 – c. 850* (Leicester, 1995), pp. 236–7.

[45] Barrow, 'Survival and Mutation', p. 158.

[46] Grave 1, from Old Minster, probably late ninth century, had 'head and shoulders . . . covered with cloth of gold' and silver Trewhiddle-style tags 'beneath the knees': M. Biddle, 'Excavations at Winchester 1964, Third Interim Report', *Antiquaries Journal* 45 (1965), pp. 230–64, 256 and 263–4; three other Winchester graves produced gold thread, in one apparently in the hands (grave 664) and another (grave 717) across the forehead: M. Biddle 'Excavations at Winchester 1968, Seventh Interim Report', *Antiquaries Journal* 49 (1969), pp. 297–329, 322.

[47] W. and K. Rodwell, 'St Peter's Church, Barton on Humber: Excavation and Critical Study, 1978–81', *Antiquaries Journal* 62 (1982), pp. 283–315, 302.

many of which are related to dying and death. Men like Wulfstan II of York (1002–23) were very interested in defining the behaviour that would disqualify people from a consecrated grave. It seems that while the 'how' of burial may not have been considered relevant to salvation, the 'where' was coming to be crucial, as the funerary landscape became polarized into hallowed and heathen. In his lawcode II Cnut, Wulfstan starts by defining *hæþenscip* as the worship of heathen gods, heavenly bodies, fire, flood, stones and trees, and the love of witchcraft and sacrifice, all of which clearly excludes one from the community of the faithful. But his list goes on to include murder and oath-breaking, adultery and failure to keep priestly vows (*had*), lying and theft.[48] *Hæþenscip* is an evolving term, not a static one, describing a wide range of social, moral and ethical as well as ritual behaviours, and Wulfstan implicitly recognizes this in his repeated references to 'one Christianity and every kind of heathen practice'.[49] Other generic words he uses for unacceptable activities performed by the baptized include *unnyt* (futile activity), *deofolgyld* (idolatry), *idel* (emptiness) and *gefleard* (delirium).[50] An anonymous homily for the third Sunday in Lent describes singing *idel* songs as *hæðenscipe* and *galscipe* (lewdness).[51] If these proscriptive texts are to be believed, a baptized and communicating church-goer could easily slip up and find himself reclassified as *hæþen*, in life and possibly also in burial. There is no simple opposition between two religious systems being constructed here.

Paganism could also be defined entirely passively, as Ælfric does in his Pastoral Letter for Wulfsige, bishop of Sherborne, when he describes a baby who dies unbaptized as a heathen.[52] If *hæþenscip* is something of which a normally devout English Christian or a new-born baby can partake, every reference to heathens in our sources needs to be evaluated separately. The men who made up the late ninth-century *micel hæþen here* (great heathen army) of the Anglo-Saxon Chronicles may have been behaving in a fashion the chroniclers found shockingly unchristian, but the phrase is not necessarily defining them as committed to a systematically pagan way of life, nor as entirely ignorant of Christianity, nor indeed as foreigners. Where the incomers were concerned, Abrams suggests that *pagani* may have come to mean Scandinavians in general, or have been used as a convenient slur 'when no longer strictly descriptive'.[53] Christians who had reneged on their ethical, social and ritual commitment may have been viewed more fearfully than pagans, as is suggested by an Irish reference to the terrifying Norse-Scots mercenaries 'who had renounced their baptism'.[54]

---

[48] II Cnut, 5–7, Liebermann, *Gesetze* I, p. 312.

[49] K. Jost, *Die 'Institutes of Polity, Civil and Ecclesiastical'* (Bern, 1959), pp. 1 and 116; Liebermann, *Gesetze* I: V Æthelred 34, p. 244; VIII Æthelred 44, p. 268; X Æthelred 1, p. 270.

[50] D. Bethurum, *The Homilies of Wulfstan* (Oxford, 1957), XVIII, lines 47–65 and 104–7, pp. 247–9.

[51] Assmann XI, pp. 138–43, lines 119–20.

[52] D. Whitelock, M. Brett and C. N. L. Brooke, *Councils and Synods of Great Britain with Other Documents Relating to the English Church. Volume I. Part 1, 871–1066* (Oxford, 1981), p. 210.

[53] L. Abrams, 'The Conversion of the Danelaw', in Graham-Campbell, *Vikings and the Danelaw*, pp. 31–44, 32.

[54] J. O'Donovan, *Annals of Ireland* (Dublin, 1860), pp. 138–9.

Ælfric and Wulfstan had a particularly chiaroscuro view of the religious landscape, and because their writings survive in unequalled quantities we tend to see that landscape through their eyes. Definitions of Christianity contained more twilit areas for those who did not spend their days in a focused cycle of prayer and preaching, and even perhaps for a few of those who did, as some anonymous homilies suggest. Conversion to Christianity has come in for focused attention in recent work, but the maintenance of Christianity in the wider community is as obscure a subject. When texts discuss the religious practices of individuals their focus is on the elite and orthodox, and, while the archaeology of the grave has great potential, its story with very few exceptions is one of religious conformity in death, telling us nothing of how that conformity was promulgated and accepted as a funerary ideal. Another source, high-profile and enduring, offers itself for interrogation: the stone monuments, like those at St Oswald's Gloucester, erected over the graves of some of the wealthy.

Most of these stones are clearly Christian in their reference, some have secular imagery, others have designs of plants, animals or knotwork which may appear purely decorative but probably encode complex references which are hard to read now and may have always been challenging.[55] A few stones refer to a body of stories and teaching from indigenous Germanic tradition, most of which have been put to explicitly Christian purpose; these are not examples of a hybrid or syncretic religion but ingenious employment of non-biblical stories in the furtherance of a Christian agenda by very thoughtful people.[56] As Murray points out in her discussion of the emergence of Christian art in the Mediterranean, it may draw on pagan art for its technique, style and imagery, but that makes it neither pagan nor syncretic, merely comprehensible to Christians brought up in a particular symbolic environment, and she specifically identifies death and the afterlife as conceptual fields in which such innovation occurred.[57] Much of the English sculpture shows that the same sculptor could work in so-called 'Anglian' and 'Anglo-Scandinavian' styles, and incorporate stories and images from a variety of sources into his iconographic programme.[58] Ascribing the growth in stone monuments connected with funerary practice only to the political disturbances of the 860s and 870s and the subsequent assimilation of the incomers needs reassessment. It is intrinsically little more plausible as a simple relationship of cause and effect than an argument that the Vikings were solely responsible for other developments in mortuary behaviour at the time, such as the growth in

---

[55] J. Hawkes, 'Symbolic Lives: The Visual Evidence', in J. Hines (ed.), *The Anglo-Saxons: From the Migration Period to the Eighth Century: An Ethnographic Perspective* (Woodbridge, 1997), pp. 311–38, 315.

[56] J. Hines, 'Scandinavian English: A Creole in Context', in P. Ureland and G. Broderick (eds), *Language Contact in the British Isles* (T(bingen, 1991), pp. 403–27, 417; J. McKinnell 'Norse Mythology and Northumbria: A Response', in J. D. Niles and M. Amodio (eds), *Anglo-Scandinavian England: Norse–English Relations in the Period before the Conquest* (London, 1989), pp. 42–52, 50.

[57] C. Murray, *Rebirth and Afterlife: A Study of the Transmutation of Some Pagan Imagery in Early Christian Funerary Art*, BAR International Series 100 (1981), pp. 11–12.

[58] Cf. also the Sutton, Isle of Ely, brooch with its 'pseudo-Viking' design but lengthy Christian and English inscription. D. M. Wilson, *Anglo-Saxon Ornamental Metalwork 700–1100 in the British Museum* (London, 1964), pp. 50 and 86–8.

popularity of charcoal burial or the formal ritual development of consecrated churchyards.

Many of the new arrivals coming directly or indirectly from Scandinavia during the ninth to eleventh centuries probably already had some exposure to Christianity. There had been various missions to the royal courts of Denmark since the early ninth century, and there must have been many unrecorded contacts, involving mission, trade, warfare, diplomacy or hostage-taking, although, as Abrams points out, a Dane who was baptized abroad would encounter difficulty sustaining his faith when back at home.[59] There were churches in Hedeby and Ribe by the middle of the ninth century, and the Sawyers argue for a century or so of religious toleration before Denmark's formal conversion in 960.[60] The people who moved eastwards across the Pennines into Yorkshire and Lincolnshire in the early tenth century had Scandinavians in their pedigrees but they had also been living among the Christian cultures of Ireland, Man and the Western Isles for several generations.[61]

Hæþenscip, *magic and heresy*

Injunctions banning paganism are a commonplace of canon lawcodes, and from the end of the tenth century they are also found in English secular law. They are likely to be a response to, and an attempt to redefine, genuine practices, although their success is questionable. They do not peter out towards the end of our period: in the mid-eleventh century the *Northumbrian Priests' Law* proscribes sacrifice and divination, witchcraft, idol-worship and maintenance of 'a sanctuary round a stone or a tree or a well or any such nonsense (*fleard*)', and in 1102 the Council of Westminster passes an ordinance that no one is to 'venerate the bodies of dead men or springs or any other things without episcopal authority'.[62] This suggests that certain activities might have been approved or frowned upon depending on who sat in the local bishop's throne, and that the people involved may have seen no contradiction between these activities and church membership. Definitions of what it meant to be a practising Christian prove elusive. In Wulfstan's opinion, the minimum requirements for admission to communion and Christian burial were a knowledge of the Paternoster and Creed, but neither of these precludes an understanding of the world as full of dangerous spirits which may need appeasing in ways the Church finds hard to accept.[63] Perhaps in response to a need for

[59] L. Abrams, 'History and Archaeology: The Conversion of Scandinavia', in B. Crawford (ed.), *Conversion and Christianity in the North Sea World* (St Andrews, 1998), pp. 109–28, 114–15.

[60] B. and P. Sawyer, *Medieval Scandinavia: From Conversion to Reformation circa 800–1500* (Minneapolis, 1993), pp. 100–1.

[61] A. Smyth, *Scandinavian Kings in the British Isles, 850–880* (Oxford, 1977), pp. 6–8 and 122–4; M. Dolley, 'The Palimpsest of Viking Settlement on Man', in H. Bekker-Nielsen *et al.* (eds), *Proceedings of the Eighth Viking Congress* (Odense, 1981), pp. 173–81, 178–9.

[62] *Northumbrian Priests' Law, Councils*, p. 463; P. Wormald, *The Making of English Law, King Alfred to the Twelfth Century; Volume I, Legislation and Its Limits* (Oxford, 1999), pp. 208–10 and 396–7; E. W. Kemp, *Canonization and Authority in the Western Church* (Oxford, 1948), pp. 53–4.

[63] Wulfstan, 'Canons of Edgar', *Councils*, p. 322.

Christian charms, the Paternoster in particular finds itself reinvented in vernacular versions, one of the most creative of which is the verse dialogue *Solomon and Saturn*. This describes the prayer as 'soul's honey' and 'mind's milk' before launching into a long exposition of its potency, in which the letters of the alphabet are personified as powerful warriors defending the soul.[64] It culminates with the suggestion that no man should draw his sword without reciting it, *ac symle he sceal singan, ðonne he his sweord geteo, Pater Noster*, giving the prayer an amuletic force which goes beyond the brief of the lawcodes.[65] *Solomon and Saturn* was clearly aimed at laymen as well as the clergy, and perhaps it was developed as a way of teaching the power of the prayer. This text, preserved in several versions, attests to a wide interest in and reverence for literacy as a quasi-magical craft, and it should alert us to the creativity and the success of the Church in its fight to capture the lay imagination.

While the lawcodes were condemning 'divination', contemporary missals and prayerbooks from such centres of orthodoxy as Winchester and Exeter were packed with information on how to foretell the future, interpret the voice of thunder, and predict a child's fate depending on which day of the week he or she was born.[66] The English translation of Halitgar's *Penitential* allows the picking of *wyrtas* (plants) as long as it is done not *mid galdre* (with charms) but with Paternoster and Creed and various prayers.[67] *Licwigelunga* (corpse-divination) and necromancy are banned in the lawcodes of Cnut, but at times such activities may have come uncomfortably close to the establishment of unauthorized saints' cults. Ælfric and William of Malmesbury held that devils could impersonate the dead, while decrying more popular beliefs that the dead themselves could walk.[68] The problem with proscribed divination may not always have been the activities *per se*, but the personnel involved, with the clergy defining themselves as the only social group allowed direct access to mystical knowledge. This issue is central to many of the concerns of this book: death and dying do not only produce practical challenges of disease diagnosis or corpse disposal, they are also, with conception and birth, the greatest mysteries of human experience, and they intersect directly with ideas about time, predicting the future, and access to secret knowledge. Medical texts also fall into this category, and many of these texts cannot be distinguished from charms or prayers, they show intimate familiarity with the liturgy, and some even require the medical application of the communion plate or

[64] K. O'Keeffe, *Visible Song: Transitional Literacy in Old English Verse*, CSASE 4 (Cambridge, 1990), pp. 54–9; R. I. Page, 'Anglo-Saxon Runes and Magic', in D. Parsons (ed.), *Runes and Runic Inscriptions: Collected Essays on Anglo-Saxon and Viking Runes* (Woodbridge, 1995), pp. 105–26, 116.

[65] Lines 163b–167a: R. J. Menner, *The Poetical Dialogues of Solomon and Saturn* (New York, 1941), p. 89.

[66] R. Liuzza, 'Anglo-Saxon Prognostics in Context: A Survey and Handlist of Manuscripts', *ASE* 30 (2001), pp. 181–230.

[67] J. Raith, *Die altenglischen Version des Halitgar'schen Bussbuches* (Hamburg, 1933), Book 2:23, p. 30.

[68] William of Malmesbury, *Regum*, pp. 134–5; *Supp.* II, XXIX, p. 796, lines 118–23.

wafers 'like those used for Mass'.[69] These activities may most usefully be seen as part of a world of para-liturgy, unrecorded by any pontifical or sacramentary but acceptable at the heart of the establishment and capable of great adaptability, as in the *Vita Wulfstani*'s vignette of Wulfstan II of Worcester insisting that his hotel bedroom be asperged with holy water and blessed with the sign of the cross, *sic fugarentur aduersa* (that the fiends might be put to flight).[70] Such an attitude invites rather than deters ritual inventiveness.

Despite the best efforts of the first and second generation Benedictine reformers between around 950 and 1000, it is clear from what Ælfric has to say about 'English books full of foolishness' that confusion (or creativity) was rife. Godden argues that Ælfric's objections to these books, which may be associated with some of the surviving anonymous homilies, centred on 'their use of sensational narratives which were clearly fictitious and in some cases of dubious morality'.[71] Ælfric insisted that *se mæssepreost sceal mannum bodian þone so þan geleafan 7 hym larspel secgan* (the mass-priest must instruct people in true faith and tell them homilies), and his series of homilies and saints' lives attempted to control the contents of the English *larspel*.[72] But by his very insistence on the value of teaching and explanation he opens up the space for the widespread, unregulated reinvention of Christian symbols and narratives, both by the vernacular preachers and by their audiences, and Ælfric's concern about orthodoxy does not seem to have been typical of his own nor of following generations of churchmen. Many of these 'dubious' texts survive in multiple versions, and it is probable that the people who had them copied approved of, or were at least interested in, their contents. Clayton argues that we do not yet know 'whether the majority of these [anonymous] texts are early and date from the pre-reform period, or, like the work of Ælfric, were the product of the Benedictine reform', but this is surely ascribing too much power and ubiquity to the monastic reformers.[73] Despite their best efforts, major churches survived unreformed, and many new parish churches were established; it is conceivable that manuscripts and other artefacts expressing ideas antithetical to reform principles continued to be produced. They were certainly copied into the eleventh and even the twelfth centuries.

Concern about Arianism in Ælfric's writing and in illustrations in eleventh-century manuscripts from Winchester and Canterbury may reflect contemporary difficulties with Trinitarian doctrine; what Ælfric calls 'belittling our Saviour' is precisely the sort of pitfall into which an under-supervised priest in a new manorial church might stumble when trying to explain the Trinity without

---

[69] J. Grattan and C. Singer, *Anglo-Saxon Magic and Medicine Illustrated Specially from the Semi-Pagan Text 'Lacnunga'* (Oxford, 1952), pp. 160–2.
[70] R. R. Darlington, *The Vita Wulfstani of William of Malmesbury* (London, 1928), p. 49.
[71] M. Godden, 'Ælfric and the Vernacular Prose Tradition', in P. Szarmach and B. Huppé (eds), *The Old English Homily and Its Backgrounds* (New York, 1978), pp. 99–117, 102.
[72] Ælfric, First Pastoral Letter to Wulfstan, ch. 175, *Councils*, p. 294.
[73] M. Clayton, 'Homiliaries and Preaching in Anglo-Saxon England', in P. Szarmach (ed.), *Old English Prose: Basic Readings* (New York and London, 2000), pp. 155–98.

undermining essential monotheistic concepts.[74] Most heresy originates in genuine efforts to understand complex mystical and ethical doctrine, or from taking biblical injunctions literally, and de Jong argues that 'it is hard to imagine the so-called popular heresies of the second half of the Middle Ages without the Gospels being interiorized on a much larger and unpredictable scale by groups of ordinary people intent on following both its letter and its spirit'.[75] This line of argument suggests paradoxically that heresy can be read as an indication that the Church is doing its job. If the tenth-century English Church, with its tradition of vernacular preaching, its numerous new local churches and its insistence on the importance of confession, was succeeding in convincing its audience of its message, then a degree of unregulated, even heretical, response is to be expected, if only at the individual level. In the next chapter we explore the question of penance, confession and ritual practice at the sick-bed and death-bed, primarily through a close reading of a mid-eleventh-century manuscript (Oxford, Bodl. Laud Miscellaneous 482), which suggests that vernacular confession was widely encouraged and already had a long history, and we may legitimately speculate on how far down the social scale these pastoral activities had percolated by 1066, and how they shaped and were shaped by lay response. The first mass burning of heretics is recorded at Orleans in 1022; while there is nothing like this in England it does suggest that the condemnation of Arius in these texts and images, like *hæpenscip*, may be more than the reflexive passing-on of patristic tradition, that they may reflect the real complexities of late Anglo-Saxon culture, as well as the anxieties of the Benedictines who saw themselves as the beleaguered defenders of orthodoxy.[76]

One of the two manuscript illustrations showing Arius is the 'Quinity' in the prayerbook of Ælfwine, dean of New Minster, Winchester, in the 1020s, which associates the arch-heretic with Lucifer and Judas, the arch-traitors (Plate 1).[77] This diminutive but innovative and challenging coloured ink-drawing shows Father, Son and Holy Ghost, crowned Madonna and Child enthroned together on a rainbow and contained within a circular frame, a giant halo that repeats the decoration of the rainbow. They are elegantly dressed and disposed, God the Father and the adult and infant Christ hold books, and their expressive hands, attentive faces and apparent eye-contact suggest an absorbing conversation is going on. The feet of the adult Christ rest on the figure of Lucifer, who plunges

[74] Ælfric's references to Arius are in *CH* I, p. 342, lines 213–14; *Supp.* I, p. 403, line 159; First English Pastoral Letter for Wulfstan, *Councils*, pp. 273–4; Ælfric's Pastoral Letter for Wulfsige III, bishop of Sherborne, *Councils*, p. 198; Manuscript illumination: Winchester (Cotton Titus D xxvii, fol. 75v.) and Canterbury (Eadui Codex, Hannover, Kestner Codex WM XXIa, 36, fol. 147v): E. Temple, *Anglo-Saxon Manuscripts, 900–1066* (London, 1976), Quinity no. 77, ill. 245; Eadui Codex no. 27, ill. 227.
[75] M. de Jong, 'Rethinking Early Medieval Christianity: A View from the Netherlands', *Early Medieval Europe* 7:3 (1998), pp. 261–76, 271.
[76] E. Peters (ed.), *Heresy and Authority in Medieval Europe* (London, 1980), pp. 57–71; R. I. Moore, *The Birth of Popular Heresy* (Toronto, 1995), p. 15.
[77] BL Cotton Titus D xxvii, fol. 75v: B. G(nzel (ed.), *Ælfwine's Prayerbook: London, British Library, Cotton Titus D. xxvi + xxvii*, HBS 108 (London, 1993); E. H. Kantorowicz, 'The Quinity of Winchester', *Art Bulletin* 29 (1947), pp. 73–85.

Plate 1: The Winchester Quinity from Ælfwine's Prayerbook (London, British Library, MS Cotton Titus D xxvii, fol. 75r). By permission of the British Library. This innovative picture of the 1020s encapsulates a polarized understanding of sacred and damned space that has parallels in descriptions of burials in tenth- and eleventh-century law codes.

from within the sacred circle towards a gaping and fanged hellmouth below. He is naked and shackled, as are Arius to the left and Judas to the right, both contorted to fit into the corners of the rectangular frame. Judas lifts his right hand to his face in a gesture of woe, while Arius appears to be biting his hand, perhaps a very early appearance of a self-harming motif specifically connected to damnation.[78] The picture works on multiple temporal levels, signalled by the presence of both the infant and the adult Christ. It represents a moment outside historical time in which Lucifer is perpetually tumbling bound into the jaws of hell, and Judas and Arius are already damned when the angels fall. Judas holds a spear whose head is drooping like a wilting flower, a close parallel to the broken spear held by the personification of death in the near-contemporary Uta Codex, a Bavarian manuscript with many Anglo-Saxon connexions.[79] The Quinity drawing was produced in Winchester, the heartland of the Benedictine reform, in a private prayer-book for a senior monk, and it represents a polarized view of the sacred and the profane, a recreation of Ælfric's fears in pictorial form. Within the sacred circle all is harmony, while outside, in the margins, lurk ambition, treachery, heresy, pain and death. Its imagery dramatizes the language used in the anathemas appended to legal documents, where anyone who breaks the terms of the agreement is threatened with being confined to hell, and sometimes specifically threatened with the company of *Iudan þe Cristes lewa wes* (Judas who was Christ's betrayer).[80]

Winchester, Canterbury and Worcester were the major focuses of the Benedictine reform movement in the mid- to late tenth century, and the textual evidence is strongly biased in their direction, both in terms of quantity and content. But despite the energy of the reform, no monasteries were established north of the Humber before Selby, in 1069–70.[81] Where does this leave the majority of the people of Anglo-Saxon England, who had no contact with the centres of reformed monasticism? Or indeed, the people living in the first century or so of the period under consideration here, before the reform was set in motion? As we have seen at St Oswald's, Gloucester, and St Peter's, Worcester, pre-reform architecture, liturgy and confraternity were capable of considerable sophistication, at the highest social level at least. Nor does the note appended to the York Gospels listing the church treasures of Sherburn-in-Elmet suggest liturgical impoverishment in the Yorkshire of the 1020s or 1030s; it includes two gospel books, two epistle books, a missal, a hymnal and a psalter, as well as chalice and paten, vestments, altar cloths, crosses and both hanging bells and hand-bells.[82]

The Benedictine reformers were a vocal group of men, with a vested interest in emphasizing their own superhuman virtues and a persistent animus against secular and particularly sexually active clergy. They revile *þa modigan preostas*

---

[78] M. Barasch, *Gestures of Despair in Medieval and Early Renaissance Art* (New York, 1976), p. 12.

[79] A. S. Cohen, *The Uta Codex: Art, Philosophy and Reform in Eleventh-Century Germany* (University Park, 2000), colour plate 4 and pp. 151–4.

[80] A. J. Robertson, *Anglo-Saxon Charters* (Cambridge, 1939), XLV, p. 94.

[81] Stenton, *Anglo-Saxon England*, p. 456.

[82] Robertson, *Anglo-Saxon Charters* II, p. 248.

(the proud priests) whom they displaced, but this does not necessarily mean that those priests had been incapable of maintaining their churches, performing the mass in Latin, preaching in the vernacular, and providing pastoral and sacramentary services for their parishioners.[83] Many churches, like St Oswald's, Gloucester, were never reformed, and even at Worcester the reform seems to have been no more than sporadically successful. There are at least two ecclesiastical cultures operating here, within the great minsters and monasteries, and there may well be a third, in the small, local churches. Blair suggests a contrast between the representatives of 'an intellectual and universalist Christian culture' and 'a participatory, locally embedded one which rural communities shared with their own priests', arguing that the latter was already well entrenched in England by around 800 but remained disturbing to representatives of the former, like Alcuin.[84] As we shall see, these different cultures within the ecclesiastical hierarchy and their various responses to issues of sexuality and purity, transgression and trust, intertwine around many of the ideas associated with the body, death and burial.

It is the first of Blair's two Christian cultures, highly educated, Latinate and orthodox, which is gravely threatened in the ninth century.[85] This has serious implications for the English Church's participation in the wider culture of Christendom, but it is less clear how it affected ordinary people's ability to have a basic Christian life, death and burial. What was the Church like before the Vikings arrived? Carver uses sculptural evidence to argue that the invasions in northern and eastern England during the 860s and 870s resulted in a 'dissolution of the monasteries', but it is questionable how many monasteries, in the strict sense, remained to be dissolved by the later ninth century. The Church may already have been 'impregnated with the values of lay society', in Wormald's phrase, and if important lay families had been investing and burying in a church for generations then it would have become the guardian of family memory and identity, in liturgical, monumental and documentary form.[86] These families are likely to have contributed the abbots as well as the land and the money to these houses, and such a church would have been receptive to lay influence long before the disruptions of the later ninth century. Carver's division of his sculpture sample, the stones of the East Riding of Yorkshire (some of which are discussed in detail in Chapter Five below), into seventh- to eighth- and ninth- to eleventh-century categories disguises the strong stylistic and iconographic continuities which are found across the period, and his assumption that the Vikings were entirely responsible for the changes in secular and ecclesiastical structure is predicated on the idea that the early to mid-ninth-century church was still

---

[83] *Ibid.* XXXVIII, p. 70; cf. M. Lapidge, and M. Winterbottom (eds), *Wulfstan of Winchester: The Life of St Æþelwold* (Oxford, 1991), ch. 16, p. 30.
[84] Blair, *The Church in Anglo-Saxon England*, ch. 3.
[85] D. Dumville, *Liturgy and the Ecclesiastical History of Late Anglo-Saxon England* (Woodbridge, 1992), p. 98.
[86] P. Wormald, 'Viking Studies: Whence and Whither?', in R. T. Farrell (ed.), *The Vikings* (London, 1982), pp. 128–53, 138; C. Cubitt, 'Monastic Memory and Identity in Early Anglo-Saxon England', in W. O. Frazer and A. Tyrell, *Social Identity in Early Medieval Britain* (Leicester, 2000), pp. 253–76.

generally monastic in the narrow sense of the term.[87] But in the account of the dispute over land at Sodbury we saw one Gloucestershire family who could not even find someone with a priestly vocation, never mind a monastic one. Furthermore, Asser prefers to understand the absence of monasteries in ninth-century England in terms of lack of interest in monasticism, not as a result of Viking assault, and he claims that many former monasteries had long lapsed into a presumably more secular way of life.[88]

The changing culture of death over two and a half centuries

The differences between the beginning of the reign of Alfred and the end of that of William I are profound. As far as the church is concerned, the main changes by 1087 are the widespread presence of reformed houses in the south, whether monks under the rule of Benedict or, as at Exeter, secular canons under the rule of Chrodegang, and the much more extensive provision of rural and urban parish churches. Where the wider culture was concerned, these developments translated into a more rigorously penitential approach to dying, a greater chance of dying with a priest present, a shorter journey to the graveyard, more access to clergy to help with or take over the funeral, and heightened awareness of the burials of the dead adjacent to the homes and places of worship of the living. Whereas the inhabitants of a minster precinct would long have been used to the intermingling of the living and the dead, it is only from the late Anglo-Saxon period that the lay inhabitants of both town and country would have been in daily contact with the graves of their predecessors. Another major factor in the transformation of society must have been the presence of priests, now living among the communities which they ministered, continuously encountered in social as well as ritual environments.[89]

There are some things we are never going to know about how the people of Anglo-Saxon England faced their deaths. It can be inferred that death in child-birth, for both mother and baby, was a frequent occurrence, but this goes almost unmentioned – is it because the sources were mostly produced by communities of men, some of whom (if by no means all) were celibate? Where the possibility of gynaecological catastrophe is mentioned, it is mostly found in the leech-books, texts that present their own challenges. They draw on an immense range of classical and indigenous traditions, covering problems from childbirth and scabies to intestinal parasites and lost cattle.[90] The number of surviving manuscripts wholly or partly concerned with this kind of knowledge suggests that medical information circulated widely, yet other than stray references to doctors, such as the baffled physicians in Asser's *Life of King Alfred*, or to the monastic

---

[87] M. Carver, 'Conversion and Politics on the Eastern Seaboard of Britain: Some Archaeological Indicators', in Crawford, *Conversion and Christianity*, pp. 11–40, 26.

[88] Stevenson, *Asser*, ch. 93.

[89] A. Murray, 'Counselling in Medieval Confession', in P. Biller and A. J. Minnis (eds), *Handling Sin: Confession in the Middle Ages* (Woodbridge, 1998), pp. 63–78, 64–5.

[90] O. Cockayne, *Leechdoms, Wortcunning and Starcraft of Early England*, RS 35 (London, 1864–6).

sick-bay in the *Regularis Concordia*, few hints are given about their social role and what, if any, training or institutional connexion they may have had.[91] Immediately after the Conquest, hospitals and leprosaria in particular begin to be founded in English towns, yet towns, needy people and indeed lepers had been present in the tenth and earlier eleventh centuries. Priests as well as physicians are called to sick-beds, and rites to ease the journey of the dying are commonly found in liturgical manuscripts, but were they only available to a very few, or had they escaped into a wider context of pastoral care? Similarly, we have no direct account of whose job it was to lay out the corpse, arrange the funeral, choose the grave-site and dig the grave, order and design the memorial (if memorial there were to be). Little or nothing is known about some crucial activities that hover on the boundary between functional and ritual, of which grave-digging is one. The elaborately structured graves show that the meaning and purpose of the grave must have been debated, and that ritual specialists were involved in their construction, but the literary and documentary sources are almost silent. These are but a few of the issues which must be raised even if only to be minimally answered.

VERCELLI HOMILY IX

This chapter concludes with a close reading of Vercelli Homily IX, a particularly rich source of images of communal and individual responses to death, the death-bed and the grave, judgement, heaven and hell. While the homilist explores the differences between life and death, they are not as important or interesting to him as the difference between experiences before and after the Last Judgement. As a result, the distinctions between living and dead bodies blur, events around death are downplayed, and Doomsday becomes the point to which significant eschatological experience is deferred, a thoroughly Augustinian concept which permeates Anglo-Saxon thought about death, and one which is central to understanding much of the material examined in this book.[92]

The Vercelli codex was compiled around sixty years after the death of Æthelflæd. In the architecture of her foundation at St Oswald's, and in the decoration of the gravestones that accompanied it, we saw a conscious evocation of the traditions of the Carolingian church of the ninth century. Vercelli IX calls on another source of inspiration, drawn from the Irish intellectual tradition.[93] The imaginative challenges presented by death were responded to with great creative energy in many different genres. Vercelli IX dramatizes this creativity; it also provides incidental detail about the cultural practices associated with death that

[91] A. Meaney, 'Variant Versions of Old English Medical Recipes and the Compilation of Bald's *Leechbook*', *ASE* 13 (1994), pp. 235–68; Stevenson, *Asser*, ch. 74, p. 54; T. Symons (ed.), *Regularis Concordia: The Monastic Agreement* (London, 1953), pp. 64–8.

[92] B. Daley, *The Hope of the Early Church: A Handbook of Patristic Eschatology* (Cambridge, 1991), pp. 131–50.

[93] C. D. Wright, *The Irish Tradition in Old English Literature*, CSASE 6 (Cambridge, 1993).

help us in the construction of analytical tools with which to make sense of other kinds of evidence.

The homilies in the Vercelli book, which is written in one hand throughout, were collected by someone with a great interest in death, burial and judgement.[94] It is the earliest surviving English homiletic manuscript, coming from the second half of the tenth century, and it is best known for its poetic content, which includes *Andreas*, *The Fates of the Apostles*, *Soul and Body*, *The Dream of the Rood* and *Elene*.[95] Although the texts on which it draws were probably originally designed for preaching to the laity at mass, the codex itself seems to have been compiled as an anthology for private reading and meditation.[96] Ó Carragáin shows how the book is structured around eschatological themes, arguing that of all the Anglo-Saxon poetic manuscripts 'it is the one where we can most clearly see the recurring, almost obsessive, preoccupations of a single compiler'.[97] Many of its texts contain graphic imagery and paradoxical ideas; Homily IX is one of these; it is also characterized by intense, sensual language. For the origins of a text like this, we may need to look outside the world of the Benedictine reformers to that of the secular clergy, who as Fowler notes 'must have enjoyed unprecedented responsibility and opportunity for freedom', and may have lived lives very similar to those of the laymen around them.[98] Fowler is referring specifically to the north of England during the archiepiscopate of Wulfstan II of York in the first quarter of the eleventh century, but his observations hold true for much of the rest of the country, in the late ninth and tenth centuries as well as the eleventh.

The composition and transmission of anonymous homilies

The homilies were reworked as they circulated between communities, and while some of these reworkings were dependent on the facilities of the scriptorium, others need not have been.[99] Teresi, in her discussion of the transmission of English homilies into the twelfth century, proposes a model in which various themes were committed to memory and permanently available to the individual preacher for retrieval and reincorporation into new homilies, a process she refers to as the 'mnemonic repertoire'. This underlines the way that the spoken and written traditions functioned in tandem, with ideas flowing in and out of minds and manuscripts, allowing a homilist to take a series of familiar ideas which he knew by heart, and combine, add to and articulate them in unparalleled ways, without necessarily committing them to parchment.[100] Although these homilies

---

94 D. Scragg, 'The Compilation of the Vercelli Book', *ASE* 2 (1973), pp. 189–207; P. Szarmach (ed.), *Vercelli Homilies IX–XXIII* (Toronto, 1981), p. xxii.

95 D. Scragg, *The Vercelli Homilies and Related Texts*, EETS OS 300 (Oxford, 1992), p. xx.

96 Clayton, 'Homiliaries and Preaching', pp. 171–5.

97 E. Ó Carragáin, 'Rome, Ruthwell, Vercelli: "The Dream of the Rood" and the Italian Connection', in V. Corazza (ed.). *Vercelli tra oriente ed occidente tra tarda antichità e medioevo* (Vercelli, 1997), pp. 59–100, 94.

98 R. Fowler, *Wulfstan's Canons of Edgar*, EETS OS 226 (Oxford, 1972), pp. xlix–li.

99 M. Godden, 'Old English Composite Homilies from Winchester', *ASE* 4 (1975), pp. 57–65.

100 L. Teresi, 'Mnemonic Transmission of Old English Texts in the Post-Conquest Period', in M. Swan

are classified as prose, their resonant images often seem more poetic than prosaic. The fluid and intertextual nature of Anglo-Saxon poetry, with its traditional vocabulary, results in what Pasternack calls 'anonymous polyphony', with each structural segment from the half-line to the entire work referring to many other poems, not quoting directly but drawing from a well of common tradition, and her analysis intersects with Teresi's ideas about the homilists' 'mnemonic repertoire' to suggest that some at least of the poems and homilies may have emerged from the same environments.[101]

Vernacular poetry provides a reflection of the assumptions and interpretations acceptable to the culture as a whole, rather than the perspective and understanding of a single poetic voice. In a study of Anglo-Saxon poets' approaches to their sources, Irvine concludes that they were profoundly creative, and terms their attitude one of 'absorption and transformation'.[102] These models also apply to the anonymous homilies, many of which had a wide and long-lasting appeal despite their occasionally erratic relationship with orthodox thinking. Nothing can be stated securely about the intended audience of Vercelli IX, although the homily with analogous passages in Oxford, Bodl. Hatton 115, envisages an audience of priests, and it seems likely that the homilist of Vercelli IX did not see his audience as devoted to celibacy, given the alluring presentation of sexuality towards the end of the text.

Vercelli IX represents the earliest extant version of a complex eschatological homily with parallels in several other homiletic collections, but it is clear that there had already been one or more English antecedents by the time the Vercelli codex was compiled.[103] Furthermore, Scragg notes the popularity of the homily, pointing out that the version in Bodley 340/342 was 'annotated and altered by a number of hands until long after the Norman Conquest', and he also points out that it may have come in for censorship: Oxford, Bodl., MS 340/342 is a copy of a Canterbury homiliary from *c.* 1000 and contains Vercelli IX; CCCC, MS 198 is a later copy of the same homiliary and substitutes an Ælfric homily in place of Vercelli IX.[104] This text, in its various incarnations, is thus enduringly successful for over a hundred and fifty years, despite its inspiration by Irish traditions of apocryphal ideas and dramatic imagery which were actively rejected by the guardians of homiletic orthodoxy.[105] This Hiberno-English literature forms a textual analogue to the Irish-inspired sculpture that was spreading widely in the north of England in the early to mid-tenth century.[106]

and E. Treharne (eds), *Rewriting Old English in the Twelfth Century*, CSASE 30 (Cambridge, 2000), pp. 98–116; Stanley, 'The Judgement of the Damned', p. 365.

[101] C. Pasternack, 'Anonymous Polyphony and "The Wanderer's" Textuality', *ASE* 20, pp. 99–122.

[102] M. Irvine, 'Anglo-Saxon Literary Theory Exemplified in Old English Poems: Interpreting the Cross in *The Dream of the Rood* and *Elene*', *Style* 20 (1986), pp. 157–81.

[103] Scragg cites parallels from Bodley Hatton 115, BL Cotton Tiberius A iii, CCCC 419/421, Bodley Hatton 113/114-Junius 121 and Bodley 340/342: Scragg, *Vercelli Homilies*, pp. 151–7.

[104] Scragg, *Vercelli Homilies*, pp. 152 and 157.

[105] Wright, *The Irish Tradition*, pp. 3–7 and 228–9.

[106] J. Lang, 'Some Late Pre-Conquest Sculptures in Ryedale: A Reappraisal', *JBAA*, 3rd series, 36 (1973), pp. 17–20; R. Bailey, 'The Chronology of Viking Age Sculpture in Northumbria', in J. Lang (ed.), *Anglo-Saxon and Viking Age Sculpture and Its Context*, BAR British Series 49 (1978), pp. 173–203.

Dissecting death

The Irish technique of clarifying ideas through lists and categories appealed greatly to the author of Vercelli IX, and he uses these devices to bring death's terrifying qualities home to his audience. While he is drawing on a well-established and extremely various tradition, no exact sources for his examples can be identified.[107] After beginning with a general exhortation to repentance and a reminder of the proximity of the last days, he sets out his main themes, *deaðes onlicnesse* and *helle gryre* (prefiguration of death, and the terror of hell, 31). He begins his attempt to describe what death is (32–40) by starting with the concept of three deaths: the first being when someone is overcome by sin, the second when the soul and body part, and the third the eternal death endured by souls in hell.[108] He thus uses *deaþ* to mean three different things, a process which can be reversed (sinfulness on earth), a moment (bodily death), and a state which cannot be reversed (damnation). Spiritual death can precede, coincide with, and come after biological death, and it is both an event and a process. There is no permanently deceased and abandoned human body, only a body in stasis, awaiting the end of time, and the grave becomes an analogue to, or even an extension of, the death-bed.

In his next section (41–58), the homilist personifies death as the relentless hunter pursuing its desperate prey, a foe from whom no one can hide, even in a fortified city (*burgum*), among family, or as one of anonymous thousands in a crowd, thus setting up ideas about death, the individual and the group to which he will return. He then goes back to death as the parting of body and soul, in order to consider what lesser separations this moment contains (68–83), and establishes three, from friends, wealth and bodily sensation and function:

> Deað ... betyneð þa eagan from gesyhðe 7 þa earan fram gehyrnesse 7 þa weloras fram spræce 7 þa fet fram gange 7 þa handa fram weorce 7 þa næsðyrelu fram stence.[109]

> Death . . . covers the eyes from sight and the ears from hearing and the lips from speech and the feet from walking and the hands from work and the nostrils from smell.

Betynan means to cover or shut in, and the description here evokes the image of death moving around the body, shutting it down little by little. He uses *betynan* in a slightly different sense in the next sentence, however, which describes a fourth and final kind of separation: *Ðonne æfter þon betyneðe ða scyldegan on helle. Wa ðam þæt bið þæt he þonne sceal bion betyned in helle!* (Then after that he shuts the guilty in hell. Woe to him that it happens that he must be shut in hell! lines 82–3). By juxtaposing these senses of *betynan*, the homilist raises the possibility that, in shutting down the senses of the body, death is imprisoning some kind of awareness inside it: the body is sealed by death just as the damned

---

[107] Wright, *The Irish Tradition*, p. 105.

[108] The conventional number of deaths is two (death of the soul from sin, parting of body and soul), but some sources cite three, four or even six: Wright, *The Irish Tradition*, pp. 88–93.

[109] Lines 79–82.

souls are trapped in hell. This is not one of the texts discussed by Godden in his article on the meanings of *mod* and *sawl*, but it supports his hypothesis about the relationship between thought, emotion and the body.

Believing that the corpse retained a degree of consciousness is not the same as ascribing agency or movement to it; although William of Malmesbury hints that some people believed this to be possible in his discussion of King Alfred's posthumous career, where the story (which William dismisses) is clearly referring to a walking corpse.[110] William claims such beliefs are widespread among the English and that they were held by senior clergy. Some support for William's idea comes in one of Ælfric's supplementary homilies, where he complains that witches go to heathen burials in the misguided belief that they can summon the dead from their graves.[111] Both William and Ælfric are impatient at the suggestion that the dead can rise from their graves without miraculous intervention, but they are quite comfortable with the ideas that a demon might impersonate a corpse, that Christ and the saints brought the dead to life, and that the dead will rise again at Doomsday. Their dismissal of beliefs in ambulant corpses may tell us something of how orthodox ideas about the resurrection body and the interim role of the corpse were reinterpreted in the wider community.

Five foretastes of hell

The homilist of Vercelli IX stays with the idea that the corpse retains some kind of consciousness (85–106), explaining that there are five earthly experiences through which we are given an admonitory inkling of the pains of hell, exile (*wræc*), senility (*oferyldo*), death (*deaþ*), the grave (*byrgen*) and torture (*tintrego*). The homilist's inclusion of death and burial in this list shows that he differentiates not between experiences of the living and the dead as we might define them but between experiences that occur before and after the Last Judgement. Thus death and burial count as experiences of this world, rather than the next. Before the Last Judgement, every human being is still part of an evolving narrative of change, time and potential salvation, as we saw with the spirits of Eanbald and Eastmund. After the Last Judgement, time is replaced by the eternal moment, and nothing will ever change again. When seen from this perspective, the differences between the living and the dead body become much less significant, and the homilist emphasizes this, as we will see, by describing the living body in terms appropriate to the dead or dying, and discussing the corpse as if it is still conscious.

In his description of exile (*wræc*), the homilist again downplays the difference between bodily life and death, as well as picking up on the ideas of the passage on the 'loss of wealth' a few lines earlier (86–9). In the parallel list of five foretastes of hell in the *Catechesis Celtica* identified by Scragg, the first item is

---

[110] William of Malmesbury, *Regum* I, pp. 134–5.
[111] *Supp.* II, XXIX, p. 796, lines 118–23.

dolor (pain or grief).[112] *Wræc* can have this meaning in Anglo-Saxon, but both on its own and as part of a compound (*wræc-sið, wræc-stow, wræc-last*) it usually carries the meaning of banishment. Describing *wræc* as a *micel cwelm* blurs the difference between loss of social position and physical death, since the latter is the commonest meaning of *cwelm* (although *cwelm* can just mean 'harm', 'death' is its primary meaning, as in *cwealm-stow*, an execution site). He thus constructs an equation which could be translated as 'pain is harm' or, more concretely and with greater cultural relevance, 'exile is death'. To achieve its full impact this imagery depends on its original audience sharing the belief that to lose one's place in networks of patronage and kinship, community and reward, is in many ways the same as being dead, picking up on the earlier images of group and individual.

The second intimation of hell also refers back to the imagery of an earlier passage. *Oferyldo* (senility) is described in terms reminiscent of the narrative of death shutting the body down, but whereas death only, if repeatedly, *betynað* the body, *oferyldo* acts through a series of striking verbs. The eyes *amolsniað* (moulder), a word which evokes putrefaction. The ears *adimmað* (grow dim) and can no longer hear *fægere sangas* (fair songs). The tongue *awlispað* (stutters) and the feet *aslapað* (are paralysed), the hands *aþindaþ* (swell), the hair *afealleð* (falls out), the teeth which once were white *ageolewiað* (grow yellow) and the formerly sweet breath *afulað* (grows foul). Many of these details are equally applicable to the corpse, and some of them, such as the feet falling asleep, are closely paralleled in accounts of dying and dead bodies, where feet are often described as growing cold.[113]

Appropriately, he then turns to death itself: *for þan ðonne se man sceal sweltan, þonne swyrceð him fram þæs huses hrof ðe he inne bið* (when a man must die, then the roof of the house where he is grows dark to him, lines 98–9). The phrase *huses hrof* is repeated in the next sentence, in the description of the grave, and Scragg suggests that antecedent versions of the homily may have had another word in place of the first use of *hrof*, in line 99. But the image may be intentional, as it makes for a striking juxtaposition of images: the dying man closes his eyes on the darkening domestic interior, before being transported to another kind of *hus* entirely. This account differs in one crucial respect from most other death-bed scenes in later Anglo-Saxon literature, such as those of Æthelwold and Edward the Confessor, where the effect of death is described from the point of view of a witness. *Testati uero nobis sunt qui ibi praesentes aderant* (those who were present have witnessed to us), writes Wulfstan Cantor of the dying Æthelwold; *erat tunc uidere in defuncto corpore* (it was then visible in the dead body), says the anonymous author of the *Life of King Edward*.[114] Edward and Æthelwold are dying the exemplary death of a saint: we are meant to look on and marvel. The homilist's perspective is quite different: here we are looking

[112] Scragg, *Vercelli Homilies*, p. 166; J. E. Cross, 'The Literate Anglo-Saxon – On Sources and Dissemination', *Proceedings of the British Academy* 58 (1972), pp. 67–100, 96.
[113] M. L. Cameron, *Anglo-Saxon Medicine*, CSASE 7 (Cambridge, 1993), p. 51.
[114] Lapidge, and Winterbottom, *Life of St Æþelwold*, p. 62; Barlow, *Life of King Edward*, p. 80.

out through the eyes of the dying person himself and experiencing in anticipation the failing of our senses when our own death comes.

With burial, as with death, we are still in the realm of experiences belonging to this world, and, again, we are not to imagine its horrors from a bystander's perspective; the point of view is that of the corpse in the grave:

> Ðonne is þære feorðan helle onlicnes byrgen nemned, for þan þæs huses hrof bið [gehnæg]ed þe him onufan ðam breostum siteð, 7 him mon þonne deð his gestreona þone wi[r]sestan dæl, þæt is þæt hine [mon siw]eð on anum [hræg]le. Hafað him þonne syððan þry gebeddan, þæt is þonne greot 7 molde 7 wyrmas.[115]

> Then the fourth likeness of hell is called burial, for the roof of the house is bowed down over his breast, and he is given the worst part of all his wealth, that is, someone sews him into a garment. After that three bedfellows have him, and they are grit and soil and worms.

The audience is invited to replace their ideas about appropriate housing, clothing and bedfellows with images of themselves in a claustrophobic, low-roofed space, where they have been immobilized, stitched impersonally into the 'worst part of their wealth'. At the end of the homily, he will describe the earthly paradise as a place of sexual delight, but here one is in the embrace of less attractive partners. The image of the house-roof pressing down on the breast suggests breathlessness: inappropriate to the corpse, but a striking way of bringing home the horror of the grave to the living.[116]

Holy and hellish communities

Having taken us imaginatively into the grave, he goes through torture and into hell, populated by the damned and the demons (equally *laðlic gastas*, loathsome spirits). These are then contrasted with an image not brought to our attention since the homily's opening lines, the church filled with people listening to him preach:

> Ac utan we, men ða leofestan, nu we syndon gegaderode on ðysne drihtenlice dæg, þæt we for Godes lufan on geornysse syn, þæt we beflion þa helle wita.[117]

> But, beloved men, now that we are gathered together on this day of the Lord, let us be zealous for God's love, that we escape the pains of hell.

He touches down for a moment here, reminding his listeners that they are *leofest* (most beloved), not yet *laðlic* (loathsome) like the damned, and they are in the right place, doing the right thing, to avoid joining the infernal congregation whom he has just described. At the very beginning of the homily, he had also, in common homiletic style, been using the second person plural; he now identifies himself with his audience to the point where individuality breaks down, and he

---

[115] Lines 101–6.
[116] Similarly, in Blickling VI, *deað* and the *byrgen* are described as sitting heavy on the dead bodies, and the earth and stone oppress (*þrycce*) them, in a way analogous to the soul being burdened with sin. R. Morris (ed.), *The Blickling Homilies of the Tenth Century*, EETS OS 58/63/73 (London, 1880), p. 75.
[117] Lines 165–8.

and the congregation appear to have one collective identity (*ure sawle*, our soul), one day of death (*ures þæs nehstan dæges*, our final day) and one journey when soul and body divide (*þære tosceadednesse ure sawle þonne hio of þam lichoman lædde bion*, the separation of our soul when it will be led from the body).

The nature of community is thus established as a major theme of the homily. There are several kinds of earthly community present in the text, including the Sunday congregation of people and priest united by their common care for *ure sawle*, the citizens who cannot defend one of their number against death, and the kin. There are also the otherworldly communities, the devils of hell and their *weagesiðas* (woe-companions, 22) among whom all social and familial ties have collapsed (140), in contrast to the joyful crowds of heaven (203–5). The absolute isolation of the grave, where no friend can help the dead person, contrasts with and separates these visions of earthly and heavenly communities.

The seductive vision of the earthly paradise

The homilist will return at the end to his thesis of the congregation as the ideal earthly community, but not before retailing a devil's eye-witness account of the pains of hell and the joys of heaven.[118] Heavenly joys, the devil (and the homilist) explain, are greater than those experienced by someone 'as precious as a royal child' (*swa dyre swa cynebearn*), as fair and wise as Solomon, sitting on a gilded mountain at sunrise in the earthly paradise, in a world of endless summer, where the pebbles are gold and the streams honey, who possesses all the treasures of earth, and *ælc niht niwe bryd to bed gelæd 7 seo hæbbe Iunone wlite* (and every night a new bride brought to bed, and she as lovely as Juno). While Wright suggests the motif may have its origins in developments of Psalm 83:11, such as Augustine's rejection of 'endless years of life enjoying temporal goods' in favour of heavenly joys, none of the analogous passages he quotes is very close, and Vercelli IX is exceptional for its emphasis on purely physical pleasure and its awareness of female beauty.[119] The *gestreona* (treasures) of the world have their place, but they are described in general terms that subordinate them to the specific and primary delights of sunshine, honey and sex.

This speech is complex in many ways. While it is put into the mouth of a devil, giving it connotations of the temptations of Christ in the wilderness, it also reminds the audience that devils are fallen angels, who once had access to but are now excluded from both the earthly paradise and heaven, thus imbuing the speech with a passionate nostalgia. The internal logic of Vercelli IX is predicated on the assumption that his audience (implicitly identified as male) will both desire and mistrust the sensuous (not to mention promiscuous) vision he conjures for them, and go on to understand the greater desirability of heaven. This is one of many passages found in the anonymous homilies, particularly those of the Vercelli Book, which are utterly unlike the intellectual exegesis-cum-story-

---

[118] Tristram, 'Stock Descriptions of Heaven and Hell', pp. 107–8.
[119] Wright, *Irish Tradition*, pp. 206–14.

telling of Ælfric, or the practical, tithe-and-Doomsday approach of Wulfstan. The aim of many of the anonymous texts seems to be to startle, delight and overawe; their *modus praedicandi* is to engage their listeners at a physical level and seduce as well as reason or intimidate them into desiring a Christian way of life and death. Several other homilies which fit this category will be discussed in following chapters; they all share a delight in worldly joys which is tempered by an awareness of their transience and futility, but has very little to do with ascetic revulsion.

Judgement and shame

The homilist follows his vision of bliss with a brief contemplation of the encounter which each soul will have with God at the Last Judgement, which again draws on themes of community, this time concentrating on honour and reputation. He advises his listeners to prepare themselves

> *þæt we us þonne ne ðurfe scamigan þonne he us nealæcð þæt he us gesion wille. For þan þæt bið mycel scamu þæt man his sylfes scamige on þam myclum gemote.*[120]

> so that we do not then need to be ashamed of ourselves when He draws near us in order to see us. Because that will be a great shame if a man brings shame to himself before that great assembly.

The use of two verbs to describe Christ first drawing near (*nealæcð*) and then examining (*gesion wille*) the soul, combined with the triple repetition of the idea of shame (*scamigan, scamu, scamige*) suggests a process of slow and painful scrutiny. This prospect of public shame at the great assembly has close affinities with a very popular motif, in which the small shame of admitting your sins to one man, your confessor, is contrasted with the alternative, the enormous shame of having them revealed before all mankind, all demons and all angels at Doomsday.[121] Godden cites Anglo-Latin antecedents from Boniface and Alcuin, and he suggests Ælfric as the likely vector by which this precise motif of 'better shamed before one than shamed before all' entered the vernacular. However, the broader idea of being shamed before all intelligent creation is one that epitomizes Pasternack's concept of anonymous polyphony in the way it shifts, reforms and appears in many different kinds of environments, even appearing in an expanded vernacular translation of the Paternoster:

> *Forgif us ure synna þæt us ne scamige eft, drihten ure, þonne þu on dome sitst and ealle men up arisað þe fram wife and fram were wurdon acenned.*[122]

> Forgive us our sins that we be not shamed afterwards, our Lord, when You sit in judgement and all people rise up who were conceived by women and men.

---

[120] Lines 206–9.
[121] M. Godden, 'An Old English Penitential Motif', *ASE* 2 (1973), pp. 221–39.
[122] Lines 84–7.

The idea taps into many profound cultural assumptions about shame, exposure, community and reputation and is too powerful to remain confined to a narrow selection of texts

Scragg describes the structure of Vercelli IX as 'episodic', but it is intricately constructed around these positive and negative images of the group and the individual, of periods of communion and fulfilment contrasted with separation and deprivation. One of the recurring images linking these communities is music and the human voice: the psalmist providing the fundamental lyric warning of death and hell (*se sealmscop us sang this* . . . lines 29–30, referring to Psalm 6:6), the *fægere sangas* that the deaf old man can no longer hear (line 92), the earthly *wuldorsangas* which are nothing compared to the glories of heaven (line 193), the sorrowful song of damned souls (*hi þonne onginnað singan swiðe sorhfulne sang*, lines 137–8), and the joyful songs of heaven (*þa þrymlican sangas*, lines 178–9). The homilist's final vision of community brings him full circle to his congregation, including himself (*we sculon*) in his exhortation to fulfil social obligations *mid ælmessum ⁊ mid godum weorcum* (with alms and good works) and to *secean ure cyrcean mid clænnesse ⁊ mid hlutran mode* (to seek our church with purity and sincere spirit). His audience has been taken on a cathartic tour of pleasure and pain, accompanied by an appropriate soundtrack; he has encouraged them to imagine themselves hanged upside-down, roasted alive, banished from their homeland, deteriorating in old age, hunted down by death, dying, suffocating in the grave, and finally enjoying the sensual luxuries of an earthly paradise which include the stimulus of a new partner every night, before returning them safely to the church in which they stand. The original author of Vercelli IX was a consummate story-teller, using glamour and excitement to dazzle his listeners into accepting his basic message of compunction and penance in the face of death and judgement.

Early on in this chapter, reference was made to Abrams's point about conduct being as important as belief. Where Vercelli IX is concerned, it is evident that that the homilist sees inner belief and communal behaviour working continuously to structure each other, and in this the homily is representative of the culture that produced it. 'Faith' or 'belief', to modern ears, imply faith in supernatural powers, removed from ordinary experience. But, as Neville makes clear, even to use words like 'supernatural' in the context of Anglo-Saxon culture and society is anachronistic: they had no word for either the natural or the supernatural world and saw no division between the two.[123] Vercelli IX associates the activity of 'seeking church' with alms and good works as well as purity of body, soul and faith, and being part of the loving community worshipping together in the awareness of Judgement. But the way that Bodley 340/342 replaces Vercelli IX with a piece by Ælfric suggests that this homily was not universally approved; like other anonymous homilies it explores ideas about the living and the dead body in a sensational mode which other Christian groups of Anglo-Saxons seem to have

---

[123] J. Neville, *Representations of the Natural World in Old English Poetry*, CSASE 27 (Cambridge, 1999), pp. 1–3.

have found unacceptable. Vercelli IX warns us that in the same faith, the same congregation, the same graveyard, people with very different approaches to Christian living and dying might be found side by side.

3

Dying with Decency

Cha pter One concentrated on the years around 900, a period of exiguous evidence. This chapter, in contrast, considers material from the later tenth and eleventh centuries in which the theories and practices surrounding death and dying are much better attested, and the bulk of the chapter is a close study of one source in particular. This is a mid-eleventh-century liturgical, confessional and penitential anthology (Oxford, Bodl. Laud Miscellaneous 482), which returns continually to the theme of the relationship between a priest and the soul in his care, especially at these moments of crisis. This manuscript has never been considered as a whole, although it is in one hand and its contents are intricately interwoven, and the argument here is that it was compiled to train priests for their part at the death-bed.

Very little English liturgical material survives from before the late tenth century, and it is hard to set what there is in its social context. It may be that all we can see directly are the ceremonies to which a tiny group of people had access, but the texts themselves assume that these rites are available for all the community of the faithful, ordained and lay. This suggests that there could have been a wide awareness of the rites, even among many of the people who may not have benefited from them directly. One of the most prominent activities enjoined in these texts is confession, which is found at the heart of the rite for anointing the sick. Looking first at the presentation of confession more generally thus allows us a better understanding of how it was used in immediate anticipation of death.

Confession

Confession (*scrift*, which also means confessor) and penance (*bote* or *dædbote*) are described in numerous homilies, prayers, sets of guidelines for priests and *ordines*. These texts present these activities as well-established parts of English Church practice, ideally undertaken by everybody, following a model established by the Carolingian reformers.[1] Confession appears to have been private (one to one, not formally public or general), depending, again ideally, on an open and intimate relationship between priest and parishioner. Vercelli Homily III assumes that the penitent will have a confessor, stressing the particular relationship with the phrase *eowrum scriftum* (your confessors), who are expected to inquire in detail about the times and places of the parishioner's sin, to ask about his thoughts,

---

[1] R. McKitterick, *The Frankish Church and the Carolingian Reform, 789–895* (London, 1977).

to use the eight chief sins as an analytical guide, and to treat every sin separately, hearing confession for each one.[2] This is very much the ideal of the Carolingian reformers, and one of the main sources for the Latin homily underlying Vercelli III is the *Capitula* of Theodulf of Orleans, a central reform text and one that was translated into English.[3]

The importance of the personal link between a priest and the souls in his care emerges in other sources as well. The use by Archbishop Wulfstan of the term *rihtscriftscire* (proper confession area) to describe the congregation belonging to a particular church suggests that he is thinking in terms of a group of people linked by a common confessor rather than a demarcated area of land. It also implies that he wanted to see the same kind of control over confession as is visible in later medieval sources, ensuring that a penitent confessed only to the priest under whose jurisdiction he fell.[4] The priest thus becomes the repository of the secrets of his community, not only their actions but also their thoughts and even their dreams. Murray describes the confessional encounter as 'individual, secret, and unscripted', and warns that 'it was precisely in that area of church life from which the historian is most systematically excluded that the dialectic of priest-lay relations was most potent'.[5] On the whole, these are valid, if frustrating, points, although the word 'unscripted' is debatable. The confessional and penitential texts allow us to see the framework within which confession was intended to be performed; even if we cannot overhear the voices of individuals detailing their lapses, we can see how these texts structure confession, and the assumptions they make about its frequency, its content, and the relationship between the two people involved.

Murray suggests that before the Fourth Lateran Council in 1215, confession was confined primarily either to the cloister or the death-bed, basing his arguments on the paucity of earlier miracle stories associated with lay confession. Although, as he points out, early twelfth-century England furnishes more evidence both for lay confession and diocesan discipline than the continental material he considers, he ascribes this directly to the Norman archbishops of Canterbury rather than to any pre-Conquest penitential tradition.[6] However, the Anglo-Saxon texts considered in this chapter suggest a well-established tradition of confession, and they register the desire to improve the existing administration of confession and penance, not the need to establish a penitential system from the ground up. Even as early as the 890s, we saw an incidental reference to *scrift* in the account of the Sodbury dispute, in Chapter One. Meens takes issue with Murray's evaluation of the continental evidence, arguing that between 800 and 1000 confession and penance were widely practised, and their rarity in narrative is a sign of the

---

[2]   This translates *Quando ergo unusquisque ad confessionem uenerit* which does not stress the personal nature of the relationship. Scragg, *Vercelli Homilies* III, lines 25–9, pp. 74–5.

[3]   Scragg, *Vercelli Homilies*, p. 72; H. Sauer, *Theodulfi Capitula in England*. (Munich, 1978).

[4]   Blair, *The Church in Anglo-Saxon England*, ch. 7.

[5]   Murray, 'Counselling in Medieval Confession', pp. 67–8.

[6]   A. Murray, 'Confession before 1215', *TRHS* 6th ser. 3 (1993), pp. 51–83, 78.

extent to which they were taken for granted.[7] Hamilton adduces evidence from continental *ordines* that, very soon after the Carolingian reforms, the Frankish Church introduced Germanic vernacular confessional texts, implying the promotion of penance among the laity.[8] The present chapter suggests that a comparable situation held good in pre-Conquest England.

These texts envision a priest hearing confession from people of widely varying social backgrounds and spiritual experience, at different points in their lives. People are encouraged to see making confession as a foretaste of their experience at Doomsday: better to be shamed before one than shamed before all, in a motif we have already examined.[9] Laud 482 is insistent that the confessor will be standing with his flock at the Last Judgement to bear witness to the validity of their confession, and priests are reminded that their own reception by God depends on the fate of their flock. Confession is thus presented as a rehearsal both for the death-bed and for the awe-inspiring events of Doomsday. For those who confess even annually, the journey to and beyond death becomes a progress towards a final destination of total self-knowledge, with acts of confession and penance as interim landmarks of introspection on this route. That final destination is the Last Judgement, represented as both confessional and courtroom, where all is revealed, and any sins unconfessed in life will be exposed to public gaze through a 'glassily transparent' body.[10]

Confession not only repairs the damaged soul, it can even resurrect the soul killed by sin, as Ælfric shows in his homily for the first Sunday after Easter, when he compares unconfessed sins to Lazarus's shroud in an extended analogy:

> Crist arærde of deaðe þone stincendan lazarum; 7 þa ða he cucu wæs þa cwæð he to his leorningcnihtum: tolysað his bendas . . . For ði sceolon þa lareowas þa unbindan fram heora synnum, þa ðæ geliffæst þurh onbryrdnysse; ælc synful man þe his synna bediglað, he bið dead on byrgene. Ac gif he his synna geandet þurh onbryrdneysse, þonne gæð he of ðære byrgene . . . Ðonne sceal se lareow hine unbindan fram þam ecum wite.[11]

> Christ revived the stinking Lazarus from death; and when he was revived, then He said to His disciples: unfasten his bonds . . . Therefore teachers must release from their sins those who are endowed with life through compunction; every sinful man who conceals his sins, he is dead in the grave. But if he confess through compunction, then he comes out of the grave . . . Then the teacher must release him from eternal torment.

The story of Lazarus underpins many of the funerary practices taking shape in the early Middle Ages, exemplified by the way the tenth-century continental sacramentaries from Fulda and Arezzo use the verb *lazarizare* to mean 'wrap in

[7]   R. Meens, 'The Frequency and Nature of Early Medieval Penance', in Biller and Minnis, *Handling Sin*, pp. 35–61, 53.
[8]   S. Hamilton, *The Practice of Penance, 900–1050* (Woodbridge, 2001), pp. 147–8.
[9]   Godden, 'An Old English Penitential Motif'.
[10] The image of the glassy body appears in *Christ III*, lines 1281b–1282, and Morris, *Blickling Homilies* X, p. 109.
[11] *CH* I, XVI, p. 310, lines 81–9.

a shroud'.[12] It brings together potent images of nakedness and innocence, the shroud as a symbol of sin and degradation, the association of sin with living death and burial, and the possibility of rotting (*stincend*) flesh being redeemed and made whole, by Christ and by the priest as Christ's representative. This imagery had been familiar in England long before Ælfric's day: Hawkes reads the iconography of the resurrection of Lazarus in eighth- to ninth-century sculpture as an embodiment of confession and Christ's promise of immortality for the faithful in John 11:25.[13]

'Let me end my days with decency': a prayer against sudden death

Many widespread ideas about confession, reciprocal prayer, and the contemplation of one's own mortality are epitomized in a prayer to be spared a sudden death which survives in three mid-eleventh-century manuscripts, one associated with Canterbury, one with Winchester and Canterbury, and one with Winchester and Worcester.[14] The Canterbury manuscript (London, BL Cotton Tiberius A iii) has been described as 'a compendium of the Benedictine Reform movements in Carolingian Francia and tenth-century England', containing the Benedictine Rule, the *Regularis Concordia* and much prognostic material, and many of its texts are drawn on throughout the present study.[15] This prayer is thus preserved in a variety of contexts associated with three of England's most important religious houses and in the case of CCCC, MS 391, in a manuscript closely associated with Bishop Wulfstan II of Worcester. The prayer's subjects are the desire for an appropriate death, the wish to be granted compunction and self-knowledge, and the well-being of Christian souls, living and dead.

It begins with a request for forgiveness and confirmation in faith, before going on to ask to be spared a *færlic deað* (sudden death).[16] The prayer anticipates

---

[12] D. Sicard, *La Liturgie de la mort dans l'église latine des origines à la réforme carolingienne* (Munster, 1978), pp. 109–10 and n. 17.

[13] J. Hawkes, 'Sacraments in Stone: The Mysteries of Christ in Anglo-Saxon Sculpture', in Carver, *Cross Goes North*, pp. 351–70, 358.

[14] A. Hughes (ed.), *The Portiforium of St Wulfstan*, HBS 89 and 90 (Leighton Buzzard, 1958 and 1960): Worcester with a Winchester exemplar, N. R. Ker, *Catalogue of Manuscripts Containing Anglo-Saxon* (Oxford, 1957), no. 67; BL Royal 2 B v: originally from Winchester but at Canterbury in the eleventh century, Ker, no. 249; BL Cotton Tiberius A iii: Canterbury, Ker, no. 186. All three manuscripts are bilingual and contain liturgical material as well as the prayer. The 'Portiforium of St Wulfstan', securely dated to 1065–6, also includes hymns, the Gallican psalter, a collectar, vernacular prognostic texts, Sunday offices and offices for the Holy Cross, the Virgin and the Dead; see R. Gameson, 'Book Production and Decoration at Worcester in the Tenth and Eleventh Centuries', in N. Brooks and C. Cubitt (eds), *St Oswald of Worcester: Life and Influence* (Leicester, 1996), pp. 194–243, 241. Cotton Tiberius A iii is a monastically oriented compilation, containing the Rule of St Benedict and the *Regularis Concordia*, both with an interlinear vernacular gloss, as well as Ælfric's *Colloquy*, together with a quantity of vernacular confessional and penitential material, prayers and prognostics. Royal 2 B v is a glossed Roman psalter with the prayers added at the end.

[15] H. Gneuss, 'Origin and Provenance of Anglo-Saxon Manuscripts: The Case of Cotton Tiberius A iii', in P. R. Robinson and R. Zim (eds), *Of the Making of Books: Medieval Manuscripts, Their Scribes and Readers* (Aldershot, 1997), pp. 13–48, 15.

[16] ℈ *min drihten ne læt me næfre færlicum deaðe of þissum earman life gewitan. Ac loc hwænne min tima beo. ℈ þin willa sy. þæt ic þis hlæne lif forlætan scyle. læt me mid gedefenesse mine dagas*

various possible ends, the worst of which is an abrupt departure from 'this wretched life', with God's attention elsewhere. *Loc hwænne min tima beo* (look when my time comes), the speaker implores, and he asks to end his days *mid gedefenesse*, 'with decency'. The prayer then goes on to refine the description of a desirable end, echoing the themes, rhythms and alliteration of confessional formulae:

> *þæt þu me of þisse weorulde ne læte. ær ic þurh þine mycclan mildheortnysse forgifenysse hæbbe ealles þæs þe ic æfre ongean þinne mæran willan geworhte. dæges oððe nihtes. gewealdes oððe ungewealdes. on worde oððe on weorce. oððe on minum þystrum geþance.*[17]

> that You do not release me from this world before I, through Your great mercy, have gained forgiveness for all that I ever undertook against Your glorious will, by day or by night, intentionally or unintentionally, in word or in deed or in the darkness of my thoughts.

The bracketing of the requests for God's attention, for a death *mid gedefenesse* (with decency), and for forgiveness achieved through confession, shows the organic connexion of these ideas. A death that happens *mid gedefenesse* is not merely a peaceful death, it is one embedded in ritual, and by the mid-eleventh century these rituals had long been highly developed. They centred on a series of controlled moments, the most important of these being the period of critical illness during which life and death hang in the balance (when confession is central), the death struggle, the washing of the body, and the placing of the body in the grave. The *ordines* expect that a priest and several other clerics are readily available, with appropriate books and equipment, and that the body can go quickly and easily from the death-bed to the church and thence to the graveyard, and that the grave will have been made ready by the time the body arrives.

The death-bed environment to which these texts aspire is that of a well-equipped monastic or clerical community, where the *domus infirmorum*, the church and the cemetery would be in close proximity. This is vividly depicted in the *Regularis Concordia*, drawn up in 971 to ensure the conformity of England's monasteries to one agreed rule.[18] Although its ultimate model, the *Rule of St Benedict*, had ignored the subject of what to do with dying and dead brethren, the original *Rule* had been revised as part of the Carolingian reform to have a greater emphasis on the death-bed and its penitential associations.[19] In the *Regularis Concordia*, the ailing monk announces his illness to his community and retreats

---

geendian. And my Lord, never let me suffer a sudden death from this wretched life. But look when my time comes, and it be Your will that I must abandon this meagre life. Let me end my days with decency. Hughes, *Portiforium* II, p. 14.

[17] *Ibid.*

[18] T. Symons, '*Regularis Concordia*: History and Derivation', in D. Parsons (ed.), *Tenth Century Studies; Essays in Commemoration of the Millennium of the Council of Winchester* (London, 1975), pp. 37–59, 39.

[19] J. McCann (ed.), *The Rule of St Benedict* (London, 1976); G. Brown, 'The Carolingian Renaissance', in R. McKitterick (ed.), *Carolingian Culture: Emulation and Innovation* (Cambridge, 1994), pp. 1–51, 25.

to the sick-house.[20] Should his condition seriously worsen, he is to be visited by the whole community singing the Penitential Psalms; he is then anointed and given the eucharist. If he fails to improve, this ceremony is to be performed every day, except for the anointing, until his death. As death draws near 'all shall assemble to assist his passing' (*conveniantque omnes ad tuendum exitum eius*). The verb *tueor*, translated by Symons as 'assist', implies something more complex than mere observation at the death-bed. Dying thus becomes a community activity, with an involved audience participating in the salvation of the dying soul, and implicitly acknowledging their own coming deaths as they do so. Individual circumstances permitting, this was the ideal death envisaged for themselves by most members of Anglo-Saxon religious communities.

Lay access to death-related ritual and ideas

It is hard to demonstrate whether such complex rites filtered very far into the lay community, and even harder to find evidence for any access that poor or isolated communities had even to a watered-down version. However, it is also hard to prove that the laity had no such access, either to the rites or to the ideas informing them. Ordinary lay piety remains one of the most obscure aspects of Anglo-Saxon society, but such evidence as there is suggests an early and widespread adoption of Christian views on the fate of body and soul.[21] While it is unlikely that a well-equipped and liturgically up-to-date team ministry attended every death-bed from *c.* 750 onwards, the idea of a death *mid gedefenesse* may have been a powerful inspiration to lay practice. Tales of the deaths of kings as well as saints like Cuthbert, Martin and Guthlac are likely to have had a wide audience; several poetic or alliterating entries in the Anglo-Saxon Chronicles deal with deaths of kings or princes, and two poems on Guthlac survive, one closely focused on his death. In Guthlac's own *Life*, it was musing on the miserable ends of Mercian monarchs which prompted his conversion from warrior to monk; Hines suggests on the basis of this passage that by the eighth century there was a widespread 'fear of damnation (and a hope of salvation) . . . in at least that stratum of Anglo-Saxon society that our sources reveal'.[22] The *Life of Guthlac* stresses the life-changing power of such story-telling, not only the sad stories of the deaths of kings, but the way that Guthlac is moved to become a warrior in the first place by thinking of the deeds of heroes.[23] The high-profile examples of the seventh- and eighth-century 'kings who opted out', in Stancliffe's phrase, and chose to die in a monastery or on pilgrimage, may also have become the subject of stories. Through such narratives the details of the *ordines*, including elements such as Martin dying on sackcloth and ashes, may have circulated among people unlikely to have direct access to elaborate rites but who became convinced of their salvific power and responded to the narratives by constructing their own version

[20] Symons, *Regularis Concordia*, ch. XII, pp. 64–8.
[21] Blair, *The Church in Anglo-Saxon England*.
[22] J. Hines, 'Religion: The Limits of Knowledge', in Hines (ed.), *The Anglo-Saxons*, pp. 374–401, 385.
[23] B. Colgrave, *Felix's Life of Guthlac* (Cambridge, 1956), pp. 78–82.

of the ideal death-bed, visible in the grave. These may have been among the mechanisms by which lay models of death-bed and burial changed, and they would not require a central directive. Burial practice is often a locus of expression of individual and group anxieties: the archaeological evidence of mid- to late Anglo-Saxon burial practice suggests that people's anxieties concentrated on a desire for a Christian burial, even if excavation cannot provide evidence that any ritual actually took place. Decisions about lay burial could be taken at the community level, as we will see in Chapter Five, and the cemeteries should be read as a projection of community identity, even if the ascribed piety of the dead inhabitants was not always an accurate reflection of their everyday behaviour in life.

The great variety in the rites

The *ordines* for the sick and dying in different manuscripts are similar in outline but very various in detail.[24] This suggests that, even after the Benedictine reform, every church was acting to some extent independently, and this situation certainly continued up to the Conquest.[25] There can be many pressures on liturgical development, such as response to developing theology, the presence of a patron such as a pope or bishop who is interested in commissioning new work, institutional changes within the Church such as the spread of monasteries, or the need to offer an alternative to unacceptable lay practices.[26] The broader cultural environment of a specific *ordo* is therefore one factor which may explain some of the differences in the variety of traditions in sick-bed and death-bed practice. From around 800 death-bed ritual had become increasingly penitential in mode, connected with the revised Carolingian liturgy established by Benedict of Aniane.[27] Paxton pinpoints the ninth-century *ordines* in the Lorsch and St Amand sacramentaries as the culmination of this tradition, and a careless reader might conclude that from around 900 the rite is unified. However, this is to underestimate the variety of rites found in ninth- to eleventh-century manuscripts, many of which perpetuate the ambiguities and contradictions he identifies in the earlier *ordines*, and it is clear that individual rather than conformist practice continued to be the order of the day.

Little English evidence this early survives, but a survey of the ninth- and tenth-century French *ordines* for unction printed by de Clercq shows that they record not just difference but incompatibility. Some enjoin the priest to anoint the sufferer's *pectus, cor, inter scapulas, in loco maximi doloris* (chest, heart, between

---

24 D. Bullough, 'Burial, Community and Belief', in P. Wormald, *et al.* (eds), *Ideal and Reality in Frankish and Anglo-Saxon Society*, pp. 177–201; C. de Clercq, '*Ordines unctionis infirmi* des IXe et Xe siècles', *Ephemerides Liturgicae* 44 (1930), pp. 100–22.

25 C. Hohler, 'The Red Book of Darley', in H. Slott (ed.), *Nordisk kollokvium II: I Latinsk liturgiforskning. 12–13 Maj 1972*, pp. 39–47.

26 K. Ottosen, 'Liturgy as a Theological Place: Possibilities and Limitations in Interpreting Liturgical Texts as Seen for Instance in the Office of the Dead', in E. L. Lillie and N. H. Petersen, *Liturgy and the Arts in the Middle Ages: Studies in Honour of C. Clifford Flanigan* (Copenhagen, 1996), pp. 168–80; Paxton, *Christianizing Death*, p. 50.

27 Paxton, *Christianizing Death*, pp. 163–4.

the shoulderblades, in place of greatest pain), others prescribe the five senses (eyes, ears, nostrils, lips, outside of hands), some combine these two, one adds *in genibus quoque et in cruribus, suris, pedibus ac plantis et pene in omnibus membris* (also on the knees and thighs, calves, feet and almost in all members). Another is particular that the oil should be placed *super humeros duos, id est scapulas, non in pectore, neque inter scapulas* (on both shoulders, that is to say the shoulderblades, not on the chest nor between the shoulderblades), thus explicitly contradicting practices enjoined elsewhere, and it goes on to say *super manus, et si presbyter est, non infra; sin aliter, et infra, et super pedes, et sub crures fiunt* (on the hands and, if he be a priest, not on the inside; if he be otherwise, inside, and on the feet, and under the shins). There are still others that do not specify any particular part of the body, implying that the decision was left to the discretion of the individual priest, perhaps in response to the nature of the illness he encountered.[28] Personnel is another significant variable. Two of these French *ordines* only mention one priest, four use plural phrases such as *unus ex sacerdotibus* and *dicentes*, thus assuming more than one priest is present. One specifies *unguatur a sacerdote vel sacerdotibus* (let him be anointed by the priest or priests), and one refers to the *alii circumadstantes* (others standing by) who need only be in minor orders, or perhaps even members of the laity, since all they do is sing the Penitential Psalms.[29] It is clear from de Clercq's synthesis that a younger manuscript may preserve an older rite, and *vice versa*, and that trying to establish a linear evolutionary model for these practices is impossible and probably misconceived.[30]

Encountering the dead: dream, memory and prayer

The prayer against sudden death, with its plea *loc hwænne min time beo* (look when my time comes), suggests that the ritual surrounding the sick and dying person can be read as an emergency signal aimed at God. The prayer is not alone in suggesting this: in the *uisitatio infirmorum* ritual in Laud 482, the prayers that the priest says over the sick person include petitions beginning *Respice, Domine, de celo . . . Aspice, Domine, eum oculis tuis* (Look, Lord, from heaven . . . Look, Lord, at him with Thine eyes). Such a prayer may be illogical when addressed to an omnipotent and omniscient deity, but it both shapes and articulates the desires of the supplicant, and provides emotional and symbolic, if not rational, satisfaction.[31] Motivations at this level, rather than the logical, underpin much death-related activity, and this is important to bear in mind when considering the development of other practices, such as the concept of consecrated churchyards,

---

[28] De Clercq, '*Ordines unctionis infirmi*', p. 110.

[29] Æthelgifu's will of the late tenth century specifies that three slavewomen are to be freed on condition that they sing four psalters every week within thirty days and a psalter every week within a year (of her death), which suggests both clerical and lay participation in the ritual in England by this period, at least. Whitelock, *The Will of Æthelgifu*, pp. 12–13 and 33–4.

[30] De Clercq, '*Ordines unctionis infirmi*', pp. 116–17

[31] R. Bocock, *Ritual in Industrial Society* (London, 1974), p. 47.

which earlier Christian cultures would have found superfluous or incomprehensible.

The prayer against sudden death concludes with a vision of the petitioner tangled in a spiderweb of prayer that goes beyond the reciprocal to embrace not only those who have maligned him but even those who may do so at some future time. It demonstrates a sense of deep responsibility towards those who trust in his prayers, making it clear that the dead as well as the living come into this category, and it is worth quoting at length:

> *Ic bidde ðe min drihten eadmodlice þæt ðu me gehelpe 7 ealra minra freonda 7 maga 7 eallra þæra þe to minre bedrædenne ðencað 7 hihtað libbendra 7 forðgewitenra 7 forgif þam libbendum gesundfulnesse on þisum life. ge on þam towardan ece myrhðe 7 syle þam forðgewitenum ealra heora gylta arfulle forgifenysse 7 heofena rices gefean a on ecnysse. Eac ic bidde ðe min drihten þæt ðu gemildsige eallum þam þat me god dydon 7 god tæhton 7 syle ece forgifenysse eallum þam þe me yfel cwædon oððe geþohtan oððe gyta to donne ðencað. Drihten heofona heah cyning gestranga hi to ðinum willan 7 gemildsa eallum cristenum folce libbendum 7 forðgewitenum eallum þam ðe fulluhtes bæð underfengon for þinum naman. AMEN*[32]

I humbly pray You, my Lord, that You may help me and all my friends and kin and all those, living and dead, who think of and trust in my prayers, and grant to the living prosperity in this life and eternal delight in that to come, and grant merciful forgiveness to the dead for all their sins and the joy of the kingdom of heaven for ever in eternity. I also pray You, my Lord, to have mercy on all who did me good and taught me good, and grant eternal forgiveness to all who spoke or thought evil about me or are yet thinking of doing so. Lord, heaven's high King, strengthen them in Your will and have mercy on all Christian people alive and dead, all those who received the bath of baptism for Your name. Amen.

This list distinguishes between the living, who currently need *gesundfulnesse* (prosperity) and the dead who need *forgifenysse* (forgiveness), although the boundaries between the two categories collapse when they are thought of in terms of eternity (*ece myrhðe . . . a on ecnysse*). Time present, time past and time future come together: the dead 'think and trust' along with the living, and the supplicant tries to anticipate the actions of any ill-wishers and win advance forgiveness for sins they are yet to commit.

The phrasing of his series of petitions is instructive. He asks for *help* for himself, his living and dead friends and kin and those who trust in his prayer, and requests God to bestow (*forgif*) prosperity and eternal joy on the living, and mercy on those who have done him good, but he reserves the term *syle forgifenysse* (grant forgiveness) specifically for the dead *ealra heora gylta* (for all their sins), and for those who have maligned or ill-treated him, some of whom are clearly still bodily alive, since they are capable of sinning further in the future. But perhaps they are only bodily alive, reminding us that sin is living death, an idea familiar from Vercelli IX and many other texts such as Ælfric's explanation that *for ðam se ðe syngað, hys sawul ne leofað* (because the soul of the sinner does not live) unless it is revived (*acucige*) by confession.[33] It also suggests that the living are

---

[32] Hughes, *Portiforium* II, p. 14.
[33] *Supp.* I, VI, p. 318, lines 139–42.

capable of seeking forgiveness for themselves, but those who are dead, whether physically or spiritually, need all the help they can get.

The image of the dead still trusting in the prayer of the living recalls the story of Eanbald and Eastmund in Chapter One. The dead are familiar presences, not gone to the remote realms of hell or heaven but still caught in an undefined place, subject to time and change, very possibly in pain, and capable of responding to prayers and gifts. The proximity of the dead and their emotional importance to the living are reinforced elsewhere in Tiberius A iii, one of the manuscripts preserving the prayer, in the material it contains on the interpretation of dreams. This is a catalogue of a vast range of dream imagery and its significance, a genre discussed in more detail in Chapter Four. Dreaming of the dead is interpreted here as very positive: *gif man mæte þæt he deadne man cysse langsum lif 7 gesæglic him bið towerd* (if one dreams that he kisses a dead person, a long and happy life is in store for him).[34] *Dead man* here refers to someone who is now dead but appears alive in the dream, rather than to a dream of a corpse; elsewhere in the same text the word *lic* is used to refer to the corpse in the interpretation of a dream of a funeral procession, in itself not a bad dream: *ne bið þæt nan laþ* (that is no bad thing). To dream of kissing someone now dead reinforces the emotional and social ties linking the living and dead members of the community across the boundary of the grave, and it may also be an anticipation of a happy reunion the other side of Doomsday. The same emotional intensity is conveyed in the poem *The Wanderer* by the lonely exile's dream of his lost lord,

> *þæt he his mondryhten clyppe 7 cysse 7 on cneo lecge honda 7 heafod swa he hwilum ær in geardagum gifstoles breac*[35]

> that he embraces and kisses his lord, and lays hand and head on his knee, as he did in the old days when he enjoyed the gift-seat

although the poignant memory is used here to bring home the inherent fragility of social relationships which are embedded in time rather than in eternity. Another dream of the dead occurs in the *Life of King Edward*, where the dying Edward sees two long-dead monks whom he had known as a boy in Normandy.[36]

In their different ways, these passages all show how the dead continued to affect the living, how their presence was continuously acknowledged through memory, dream and prayer. Their proximity was no abstract theory but a profoundly felt reality based on experiences of many kinds. The prayer against sudden death allows us to see how closely people might identify with the dead, and how afraid they could be of going unconfessed to the grave. The fear with which the prayer opens is balanced by its comprehensive pleas for help, joy, mercy and forgiveness. The petitioner attempts to solve the problem of unexpected death for himself by asking to be granted a continually confessional mode of life, *onhliht minre heortan geþanc mid lifes andgite 7 onhliht mine word 7 dæda 7 minne lichoman*

---

[34] Fol. 42r; cf. *Gif he þince þæt he deadne man cysse, þæt biþ lang lif ⁊ god*, fol. 39r.
[35] Lines 41–4.
[36] Barlow, *Life of King Edward*, p. 116.

7 sawle 7 eall min lif mid gastlicum andgyte (illuminate the thought of my heart with understanding of life and illuminate my words and deeds and my body and soul and all my life with spiritual understanding).[37] He attempts to solve it for others, living and dead, friend and foe, by embedding them in his all-embracing prayer.

Theory and practice at the death-bed: Bodley Laud miscellaneous 482

So far we have explored questions concerning the importance of confession, the development and practice of the rites for the sick and dying, the availibility of these rites to the laity, and the relationship between a priest and the souls in his care. These questions were also of paramount concern to the compiler of Laud 482, which in its sixty-seven folios combines a comprehensive anthology of vernacular confessional and penitential material with the *ordines* for the sick, dying and dead, rubricated in English. Laud 482 comes from the same circles as the prayer against sudden death: it shares some material with Tiberius A iii, and it has a scribe in common with the *Portiforium of St Wulfstan*, a strong argument for a Worcester provenance.[38] It is an unusually small, narrow manuscript, written in one hand throughout; the leaves toward the end are worn and the very last ones, including the last stages of the funeral service (the funeral mass and the burial itself), have been lost. Apart from the Latin prayers in the *ordines*, it is entirely in English. Very little of the content is exclusive to this manuscript, but as a compilation it is unique, primarily because of these very full vernacular rubrics and the way that they interact with the penitential and confessional material in the first part of the manuscript. Almost all of the texts in Laud 482 have appeared in print in various places, but the manuscript deserves to be considered as a whole because of its unity of layout, scribe and subject matter.[39]

The vernacular penitential texts represented in Laud 482 have a complex stratigraphy that may go back over a century and a half to the reign of Alfred. Their compilation embodies successive generations' translation and remodelling of key texts governing the rites of penance, confession, sickness, dying and death. The first item in the manuscript (fols 1–19) is the English translation of Halitgar's ninth-century *Penitential*, which has been tentatively assigned to Worcester or Ramsey under Bishop Oswald, in the mid- to late tenth century.[41] But we should be wary about assuming that these texts only belonged to Benedictine reform circles. Means argues that the continental transmission of Halitgar's *Penitential*

---

[37] Hughes, *Portiforium* II, p. 14.

[38] Gameson, 'Book Production at Worcester', 241.

[39] The *ordines* are printed in B. Fehr, 'Altenglische Ritualtexte für Krankenbesuch, heilige Ölung und Begräbnis', in H. Boehmer *et al.*, *Texte und Forschungen zur Englischen Kulturgeschichte* (Halle, 1921), pp. 20–67; the English *Penitential* is in Raith, *Die altenglische Version des Halitgar'schen Bussbuches*; the *Scrift Boc* and some of the brief penitential texts are in R. Spindler, *Das altenglische Bussbuch* (Leipzig, 1934); other confessional texts are printed in R. Fowler, 'An Old English Handbook for the Use of a Confessor', *Anglia* 83 (1965), pp. 1–34.

[41] Raith, *Die altenglische Version des Halitgar'schen Bussbuches*, pp. xxxviii–xxxix; Spindler, *Das altenglische Bussbuch*, pp. 111–25.

TABLE 1. CONTENTS OF BODLEY LAUD MISC 482

PART ONE

1	fols 1–19	A vernacular Penitential in four books. I is a series of authoritative quotations about the meaning of penance and confession. II and III (fols 5r–14r) are a conventional list of tariffs; IV is a summary of the major points of the preceding three books. (This text is also known as the 'Penitential of Pseudo-Egbert'.)
2	19–20	'12 things through which God forgives men their sins' (repeated in an abbreviated form as no. 10 below)
3	20	Brief text on the need for penance (repeated at the end of no. 9 below)
4	20–1	Canons 1–11 of the Synod of Rome, 721, dealing with sexual sin
5	21–7	Penitential material
6	27	A computistical note on ember days
7	27–8	Extracts from penitential material
8	28	Passage on confession, Fowler's 'Handbook', V, para 1[40]
9	28–30	Texts on confession, particularly on ways of commuting penance, concluding with a repetition of no. 3 above
10	30	A briefer version of the '12 things through which God forgives men their sins' (see no. 2 above)
11	30–40	Texts on penance and confession, known in CCCC 190 as *Scrift Boc*
12	40–2	Passage on penance and confession, Fowler's 'Handbook', V, paras 3–7
13	42–3	Commutation of penance, Fowler's 'Handbook', VI, ending FINITUM EST

PART TWO

14	44	*Originally blank*
15	45–6	Passages on penance and confession, Fowler, 'Handbook, III, lines 1–98, V, para 2, and III, lines 100–11
16	46–7	Formula for absolution following confession
17	47–8	*Ordines* for visiting the sick, celebrating mass in a sick person's house, attending the dying, and burying the dead, extensively rubricated in English

shows that it was used by 'simple priests in the daily work of pastoral care' as well as bishops, and Frantzen suggests that the English manuscripts of Latin penitentials indicate 910–30, the pre-reform generation, as the period when these texts were widely reintroduced to English religious life.[42]

[40] Fowler, 'Old English Handbook'.
[42] Meens, 'The Frequency and Nature of Early Medieval Penance', pp. 41–5; A. Frantzen, 'The Tradition of Penitentials in Anglo-Saxon England', *ASE* 11 (1982), pp. 23–56, 49–52.

The English translation of Halitgar was influential; it survives in several manuscripts, Ælfric knew it, and it was one of the vernacular sources on which Wulfstan drew in his 'Canons of Edgar'.[43] The same manuscripts, including Laud 482 (fols 30–40), preserve copies of another self-contained confessional and penitential text, which refers to itself as *Scrift Boc* in CCCC, MS 190. Frantzen argues that this represents an earlier stratum of vernacular penitential material, though 'probably not earlier than the reign of Alfred'.[44] Laud 482 also contains sections of the text that Fowler calls a *Handbook* for a confessor, which circulates in the same scribal pool, and he suggests that the *Handbook* came from the circle of Wulfstan of York at the beginning of the eleventh century.[45] Frantzen stresses the way that the *Handbook* texts form a 'compact guide, devoted chiefly to murder, fornication and superstitions . . . the most practical of the vernacular penitentials'.[46] Practicality seems to have been the guiding principle of the man who compiled the texts of Laud 482: they function together to facilitate the proper interaction of belief, speech, action and use of material culture, on the part of both the priest and the parishioner to whom he is ministering. The compiler of Laud 482 inherited a well-established tradition of accumulating vernacular material on penance; it is argued here that his specific intention was to highlight within that tradition the material vital for the priest attending the sick and dying.

Unlike most of the manuscripts in which these texts circulate, Laud 482 is peculiarly unified in theme and written by a single scribe. It clearly divides itself into two parts, the first finishing at the bottom of fol. 43v with the rubric FINITUM EST, followed by an originally blank folio. The text on fol. 45r begins with an outsize red þ, suggesting that the passages on confession which begin here are introductory to the liturgical texts, into whose vernacular rubrics which they segue. Parts One (fols 1–43) and Two (fols 45–67, with the final folios missing) complement each other: each is designed to clarify the function of confession within the liturgy appropriate to sick-bed or death-bed, but whereas Part One consists of confessional and penitential texts often presented to show how they may be relevant to those bedsides, Part Two reframes the *ordines* to show how they may be administered to maximum confessional and penitential effect. The interplay of the *ordines* and their English rubrics, embedded in, interspersed with and cross-referencing passages on confession and penance, makes this manuscript a source of unrivalled richness for unpicking the ideas about Christian death and dying of most concern in the generation of the Norman Conquest.

---

[43] The English *Penitential* (fols 1–19) edited by Raith (pp. 1–70) also appears in whole or in part in Brussels Bibliothèque Royale, MS 8558–63 (2498), CCCC, MS 190, CCCC, MS 201, CCCC, MS 256, Oxford, Bodl. Junius, MS 121, and Tiberius A iii; A. Meaney, 'Ælfric's Use of His Sources in His Homily on Auguries', *English Studies* 66 (1985), pp. 477–95; Fowler, *Wulfstan's Canons of Edgar*, pp. xlii–xliii.

[44] The *Scrift Boc* is also found in CCCC 190, Bodley Junius 121, Brussels Bib. Roy. 8558–63 (2498), Tiberius A iii, CCCC 265 and CCCC 201.

[45] Fowler, 'Old English Handbook'. Fowler draws attention primarily to Brussels 8558–63 (2498), CCCC 265, CCCC 201, Tiberius A iii and Junius 121.

[46] Frantzen, 'Tradition of Penitentials', p. 48.

Categorizing Laud 482

Recent scholars who have discussed Laud 482 find it hard to categorize satisfactorily. Gneuss files it under 'Manual' in his list of Anglo-Saxon liturgical material, but it does not fit easily under this heading. A manual contains the rites which the priest often needs to administer at short notice in an informal environment. While Laud 482 is an eminently portable book, and does contain three of the relevant *ordines*, they take up less than a third of its content and their rubrics read more like an exposition of the rite than the conventional abbreviated notes that would serve as an *aide-memoire* to a priest in the field. The other eight manuscripts which Gneuss describes as manuals contain a much wider range of liturgical material; while this does not in itself disqualify Laud 482 from being a manual, it suggests it may have been intended to serve a different function.[47] Keefer also finds Laud 482 hard to categorize, including it under the general heading of 'Manuals', which she subdivides into 'sacramentaries/missals', 'pontificals/benedictionals', 'books relating to the daily office' and 'other'. The last category contains one manuscript: Laud 482. Later she calls it a 'manual miscellany' and suggests it may have been 'an instruction booklet for a priest whose Latin is poor'.[48] Keefer accurately identifies the oddness of Laud 482, and her suggestion that it may have been used for instruction is an extremely fruitful one, whose implications will be explored below. Given the ubiquity of English in the late Anglo-Saxon Church, however, we should not assume here that it was compiled as a compromise solution.

Gneuss and Keefer see Laud 482 primarily as a book from which the *ordines* for the sick and dying would be performed. Frantzen, on the other hand, sees it as oriented towards the needs of a confessor, but, again, as the kind of book that a priest would use in the field.[49] But the texts are integrated in such a way that neither the penitential nor the ritual element dominates, and it is probable that all this material was intended to work in harmony. Leading themes of Laud 482 include the challenging nature of the relationship between priest-confessor and parishioner in life and at death, the varying needs of different members of the flock, and the trials and temptations faced by the ordained as well as the lay. Laud 482 would be a very suitable book from which to teach these priests their responsibility to the dead as well as the sick and dying.

The confessional and penitential texts of Laud 482

It is clear from the opening folios of each section of the manuscript that the penitential and confessional material of Part One and the *ordines* of Part Two are interrelated. In the introductory material to the Penitential, there is a passage based

---

[47] H. Gneuss, 'Liturgical Books in Anglo-Saxon England and Their Old English Terminology', in Lapidge and Gneuss, *Learning and Literature in Anglo-Saxon England*, pp. 91–142, 134–5.

[48] S. L. Keefer, 'Manuals', in R. Pfaff (ed.), *The Liturgical Books of Anglo-Saxon England*, Old English Newsletter Subsidia 23 (1995), pp. 99–109, 104.

[49] Frantzen, 'Tradition of Penitentials', p. 26.

on James 5:14–16 on the importance of unction which is repeated almost word for word on fol. 47, as part of the prefatory material introducing the *ordo* for the visiting of the sick:

TABLE 2. COMPARISON OF THE TWO PASSAGES ON ST JAMES

fol. 4	fol. 47
Be Iacobes ærendgewrite þæs halgan apostoles, on þam segð hu man sceal for þæne seocan man gebiddan ⁊ hine mid ele smyrian – Her tæcð S Iacobus, þæt gif hwa geuntrumad beo, þæt he geladige him his sacerd to ⁊ oðre godes þeowas, þæt hi him ofer rædan ⁊ se untruma his þearfe him secge ⁊ hine smyrigean on godes naman mid þam halgan ele; ⁊ þurh þæra geleafulra manna bene ⁊ þurh þa smyrenesse he mæg beon gehealden, ⁊ drihten hine aræreð, ⁊ gif he synful bið he beoð him forgifene. þy sceal ælc geleaful man, gif he mæg, þa smyrenesse begitan ⁊ þa gerihto þe þærto gebyriað; forþam hit is awriten, þæt ælc þæra manna þe þas gerihto hæfð, þæt his sawl bið gelice clæne æfter his forðsiðe ealswa ðæt cild bið þe æfter fulwihte sona gewit.	*þonne gif hwa to þam geuntrumod beo, þæt he haliges smyrels beþurfe, tæcð se halga apostol Sanctus Jacobus, hu man ymb þæt don sceal. Se untruma sceal ladian him his sacerd to, ⁊ oðre godcundes hades men, þe cunnon hym ⁊ wyllon ofer-rædan, ⁊ wyllað him his gastlice þearfe buton forwande secgan. þonne sceal se untruma heom his þearfe secgan, ⁊ hy hine þonne smyrian, on Godes naman mid þam halgan ele, for þam þurh þæra geleaffulra bene, ⁊ þurh þa smyrennesse he mæg beon gehealden, ⁊ drihten hine arærað, ⁊ gif he synfull bið, hy beoð him forgifene. Ðis sceal ælc geleafull man don, gif he mæg þa smyrunge begitan, ⁊ þa gerihta þe þær-to gebyriað; for-þon hit is awriten, þæt ælc þæra manna þe þas gerihta hæfð, þæt his saul bið gelice clæne æfter his forðsiðe, swa þæt cild bið, þe æfter fulluhte sona gewiteð.*
On the writing of James the Holy Apostle, in which it says how a sick man is to be prayed for and anointed with oil – here teaches St James, that if anyone is ill, he should call his priest and other servants of God to him, that they may read over him and the sick man may say his need to them and they may anoint him in God's name with holy oil; and through the prayers of the faithful men and through the unction he may be healed and God raise him up, and if he is sinful he will be forgiven. By this shall every faithful man, if he may, obtain unction and the rites that pertain thereto; because it is written that every man who has these rites, his soul will be as clean after his death as that of the child who dies immediately after baptism.	Then if anyone is so sick that he has need of holy unction, St James the Holy Apostle teaches how it is to be done. The sick man must summon his priest and other men in holy orders to him, who know him and are willing to read over, and are willing to say him his spiritual needs without shame. Then the sick man must say his need to them, and then they must anoint him in God's name with holy oil, for through the prayers of the faithful and through the unction he may be healed, and God will raise him up, and if he is sinful he will be forgiven. Every faithful man must do this if he is to obtain the unction and the rites pertaining thereto; because it is written that each man who has these rites, his soul will be as clean after his death, as that of the child who dies immediately after baptism.

There are some minor differences here, but overall the correspondence is very close, and the simile comparing the soul of the man who dies after unction to the child who dies immediately after baptism is found only in these two places and in the other manuscripts of the *Penitential*.[50] This passage provides a thumbnail explanation of the origins, purpose and importance of unction, and is strategically located near the beginning of each part of the manuscript. Its first citation is in the context of a section on what might be called 'the theory of penance', its second comes in the more practical environment of the *ordo*. It also introduces a number of themes crucial to the manuscript in the image of the paradigmatically innocent dead baby, whose christening and death are conflated.[51] Presented as a quotation, *for-þon hit is awriten,* this is the first in a series of *sententiae* that Laud 482 includes, reminding the priest of the seriousness of his actions and serving as a fund of authority if he needs to reassure his patient. Another theme emphasized in this passage is the possibility of imminent death. Although the rite is designed to heal, *7 þurh þa smyrennesse he mæg beon gehealden, 7 drihten hine arærað* (and through the anointing he may be healed and the Lord raise him up), the compiler of Laud 482 is very aware that the patient may die, leading him to emphasize the salvific element. The possibility that someone might experience these *gerihta*, recover, and go on to sin again is not admitted (in contrast to Part One (fol. 30) drawing on Proverbs 26:11 and 2 Peter 2:22 to compare the unregenerate sinner to the dog returning to his vomit).

The occurrence of this passage at the beginning of the *Penitential* is the first link between Parts One and Two, but it does not stand alone. The first item in the table of contents for Book I of the Penitential is *Be þam men þe on his ytemestan dæge his synna gecyrran wyle to dædbote þæt him man þæs ne wyrne* (About the man who, on his final day, wants to turn from sin to penance, which may not be refused him). This is followed by *Be þam men þe gyrnð dædbote 7 wegnyste for deaðes ege 7 be þam þe him his spræc ofnimð ær him his scrift to cume* (About the man who desires penance and the viaticum for fear of death, and he who loses the power of speech before his confessor arrives). Book I, 13 raises the question of those who have been excluded from taking communion, and die under this ban, concluding *Be þisum þingum ne cunne we smeagan nan oðer þing, butan hit sy on godes dome gelang; forþam on godes anwealde wæs, þæt he butan husle gewat* (On these subjects we are unable to conjecture further, unless it may come from God's judgement, because it was under God's jurisdiction that he died without the eucharist). This last seems like a harmless remark here, but it could conflict with legal texts, many of which deny excommunicants the right to burial in a churchyard. Thus from the opening folios of Laud 482 the priest is reminded of the challenging environments in which he is likely to be hearing confession

---

[50] The near identity of these two passages is even clearer when compared to Ælfric's Pastoral Letter for Wulfsige, ch. 89, where he translates the same passage but uses quite different English vocabulary and phrasing. *Councils*, p. 214.

[51] J. Lynch, *Christianizing Kinship: Ritual Sponsorship in Anglo-Saxon England* (Ithaca and London, 1998), p. 129, citing Æthelwulf, *De Abbatibus*, pp. 27–32, for a vision of the otherworld in which the dreamer is guided by his own dead babies, still in their baptismal robes.

and administering penance. The text reiterates the need for generosity and under-standing on the part of the priest: if witnesses at a death-bed attest that the speechless and dying man *scriftes gyrnde Ᵹ husles* (desired confession and communion) then the priest is to carry out the rite. The priest is not to conclude that a man is damned if he dies excommunicate and without the viaticum. Although these concepts are a standard part of the penitential package, they take on new immediacy when copied out in conjunction with the *ordines* and their expanded rubrics.

There are further aspects of Laud 482 which suggest it was compiled by men with great expertise in the administration of confession and penance. It includes several ways of commuting penance for those incapable of sustaining a rigorous fast, or even of kneeling down. At the end of Book II of the English Penitential there is a passage advising that the penalty for theft should depend on the value of the stolen goods, making the confessor's role analogous to that of a secular judge. Penance is attuned to the wealth and status of the penitent in the passages on fols 40–2, immediately followed by a passage suggesting that the wealthy also have the option of paying the poor to do their penance for them (otherwise only found in CCCC 201). Fowler comments that this passage is 'apparently unique in its lax provisions for rich men, [and] contradicts the principle on which commutation is based'.[52] This notwithstanding, the passage gives a realistic idea of the difficulty churchmen had in trying to impose penance on influential and unwilling members of the laity, and suggests that Laud 482 was part of a movement in the late Anglo-Saxon Church that brought an intensely pragmatic and experienced attitude to penance. Murray analyses later medieval penitential handbooks and anecdotes about the confessional, and concludes that the administration of penance involved endless negotiation and much basic instruction in the articles of faith, that it was a learning experience for both parties, and that successful compromises were often reached.[53] Many of the texts anthologized in Laud 482 suggest that the same was already true of the English Church by the eleventh century.

Medicine for the soul

It is this section on commutation which concludes with FINITUM EST, followed by an originally blank folio. After this, the tone changes somewhat. Part Two begins with a series of passages referring to the role of the confessor as *sawla læce* (soul's doctor), and exploring the medical metaphor in some detail, speaking of *yfel wunda* (evil wounds), *god sealfe* (good ointment), *aspiwe þæt attor* (vomit the poison) and *godne drenc* (good emetic). Although the equation of confession and penance with medicine for the soul is another commonplace of the genre, it is interesting that this metaphor has not been explored in any detail earlier in Laud 482; it only occurs now, introducing the *ordo* for visiting and anointing the

---

[52] Fowler, 'Old English Handbook', p. 14.
[53] Murray, 'Counselling in Medieval Confession', pp. 72–7.

sick starting two folios later. Again, this suggests that the texts in Laud 482 were put together according to a coherent underlying plan.

Another recurrent theme of the introductory material to the *ordines* is that of fitting the penance to the penitent, as in Part One. However here it is embedded in the passages about spiritual medicine, with several references to being gentle with the physically weak or ill, and the confessor is represented more as a triage nurse than a judge, assessing the extent of the spiritual danger and prescribing the appropriate remedy. It first warns the priest against condemning the sinner and plunging him into despair, *ðeah hwæðre ne fordeme ne hig ormode ne gedon* (do not judge so that they cause despair). This is a risk that Ælfric also explores, in his *De Doctrina Apostolica*, but *his* warning, in contrast, puts the onus of responsibility for avoiding despair on the shoulders of the sick person him-self, not on those of the confessor.[54] Laud 482 then considers the confessional expertise of the sinner and his degree of self-awareness. Phrases such as *will 7 cunne* (desire and know), *ðu ongite* (you should understand), and *gif he ðonne ne cunne* (should he not know it) attest to an understanding of confession as the negotiated learning experience envisaged by Murray for the later Middle Ages. The text also constructs confession differently depending on the penitent's experience. The confessor is to be a *gescadwis dema* (discerning judge) and respect someone who is spiritually educated and treat him *lufelice 7 mildheortlice* (lovingly and mercifully), whereas a person who lacks self-knowledge is to be treated more severely, and have his sins 'wrung' (*atredan*) out of him. It goes on to refine this basic distinction with a list of factors founded on status and lifecycle, concluding with an epitome in a heightened, alliterative mode: *þi man sceal gesceadwislice toscadan ylde 7 geoguðe, welan 7 wædlan, hale 7 unhale 7 hada gehwilcne* (By this one shall discriminate discerningly between old and young people, rich and poor, healthy and sick and of every kind). This sounds as if it were designed to be easily committed to memory, perhaps through being read aloud.

The value of tears

Before moving on to look at the *ordines* in detail, there is one more text in Part One which, like the prayer against sudden death, paints a picture of complex and powerful death-related emotion. This is the list of the twelve ways to earn God's forgiveness, which appears twice, once in an expanded form on fols 19–20, immediately after the Penitential, and again, more briefly, on fol. 30v, in a form much closer to the Latin original.[55] The first list glosses, expands and provides examples and even quotations whereas the second list is telegrammatic in its brevity. Two of the items on the first list are of particular interest here because they bring home the emotional pressure put on the living to identify with and help the dead:

---

[54] *Supp.* II, pp. 622–35, lines 131–5.
[55] Penitential of Pseudo-Cummean, quoted in Spindler, *Das altenglische Bussbuch*, p. 155.

Seo eahtoðe forgifenes is þæt man of ðisse life fare to wite, 7 his freond ðonne ðe on ðisse life beoð hine magon alysan 7 him to forgifenesse æt God geearnian mid godcundum ðeowdome 7 mid heora woruldæhton.

The eighth forgiveness is that a man goes from this life to punishment, and his friend who remains in this life may release him and earn him forgiveness from God with divine service and with worldly possessions.

The principle here is clearly that it is better to assume that your friend has gone to torment, and to respond accordingly with masses and alms, rather than to risk assuming wrongly that his soul is in no need of forgiveness. *Wite* often means the pains of hell, but it cannot do so here or else the masses and alms would be wasted, and clearly the writer has an unspecified but unpleasant interim destination in mind. This awareness of the vulnerability of the dead adds an extra poignancy to the fourth type of forgiveness: *Seo feorþe forgyfenes is ðurh sealmsang 7 teara agotenesse, ðat gehwa for his synnum hreowsige 7 weope, swa gehwa deð for his freondes forðsiðe* (The fourth forgiveness is through singing of psalms and effusion of tears, so that someone repents and weeps for his sins as he does for the death of his friend). Both these passages make an unembarrassedly personal appeal by referring to *freondas* and the loving obligations they have to each other. Weeping for your dead friends involves not only weeping for all that you yourself have lost at their death, but also tears of fear on behalf of their souls, inspiring acts of piety. The *teara agotenesse þæt gehwa for his synnum hreowsige 7 weope* is reminiscent of the petition in the prayer against sudden death for *teara genihtsumnysse ðæt ic mæge ða misdæda bewepan 7 behreowsian* (abundance of tears that I may weep and repent the misdeeds). Tears shed for friends who have died metamorphose into tears shed for the self who is about to die, and they represent not merely reactive grief but proactive and beneficial compunction and prayer.

Laud 482: the Ordines

The centrality of confession to salvation is reiterated in a confessional formula, conventional in type but in this precise wording unique to Laud 482, which is the last entry before the repetition of the account of St James's establishment of unction, and the beginning of the *ordines* proper. It contains a formula for absolution which acknowledges the reciprocal nature of the relationship between confessor and person confessing: *for þan me is neod þearf þæt ic þe riht lære 7 þe is neod þearf þæt þu riht do* (because it is necessary for me to teach you properly and for you to act properly). The parishioner is then encouraged to be aware of his nakedness before God, to see himself both as the newborn baby he was and the corpse he soon will be, images that haunt this manuscript (the corpse is stripped naked in the rubric for the *commendatio animae* a few folios later). He is to be sensitive to the proximity of death and judgement, and to understand the priest's role in confession as a foretaste of the way that his soul will be open to God's eyes (*godes ælmihtiges eagum*).

We have seen this at work in Part Two's introductory material to the *ordines*, but it is also found at their heart. One of the several unusual aspects of Laud 482 is the quantity of direct speech its rubrics contain. This is particularly noticeable in a second confessional formula found embedded in the *uisitatio* rubric, after the sick man has been encouraged to bequeath his possessions. The parishioner then confesses, and is to draw to a close with these few words, addressed to God, all the saints, and 'you', the priest, his personal witness and intercessor: *Nu andette ic minum drihtne 7 eallum his halgum 7 þe, þe min gastlice scrifte eart* . . . (Now I confess to my Lord and all his saints and you, who are my spiritual confessor). The rest of the prayer is directed only to the priest, using the second person singular throughout. The sick person promises to obey *þinre tæcinge* (your teaching) and concludes *ic bidde þe, þe min gastlica lareow eart, þæt þu me foreþingie 7 beforan mines drihtnes þrym-setle on domes dæge minre andetnesse gewita sy* (I pray you, who are my spiritual teacher, that you intercede for me and testify to my confession before my Lord's throne on Judgement Day). Here we see another powerful bond connecting the living and the dead, or the person about to die: the reunion at the end of the time.

The narrative in this prayer dramatizes Doomsday in a way that resonates with the language of those Anglo-Saxon wills that ask for earthly protection and intercession. The will of Ælfflæd, widow of Byrhtnoth of Essex, sets up several such networks, asking King Æthelred to protect her bequests 'for the love of God and my lord's soul and my sister's soul', and going on to ask ealdorman Æthelmær that

> *he beo on minum life min fulla freod. 7 forespreca. 7 mira manna 7 efter minum dege beo þara halgan stowe. 7 þeræ are ful freod. 7 forespeca æt Stocæ þe mine yldran on restaþ.*[56]
>
> during my life he shall be a true friend and advocate and to my men, and after my death, be a true friend and advocate of the holy foundation at Stoke, where my ancestors lie buried, and its property.

Ælfflæd needs a powerful intercessory voice to plead for her rights on earth, before and after her death, just as the person facing death needs one at Judgement. This confessional formula thus repeats ideas of patronage and advocacy familiar at every level of Anglo-Saxon society, projecting the structure of both royal and legal court on to the vision of Doomsday. The priest is given the weighty role of playing the intercessor for the dying person, bearing witness to God on his behalf.

Summary of the rites and rubrics

Given the amount of material about the sick and dying contained in fols 1–43, the relevance of Part One to Part Two's *ordines* would be apparent even if the latter had normally terse rubrics instead of greatly expanded ones. However, what the compiler of Laud 482 has done is to interleave the stages of these rites with material culled from Latin rubrics, penitential and confessional material,

---

[56] Whitelock, *Wills* XV, pp. 38–9. The irregular spellings are those of the MS.

the Gospels and other scriptural sources, to produce a text which reads like a students' edition, full of explanatory notes and useful references. These rites are complex, both in performance and in the theology underpinning them, and Laud 482 would be very useful in conveying this complexity. The *uisitatio*, in particular, has to be an ambiguous ritual, predicated both on the assumption that God can hear and will sometimes answer the prayers and heal the disease, and on the need to prepare the soul for death. An inarticulate or confused priest would be incapable of conveying to his parishioners the importance of summoning him at these times of crisis, and he would have been seen as a terrible liability by anyone who had internalized the lessons taught by Laud 482.

After the explanation of St James's teaching on unction, there is a long passage on the appropriate vestments and accoutrements – candles, incense, holy water, oil, *ordo* – that the priest and the other men in holy orders need to wear or carry. The rite then moves through the entry into the house, the asperging of house and patient, and the appropriate prayers (including *Respice, Domine, de Celo*), anthems and collect, which have minimal English rubrication, before moving on to confession, which is treated in another long English passage. This gives the questions and responses of both priest and patient, and distinguishes between the modes in which confession should be handled for the ordained and for the laity; it raises the issue of how to respond if the sick man refuses to confess, and again stresses the need for the priest to be humble and reassuring. It then gives the litanies which are to be sung while confession is taking place, after which there is another discussion of the function of confession with a reiteration of the priest's responsibility to God for this soul, and a forcefully expressed passage explaining that the priest must avoid sounding as if he is condemning the sinner rather than the sin, supported by a string of scriptural citations. It then provides the catch-all confessional formula examined above, to be spoken by the sick man directly to the priest and asking for his intercession at the Last Judgement.

This is followed by the blessing of the ashes, which are then mixed with holy water and used to make the sign of the cross on the sick man's breast. Then comes the blessing of the haircloth, which is laid out on the ground and sprinkled with holy water and ashes, followed by anthems, psalms and collects. Unction takes place, then more prayers and the administration of the eucharist, with a note in English to the effect that the mass which follows in the manuscript may be said for the next seven nights, and the *uisitatio infirmorum* concludes with ten collects and a benediction.

The *missa pro infirmo in domo* which follows has very few rubrics, although it does conclude with the direction that if the sufferer is ordained, on his return to health he must bow down to the community and prostrate himself before the altar on the first time he goes to church, while the brethren pray and the priest chants a collect. The *agenda mortuorum*, on the other hand, is extensively annotated. It starts with a long English passage explaining how the priest must establish whether the sick person knows his Creed and Paternoster, and how, if not, the essentials of the faith must be explained to him. This is followed by the administration of the eucharist. The narrative then becomes more complex, as there is necessarily an unknown length of time before the patient dies. The rubric first assumes a scenario in which he dies at once, and describes how the body must be stripped and laid out. It then lists the psalms, litanies and prayers which are to be sung, with the note that if there is time before the sick man dies, the Gospel accounts of Christ's passion are to be read. This is followed by prayers, the *Kyrie* and a collect, at which point the manuscript breaks off.

Laud 482 and other English Ordines

Only two other English service books, the mid-eleventh-century Red Book of Darley (CCCC, MS 422) and the early eleventh-century Missal of Robert of Jumièges, also contain rites with systematic vernacular rubrics.[57] Robert, the earliest of these three, has the smallest quantity of English, its rubrics are simple instructions and it does not differentiate between the rite as performed for the lay and for the ordained. Confession is referred to in a cursory fashion, implying an assumption that the sick man would be familiar with it, and there is nothing in Robert which suggests that the rite was intended for anyone outside the ordained community. Darley is a very different kind of book. Its rubrics are much less full than those of Laud 482, they do not include the *missa pro infirmis in domo*, and in the *agenda mortuorum* English is interlineated with Latin rather than standing alone. However, in several places its phrasing is close enough to Laud 482 to suggest a common history, and they also share a unique detail in the ritual of unction, in which special attention is paid to the hands and the feet. The two passages need to be quoted in full for proper comparison. Darley, the briefer and less detailed of the two, reads:

> To uteweardum handbredum. 7 þonne hi gesmyrod beoð, þonne do him linene glofa on handa 7 hæbbe hi oð þone eahteðan dæg, gif his lyf swa lang byð. Gif hit þonne [ne] beo, hæbbe hi mid him to byregene. To uteweardum fotum. 7 þonne hi gesmyrod beoð, þonne do him on linene meon 7 do þærymbe swa swa embe þa glofa.

On the outside of the hands. And when they are anointed, put linen gloves on his hands and let him have them until the eighth day, if his life be so long. If not, he may have them in the grave. On the outside of the feet. And when they are anointed, then put linen socks on him and do with them as with the gloves.

Laud 482 follows the same outline with more refinements:

> To uteweardum handum, gif hit mæsse-preost bið, 7 to innewardum gif hit læwede man sy. 7 þonne hy gesmyrede beoð, do him man linene glofan buton ælcon þymule on handa 7 hæbbe hy oð þone eahteoþan dæg, gif his lif swa langum bið. And gif he forðfare, hæbbe hy mid him to byrgenne. To uteweardum fotum. 7 þonne hy gesmyrede beoð, do him on linene meon, 7 hæbbe hy on eal swa we ær cwædon be þam linenum glofum, þæt is to byrgenne, gif him swa getimað.

On the outside of the hands, if it be a mass-priest, and on the inside if it be a layperson. And when they are anointed, put on linen gloves without thumbs on the hands and keep

---

[57] R. I. Page, 'Old English Liturgical Rubrics in Corpus Christi College, Cambridge, MS 422', *Anglia* 96 (1978), pp. 149–58; T. Graham, 'The Old English Liturgical Directions in Corpus Christi College, Cambridge, MS 422', *Anglia* 111 (1993), pp. 439–46. H. A. Wilson, *The Missal of Robert of Jumièges*, HBS 11 (London, 1896).

them on for eight days, if his life last so long. And if he die, he is to have them with him in the grave. On the outside of the feet. And when they are anointed, put linen socks on, and keep them on just as we already said about the linen gloves, that is for the grave, if that is what happens to him.

This detail of the gloves and socks is only found in these two manuscripts and presumably reflects a particularly English practice. Though Darley does not mark the difference between priest and layman here, it shares Laud 482's insistence on the socks and gloves, the concern that the sick person should wear them for a week and the insistence that if the patient dies during this period then the body is to be buried wearing them. This is symptomatic of Darley's overall relationship to Laud 482: it follows the same outline but is a pared-down version. It refers to the priest carrying out his task *mid gelimplicre eadmodnisse* and *mid ealle liðnysse* (with appropriate humility, and with all gentleness), but does not mention the danger of an arrogant or judgemental priest panicking the parishioner, nor does it mention the validity of last-minute repentance, or back this up with the numerous scriptural citations of Laud 482. Darley goes into some detail about the process of confession, and provides the basic formulae in English, but the only thing the parishioner is given to say is *To þam þæt ge me smyrian sceoldon* (that you should anoint me), nothing like the long speech given to the patient in Laud 482. This comparative simplicity is also noticeable in the Latin: the prayers following the litany in Darley are shorter and less elaborate, and the moments of unction are unmarked, whereas in Laud 482 each part of the body has its own prayer, psalm and collect. Darley contains a fuller range of rites, including baptism, and Gneuss and Keefer both catalogue it under 'missal and sacramentary'. Its rubrics, while more ample than the average, focus on the practical elements rather than the theoretical, making Darley look much more like a book for use in the field.

One last English manuscript to compare with Laud 482 is the Lanalet Pontifical, although this contains no vernacular rubrics.[58] Its *uisitatio* rite has comparatively ample Latin rubrics, however, stressing that the priest must comport himself *non tumide mentis* (without arrogance of mind) and *cum omnia lenitate* (with all gentleness); it differentiates between the way confession is to be heard from the *spiritualis* and the *secularis*, and it stresses that holy oil is to be applied *humiliter*, with every stage of the unction marked by a prayer, antiphon and psalm. The rite for the sick is followed by the *absolutio penitentis*, which concludes with the same popular formula found towards the end of the *uisitatio* in Laud 482, *Absoluo te uice beati Petri apostoli apostolorum principis, cui dominus potestatem ligandi atque soluendi dedit . . .* (I absolve you in the name of blessed Peter the apostle, prince of the apostles, to whom the Lord gave the power of binding and loosing). Furthermore, the Lanalet *uisitatio* begins with a Latin description of what the clergy must wear and carry which is very close to Laud 482, quoted in full here to facilitate comparison with Laud 482 as well as for its intrinsic interest:

---

[58] G. H. Doble (ed.), *Pontificale Lanaletense*, HBS 74 (1937).

Dum inuitati sacerdotes ad infirmum fuerint uisitandi ungendique causa, qui eorum ad illud officium dignis iure censetur induat se super humerali alba et stola cum phanone atque planeta si affuerit sin alias casula non induatur. Diaconus uero qui euangelii textum ferat et oleum infirmorum et ceroferarii secundum ordinem suum se induant. Unus ceroferariorum dextra cereum. sinistra aquam benedictam teneat. alter uero dextra cereum. leuat urribulum [sic] cum incensu. Sic induti cum domum in qua infirmus iacet intrare uoluerint. Sacerdos leua codicem quo huius officii orationes habentur teneat. dextra signo se dominice crucis muniat, quatinus cum summa humilitate et timore dei quod inceperit perficere ualest.[59]

When the priests are to be invited to the sick person for the sake of visiting and anointing, he who is esteemed by rule most suitable for that office should put on superhumeral, alb and stole, with maniple and a *planeta* chasuble if there is one, if not no chasuble should be worn. The deacon, who should carry the evangeliary and the oil for the sick, and the acolytes (candle-bearers) should dress themselves according to the ordo. One of the acolytes should have a candle in his right hand and holy water in his left. The other should have a candle in his right and in his left a thurible with incense. Thus dressed, they are to desire to enter the house in which the sick person lies. The priest should hold the book in which the prayers for this office are contained in his left and with his right hand protect himself with the sign of the lordly cross, in as much as what he is to begin he should be able to complete with the greatest humility and fear of God.

By no means all Latin rubrics are as elaborate as Lanalet; the Winchcombe Sacramentary, for example, has elaborate *ordines* but minimal rubrication.[60] When Robert, Darley and Lanalet are compared to Laud 482, it becomes clear that Laud 482's handling of the rites is part of a continuum. The eleventh-century English Church shows great interest in elaborate ritual and the relationship between priest and parishioner, in finding appropriate rites for laity and clergy, in vernacular translation, and in the validity of confession, but Laud 482 takes all of these concerns to the extreme. If the Worcester provenance is correct – and on the basis of the capitalization of Peter and only Peter in the *uisitatio* litany it may be possible to be more specific and identify the cathedral – then Laud 482's compiler probably had a respectable research library on which to draw, allowing him to bring together everything he found most useful.

This care for detail can be seen at work in the passage which introduces the *uisitatio*. The English of Laud 482 is very close to the Latin of Lanalet quoted above, suggesting a comparable source, but there are several phrases which are expansions or additions. Whereas the deacon in Lanalet is simply to dress according to his order, in Laud 482 this is expanded to *scryde hine . . . swylce he godspel rædan* (let him dress . . . as thought to read the Gospel). In the final sentence *quod* is more explicitly *þa godcundan þenunge* (the divine service), and the phrase *butan æghwylcere modes toþundenesse* (without any swollenness of spirit) is added to the closing exhortation to perform the rite with humility, in addition to which *timore dei* (fear of God) changes to the more positive *mid Godes fultume* (with God's help). These may indicate only that Laud 482's Latin

[59] P. 131.
[60] A. Davril, *The Winchcombe Sacramentary*, HBS 109 (1995).

source included elements different or absent from Lanalet, but two other phrases suggest a process of engaged translation and annotation. At the end of the list of vestments, *planeta* is glossed with *þæt is godwebben cæppe*, explaining the obscure technical Latin word with a resonant Old English one, *godweb*, a cloth described elsewhere as taffeta-like or interwoven with gold. As the text suggests, it is unlikely that every priest would have had access to such a magnificent object. The glories of *godweb* are contrasted to the miseries of the grave in several homilies, and some possible implications of this are explored further in Chapter Four.

The other difference is also informative. Lanalet begins the sentence instructing the clergy to go to the patient's house *sic induti*; in Laud 482 this reads *ðus gescrydde 7 gescrypede* (thus dressed and kitted-out). *Sic induti* is itself superfluous to the meaning of the passage, and it is suggestive that in Laud 482 it becomes an alliterative pairing of past participles, and that *gescrypede* is a nonceword. Discussing Hrothgar's so-called 'sermon' in *Beowulf*, Clemoes notes that 'coupling of finite verbs which are synonyms or near-synonyms' is 'characteristic of expository discourse' and 'clerical didacticism'.[61] In similar vein, Orchard shows how Wulfstan of York 'adds such doublets' to his English translations from Latin, which he reads as Wulfstan cultivating a style derived explicitly from the oral and the traditional.[62] Although this alliterative pairing in Laud 482 is a slender piece of evidence, it suggests that the rubrics may have been designed to be read aloud and committed to memory, perhaps in the context of teaching priests the meaning of their role.

Envisioning the death-bed

This introductory rubric reveals a concern with the material culture of these rites, a concern that is also evinced in the rite of unction, with its linen socks and gloves, and with the hair-shirt that is blessed with ashes and 'laid aside till it be needed' (*lecge hy neah þam untruman oð hire man beþurfe*) immediately before the anointing. While sackcloth and ashes have a long history in burial rites going back to the *Vita Martini* and beyond that, in a penitential mode, to the Book of Job, it is striking to find it here in a rite so explicitly for the lay as well as the ordained. This unusual care for the appropriate tools and accessories also appears in the *commendatio animae*, when the patient has died:

> 7 syððan mid gedreoge hine unscrydan, þonne he gewiten bið. 7 þa, ðe þær ætstandað, hine eastwardne astreccan and on þære hæran alecgan 7 æfter þam hine utan besittan 7 þa eagan belecgan 7 þone muð belucan 7 gif he belocen beon nylle, þonne befo man þa ceacan up to þam heafde mid sumam bende and þa sawle mid lof-sange Gode bebeodan.

and afterwards with modesty undress him, when he is departed. And then those who are standing by should lay him out eastward and lay him on the haircloth and after that sit

[61] P. Clemoes, *Interactions of Thought and Language in Old English Poetry*, CSASE 12 (Cambridge, 1995), pp. 44–5.
[62] A. Orchard, 'Crying Wolf: Oral Style and the "Sermones Lupi"', *ASE* 21 (1992), pp. 239–64, 249.

around him outside and cover the eyes and fasten the mouth and if it does not want to be closed, then someone should tie the jaw up to the head with a strip of cloth and commend the soul to God with praise-song.

The cryptic remark in the *uisitatio* about the hair-cloth being kept to hand 'until there was need of it' now becomes clear: the corpse is to be laid out on it and perhaps also shrouded and buried in it. The intensely practical focus of these rubrics is again prominent here, with the concern that the body should be stripped *mid gedreoge*, modestly, that it should be laid out *eastwardne* (a foretaste of its position in the grave), that eyes and mouth should be closed, and if the mouth is hard to close then the jaw is to be tied up to the head with a strip of cloth. We are thus given a vivid visual image of the corpse, perhaps with the protective linen still guarding its hands and feet, the band around its jaws, lying supine on the hair-cloth, smudged with ashes and with an ash cross daubed on the breast. This passage is unparalleled in any other rubric, or indeed in any other account of the death-bed in Anglo-Saxon literature, and the next English reference to the corpse being laid out eastwards and binding the jaw comes in the late twelfth-century fragmentary *Soul and Body* poem copied out by the Tremulous Worcester Hand who also glossed Laud 482.[63] What is notable here is that Laud 482's compiler thought such details worth mentioning, implicitly extending the boundaries of what was appropriate for a rubric, bringing these actions into the ecclesiastical ritual field. He is unlikely to have been the first to do so; given the development of penitentially oriented ritual around the death-bed over the previous two hundred and fifty years it is clear that the question of Christian dying exercised the imaginations of many senior churchmen across Christendom, and in this they may have been representative of many other people in their societies. Other kinds of evidence for this, such as that from burials, will be looked at more closely in the next chapter.[64]

Secular activities around the corpse

The strictly liturgical activities (asperging and so forth) are clearly assigned to priest, deacon and other men in orders, but the rubric here is coy about who should actually strip and lay out the body, referring only to *þa ðe þær ætstandað* (those who stand by). Are these the minor clergy or, in a lay environment, do we see here the shadowy presence of family and neighbours? There is also the tantalizing reference in the Worcester *Soul and Body* to a *wrecche wif* who 'despises misfortune' (*forhoweþ þene earfeþsiþ*), whose task it is to bind the mouth and the 'dim eyes' of the corpse'.[65] Then there are the *alii circumadstantes*, cited by de Clercq, who sing the Penitential Psalms, and the bystanders present

---

[63] *He biþ eastward istreiht; he biþ sone stif... Forbindeþ þæs deadan muþ ꝥ his dimme egen.* Moffat, *The Soul's Address*, Fragment A, lines 31 and 42, pp. 63–4.
[64] V. Thompson, 'Constructing Salvation: A Penitential and Homiletic Context for Late Anglo-Saxon Burial Practice', in Lucy and Reynolds, *Burial in Early Medieval England and Wales*, pp. 229–40.
[65] Moffat, *The Soul's Address*, Fragment A, lines 41–2, p. 64.

at the dying person's bedside in Laud 482's *Penitential* I, 4, who attest to the now-speechless patient's desire for *scrift* (confession) and *husel* (communion). The monks of the *Regularis Concordia* are unlikely to have been the only Anglo-Saxon community who gathered around a bedside to ease one of their number through death. In several places Ælfric mentions the *licmenn* attending a corpse, like those who watch over Fursey after his death from evening until cockcrow, and who uncover the supposed cadaver's face (*his neb þærrihte unwrogon*) when they notice him stirring, and this word may conceal a group of men with an official, ritual function.[66] The activities of 'those who stand by' move between the precise (tying up the jaw) and the (to us, at least) vague: they are to *utan him besittan* (sit out around him), with a later reference to *syððan hy hine utan betrymedne habbað* (after they have sat out around him). Both *besittan* and *betrymian* are words which elsewhere have connotations of defence and siege, and we may catch a glimpse here of a secular wake intended to defend the corpse.[67] There are traces here of a ritual space that liturgical practice had not colonized, but that Laud 482's compiler, at least, did not think he needed to condemn.

He may have wished to modify lay activities around the corpse, however, since his emphasis that the corpse be stripped *mid gedreoge* suggests that the reverse could be the case. Burchard of Worms, writing his penitential at the beginning of the eleventh century, lists singing, dancing, drunkenness, laughter and the appearance of rejoicing as unacceptable practices when watching over a corpse, and there is a little evidence from Ælfric that similar activities could take place around the Anglo-Saxon death-bed.[68] In his Pastoral Letter for Wulfsige of Sherborne, he warns priests against joining in 'the heathen songs and loud laughter of the laity' (*þa hæðenan sangas þæra læwedra manna & heora hludan cheahchetunga*) and eating and drinking in the presence of the corpse, all of which he terms *hæðenscype*.[69] He takes it for granted that these activities will be taking place, even when the priest has been invited to the death-bed (*þænne ge þærto geladode syn, þonne forbeode ge þa hæðenan sangas*). These injunctions, in both Burchard and Ælfric, have antecedents in canon law, but Ælfric is not passing this on merely as an item of received wisdom. He returns to the subject in his *Life of St Swithin*, drawing a similar and much more detailed picture:

---

[66] *CH* II, XIII, p. 59, line 193; *CH* II, XX, p. 191, line 51. In the latter he is using *licmenn to* translate the *circumstantibus* of the anonymous *Vita Fursei*: *CH Comm.*, p. 532.

[67] *Besittan* occurs in a similar context in *CH* I, XV, p. 299, line 9: *Bebeod nu for ði besittan his birigene* and significantly in *CH* II, p. 414, line 135: *þæra sawla fynd sind þa hellican gastas þe besittað þæs mannes forðsið*. Another related word may be *bestandan*, which Ælfric uses specifically to refer to a heathen wake in his *Life of Thomas*, and in a more neutral funerary context in his sermon for the feast of Gregory the Great: *LS* II, XXXVI, p. 407, lines 125–8: *Men heold þæt lic on þa hæþenan wisan and se broðor wolde wurðlice hine bestandan and kynelice macian mid mærðum his byrgene. CH* II, IX, p. 76, lines 124–5: *Fæderas and moddru bestandað heora bearna lic*, translating *filiorum funera parentes aspiciunt. CH Comm.*, p. 409.

[68] Book xix of the Corrector of Burchard of Worms, McNeill and Gamer, *Medieval Handbooks of Penance* pp. 333–4; A. Meaney, 'Ælfric and Idolatry', *Journal of Religious History* 13 (1984), pp. 119–35, 132–3.

[69] *Councils*, p. 218 and n. 2, citing Leo IV, *Homiliae* (*PL* 115, p. 681): *Carmina diabolica, quae nocturnis horis super mortuos vulgus facere solet, et cachinnos quos exercet, sub contestatione Dei omnipotentis virtute.*

Hwilon wacodon menn swa swa hit gewunelic is ofer an dead lic, and ðær wæs sum dysig mann plegol ungemetlice, and to þam mannum cwæð swylce for plegan, þæt he SwyÐun wære.[70]

At one time men were watching a dead body, as is customary, and there was a certain foolish man, making fun in an inappropriate way, and he said to the men, as if in play, that he was Swithin.

The wake is only here to provide incidental detail for the miracle story in which Swithin punishes his impersonator by felling him with a stroke. Ælfric could have left the story there, but instead he chooses to expand its moral:

Is eac to witenne þæt menn unwislice doð þa ðe dwollice plegað æt deadra manna lice and ælce fulnysse þær forð-teoð mid plegan, þonne hi sceoldon swyðor be-sargian þone deadan and biddan for his sawle butan gewede georne. Sume menn eac drincað æt deadra manna lice ofer ealle þa niht swiðe unrihtlice and gremiað god mid heora gegaf-spræce, þonne nan gebeorscype ne gebyrað æt lice ac halige gebedu þær gebyriað swiþor.[71]

It is also to be known that those men behave unwisely who play in stupid ways by the bodies of dead men, and bring in foul behaviour with their play, when they must rather mourn the dead and dread for themselves the coming of death, and pray for his soul without any foolishness. Certain men also drink by the bodies of dead men throughout the night, most inappropriately, and blaspheme against God with their idle speech. Beer-drinking is not fitting around the corpse, but instead holy prayers are appropriate there.

Ælfric considers it customary to watch over the dead, and in the absence of an appropriate Latin liturgical rite to fill this space he attempts to regulate and sanitize behaviour he considers *ungemetlice* around dead bodies, to eliminate the horse-play, eating and beer-drinking that he sees as normal unenlightened practice.[72] His interest in the topic suggests an area of secular activity around the corpse which has been rendered almost entirely invisible to our eyes, and his rash sinner's impersonation of Swithin suggests that this boisterous behaviour included parodying the actions of the churchmen. Lively singing and beer-drinking may have been enacted as an anticipation and inversion of the solemnities of the funeral mass. There is little Anglo-Saxon evidence for the anti-clerical satire of the later Middle Ages, but this passage hints that it existed.

Burying the difficult body

Even in those texts which attempt to prescribe an ideal death-bed, difficulties of various kinds are acknowledged. In the passage just cited from his Pastoral Letter for Wulfsige, Ælfric is also adamant that the priest is not to rejoice at a man's death, nor is he to go to a dead body to which he has not been summoned. At whose death might the priest rejoice? Does this refer to his happy anticipation of earning *sawelsceatt*, or could the dead man be a parishioner with whom he had

---

[70] *LS* I, XXI, p. 459, lines 290–3.
[71] *LS* I, XXI, p. 459, lines 307–17.
[72] Wulfstan supports this in the Canons of Edgar, *Councils*, pp. 335–6.

quarrelled and was glad to see die?[73] Another difficulty is presented by the corpses of those who had not invited a priest to hear their confession, who did not have *gewitnesse* to attest to their desire for confession and communion, or who may not have been part of a family, religious community, or gild who would see to their burial. One possible solution to this problem is suggested in the passage on appropriate forms of penance for different social classes on fols 40–2 of Laud 482. This advises that care for the poor (including the poor corpse) is an appropriate charitable activity for the less well-off, in an expanded version of the corporal acts of mercy, which includes giving house-room, food, fire, clothes, bed and bath to the poor, as well as comforting the *sarigmode 7 seoce* (sorry-hearted and sick) and burying the dead (*7 deade bebirige*). This would presumably extend to the body of the pilgrim, penitent, tramp or traveller found dead in a ditch. The corporal acts of mercy, derived from Matthew 25:34–46, are central to the construction of Christian social identity, and may have been a powerful influence on burial practice.[74] If the idea took hold that burying the dead was *per se* a Christian and charitable act, this may have reinforced the idea that Christian identity should be stressed in the grave.

Other types of problematic corpse also crop up. In his first Pastoral Letter to Wulfstan, Ælfric argues that a priest who has died brawling or in a battle merits no more than maimed rites: *þæt man nateshwon ne mot him mæssian fore ne him fore gebiddan; ac bebyrian swaþeah* (on no account may mass be celebrated for him or prayers be offered for him, but yet one may bury him).[75] One of the surviving manuscripts of this letter was revised by Archbishop Wulfstan, who added *on clænan legere, 7 lætan swa siððan eal to Godes dome* (in a clean grave, and leave everything else to God's judgement).[76] Murderers, including homicidal priests, are also treated in penitential literature, and appear in several passages in the *Penitential* and *Scrift Boc* in Laud 482. Moving beyond this to the subject of those who actively refuse reconciliation or the last rites goes beyond the brief of the present chapter and is discussed below in Chapter Six, in the context of capital punishment and those people who were denied consecrated burial, a discussion which also looks at what Wulfstan may have meant by *clænan legere*.

---

[73] William of Malmesbury has a story about Ælfheah, bishop of Winchester, cursing a man who failed to take Ash Wednesday seriously; the man was found dead the next day: *Postero enim mane in cubiculo repertus est exanimis, incertum an a diabolo guttur elisus.* William of Malmesbury, *Pontificum*, p. 164. The Council of Toledo (732) bans bishops and priests from singing requiem masses for the living in the hope that they would die or otherwise come to harm: *PL* 84, cols 557–8. Thomas suggests English fifteenth-century evidence will support the same interpretation: K. Thomas, *Religion and the Decline of Magic* (London, 1971), p. 34.

[74] Bede includes burial in his list of caritative works, *Opera Homiletica*, ed D. Hurst, CCSL 122 (1955), p. 64. This is reiterated in the *Capitula* of Theodulf XXI (*mortuum sepelire*) and its vernacular translation (*deade byrge*): Sauer, *Theodulfi Capitula*, pp. 326–7.

[75] *Councils*, p. 297.

[76] Only in CCCC 201, *ibid.*

The priest's soul at stake

These texts suggest that the priest's relationship with his parishioners was profoundly reciprocal and one of mutual dependency. Although confession and repentance could not be forced on the recalcitrant, no excuses would be accepted at Doomsday from a slack priest who put both his own soul and those of his flock in jeopardy. The *Penitential* brings this home in several places, including its opening chapter, where it enjoins a priest not to flinch (*wandige*) in his interrogation of anyone, no matter how mighty, but to follow the guidelines in his book and to remember that if he chooses not to instruct the sinful, then Christ will be calling him to account (fol. 1v). The topic is picked up again in Book III of the *Pentiential*, where the verb *wandian* recurs in a passage which clarifies the nature of the priest's stake in his parishioners' souls:

> *þæt heora nan ne wandige for nanes mannes ege ne for lufe ne for sceame ne for nanum sceatte, þæt hy ne bodian ælcon men hwæt him sy to donne 7 hwæt to forganne, gif hy sylfe wyllað þæt heom be geborhgen on domesdæg beforan gode sylfe.*

> That none of them hold back through fear of any man, or love, or shame, or for any money, that they fail to instruct everyone what they should do and what forgo, if they wish themselves to be protected on Doomsday before God Himself.

The dative plural *heom* who are to be protected 'on Doomsday before God' refers back to *hy sylfe*, the priests, rather than to the parishioners (*ælcon men*). The recurrent emphatic pronouns of *hy sylfe* and *gode sylfe* (grammatically superfluous) stress the face-to-face nature of the Doomsday confrontation. The passage continues on this theme, drawing its text from the fulmination against the shepherds of Israel in Ezekiel 34: *Eall þis is gecweden be biscopon 7 be mæssepreoston þe godes folc on domesdæg to þam dome lædan sceolon: ælc þæne dæl þe him her on lif ær betæht wæs* (All this is said about bishops and priests who shall lead God's people to the Judgement; to each the share assigned to him previously here in life).[77] These texts refer to the priest's entire career in the light of the Day of Judgement rather than any particular environment where he might fail in his mission. But the confessional and penitential texts on fols 21–7 have already spelled out the fate of culpable priests who refuse confession to the dying (*gif hwylc mæssepreost untruman men spræce forwyrne*) and will have to explain their actions to God (*sy he on domesdæg þære sawle scyldig*). Not only have they denied a soul salvation, they have also disobeyed orders: *forþam drihten sylf cweð on swa hwilcum dæge swa se synfulla man gecyrd bið life he leofað 7 deaðe he ne sweltað* (because the Lord Himself said that on the day that someone turns to life he lives and will not die). The judgemental priest postulated in this passage is the opposite of the ideal priest, who trusts the witnesses telling him of a speechless man's wish for confession, and lets the reported speech, that he *scrift gyrnde 7 husles* (asked for confession and communion), stand for the thing itself. The passage goes on to warn that true repentance may happen even

[77] III, 16.

at the *ytemestan tide* (last minute) and adduces an irrefutable example from the Gospels: *Swylce se sceaða on þære ytemestan tide andetnesse on anre berht hwile geearnode þæt he moste beon on neorxenawonges gefean fram ælmihtigum gode alæded* (Thus the criminal on his final day earned with confession in the twinkling of an eye that he would be led by Almighty God to the reward of paradise).[78] The complex and problematic figure of the good thief (only found in Luke 23) exemplifies the sinner whom the world had judged and found irredeemable, but who was saved through his own volition at the last moment, who is also cited as an exemplum of martyrdom in the lists of 'Twelve ways to forgiveness'.

Murray identifies 'the period when confession should come of age as a widespread pastoral practice for the laity' as between *c.* 1000 and 1215, the year of Innocent III's definitive legislation on lay confession at the Fourth Lateran Council.[79] He is discussing the practice on a European scale, but the English evidence supports the earliest date he suggests, or earlier. Although the texts in Laud 482 are inspired by an ideal model of universal confession and penance, their pragmatism and sensitivity suggest that they emerge from direct experience. They reflect the difficult nature of the events with which they are grappling, including the unpredictability of death, the way that the *uisitatio infirmorum* must always be ready to become the *commendatio animae*, the possibility of a priest being incompetent or arrogant, and the challenge of explaining Doomsday to the laity. Other difficulties include recalcitrant parishioners, people who die mid-penance, priests who have sex or commit murder, and mulish penitents who are prepared to go to almost any financial length to escape having to fast or pray in person. Of course, Laud 482 is not a snapshot of pastoral care for the sick, dying and dead in Worcester in the 1060s. What it *is*, is an anthology of the ideas and traditions about Christian death developed in English over the previous century and a half that one man thought vital, from the largest eschatological issues to the smallest details of caring for the dignity of the corpse.

A possible context for Laud 482

Barlow argues that the penitentials' lists of sins were outdated by the eleventh century, that penance must have depended entirely on the discretion of the individual priest, and that the system was 'coming to a dishonoured end'. But even he makes one exception: 'as with all systems, everything depended on the operator. St Wulfstan bishop of Worcester was a famous confessor'.[80] Worcester Cathedral has already been suggested as the most probable provenance for Laud 482, and it is likely to have been compiled in the episcopate of Ealdred (1046–62) or early in that of Wulfstan II (1062–95).[81] Both men had great concern for liturgical good

---

[78] Fols 25v–26r.
[79] Murray, 'Confession before 1215', p. 63.
[80] F. Barlow, *The English Church, 1000–1066* (2nd edn, London, 1979), pp. 268–9.
[81] M. Lapidge, 'Ealdred of York and MS. Cotton Vitellius E. xii', in M. Lapidge, *Anglo-Latin Literature, 900–1066* (London, 1993), pp. 453–67; Gameson, 'Book Production at Worcester', p. 218.

practice and innovation. Ealdred was an assiduous supporter of commemoration of the dead as well as an expert in royal liturgy: he is likely to have buried Edward the Confessor before crowning Harold Godwinson on the same day and in the same church in January 1066. It is possible that the poem lamenting Edward's death in the C and D Chronicles was composed in Ealdred's circle, perhaps to be performed as part of the funeral.[82] Wulfstan sponsored daily masses for the dead, and his attempt to stop people riding through churchyards is well known.[83] Both were also concerned with the quality of pastoral care; either man could have overseen a church and *familia* conducive to the production of this manuscript, in a library likely to have had many texts associated with Oswald and the earlier Wulfstan, both of whom had also been bishops of Worcester. Whether we see Laud 482 as a private anthology, lecture notes, or a textbook to be circulated among the priesthood, read, committed to memory or copied and then passed on, it would have been an invaluable tool for those men in the episcopal household responsible for priests' activities at sick-bed, death-bed, grave-side, and, in the end, *beforan mines drihtnes ðrym-setle on domesdæg* (before my Lord's throne on Doomsday).

Postscript: the Newent Stone Book

Ideas about burial, salvation and judgement in eleventh-century West Mercia were not confined to the precincts of Worcester Cathedral, nor to the written word. In 1912 excavations in the churchyard at Newent in Gloucestershire uncovered a small, thick, rectangular stone (Plate 2), measuring approximately twenty centimetres by sixteen and a half, resting under the head of a skull, although the circumstances of excavation were such that it is impossible to be sure that this was its original position. There is no documentary evidence for a pre-Conquest church at Newent, but a ninth-century cross-shaft was found in the churchyard in 1907, which, together with this small stone slab, suggests that there may well have been one. The slab is carved on all six surfaces, and while the iconography is complicated, one broad face clearly shows the Crucifixion and the other should probably be identified as the Last Judgement.[84]

In the centre of this latter scene there stands a large figure carrying a cross and a crosier, to his upper right a recumbent figure has the name EDRED carved above it, and the lettering dates it to the eleventh century. The narrow faces of the stone are also carved with names, reading MATTHEW MARK LUKE JOHN EDRED. The cross in the crucifixion scene is carved with four small circles; Zarnecki suggests that these are skeuomorphic rivets and that what he calls the

[82] V. Thompson, 'The Understanding of Death in England from *c.* 850 to *c.* 1100', unpublished Ph.D. thesis (University of York, 2000), p. 235.
[83] Lapidge, 'Ealdred of York', p. 461; Darlington, *Vita Wulfstani*, p. 53.
[84] G. Zarnecki, 'The Newent Funerary Tablet', *Transactions of the Bristol and Gloucester Archaeological Society* 72 (1953), pp. 49–55. Both sides of the stone are illustrated here, and Bailey illustrates the Crucifixion in *England's Earliest Sculptors*, pl. 41.

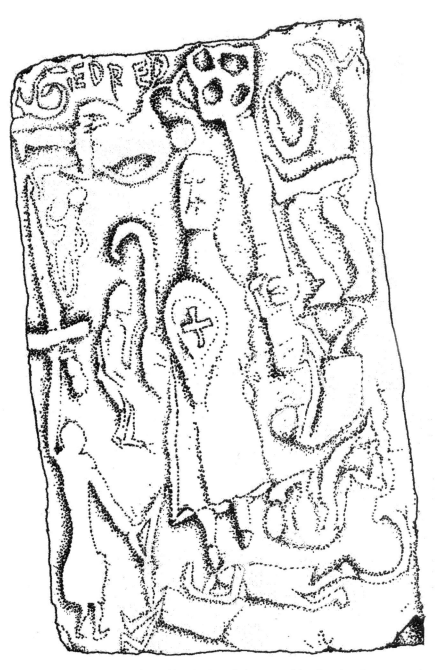

Plate 2: The Newent Stone Gospel Book, Last Judgement side, showing the resurrection of Edred in the top left-hand corner. On display in the Church of St Mary the Virgin, Newent, Gloucestershire. Approx. 20 cm × 16.5 cm. Illustration: A. Pluskowski. This carving has the names of the Evangelists carved round its sides and represents a gospel book in stone. It is likely to have been made for Edred's grave as it names him twice.

'funerary tablet' may have had a metalwork model; he mentions the analogy with bookbinding without pursuing the thought. But this carving is in fact a stone rendition of a gospel book, with ornate plaques of the Crucifixion and Last Judgement fastened to front and back covers and the contents represented by the names of the evangelists carved around the narrow sides, followed by the name of the book's owner.[85] Here, surely, we have a Christian grave-good for use in another life, a very personal object and one of great sophistication. The carving is certainly no cruder than that on the coffin of St Cuthbert, an artefact of great complexity, and the Newent Stone provokes unanswerable questions about how often similar images of books and other sacred objects were made in less durable materials. The iconography of the Newent Stone Book makes good sense interpreted in the light of the funerary ritual of Laud 482, its close contemporary and compatriot.

By the eleventh century the reading of the Gospel narratives of Christ's dying and death was embedded in the funerary *ordo*. The priest was to start the reading when he suspected death was approaching, and to keep going, varying it with litanies, psalmody and other holy readings, until the parishioner had died. This was necessarily an open-ended part of the rite, and Laud 482, as we might expect, is insistent that it was done properly: *7 gif man fyrstes hæbbe, þonne ræde man Cristes þrowunge 7 oðre halige bec, þæt þær symble buton tolæted-nesse sealmsang oððe haligra boca ræding* (if there should be a wait, then the Passion of Christ is to be read and other holy books, that there may be continuous psalmody or reading of holy books without a break). The model gospel book thus fossilizes the rite, providing a permanent guarantee that the dead person died *mid gedefenesse*. Laud 482 insists that, should the dying person be ignorant of the nature of the Trinity, it is to be explained to him *þæt he sceal gelyfan, þæt fæder 7 sunu 7 se halga gast is an God* (so that he may believe that Father and Son and the Holy Spirit is one God). The Crucifixion scene from Newent affirms Trinitarian doctrine with the Hand of God descending to bless Christ, flanked by two birds who represent the Holy Spirit, doubled for symmetry. The priest is to go on to explain the nature of the Last Judgement: *þæt he sceal on domes dæge mid sawl and lichaman arisan 7 æt Godes dome standan* (that he must rise with soul and body and stand at God's judgement). Just this is happening on the other side, illustrated here, where the recumbent figure represented by the name EDRED is raising his right hand to Christ. The likelihood is that the Newent Stone Book was carved specifically for Edred's grave. At the bottom left of the Crucifixion scene there is a sarcophagus outline containing a human figure, and Zarnecki suggests this is Adam, buried at the foot of the Cross. If so, it is the earliest surviving such image from the Anglo-Saxon world. Should this be Adam's corpse, it evokes images of creation and new beginnings, as well as the Fall, death and the harrowing of hell, and the iconography of the Stone Book again connects with the funerary rubrics of Laud 482. The manuscript's battered final folio instructs

---

[85] Cf. the gold and enamel Christ in Majesty surrounded by the evangelist symbols of the Uta Codex gospel lectionary of *c*. 1025. Cohen, *Uta Codex*, colour plate 1.

that prayers and collects are to be sung after the reading of the Passion, when the priest decides that body and soul have finally parted company: *gif he þince, þæt he his gast agifen hæbbe his drihtne, þe hine gesceop 7 geworhte* (if it seems to [the priest] that [the dying person] has given his soul to his Lord, who shaped and made him). The journey of human life has come full circle.

4

The Body under Siege in Life and Death

THE LIVING AND DYING BODY

The Newent Stone Book (discussed at the end of Chapter Three) represents one means of trying to protect the vulnerable body and soul. In this chapter we look at many others, ranging from medical recipes and charms to coffins and grave structures. A wide range of sources represent the body and soul as under constant attack from a host of invisible assailants, whose effects are perceived as sin, disease and decay. However, contemporary literature often shows a reluctance to assume that disease is the direct consequence of sin. In the poem *Christ III*, the narrator bewails the fact that we cannot see in our bodies the effect of sin on our souls, which would prompt us to repentance: *Eala, þær we nu magon wraþe firene geseon on ussum sawlum, synna wunde, mid lichoman leahtra gehygdu, eagum unclæne ingeþoncas* (Alas, if only we could see in our souls the terrible crimes, the wounds of sin, in the body the evil thoughts, with our eyes the unclean inner thoughts).[1] The body is sometimes the soul's ally, and sometimes its worst enemy. It can be inherently treacherous on multiple levels, in its refractory, unpredictable nature and its concealment of sin when alive, as well as in its sudden revelation of unconfessed sin on the Day of Judgement.

The body endangered from without

Judging by the vernacular medical texts, the Anglo-Saxons never really embraced the humoral theory of disease, preferring to look outside the body for the sources of illness.[2] Outside the Latin tradition represented by the glossed *Liber Scintillarum*, only Byrhtferth's *Enchiridion* and the late *Peri Didaxeon* provide an analysis of the humours.[3] Beyond this there are only stray references, such as the prescription of blood-letting for a disease caused by an evil humour or vapour in Bald's Leechbook.[4] *Wætan*, which Cameron translates as 'humour', is almost always cited as a symptom rather than a cause and is better understood as 'flow' or 'discharge'; usually only specified as *yfel wætan* (abnormal flow), it can refer to blood, pus or diarrhoea. Whereas the humoral system focuses on internal

---

[1]   *Christ III*, lines 1312–15.
[2]   Cameron, *Anglo-Saxon Medicine*, pp. 159–61; K. Jolly, *Popular Religion in Late Saxon England: Elf-Charms in Context* (Chapel Hill and London, 1996), p. 105.
[3]   Cockayne, *Leechdoms* III, pp. 82–4.
[4]   *Ibid.* II, p. 20.

imbalance as the proximate cause of disease, the emphasis in Anglo-Saxon medicine is on external cause, a tendency noted by Grattan in his singling out of 'flying venoms', 'worms' and 'elfshot' as typical culprits identified in the medical text known as *Lacnunga* (London, BL Harley, MS 585).[5] This characteristic is shared by disease and decay, for, as we will see in Chapter Five, vernacular descriptions of the rotting body focus on the assault by worms and other creatures almost (though not quite) to the exclusion of catabolic decay, and the worms are often presented as the agents of punishment, eliding with the tormenting serpents of hell. These attacks on the living and dead body have further parallels in the onslaught on the soul carried out by bow-and-arrow-wielding demons, an originally biblical image that recurs in texts from *Beowulf* to Ælfric.[6] The human condition is to be battling perpetually to preserve innocence and integrity in a fallen universe.[7]

This vision even underlies Ælfric's depiction of Adam in Eden, where fire will not burn him, nor water drown him *ne nan wildeor ne mihte, ne nan wyrmcynn ne dorste derian þam menn mid hys muðes slite* (nor could any wild beast, nor dared any of the *wyrm*-kind to injure the man with the bite of its mouth).[8] Although Ælfric's source is the *De Correctione Rusticorum* of Martin of Braga, he is on his own here, expanding Martin's cursory phrase *sine morte* into a dramatically alliterative passage. He combines the tradition of the *locus amoenus*, which describes an attractive landscape in terms of the unpleasant features it lacks, with the catalogues of causes of death found elsewhere in Anglo-Saxon literature.[9] Ælfric does not suggest that there were no dangerous beasts in Eden; instead he writes as if these fatal dangers all existed but were inhibited by God from affecting the innocent Adam. As a result, this passage conjures up an image of the fragile human creature menaced from all sides: a post-lapsarian understanding projected back on to the pre-lapsarian world. Ælfric goes on to say that, after Adam's fall, the *lys* and *flean* (lice and fleas) could attack him, whereas previously even the *draca* (dragon) had not dared, not only underlining the humiliation of the Fall but suggesting that these creatures great and small were opposite ends of the same aggressive spectrum. In one of his homilies, Wulfstan picks up the theme of the corruption of Creation at the Fall, and argues that *clæne wæs þeos eorðe on hyre frumsceafte, ac we hi habbað syððan afylede swyðe 7 mid urum synnum þearle besmitene* (clean was this earth at its creation, but we have since made it filthy and with our sins have thoroughly soiled it), identifying all humanity as guilty and using the words *clæn* and *besmitene* to refer to the earth in a way that resonates with the many references to 'clean' burial.[10] The *eorð* here is analogous to the human body, itself made of earth, clean at its creation and now

---

[5] Grattan and Singer, *Anglo-Saxon Magic and Medicine*, p. 52.
[6] Jolly, *Popular Religion in Late Saxon England*, pp. 136–7.
[7] M. Eliade, *The Sacred and the Profane: The Nature of Religion* (New York, 1959), esp. pp. 49 and 175–80.
[8] *Supp.* II, XVII, p. 678, lines 39–40.
[9] C. L. Wrenn, *A Study of Old English Literature* (London, 1967), pp. 30–1.
[10] Bethurum, *Wulfstan* III, p. 124, lines 28–9.

defiled by human sin, and the body is referred to in the poem *Soul and Body* as an 'earthen vessel' (*eorð-fæt, lam-fæt*). Microcosm and macrocosm, the body above and below ground, are all subject to the same rules and the same torments. The ubiquity of this theme suggests that it was not only confined to clerical circles. It is a useful way of thinking about graves and (as we shall see in Chapter Five) the iconography of many funerary monuments.

Medical and magical approaches to dying

Medical practice and liturgical practice come very close to each other in the *uisitatio infirmorum*, although Laud 482 distinguishes between the realms of doctor and priest. Outside the world of the *ordines* it is clear that medicine and ritual of various kinds had even more in common, although the extant leech-books have almost nothing to say about activity at the death-bed. Prognoses usually end with a variation on the formula *he bið sona hal* (he will shortly be well), but sometimes another outcome is allowed for, as in this cure for dysentery from *Leechbook III*:

> *Gif se briw 7 se drinc inne gewuniað þu meaht þone man gelacnian, gif him offleogeð him bið selre þæt þu hine na ne grette; him biþ his feorhadl getenge.*[11]
>
> If the gruel and the drink remain inside, then you may cure the man, if they flow out, it is better for you that you do not deal with him; his fatal illness is upon him.

Dying is understood here as a biological inevitability, resulting inexorably from a particular phase of a disease, described as *feorhadl* (life-sickness). All the doctor can do is stand back and there is no indication in this kind of text that the patient's disease or death are the merited result of sinful actions.

The only major exception to this general principle, that the leechbooks show little practical or philosophical interest in dying and death, is a series of charms dealing with danger to unborn children. They are preserved in the *Lacnunga* manuscript (fols 184–5), a collection of medical remedies derived from classical sources and Irish and Germanic secular and Christian charms. Crawford draws attention to the way that pregnancy is singled out for treatment with charms and rituals, in contrast to the normal, symptom-based approach to diagnosis and treatment that these texts evidence, and suggests that this indicates 'a sense of helplessness'.[12] It is also plausible that some of the rituals associated with pregnancy and childbirth derive from other types of source than those looked at so far, and represent a different understanding of the relationship between the body and the wider world, derived neither from the liturgical nor the main leechbook tradition.[13] Perhaps they are a glimpse of a usually female preserve, not often caught in writing.

---

[11] Cockayne, *Leechdoms* II, p. 320.
[12] Crawford, *Childhood in Anglo-Saxon England*, p. 59.
[13] *Bald's Leechbook* has lost the section on gynaecology listed in its table of contents, which, had it survived, might have presented a different picture.

The first charm is structured around three petitions spoken by the woman. The first of these is to be uttered at a grave when she realizes that there is a problem, the second at the marital bed when she is pregnant, and the third at the altar when the problem has been resolved. She is to step over the grave three times, saying, *þis me to bote þære laþan lætbyrde; þis me to bote þære swæran swærtbyrde; þis me to bote þære laðan lambyrde* (This be a remedy for me for the loathsome late [slow] birth; this be a remedy for me for the grievous dismal birth; this be a remedy for me for the loathsome imperfect birth). When her husband is in bed she is to say, *Up ic gonge, ofer þe stæppe; mid cwican cilde; nallæs mid cwellendum; mid fulborenum, nalæs mid fægan* (Up I go, step over you; with a living child, not with a dying one; with a full-term one, not a doomed one). Finally at the altar, she says, *criste ic sæd this cyþed* (I said this charm to Christ).[14] The charm demonstrates a belief in meaningful likeness.[15] The first part draws a parallel between the pregnant woman containing the foetus and the grave containing the corpse. The language of the petition is incantatory, with its repetition of *bote . . . bote . . . bote* against the alliterative *laþan lætbyrde . . . swæran swærtbyrde . . . laðan lambyrde.* In the second part the body of her resting husband is associated with life, in contrast to the dead man's grave, as well as the potential death-bed and grave of both mother and child, against which the charm is a prophylactic. The adjectives describing the child in the womb reflect this double danger, in that while *fæg* means 'dying, doomed, mortal', *cwellend* can also have the meaning of 'killing', the danger the child poses to its mother. Like the first part of the charm, the second part also uses alliteration; it opposes living and dying children, the *cwic, fulboren cild* substituted for the *cwellend* and *fæg* one. The final part of the charm introduces a third focus, the altar, which the mother is only to approach after she feels the child alive in her womb. Her acknowledgement of the source of the healing has none of the poetic force of the earlier petitions and reads as something of an afterthought. Nonetheless, the altar, with its sacrificial and reliquary associations, fits into the symbolic pattern established by the grave and the bed in the first two parts of the charm. It is not clear whether the first part of the charm refers to a child who fails to quicken and is feared to have died in the womb, or to an otherwise successful pregnancy that has gone over term. The outcome in either case may have been seen as equally dangerous: the word for terminal illness, *feorhadl*, used in the gloomy prognosis for dysentery above, is also used in Tiberius A iii to describe the risk to a pregnant woman when her child is still unborn in the tenth month.[16] In either case, the recourse to the grave is an appeal to the experts, the dead, to help against the threat of death. The grave itself becomes a therapeutic tool, in both this charm and the following one.

The next charm also links birth and death. Again, a woman *se hyre bearn afedan ne mæg* turns to ritual and symbol for help. She is to take earth from the

---

14 Grattan and Singer, *Anglo-Saxon Magic and Medicine*, p. 188.
15 W. Nöth, 'Semiotics of the Old English Charm', *Semiotica* 19 (1977), pp. 59–83, 66.
16 *for þam þe hit in þam magan wyrð hit to feorhadle.* Cockayne, *Leechdoms* III, p. 146.

child's grave, wrap it in black wool and sell it to a merchant, saying *ic hit bebicge, ge hit bibicgan, þas sweartan wulle 7 þysse sorge corn* (I sell it, you buy it, this black wool and these sorrow-seeds).[17] The compressed, telegrammatic style in which these charms are written means that it is hard to tell whether, in the latter, the grave belongs to the child whom she could not 'feed' or whether it is assumed she has already lost one of her children. In either case, the charm might represent an attempt to disarm the spirit of the dead child, with the earth of the grave representing the dead child's body, and the black wool an inverted reference to the white clothes of baptism, with the *sorge corn* a metaphor for the dead child. These two charms attest to a culture of unregulated and quasi- or non-liturgical activities around the grave, and they may only have been preserved because they relate to gynaecological problems with which conventional medicine found it hard to cope. Their association with soil and with graves may mean they are as close as the written record will let us get to the practices represented by those mysterious phrases in the lawcodes condemning *licwigelunga* (corpse-divination) and denouncing the 'drawing of children through the earth' as *micel hæþenscip*, although neither of the charms discussed here contains anything incompatible with Christianity, and both seem to be informed by Christian ritual activities.

'Suffering in the body': sin, disease and a close look at leprosy

In his homily on the *Nativity of the Innocents*, Ælfric suggests that medicine for the body is unlikely to work unless it is accompanied by penitence, providing the awful warning of the slow dying of King Herod, who fails to respond to the penitential prompting of his disease-ridden body.[18] Herod is an extreme case, however, among the arch-sinners. Elsewhere, Ælfric sees sin as only one of many causes of illness, although he understands disease and cure both as coming ultimately from God, like everything else.[19] His longest discussion of the subject is in his homily for the feast of St Bartholomew, where he deals both with the false healing powers claimed for heathen gods, and the thorny issue of God's purpose in sending illness. He cites Revelation 3:19 to show that disease may be a sign of God's favour,[20] and interprets the many ailments with which Christians are stricken as a trial of their strength as much as a punishment, and as an opportunity for God to work miracles as well as a way of keeping Christians from becoming too proud.[21] Sin, disease and decay are linked in that they are all proof that we inhabit a fallen universe, albeit one in which God is intimately involved, but disease and decay are not reflexive symptoms of sin. Ælfric's multi-causal explanation of disease suggests a reluctance, if not a refusal, to reach a hasty judgement in any individual case. When Wulfstan considers the question of the

---

[17] *Ibid.* III, p. 68.
[18] *CH* I, V, pp. 221–2, lines 144–7.
[19] *CH* I, Preface, p. 75, lines 78–84; *CH* I, XXXI, pp. 448–50, lines 224–334.
[20] *Ego quos amo arguo et castigo aemulare ergo et paenitentiam age.* Those whom I love I rebuke and discipline, so be earnest, and repent.
[21] Meaney, 'Ælfric and Idolatry', pp. 119–35.

purpose of illness, his analysis is much simpler than Ælfric's, and he only gives one reason, but the one he chooses is the image from Job of the devil being permitted by God to test people's faith, a model which implies that disease may be a measure of virtue as easily as sin.[22] Similarly, Asser presents Alfred's illness not as a punishment but as the answer to prayer and the solution to the carnal lusts which had distracted him in his youth.[23]

This reluctance to equate disease and sin is also evident in the treatment of lepers in Anglo-Saxon graveyards. Lees has argued that late Anglo-Saxon England was a 'persecuting society', defining its Christian identity by rejecting 'the pagan, the excommunicant, the leper [and] the Jew'.[24] But the place of the leper on her list is questionable on both archaeological and textual grounds, and almost certainly anachronistic: the later medieval idea of the infectious, sexually transgressive and morally corrupt leper who requires segregation is not visible in pre-Conquest sources.[25] A very high-status female leper was found in a seventh-century Cambridgeshire cemetery, and Raunds produced one definite and one probable leper, both buried normally and within the cemetery limits.[26] The definitely leprous young man was one of the twenty per cent buried in a coffin and he lay towards the southern boundary of the cemetery, while the possible leper had stones packed around his head in a very common arrangement, and lay much closer to the church. By the time these two men were buried, after the beginning of the tenth century, the location of a burial was coming to carry extra ideological baggage expressed in civil and ecclesiastical lawcodes which prescribe burial outside consecrated ground for certain crimes and sins, including sexual misconduct (discussed in detail in Chapter Six below). Nowhere, however, do these codes mention lepers. In the churchyard, within the community of the faithful, is precisely where one would expect to find these people.

Ælfric is the only homilist to discuss the meaning of leprosy in any detail, and both of his stories stress physical contact with them. The sermon for the third Sunday after Epiphany gives an account of Christ's miraculous healing of a leper by touch, thus replacing the Mosaic law of segregation with the new law of inclusion.[27] Lees reads this story as a rejection of the literally leprous body, claiming that 'the leper's disfigured body is a mark of disfiguring faith', and that the 'diseased body . . . is expelled from the community until it is healed'. But Ælfric's emphasis is on the leper as a representative of humanity, and in the other story a monk takes pity on a leper who turns out to be Christ.[28] No Anglo-Saxon lawcode refers to leprosy and no English saint encounters a leper before Wulfstan II of Worcester, whose *Life* was written after 1095, by which time leprosaria were

---

[22] Bethurum, *Wulfstan* VI, pp. 147–8, lines 77–95.

[23] Stevenson, *Asser*, ch. 74.

[24] C. Lees, *Tradition and Belief: Religious Writing in Late Anglo-Saxon England* (Minneapolis and London, 1999), p. 131.

[25] S. N. Brody, *The Disease of the Soul: Leprosy in Medieval Literature* (Ithaca, NY, and London, 1974).

[26] J. Hines and T. Malim (eds), *The Anglo-Saxon Cemetery at Edix Hill (Barrington A)*, CBA Research Report 112 (1998); *Raunds*, p. 69.

[27] *CH* I, VIII, pp. 242–4, lines 25–86.

[28] *CH* I, XXIII, pp. 369–70, lines 135–44; *CH Comm.*, pp. 60–3 and 190–1.

becoming familiar institutions. But there is no explicit evidence for institution-alization of lepers until the 1070s, and Anglo-Saxon text and grave alike suggest that they remained part of the pre-Conquest community.[29] The vocabulary of leprosy bears this out: there are two separate terms, *hreof* (which refers to all painful skin conditions, in animals as well as people) and *licþrowere* (literally, 'one who suffers in body'), a learned word and perhaps a neologism in the late tenth century. Its very stress on lepers' suffering *in body* rejects any attempt to read the metaphor of the leprous soul at the literal level.

Death foretold: the role of the prognostics

Although the Church condemned divination, senior ecclesiastics were fascinated by the idea of reading the future. This is evident from the prognostics, which are based on interpreting such phenomena as the thunder, the phases of the moon and dreams, and survive in numerous eleventh-century manuscripts. Flint calls these 'compromise magic', arguing that priests might be tempted to take part in activities 'in the no-man's-land between accepted and rejected magic', and that the Church recognized the potency of such ideas, assimilating them rather than attempting eradication.[30] Liuzza provides a full survey of the prognostics in their manuscript contexts, stressing the orthodox environments in which they are found; he also suggests that they occur primarily in eleventh-century collections because they were 'a consequence, though no doubt an unintended one, of the tenth-century monastic reform – not at its margins but in its midst'.[31] This is likely to be true for these specific texts, but it does not mean that the desire to read the future was limited to centres like the New Minster, Winchester.

Death and disease are foretold through many different portents in these texts. Prognostics is an ancient genre, and the routes by which the various Latin and English versions entered our manuscripts are not clear. Their classical back-ground betrays itself in references to olive trees, camels, lions and elephants, but their popularity at the highest level suggests that they were seen as immediately relevant, and not only to monks. One text on dreams pronounces *gif he þince þæt he mid his freondes wif hæme, þæt biþ adl* (if he should think that he has sex with his friend's wife, that forecasts illness) but *gif he þince þæt he mid his agenes wif hæme, þæt bið god swefen* (if he should think he has sex with his own wife, that is a good dream.).[32] Though they are preserved in manuscripts produced in

---

[29] Moore concludes that no English leprosarium is likely to have been founded earlier than *c.* 1075. R. I. Moore, *The Formation of a Persecuting Society* (Oxford, 1987), p. 52. One possible exception is the recently excavated cemetery at St John Timberhill in Norwich, which appears to have a high proportion (around 20%) of people with leprosy severe enough to affect their bones, and an above average number of disabled people. This could be a Anglo-Saxon hospital cemetery, since the burials date from the end of the tenth to the mid-eleventh centuries (pers. comm. Liz Shepherd Popescu).

[30] V. I. Flint, *The Rise of Magic in Early Medieval Europe* (Oxford, 1991), pp. 113–16; J. N. Hillgarth, 'Popular Religion in Visigothic Spain', in E. James (ed.), *Visigothic Spain: New Approaches* (Oxford, 1980), pp. 3–60, 47.

[31] Liuzza, 'Anglo-Saxon Prognostics in Context', pp. 195–6.

[32] Cockayne, *Leechdoms* III, p. 215.

monasteries, the assumption that the dreamer could be not only sexually active but also married indicates that these guides were not intended solely for monastic use, and the prediction that dreaming of having sex with a friend's wife is a bad sign may be based on common sense and bitter experience. In his *Life of Æthelwold*, Wulfstan of Winchester describes one possible environment for dream-interpretation, with or without the use of textbooks, when he portrays Æthelwold's pregnant mother asking advice about her dreams from Æthelthryth, a Winchester wise woman and probably a nun.[33] The text on reading dreams in Tiberius A iii is laid out in a format that suggests that it was designed to be easy to use, beginning with a table enabling assessment of the dream's reliability, depending on the phase of the moon when it was dreamed. These texts could be used as reference books in ways closely analogous to the penitential tariff lists, and possibly in the same environment. The common references in penitentials to sexual dreams, including those of clerics *slæpende in cyrcean* (sleeping in church, Laud 482, fol. 26r), suggest a culture in which people were encouraged to tell their confessors about these disturbing experiences, and perhaps by extension all particularly striking dreams.

Magical, medical and prognostic ways of interpreting the world express a common desire to be admitted to privileged knowledge, inversely reflected in the lawcodes' various prohibitions of lay fortune-telling, witchcraft and divination by means of corpses. This desire for knowledge of and power over the future is also manifest in the importance placed by Byrhtferth and Ælfric on priests having a proper understanding of computus, and the penalties prescribed by the *Northumbrian Priests' Law* for priests who celebrated feasts on the wrong day. The mastery of the calendar and the ability to predict the date of Easter were among the most arcane and complex intellectual tasks demanded of priests, and Byrhtferth makes it clear from his dismissive references to *uplendisc* (backwoods) priests in his *Enchiridion* that his expectation of their ability to reach the necessary standard was not always high.[34]

Priests also had access to revelations about the end of the world, the meaning of body and soul after death and the Last Judgement, and, as Vercelli IX shows, they were capable of mediating these to their congregations in dramatic and unexpected ways. Both Church and State claimed to be able to curse as well as bless in eternity, with lawcodes and charters arrogating the power to exclude wrongdoers 'from God's blessing and ours'. It would not be surprising if a charismatic and articulate priest or monk was perceived by some of the laity as a quasi-magical figure with powers over life, death and the future. Liuzza's argument that, since the prognostic texts are found mostly in Latin and postdate the Benedictine reform, they are therefore a consequence of the reform is only part of the story. The explosive proliferation of these texts represents the Church extending its field of influence over areas of human activity, such as dreaming and

---

[33] Lapidge and Winterbottom, *Life of St Æþelwold*, p. 4.
[34] M. Lapidge and P. S. Baker (eds), *Byrhtferth's Enchiridion*, EETS SS 15 (London, 1995), p. 106.

fortune-telling, which previously it may have found disturbing, but which it had not hitherto tried to commandeer.

Knowledge reserved to God

Not all texts share the prognostics' confidence that one can know the future, either on earth or after death: the idea that 'God alone knows' what is going to happen links several of the gnomic poems like a refrain. Where the soul after death is concerned, the Cotton *Maxims* picks up on a theme we have already seen in the confessional material, that no one can be sure of its fate:

> *Meotod ana wat hwyder seo sawul sceal syððan hweorfan, and ealle þa gastas þe for Gode hweorfaþ æfter deaðdæge, domes bidað on Fæder fæðme. Is seo forðgesceaft digol and dyrne; Drihten ana wat, nergende Fæder.*[35]

> God alone knows whither the soul shall turn afterwards, and all the spirits who turn to God after their death-day, they wait for judgement in the Father's embrace. The future is dark and hidden; the Lord alone knows, the saving Father.

Several other poems introduce the idea that knowledge about death (plague, battle) is the exclusive preserve of God, while *The Fortunes of Men* has the widest definition of unknowability, associating it not only with death and the afterlife but with human life from its earliest stages. The parents in this poem care for their child but *God ana wat hwæt him weaxendum winter bringað.*[36] These cautious poetic ideas about the *digol, dyrne* (dark, hidden) future sit uneasily beside the breezy predictions enshrined in the prognostics, that a child born on a particular day will grow up to be a thief, or that a given year will see the deaths of the elderly, bees, women, kings, the young, princes or sheep.[37]

Cavill discusses the *God/Metod/Drihten ana wat* group of passages together to illustrate the dynamic relationship that different Anglo-Saxon poets have with traditional material, showing how this theme, that certain kinds of knowledge are reserved to God, can be reworked to suit different contexts. This suggests that the audiences of these poems found the idea acceptable and perhaps also reassuring. He goes on to consider the specifically gnomic poems in the context of the sociology of knowledge to show how these texts construct reality, arguing that their perception of the world suggests that they have a popular rather than an institutional genesis, although they embody a fully naturalized view of Christianity, with an omnipotent and omniscient God contrasted with the limited realm of human knowledge and power.[38] His argument for their secular origins is supported by the complete absence of references to the Church hierarchy (and indeed to Christ) in these poems, despite their internalization of a Christian understanding of morality and deity. If he is right about how the gnomic poems

---

[35] *Maxims II* (Cotton), lines 53b–63a.
[36] God alone knows what the winters will bring him as he grows up. *Fortunes of Men*, lines 12–13, cf. *Battle of Maldon*, lines 94b–95; *Maxims I* (Exeter), lines 29b–30; *Christ and Satan*, lines 32b–33.
[37] Cockayne, *Leechdoms* III, pp. 150–215.
[38] P. Cavill, *Maxims in Old English Poetry* (Woodbridge, 1999), pp. 171–83.

work to socialize their listeners, enshrining 'common sense' and providing an interpretative framework for unfamiliar experiences, then their insistence that people cannot know the future takes on new significance as a stubborn refutation of the power of Church and State to predict or engineer either salvation or damnation.

Control of secret knowledge

These disparate sources have turned up several points central to the present argument, clustering around ideas of power and mystery. Disease is not part of an individual's whole being, but the result of an assault, which even if sent by God is no straightforward guide to spiritual health. A leper is only someone with leprosy, not a physical, moral and sexual threat, and there is as yet no certain evidence, archaeological or textual, for either segregation or persecution. The medical texts show little interest in death, other than to acknowledge its approach, but the *Lacnunga* pregnancy charms attest to an interest in the places of the dead and the earth of the grave as therapeutic tools. Although the classical understanding of disease causation had been imported into England along with many other aspects of Mediterranean culture, ideas about the humours circulated very narrowly. Even the more academic end of the Church did not assimilate ideas about disease, cure, sin and the body into a theological unity. This created a vacuum which was filled by a great deal of paraliturgical activity, whereby the language, buildings, spaces and tools of the Church were deployed in endlessly inventive ways, with the Creed and Paternoster, the Cross and its legends, the names of the Evangelists and Christian holy sites invoked for their curative powers.[39] The prognostic texts also come under the heading of paraliturgical activity, providing evidence of the ways that the eleventh-century Church actively adopted and redefined practices which it condemned when undertaken by the laity. The Church's attitude to divination is analogous to its attitude to burial, another activity which increasingly comes to be controlled by Christian specialists. In both of these we may see part of the process by which the Church furthered the creation of a fully Christian society, in which every activity is coloured by a particular ethical and spiritual understanding. If this is true of the texts interpreting dreams, it suggests that men like Ælfwine, the dean and later abbot of New Minster whose private prayer-book includes the Quinity miniature as well as a prognostics anthology, saw it as their job to oversee the sleeping as well as the waking minds of the souls in their care.

---

[39] For example Creed and Paternoster, *Lacnunga*, p. 74, *Leech Book III*, p. 350, Bethlehem, *Lancnunga*, p. 60; Rome, *Lacnunga*, p. 66; Evangelists, *Lacnunga* p. 24, *Leech Book I*, p. 140 (all from Cockayne, *Leechdoms* II).

THE MAKING AND MEANING OF GRAVES

The corpse as an object of fear

In the second half of this chapter, we turn from the threatened living body, assailed
by disease and sin and in a perilous state of unknowing, to the equally threatened
dead body. Carver has compared the rich seventh-century graves and associated
structures at Sutton Hoo to the artistic genres of epic and drama, and he sees the
burial ground as 'a theatre, in which each burial is a composition, offering, with
greater or lesser authority, a metaphor for its age'.[40] What textual analogies
offer themselves for ninth- to eleventh-century graves? We might take the cue
offered by the *ordo in agenda mortuorum* from Laud 482, and see the grave as
the reification of penitential prayer. But Carver's analogy also argues against
generalization, implying that every grave should be read as carefully as every
poem.

The specific, and ubiquitous, theme of the corpse menaced by worms is
discussed separately in Chapter Five; the present discussion concentrates more
on the threat posed to the body by the soil itself and the insecurities about literal
and metaphorical corruption this presents. Another kind of threat is posed to
the living by the corpse; there are numerous anthropological parallels for the
idea that, while still in the process of decay, the corpse is seen as profoundly
disturbing, but that this quality is lessened once it has been reduced to a skeleton.[41] Precisely this distinction is found in an anonymous homily (Assmann XIV)
which introduces the theme of repentance by observing that *we magan geseon,
þonne man binnan mynster byrgene delfeð 7 þa ban þæron findeþ, hwilce we
beon scylan* (we can see, when a grave is dug in a minster and bones turn up, what
sort of thing we are going to be).[42] This sentence is remarkable for its matter-of-
fact assumption that new graves are likely to be cut into soil containing old graves,
and that human remains are a familiar sight to the homilist's audience. Excavation
bears this out: the area north of Æthelflæd's church of St Oswald in Gloucester
received seven superimposed generations of burials between *c.* 900 and *c.* 1120,
and those churches which had been funerary centres since the seventh century
would have created an even more complex palimpsest.[43] The homilist of Assmann
XIV goes on to describe the very different appearance of newly buried bodies,
before time has rendered them innocuous: *heora lichaman licgað on eorðan
7 beoð to duste gewordene 7 þæt flæsc afulað 7 wirmum awealleð 7 nyðer
aflowed in þa eorðan* (their bodies lie in the earth and turn to dust and the flesh
goes bad and wells with worms and flows down in the earth).[44] He starts with
a comparatively neutral image, the dry bones, to introduce his theme of our

---

[40] M. Carver, *Sutton Hoo: Burial Ground of Kings?* (London, 1998), p. 139.
[41] Hertz, 'Collective Representation of Death'; L. Danforth, *The Death Rituals of Rural Greece* (Princeton, 1982), pp. 35–6.
[42] Assmann XIV, pp. 164–9.
[43] Heighway, *Golden Minster*, p. 195.
[44] Assmann XIV, p. 164.

common physical fate, lulling his hearers, so that when he follows up with the graphic picture of the rotting corpse the impact is that much more shocking.

The corpse may be an object of fear as well as one of disgust. A recurrent theme of the present study is the way that the dead and buried body is imagined as still having some kind of life, and a complex response is suggested both by Assmann XIV, and by the fragmentary *Soul and Body* poem from Worcester. This latter describes the dead person's friends fleeing from his corpse: *nulleþ heo mid honden his heafod riht wenden; heom þuncheþ þet hore honden swuþe beoþ afuled gif heo hondleþ þene deade* (they do not want to put his head straight with their hands; it seems to them that their hands will become very foul if they handle the dead).[45] Their flight is followed by the arrival of the *wrecche wif* referred to above, who lays out the body. The poem goes on to describe how eager the dead man's heirs are to have the body out of the house (B15), and the ritual cleansing of the house that occurs after the body has departed. The *flor* and *flet* (floor, and platform) are swept and cleaned, the walls are asperged with *holiwatere*, the survivors *bletsien ham georne to burewen ham wiþ þe* (bless themselves eagerly to protect themselves against you [i.e. the corpse]), and the dead man's bedstraw is brought out to be burnt.[46] Again, we seem to be in a paraliturgical world: while the *ordines* follow the journey of the corpse to the grave, the bereaved construct their own ritual, a large part of which involves cleansing and protection.

The language of death

Assmann Homily XIV is precise in its use of words to describe the stages of burial and decay, and such precision is also evident in many other writers' choice of words for the grave and grave-furniture. This lexicon is not consistently applied across the whole corpus of surviving writing, but nonetheless some strong patterns emerge. Most notably, the different Anglo-Saxon words have positive or negative associations which Modern English equivalents fail to convey.

Legere is the word most often used for the grave in the lawcodes. This can also mean 'sickness', 'sickbed' and 'place of rest': it is where a man *bedryda fram cildhæde* (bedridden from childhood) spends his life in Ælfric's homily for Sexagesima Sunday, where he translates *in dolore* with the more concrete English word *legere*.[47] There are also the compounds *legerbed* and *legerstow*; Ælfric uses the former to mean death-bed in his description of the priest Hereberht awaiting death, *on legerbedde licgende*.[48] In the Vercelli *Soul and Body* poem *legerbed* is used to refer to the grave of the saved body (156), whereas the damned body lies in an *eorðscræf* (117), a word whose negative implications are explored below. *Legerstow* appears in the lawcodes II Athelstan and I Cnut, where it probably means a consecrated churchyard, but it can also simply refer to the grave.[49] The

---

45 Moffat, *The Soul's Address*, Fragment A, lines 37–40, pp. 63–4.
46 *Ibid.* p. 65, Fragment B, line 15 and p. 70, Fragment D, lines 10–14.
47 *CH* II, VI, p. 58, line 180.
48 *CH* II, X, p. 90, lines 321–2.
49 Liebermann, *Gesetze* I, p. 282.

will of Ordnoth and his wife leaves an estate to Old Minster, Winchester, on condition

> *þæt man unc gefecce æt uncrum endedege mid þes mynstres crafte 7 unc swylce legerstowe forescewian swylc unc for gode þearflice sy 7 for worulde gerysenlic.*[50]

> that we are collected on our last day with the skill of the minster and that a grave be prepared for us which does what is necessary for us where God is concerned and seemly in the eyes of the world.

Legerstowe here means a single, or at most a double burial, and one notably embedded in *gedefenesse*: Ordnoth and his wife are hoping to guarantee their access to high-quality care (*þes mynstres crafte*) and a socially as well as spiritually appropriate tomb (*swylce legerstowe*). This will is unusual in its acknowledgement of how a burial has a worldly aspect (*for worulde*) as well as a religious one (*for gode*). The overlapping meanings of *legere* also suggest that when a dutiful priest is described as entitled to the rights of a thegn *ge in life ge on legere* this could refer to his treatment when he lies dying, instead of or as well as the conduct of his funeral and the appearance or location of his grave.[51] It has connotations of a foreseen death and a peaceful place for the corpse, and it is never used to refer to landmarks in charter bounds.

Græf, a comparatively rare word, is an apparently neutral reference to the grave-cut. It is found almost exclusively in the lawcodes, in association with the idea that soul-tax should be paid *æt openum græfe* (at the open grave).[52] *Byrgen*, by contrast, is a very common word. It has connotations of monumentality and perhaps specifically a connexion with stone, as it glosses *monumentum, sepulcra* and *tumba*, and it is often used to refer to Christ's tomb. The homilist of Assmann XIV (quoted above) makes it clear that a *byrgen* is something that may be dug, but he perhaps chose this word rather than *græf* or *pytt* (another neutral word for grave-cut) because *byrgen* implies something constructed, probably made of stone, and therefore clean, hard, dry and enduring, like the bones. When he wants to shock, he emphasizes the organic body decaying in the equally organic soil, reiterating *on eorðan* and *in þa eorðan*.

Another grave-related word which occurs in many compounds is *þruh*. This refers to a highly artificial object, presumably a sarcophagus, and is found primarily in saints' lives. It can stand alone, or be prefixed by *lic-* (body-, only in Werferth's translation of Gregory's *Dialogues*), or other words which specify its material rather than its contents, including *marman* (marble: Clement and Æthelthryth), *stænan* (stone: Apollinaris and Swithin), *treowene* (wood: Chad) and *læden* (lead: Guthlac). *Cyst*, the word used for coffin in a homily in Oxford, Bodl. Hatton, MS 115, is not a very common word, but this may reflect the fact that funerals are not often recorded unless they are the obsequies of those too

---

[50] Whitelock, *Wills*, pp. 16–18.
[51] V Æthelred 9–9.1, Liebermann, *Gesetze* I, p. 240, repeated in VI Æthelred 5–5.3, Liebermann, *Gesetze* I, p. 248.
[52] Liebermann *Gesetze* I: V Æthelred 12, p. 240; VI Æthelred 20, p. 252; VIII Æthelred 13, p. 265; I Cnut 13, p. 294.

grand for an ordinary coffin. When St Æthelthryth dies, in accordance with her wishes she is buried in a *treowene cyste* (wooden coffin); only at her translation is she moved into a *marm-stane þruh* (marble sarcophagus). The use of *þruh* to describe Chad's coffin suggests that, although wooden, it was more elaborate than a mere *cyste*, a hypothesis borne out by the detail that it was *gewarht ufan on huses gelicnesse* (carved out in the likeness of a house).[53] Napier Homily XLIII concludes its detailed instructions about performing the corporal acts of mercy with *forðferede þearfan mildheortlice cystian 7 syððan bebyrian* (mercifully supply a dead pauper with a *cyst* and then bury), suggesting that by the late Anglo-Saxon period a *cyst* was seen as an important part of the rite.[54] *Cyst* may be translating Latin *feretrum*, the word used commonly in rubrics for the object used to convey the corpse; Sicard analyses numerous continental rubrics in the attempt to define *feretrum* more closely and concludes that it can only be understood as 'quelque chose de portable', which would perhaps exclude a *þruh*.[55] The verb *cystian* in Napier XLIII could therefore mean 'carry in or on a wooden structure' rather than necessarily 'bury in a coffin', and the syntax separates *cystian* and *bebyrian* in a way that suggests the former. Does the charitable deed commended here anticipate later developments such as the re-usable parish coffin or bier? One last word to consider is *pytt*. The anonymous homily in Hatton 115 contains a reference to unrepentant sexual sinners being buried in the *hæþen pytt*, discussed in detail below in Chapter Six, but this is a unique phrase, and *pytt* is usually reserved for natural features, only rarely being used to mean 'grave'.

Legere, græf, byrgen, þruh, cyst and *pytt* thus have predominantly positive or neutral associations, but there is also a vocabulary for less acceptable burials, most notably *scræf* and *byrgels*. *Scræf* is a complex word; in prose it refers to neutral landscape features, such as caves, more often than it does to man-made trenches, and it does not appear in charters, while in poetry it often refers to hell.[56] *Scræf* is often an element in compounds, the commonest of which is *eorðscræf*, used to describe the grave in *The Wanderer* (84), the damned body's grave in *Soul and Body* (117), and the ambiguous cave/grave space inhabited by the speaker in *The Wife's Lament* (28).[57]

The most consistently negative word, with many occurrences in charters, is *byrgels*. The Cotton Cleopatra glossator translates it as *bustum*, a word which comes to mean 'grave' in Latin but also has the earlier sense of 'funeral pyre'.[58] This implies that traditions about cremation burial were still being recounted and associated with barrows, as *Beowulf* also suggests. The great majority of charters which refer to *byrgels* specify these as *hæþen*, implying an awareness of the

---

[53] *LS* I, XX, p. 436, lines 69 and 79–80; *HE* iv.3, *in modum domunculi*.
[54] Napier XLIII, pp. 205–15, 209.
[55] Sicard, *Liturgie de la mort*, p. 112.
[56] *Exodus*, line 537, *Christ and Satan*, lines 125, 414, 628, 724; *Juliana*, line 684; *Judgement Day II*, lines 140, 230.
[57] S. Semple, 'A Fear of the Past: The Place of the Prehistoric Burial Mound in the Ideology of Middle and Later Anglo-Saxon England', *World Archaeology* 30:1 (1998), pp. 109–26
[58] Gloss 1524 in Cotton Cleopatra A iii.

ancestry of both the word and the feature encountered in the landscape.[59] *Byrgels* also stands in contradistinction to other words referring to places of multiple burial, *lictun, cyrictun, cyricheige*, since all of these refer to enclosed spaces, and *mynster*, probably a graveyard within the minster complex, not the interior of the church. *Byrgels* occurs very rarely in Ælfric's work, and it usually has overpoweringly negative associations. In his homily for Palm Sunday he chooses it to refer to where Judas was buried after he hanged himself (*ælðeodigum to byrgelsum* translating *sepulturam peregrinorum*), and another use is in the passage of his own composition, describing witches practising necromancy at heathen burials and summoning the devil in the guise of the dead man.[60] A third appearance is in the *Colloquy*, in a reference to elaborate tombs containing stinking human remains, where *byrgels* translates *sepulchrum*, a neutral Latin word made negative by context. In telling contrast, Ælfric uses the positive word *byrigen* to gloss *sepulchrum* when it stands alone in his *Glossary*.[61]

Ælfric is similarly precise with other burial-related words; he does not use *hlæw* (barrow) anywhere in his work, although other writers use it to describe both barrows and natural hills. This might only mean that Ælfric had no occasion to use this word, but a policy of active avoidance is suggested by his treatment of *beorg* (*beorh*), a word close in meaning to *hlæw*. He does not use *beorg* in his prose, but in the *Glossary* he uses it to translate *collis* (hill) and *agger* (rampart), whereas the Antwerp and Harley glosses both translate *beorg* as *tumulus*, an explicit funerary reference. This suggests that Ælfric is consciously rewriting language in order to reshape his readers' responses to the landscape, figuratively removing the heathen corpses from their burial mounds and leaving behind a sanitized vista of 'hills' and 'ramparts'. Barrows were still potent presences in Ælfric's Wessex; those he encountered personally were probably Bronze Age or early Anglo-Saxon and used for the burials of outcasts, and he may also have known that in Scandinavia and the northern isles of Scotland barrow burial was current practice.[62]

It is hard to know what words might have been used to describe commemorative or funerary carvings, but one which suggests itself is *becun* (beacon, sign). This appears on a series of commemorative stones, which are found across the north of England and are mostly ascribed to the mid-ninth century or earlier, although there is one from Crowle (N. Lincolnshire) which is plausibly ascribed to the early tenth century.[63] Many of the *becun*-inscriptions use alliterative

---

[59] Reynolds provides a complete annotated list of the appearance of *hæþen byrgels* and other relevant landmarks in charter bounds: 'Burials, Boundaries and Charters', pp. 189–94.

[60] *CH* II, XIV, p. 142, line 157; *Supp.* II, XXIX, p. 706, line 119.

[61] *Swa swa bergyls metton ofergeweorke, withinnan fule stence*: G. N. Garmonsway (ed.), *Ælfric's Colloquy* (London, 1939), line 257, p. 43. The consistency and sensitivity to the vocabulary of burial evident here supports Lendinara's argument that Ælfric himself glossed the *Colloquy*: P. Lendinara, *Anglo-Saxon Glosses and Glossaries*, pp. 207–88.

[62] Semple, 'A Fear of the Past', pp. 109–26; O. Owen and M. Dalland, *Scar: A Viking Boat Burial on Sanday, Orkney* (East Linton, 1999), pp. 24–5, 188; J. Graham-Campbell, *Cultural Atlas of the Viking World* (Oxford, 1994), p. 41.

[63] R. I. Page, *An Introduction to English Runes* (2nd edn, Woodbridge, 1999), pp. 139–57. Bewcastle

memorial formulae, often in runes or a mixture of roman and runic alphabets, which typically name both the person commemorated and the stone's sponsor, 'X set up this *becun* in memory of Y'. In most cases *becun* alliterates with *gebiddæ* (pray for). On the cross-shaft from Yarm (N. Yorkshire) *signum* and *sacerdos* alliterate, the Latin words embedded in an otherwise English verse, and this suggests that *becun* is thought of as the English equivalent of Latin *signum*. The words in the Yarm inscription are interspersed with crosses, and both words and signs may be a prompt to viewers to cross themselves as well as a reference to the vision of Constantine (*in hoc signo uinces*), with the stone, the lettering and the incised crosses encoding many layers of self-referentiality.[64]

The one later example, the badly worn inscription from the stone at Crowle, opens with *licbæcun*, which has been plausibly interpreted as 'body-beacon' (although, reading *lic* as the adjectival ending of an otherwise missing word, it could be a fragmentary '-ly beacon'). This suggests that the tradition embodied by the Anglian stones continued into the Anglo-Scandinavian period. The earlier stones seem primarily designed to catch the attention of and elicit prayer from the onlooker through a multiplicity of devices. They ask for prayer for the souls of the individuals whom they name but they need not have marked a grave. The Crowle stone, if read as 'body-beacon', is presumably a gravestone as well as a memorial, with both the whole stone and the inscription drawing attention to the place where the body is buried. It may thus represent an old formula reinvented to apply to the newly popular genre of stones which mark graves rather than only eliciting prayer.

The language of the grave has its share of flexibility and ambiguity but it is clear that most of these words have core meanings around which they cluster. *Byrgen* and *byrgels* are phonetically similar, but they are used almost mutually exclusively, with the former having the positive meaning of a monumental burial, and the latter signifying the antithesis of a Christian site, with overtones of a cremation pyre, at least to the compiler of the Cotton Cleopatra gloss. Different writers may use these words in different ways, but they do so with internal consistency. This is not a lexicon precise enough to be applied archaeologically, perhaps, but it gives us a graphic idea of the funerary landscape through which people moved, the graves, structures and enclosures of ordinary burial, punctuated by the extremes of the shrines of the saints and the peripheral burials of the ancestors, the outcast and the condemned.

The material culture of burial

As we saw in Chapter Two, it is often asserted that late Anglo-Saxon burials are unfurnished, though it is sometimes hard to work out precisely what is meant by this. Certainly, they have far fewer items in them than the wealthy graves of their

---

(*sigbecun*), Dewsbury (*becun*), Great Urswick (*becun*), Thornhill x 2 (*becn, becun*), Falstone (*becun*), Overchurch (*becun*), Wycliffe (*becun*), Yarm (*signum*), Leeds (*-cun*). Crowle is discussed and illustrated in Everson and Stocker,*Lincolnshire*, pp. 147–52 and ill. 144–50.
64 J. Lang, *Northern Yorkshire*, CASSS VI, pp. 274–6.

fifth- to early eighth-century predecessors, but there is a circularity to an argument which denies that shrouds, shroud pins and coffins are grave-goods and then asserts that Christian burials have no grave-goods. It is methodologically suspect to treat Christianity as if it were in a different category from all other religions, or indeed to argue as if all Christians believed exactly the same things. It is also unclear whether this division which defines some artefacts as grave-goods and others as 'something else' is a dichotomy which would have been understood in the early medieval period. Many Anglo-Saxon burials were undoubtedly only furnished with, at most, a shroud and/or a coffin, but we should at least entertain the idea that these objects could have been designed to help in the journey to salvation. In addition, there is sporadic but insistent evidence that some burials were more complex, probably for a variety of reasons, which often seem to be oriented towards salvation rather than status. The *Regularis Concordia* of the 970s is particular that a monk is to be buried in clean clothing (*mundis uestimentis*), listing shirt, cowl, stockings and shoes, with a stole if he is a priest.[65] Laud 482's rubrics insist that the linen socks and thumbless gloves protecting the anointed hands and feet were to remain on the corpse, and that the haircloth, sprinkled with holy ashes and water and set aside during the *uisitatio infirmorum*, should reappear so that the corpse may be laid out on it. There is also the 'certain band' with which the corpse's mouth is kept closed. This last may be a concession to the sentiments of the living, but the linen hand- and footwear and the ash-strewn sackcloth are certainly an attempt to affect the dead person's prospects of salvation, whether or not these objects were envisaged as rising with the body at Doomsday.

Some late Anglo-Saxon texts focus on the demeaning aspects of burial and its associated material culture. The homilist of Vercelli IX envisages the corpse being stitched into 'the worst part of his wealth' (which, if it reflects common practice, suggests why many sites produce no shroud pins). Likewise, Ælfric envisages the fabric in which the dead are buried as unappealing:

> *Man bewint þone deadan gewunelic mid reafe, ac ðæt reaf ne arist na ðe hraðor mid þam men, for ðan he ne behofað þas huxlican reafan, ac þære gastlican gyrlan ðe him God foresceawað.*[66]

> The corpse is wound customarily in a cloth, but the cloth does not rise readily with the person, for it is not fitting to have shameful cloth but the spiritual garments that God provides for him.

He distinguishes here between *reaf* and *gyrla*, the former being shameful, the latter spiritual, and he envisages the corpse being wrapped or wound in its *reaf*, suggesting a shroud. This is one of the two passages in which Ælfric insists, independently of his source, that the grave-clothes do not rise with the body, implying in turn that some people thought they might. Both Ælfric and Vercelli IX correspond with Laud 482's vision of a penitential death-bed, and they suggest that this elides into an equally penitential environment in the grave.

---

[65] Symons, *Regularis Concordia*, pp. 64–8; Rowell, *Liturgy of Christian Burial*, p. 58.
[66] *Supp.* I, XI, pp. 433–4, lines 339–42.

Other homilies dwell not on the ignominy of a *huxlican* burial but on the futility of a magnificent one, focusing on luxurious materials such as *godweb*. The importance of *godweb* was touched on in the last chapter, where the priest in the rubrics of Laud 482 and the Lanalet Pontifical was enjoined either to wear a *godweb* cope (*planeta*) or no cope at all when he went to anoint the sick. *Godweb* was not reserved to clerical use: Æthelgifu leaves three dresses of this material in her will of the late tenth century.[67] In Blickling Homily X the dead man's bones lament that *Nu þu miht her geseon moldan dæl 7 wyrmes lafe, þær þu ær gesawe godweb mid golde gefagod* (Now you may see a portion of earth and worms' left-overs, where once you saw *godweb* patterned with gold).[68] Blickling Homily VII visualizes the dead rising from their graves *on swylcum heowe swa hie ær gefrætwodon, næs na mid golde ne mid godwebbenum hræglum, ac mid godum dædum 7 halgum* (with the appearance that they were adorned with before, that is not with gold or *godweb* clothes but with good and holy deeds).[69] Both the Blickling references are ambiguous, allowing us to visualize the *godweb* adorning the living or shrouding the corpse.

Lavish burial is explored in most detail in a passage surviving in various forms in five related homilies, quoted below from Napier Homily XLIX, the most elaborate.[70] Although he explores an aesthetics of treasure common to all early medieval Christian culture, the homilist also describes several objects which are not part of the usual literary hoard.[71] While much has been made of the *Beowulf* poet's evocation of fifth- to seventh-century burial culture, 'classicizing the past' as Owen-Crocker puts it, this passage, which may describe the Christian funerary ritual of the same period, seems to have escaped detailed critical attention.[72] It starts conventionally by describing the futility of adorning ourselves with *godweb*, gold and gems since it all ends in the grave, phrased so that it is unclear whether the people, the treasure, or both, are destined for burial. This passage, like those in the Blickling homilies, could be read as contrasting the living in *godweb* and the dead *on eorðan*, but the next sentence presents a more complex picture:

Ðeah þe ða mihtegestan and þa ricestan hatan him reste gewyrcan of marmanstane and mid goldfrætwum and mid gimcynnum eal astæned, and mid seolfrenum ruwum and beddum eall oferwrigen and deorwyrþum wyrtgemengnessum eal gestyred, and mid goldleafum gestrewed ymbutan, hwæðere se bitera deað þæt todæleð eal.[73]

67 *⁊ selle man Lufetate ⁊ Ælfgifu ⁊ Godwife hire iii godwebbenan cyrtlas*: Whitelock, *Will of Æthelgifu*, pp. 13 and 82–3. Whitelock concludes that *godweb* may only refer to purple-dyed wool, but, given that the townswomen of York at this period were trimming their clothes with and making caps of silk, Æthelgifu may well have had silk dresses. P. Walton, *Textiles, Cordage and Raw Fibre from 16–22 Coppergate* (London, 1989), pp. 360–82.
68 Morris, *Blickling Homilies* X, p. 113; J. E. Cross, '"The Dry Bones Speak"-Theme in Old English Homilies', *JEGP* 57 (1956), pp. 434–9.
69 Morris, *Blickling Homilies* VII, p. 95.
70 Napier XLIX, p. 263; Scragg, *Vercelli Homilies*, p. 191.
71 M. Hardt, 'Royal Treasures and Representation in the Early Middle Ages', in W. Pohl and H. Reimitz, *Strategies of Distinction: The Construction of Ethnic Communities, 300–800* (Leiden, 1998), pp. 255–80.
72 G. Owen-Crocker, *The Four Funerals in Beowulf* (Manchester, 2000), ch. 6, *passim*.
73 Napier XLIX, p. 263.

Even though the mighty and the most powerful order a resting-place to be made for themselves of marble and with gold ornaments and all set with gemstones and with tapestries of silver thread and piled with mattresses and all scattered with priceless spices and with gold leaf all strewn about, yet bitter death takes all that away.

Reste can, of course, mean a bed, but *marmanstane* is a sufficiently unusual material for a *reste* to be made from to alert us to the word's other potential meaning of tomb, and it evokes the marble sarcophagi (*marmanþruh*) of saints, while the valuable spices suggest sweetening the air of the tomb, or even the exotic practice of embalming. The homilist is constructing an intentionally ambiguous image, his audience as yet unsure whether they are to imagine a luxurious bed or a sumptuous burial. He may also be striking a satirical note, deploying the aesthetic of saints' shrines to describe the resting-places of the merely rich and powerful. In his next sentence, he brings the body and the treasure together, *þa gimmas toglidene and þæt gold tosceacen and þa lichama tohrorene and to duste gewordene* (the gems fallen and the gold scattered and the body broken and turned to dust), in a list that puts them all in the same conceptual space, showing us the disintegrating body still lying among the fallen gold and tumbled gems. The *godweb*, the silver-thread tapestries or palls, the mattresses and spices have disappeared from the list, perhaps included in the generic organic *duste*.

The objects on this list are not the usual early medieval *desiderata*. Mattresses (*beddum*) do not figure on inventories of royal treasures, and the silver-thread rugs or tapestries are also unusual. There are no other extant Anglo-Saxon references to gold-leaf outside this cluster of related homilies, and with the costly spices the vision is reminiscent of the gold-leaf crosses, silks and herb-filled pillows found in Merovingian burials. Effros describes one well-preserved tomb from late fifth-century Marseilles in which a woman dressed in silk and taffeta clothes was lying on herbs and crowned with flowers, with a gold cross on her forehead; votive gold-leaf crosses, herbs and spices are typical of aristocratic burial customs.[74] Burnell and James draw attention to the fragility of these gold-leaf crosses, stressing that they must have been made specifically for the dead, and also to their apparent potency in protecting the corpse, in that they were left untouched in graves that had otherwise been ransacked by grave-robbers.[75] The Bavarian, Alemannic and Lombard graves they discuss long predate our homily in its surviving form, and perhaps its author was drawing on a tradition that originated in a late antique environment where such burials were practised. Nonetheless, his attention to detail suggests that he and his audience were responsive to this kind of description of treasure, and we might remember the burials with gold thread from York and Winchester. Wormald interprets the brief legal text known as *Walreaf* as a condemnation of grave-robbing, which implies that when it was

---

[74] B. Effros, *Caring for Body and Soul: Burial and the Afterlife in the Merovingian World* (University Park, 2002), pp. 21, 48–9, 72–6, 158.

[75] Burnell and James, 'Archaeology of Conversion', pp. 93–5.

recorded in around the year 1000 some English graves were seen as potential repositories of valuables. [76]

But Napier XLIX is not describing a furnished grave in the conventional, archaeological sense. Its images of enduring treasure are the raw materials of gold and gems, not the swords and rings and silver cups so highly valued in late Anglo-Saxon wills. This homily caters to some of the same aesthetic appetites that were fed by the descriptions of the lavishly equipped funerals of Scyld Scefing and Beowulf, but its author is not reconstructing the same kind of antiquarian vision, nor indeed is he drawing on contemporary Scandinavian practice.[77] Although Cramp suggests that there was a 'persistent memory of rich Roman burials', Anglo-Saxon accounts of the rediscovery of these focus on the sarcophagi rather than their contents, osteological or artefactual.[78] It is possible that the homilist's description is informed by an awareness of the long-ago splendour of Merovingian or even early English Christian burials, in the same way the *Beowulf* poet reconstructs Germanic burials of the same period. It is also possible that he had the mighty and powerful of his own generation in his sights. Either way, it is clear that the burial he evokes so clearly only to repudiate is not a pagan one. There is no sense that these trinkets and textiles are the signs of a different belief system, they are simply a waste. The mood is close to the passage in *The Seafarer*, where the poet acknowledges the man's yearning to scatter gold in his brother's grave (*þeah þe græf wille golde stregan*), but nonetheless asserts its uselessness.[79] Wills, homily, epic and elegy alike recognize the tremendous emotional pull of beautiful man-made objects, although Napier Homily XLIX and *The Seafarer* only do so in order to lead the audience to an acknowledgement of their ultimate futility. The homilist may be describing an expensive burial but he is certainly not advocating one. We have the inverse of the situation Young describes in regard to Merovingian practice: 'furnished burials which the documents do not and the archaeology does reveal'.[80] In contrast, Anglo-Saxon texts attest to a continuing fascination with wealthy burials which prove archaeologically elusive.

The long rubric in Laud 482 that explains the importance of confession in the *uisitatio infirmorum* specifies that, if the sick person *wuruldcund man sy, þonne secge him se mæsse-preost, þæt he mot ærost his hiwrædenne dihtan, þæt is, þæt he sceal his þing becweðan 7 his synna smealice geyppan* (be a layman, then the mass-priest must tell him to put his household in order, that is, that he must bequeath his things and completely reveal his sins). Possessions and sins here are syntactically linked, both governed by 'must' and glossing *hiwræden* (household).

---

[76] *Walreaf is niðinges dæde: gif hwa ofsacen wille, do þæt mid eahta and feowertig fulborenra þegena.* Liebermann, *Gesetze* I, p. 392; Wormald, *The Making of English Law*, p. 372.

[77] E. Roesdahl, *Viking-Age Denmark* (London, 1982), pp. 171–5; M. Iversen, 'Mammen: A Princely Grave from 971 and a Craftsman's Hoard', in Dickinson and James, *Death and Burial*, pp. 73–8.

[78] R. Cramp, 'The Monumental Stone', in *Raunds*, p. 103.

[79] I. Gordon, *The Seafarer* (Manchester, 1979), pp. 45–6.

[80] B. K. Young, 'Merovingian Funeral Rites and the Evolution of Christianity: A Study in the Historical Interpretation of Archaeological Material', unpublished Ph.D. thesis (University of Pennsylvania, 1975), p. 10.

The prospect of death is thus presented to the layperson as an opportunity to unload material burdens as well as to cleanse oneself spiritually in preparation for going to Judgement naked but for one's good deeds. It also suggests a space in the rite for the dying person to share out small personal possessions among the bystanders, rerouting objects which might earlier have been buried.[81] One of the intentions of Napier XLIX may thus have been to reinforce the tension between the extremes of luxurious and penitential material culture, the *hæran* (hair-shirt) prescribed by one's confessor in opposition to the princely silks and taffetas worn and bequeathed by ladies like Æthelgifu. Ideally, this tension could be resolved only through its inversion at the sick-bed and death-bed, where the *godweb*-clad priest blesses the sackcloth in which the corpse is to be wrapped.

The gilds

In an article on fifth- to eighth-century practice, Geake explores the social context of burial in the hope of illuminating 'the seemingly immense effect of the coming of the Church on burial practices, which took place apparently without any detectable institutional intention'.[82] She argues that the number of decisions involved in early Anglo-Saxon burial practice hints at the existence of community burial specialists, very plausibly women, who were guardians of the group's memories and customs and in communication with each other. Geake's field of enquiry extends no later than *c.* 750 but her questions are of the greatest relevance to the present study. If we are looking for lay individuals or groups to whom, eventually, the job of organizing burial may have devolved, one obvious candidate is the gilds.[83] Four sets of gild statutes survive, and the lawcode VI Athelstan, which defines itself as the *friðgegyld* (peace-gild) of the bishops and reeves of London, is also relevant here. The will of Ealdorman Æthelmær refers to the gilds of the mass-priests and the deacons at Winchester, suggesting that such associations were a normal part of ordained as well as lay life.[84] The surviving statutes are all lay-oriented, however, and the only religious obligation which all enjoin is care for the bodies and souls of dying and dead gild members.[85] None is earlier than the tenth century, and they are not the immediate successors of the community burial specialists postulated by Geake. They do show, however, that responsibility for burial and commemoration could be shouldered at community level.

---

[81] Wynflæd mentions jewellery, books and *swylcum lytlum* (other small things): Whitelock, *Wills* III, pp. 10–15.

[82] H. Geake, 'The Control of Burial Practice in Anglo-Saxon England', in Carver, *Cross Goes North*, pp. 259–69.

[83] G. Rosser, 'The Anglo-Saxon Gilds', in J. Blair (ed.) *Minsters and Parish Churches: The Local Church in Transition 950–1200*, Oxford University Committee for Archaeology: Monograph no. 17 (Oxford, 1988), pp. 31–4.

[84] Whitelock, *Wills* X, pp. 25–7.

[85] VI Athelstan, Liebermann, *Gesetze* I, pp. 173–83; S. Reynolds, *Kingdoms and Communities in Western Europe, 900–1300* (Oxford, 1984), pp. 67–78.

The statutes which survive are from Exeter (Devon), Bedwyn (Wiltshire), Cambridge (Cambridgeshire) and Abbotsbury (Dorset).[86] By the time that their statutes were written down, the gilds had become associated with churches, but they may have had their distant origins in pre-conversion fellowships.[87] Cambridge defines itself as the 'thegns' gild', and this, with the London reference to the bishops and reeves, suggests that these gilds drew on the upper gentry. All were voluntary associations, concerned with violence and peace-keeping, with the gild-membership creating reciprocal networks of obligation similar to those imposed by kinship. Exeter and Cambridge are unambiguously urban environments, while Bedwyn might be designated failed urban: it had a mint in the mid-eleventh century, and there is evidence of burgage plots, but it never developed into a fully fledged town.[88] At Abbotsbury, the connexion with the newly founded abbey is much more explicit than in any of the other statutes, and abbey and gild have the same patrons. VI Athelstan, of course, comes from London. This does not preclude there being rural gilds; Rubin draws attention to the similarity of gild and fraternity associations in rural and urban environments in the later Middle Ages, and suggests that the 'impulse to socialize' was structured around gender, age and life-cycle distinctions, equally important in rural and urban communities. She also argues that the late medieval rural population were just as ambitious for their dead as their city-dwelling contemporaries.[89]

The Bedwyn statutes show the value placed by the Anglo-Saxon fraternities on proper treatment of the dead by citing the responsibilities of gild brothers at a death before any other obligation is mentioned; they are to pay for masses or psalms when a member dies, provide food on the thirtieth day after death and contribute towards the payment of soul-tax. Cambridge first mentions the oath sworn among the members of the thegns' gild, then moves directly on to burial, establishing that the gild members are to bring the dead man to the site where he wanted to be buried, pay for half the funeral feast and subscribe towards the distribution of alms. Exeter discusses arrangements for gild meetings and the celebration of mass, then the obligation of each gild member to pay for masses or psalms at a death. Abbotsbury sets out the dates of meetings and the brothers' responsibility for providing food and drink, then discusses unruly behaviour, before moving on to burial. Here, the members are to pay a penny each *æt þam lice for þære sawle*, which sounds as if they are in the presence of the corpse: perhaps gild-members could be among the bystanders whose presence we glimpsed in Laud 482. If a member has fallen ill (*untrumod*) up to sixty miles

---

[86] Whitelock, *EHD* I, pp. 557–60; *Councils*, Exeter, pp. 57–60; Abbotsbury, pp. 516–20.

[87] E. Coonaert, 'Les Ghildes médiévales: (Ve–XIVe siècles): définitions, évolutions', *Revue historique* 199 (1948) pp. 22–55, 43.

[88] A. Reynolds, 'Avebury: A Late Saxon *Burh*?', *Antiquity* 75 (2001), pp. 29–30; J. Haslam, 'The Towns of Wiltshire', in J. Haslam (ed.), *Anglo-Saxon Towns in Southern England* (Chichester, 1984), pp. 87–147, 96–102; J. Williams, 'A Review of Some Aspects of Late Saxon Urban Origins and Development', in M. Faull (ed.), *Studies in Late Anglo-Saxon Settlement* (Oxford, 1984), pp. 25–34.

[89] M. Rubin, 'Religious Culture in Town and Country: Reflections on a Great Divide', in D. Abulafia (ed.), *Church and City, 1000–1500: Essays in Honour of Christopher Brooke* (Cambridge, 1992), pp. 3–22, 7–8.

away, they are also responsible for bringing him home with an escort of fifteen men, while a dead member merits thirty, a time-consuming and high-profile commitment.[90] Both the dying and the dead gild-member are to be brought to the place where he wanted (*gyrnde*) to be *on his life*. Should he instead die in the vicinity, the gild steward is responsible for learning where he wanted to be buried and for publicizing the death among the brothers so that they can escort the body to the church and pray for the soul. This emphasis in Abbotsbury and Cambridge, that the dead brother is to be brought to the church he previously designated, suggests that gild-members need not be buried in the local minster churchyard, even at Abbotsbury, where St Peter's is such a focus. They seem to be exactly the class of people who would be founding proprietary churches, and perhaps the choice here is only between their own church and the local minster. But it may reflect a more complex consumer culture in which a wealthy person's family would pay the minster the *sawelsceatt* and then feel free to bequeath the corpse to another major church, and just such an investment in a portfolio of prayer and commemoration is visible in some of the wills.[91]

These texts embed death in life and community. The emphasis throughout is on reciprocity and obligation, with the statutes evincing great care that gild members should not insult each other (Exeter, Abbotsbury), and the Abbotsbury text demanding that the culpable brother is to recompense the whole fraternity, not merely the man he has offended, underlining the sense of corporate identity. VI Athelstan represents the darker face of this emphasis on harmony, setting out the members' obligation to hunt down thieves and their supporters, to administer the ordeal and carry out the death penalty, as well as reminding everyone that their oath obliged them to give a *gesufelne hlæf* (bread and relish) for a dead member's soul and to sing fifty psalms or pay for them to be sung. The law of the lynch mob enshrined in VI Athelstan, with its mission statement that *we wæron ealle swa on anum freondscype swa on anum feondscype* (we are to be as united in one friendship as we are in one enmity), is a powerful reminder of the potential strains on social bonds, and the need for people to construct these fictive kinship relations with their gild 'brothers', and to be able to rely on each other's *wedd* (pledge).

Abbotsbury demonstrates particularly close links with its minster, recently founded by Cnut's minister Urki who is also the sponsor of the gild. The statutes stress that the gild exists *Gode to lofe ⁊ sancte Petre* and that the members are to give either a penny or a penny's worth of wax to the church three days before the feast of St Peter (28 June), in addition to which they are required to donate food for the *gemæne ælmyssan* (common alms-giving) on the eve of St Peter. This suggests that St Peter's day was the occasion for a public demonstration of gild identity and charity, simultaneously reinforcing the status of the gild-members and their links with the wider community, especially the poor. Abbotsbury

---

[90] H. Loyn, 'Towns in Late Anglo-Saxon England: The Evidence and Some Possible Lines of Enquiry', in Clemoes and Hughes, *England before the Conquest*, pp. 115–45, 123–4.

[91] For example Whitelock, *Wills* I, Theodred, pp. 2–5, II, Ælfgar, pp. 6–9, III, Wynflæd, pp. 10–15.

concludes with a very personal plea directed to Peter on the gild members' behalf, *þæt he us geþingie ⁊ urne wæg geryme to ecere reste, forþan we for his lufon þis gegyld gegaderodon* (that he intercede for us and prepare our road to eternal rest, because for his love we have brought this gild together), followed by a translation of the *traditio clavium* passage (Matthew 16), and concluding with the hope that *he us bewite a her on worulde ⁊ æfter forðsiðe ure sawla gehelp* (that he take care of us here on earth and after death help our souls). This gild embodies inter-cessory prayer as well as community spirit, with Peter an even more important patron than Urki, and the focus on Peter as intercessor and heavenly key-holder unites the living and dead gild members under his protection.

The society imagined in these statutes is structured around communal feasting, worship, charity and burial. The obligations expressed to the dead are no less binding than those to the living or the dying: Exeter specifies that at every meeting the priest is to sing two masses and the ordinary members two psalters of psalms, the first for the 'living friends' and the second for the dead. Gild identity survived death, these texts suggest, and death prompted a particularly visible assertion of gild identity at Abbotsbury, with fifteen to thirty men riding through the Dorset fields, surrounding a cart carrying the dying man or the corpse. The dead mem-bers were continually remembered and reincorporated into the gild through the psalms and masses sung in their name. Urban gilds may have needed to preserve their statutes in written form in a way that rural communities found unnecessary. The larger population in a city, with its high turn-over and greater proportion of strangers, generated tensions which strained social bonds in a culture which relied so heavily on personal connexions, reputation and oath-worthiness. Furthermore, the complex urban environment might offer a range of burial options, making it all the more important that the gild-members announce their chosen place of burial, and be able to trust their fellows to put their wishes into force. The invitation to prayer copied into the York Gospels asks the congregation to pray for *ure godsybbas and ure cumæðran, and for ure gildan and gildsweostra* (our spiritual kin and our co-mothers [i.e. the mothers of our godchildren and the godmothers of our children] and our gildbrothers and gildsisters), which gives an idea of the closeness of the quasi-familial ties between the gild-members, as well as reminding us that they might be female.[92]

þonne man binnan mynster byrgene delfeð: the problem of grave-diggers

These texts remain mute about who was responsible for digging the grave, perhaps because it was self-evident, or nobody's job in particular, or differed from church to church. In a manner typical of most *ordines*, the *Regularis Concordia* dismisses the questions of corpse-washing, coffin-manufacture, the acquisition of burial-clothes, and grave-preparation with airy references to *lauetur corpus a quibus iussum fuerit* (the body is washed by those ordered to do it) and *sepulturae*

---

[92] W. H. Stevenson, 'Yorkshire Surveys and Other Documents of the Eleventh Century in the York Gospels', *EHR* 27 (1912), pp. 1–25, 11.

impedenda (things necessary for burial). Here we may really regret the loss of the last few pages from Laud 482, with the committal of the body to the earth, for surely the person who bothered to write about the cloth binding the corpse's jaws would have said something about the grave itself.[93] Just to know how he translated *feretrum* (coffin or bier) would have been instructive. The evidence of the burials both supports and undermines the idea that there were designated grave-diggers: the variety of graves suggests that there was no central directive, but their permutation within certain parameters militates against burial being entirely unguided. At St Mark's, Lincoln, Gilmour and Stocker argue that the evidence for fenced plots in the graveyard suggests 'a strong organizing hand at work in the parish administration', and they take the existence of a sexton for granted.[94]

After the Reformation, the sexton comes into focus as the man with responsibility for caring for the church and keeping it locked, ringing the bell and digging graves. We might postulate a similar role for his predecessor, the *hostiarius*, in the pre-Conquest Church, at least at the larger minsters. In Ælfric's Pastoral Letter for Wulfsige, bishop of Sherborne, he remarks that the *hostiarius is þære cyrican durewerd; se sceal mid bellan bicnigan þa tida and þa cyrcan unlucan geleaffullum mannum and þa ungeleaffullan belucan wiþutan* (the *hostiarius* is the church's doorkeeper. He is to mark the hours with a bell and to unlock the church to the faithful and to lock the unbelievers out).[95] This derives ultimately from Isidore of Seville's definition of the doorkeeper which also informs the rites for consecrating *hostiarii*.[96] In Lanalet (and there are similar texts in other Anglo-Saxon pontificals), the doorkeeper is identified with Christ when He opened and closed the doors of Noah's Ark and when He liberated the patriarchs and prophets from hell on Easter Saturday, and Wulfstan refers to the former tradition in his *Institutes of Polity*.[97] The ordination rite involved the bishop taking the keys from the altar and giving them to the new door-keeper, an implicit parallel with Christ giving the keys to Peter in Matthew 16, and in prayers for intercession Peter is often given titles such as *clauicularius* and *ianitor*, key-holder and doorkeeper.[98] Bell-ringing and the dead are explicitly connected in a note written into Ælfwine's prayerbook enjoining that when a bishop dies *þonne hringe man ealle bellan* (then all the bells are to be rung).[99] In the early Church, burial was the preserve of specialist *fossores*: these fade from view long before our period but there is some evidence from eastern Christendom

[93] Symons, *Regularis Concordia*, p. 65.
[94] B. J. Gilmour and D. A. Stocker, *St Mark's Church and Cemetery* (Trust for Lincolnshire Archaeology, 1986), pp. 91–2.
[95] *Councils*, p. 202.
[96] Isidore, *Etymologiae*, Book VII 'De Deo, Angelum et Fidelium Ordinibus', 32, *PL* 82, col. 293.
[97] *Ostiarius fuit quando conclusit et aperuit arcam noe et portas inferni aperuit. unde modo ostiarii dicuntur. qui aecclesiae hostia et sacrarii. et tangere signum ut occurrant omnes. custodire iubentur.* Doble, *Pontificale Lanaletense*, p. 49; *Crist wæs hostiarius þa he beclysde Noes arce wið þone geteondan flod ᛉ eft untynde*: Jost, *Institutes of Polity*, p. 226.
[98] For example *Ianitor*: Günzel, *Ælfwine's Prayerbook*, p. 138; *clauicularius*, Hughes, *Portiforium* II, p. 8; B. J. Muir, *A Pre-Conquest English Prayer-Book*, HBS 103 (1988), p. 53.
[99] Günzel, *Ælfwine's Prayerbook*, p. 157.

to suggest that there they had been assimilated into the lowest ranks of the clergy by the sixth century.[100] The role of the *hostiarius* remains hypothetical, but the large churches with important burials to manage are unlikely to have left grave-digging entirely to chance, and many burials show signs of ritual involvement. An Anglo-Saxon *hostiarius* was in the lowest of minor orders and able to marry, but responsible for guarding the sacred spaces and for announcing deaths as well as services by ringing the church-bell. He was directly involved with the laity, admitting the faithful and excluding the sinners in a role that associated him symbolically with both Christ and St Peter, as well as the doors of heaven and hell. These men had the potential to bridge divides, between life and death as well as between lay and ordained, and, as we shall see, door and key imagery is sometimes explicitly invoked in the material culture of the grave.

Burials and gravestones

Bringing together the literary and documentary references to graves with the excavated remains of burials is fraught with methodological challenges. This reading concentrates on a select group of cemeteries which can be fairly closely dated and thus allows the testing of some of the hypotheses aired above about the interplay between external guidance and local custom, between church, kin, gild and community. Even within this small group of cemeteries, there is great variety, both between graves at the same site, and between sites, although certain themes, such as the presence of quantities of charcoal, wooden coffins that may have elaborate iron fittings, and large stones around or beside the head, recur in various combinations from site to site. This pattern might be compared to Anglo-Saxon fifth- to seventh-century funerary practices, of which Pader concluded that every cemetery had its own symbolic language.[101] Such activities are predicated on the existence of people who are both guardians of tradition and vectors of new ideas concerning the theory and practice of burial. The burials considered here come from a range of sites, urban, rural, minster and monastic, and each kind of cemetery may have had its own ritual specialists.[102]

---

[100] E. Conde Guerri, *Los 'fossores' de Roma paleo-cristiana: estudio iconografico, epigrafico y social*, Studi di Antichit(Cristiana, 33 (Vatican City, 1979).

[101] E. J. Pader, *Symbolism, Social Relations and the Interpretation of Mortuary Remains*, BAR Supplementary Series 130 (Oxford, 1982).

[102] Gilmour and Stocker, *St Mark's Church and Cemetery*; W. White, *The Cemetery of St Nicholas Shambles* (London, 1988); B. Kjølbye-Biddle, 'A Cathedral Cemetery: Problems in Excavation and Interpretation', *World Archaeology* 7 (1975), pp. 87–108; B. Kjølbye-Biddle, 'Dispersal or Concentration: The Disposal of the Winchester Dead over 2000 Years', in Bassett, *Death in Towns*, pp. 210–45; B. Ayers, *Excavations within the North-East Bailey of Norwich Castle, 1979*, East Anglian Archaeology 28 (1985); Shoesmith, *Castle Green*; Barrow, 'Urban Cemetery Location'; Carver, *Excavations at York Minster*; *Raunds*; M. Carver, 'Early Medieval Durham: The Archaeological Evidence', in N. Coldstream and P. Draper (eds), *Medieval Art and Architecture at Durham Cathedral* (London, 1980), pp. 11–19; Rodwell and Rodwell, 'St Peter's Church, Barton-upon-Humber'; P. Rahtz and L. Watts, 'Kirkdale Anglo-Saxon Minster', *Current Archaeology* 155 (December 1997), pp. 419–22.

In his discussion of the numerous stone arrangements in graves from Raunds, Boddington calls them 'protective', 'aesthetic' and indicative of 'compassion and care', and he attributes them to the 'spontaneous activities' of the families of the dead.[103] But it takes a highly formal spontaneity to produce one hundred and eighty-eight graves of this kind, evenly distributed and constructed over perhaps two hundred years. These and other diagnostic late Anglo-Saxon burial techniques centre on the body as the basis of identity, the flesh and bone itself rather than any ascribed and enduring symbols of rank, gender, ethnicity or occupation, suggesting that belief in the vulnerability of the corpse and its equal share, with the soul, in the struggle for salvation, was paramount.[104] That burial practices tell us more about the mourners than the dead is an often-repeated truth; if these burials were overseen by laymen then they are a powerful affirmation of the hypothesis that discursive Christianity was the principle structuring this culture's world-view.[105] Above ground, rank could be asserted in a number of ways, by the position of the grave or with a stone grave-marker, but with only a very few exceptions it is not obvious in the grave. Furthermore, many of those exceptions, such as the stone sarcophagi which have turned up at a range of sites, represent an exaggerated and expensive version of the common practice.[106] The focus on the body itself as the significant element remains.

Charcoal burial

In this kind of burial, charcoal (usually oak) is spread uniformly within the grave-cut and the corpse, either coffined or uncoffined, laid on top.[107] Early evidence for the practice comes from Oxford, where one example from St Frideswide's had a date of 825–50, and another of similar date was found at Winchester.[108] The eighth- to tenth-century levels in the cemetery at Exeter contained at least fifteen charcoal burials; after the cemetery was re-aligned, possibly following the building of a church in the tenth century, more than forty charcoal burials were found.[109] Burials of this kind begin in ninth-century contexts at many sites,

---

[103] *Raunds*, pp. 48 and 69.

[104] Current doctoral research by Jo Buckberry of the University of Sheffield on correlating skeletal remains to types of late Anglo-Saxon graves suggests that there is no obvious equation between age or gender and type of burial.

[105] Brown, *The Death of Christian Britain*, pp. 115–69.

[106] M. Biddle, 'Excavations at Winchester 1966, Third Interim Report', p. 254; M. Biddle, 'Excavations at Winchester 1966, Fifth Interim Report', *Antiquaries Journal* 47 (1967), pp. 251–79, 270–1; Biddle, 'Excavations at Winchester 1968, Seventh Interim Report', pp. 321–2.

[107] Burials containing charcoal are found earlier and later than this period, and outside England, but the parameters of the practice are often different, with charcoal only found in a small area of the grave, or ashes from the hearth being used, or fires lit in the grave before or after the deposition of the body. When very similar burials are found, such as the ones in an eleventh-century context from Lund, Sweden, they have been ascribed directly to the influence of English ecclesiastics. Young, 'Merovingian Funerary Rites', pp. 118–31; Roesdahl, *Viking-Age Denmark*, pp. 177–9.

[108] T. G. Hassall, 'Excavations at Oxford 1972, Fifth Interim Report', *Oxoniensia* 38 (1973), pp. 268–98, 270–4.

[109] C. G. Henderson, 'Exeter', in J. Schofield *et al.* (eds), *Recent Archaeological Research in English Towns* (London, 1981), pp. 36–7.

continuing throughout the tenth and eleventh centuries and tailing off in the twelfth, implying they remain acceptable across this period despite great changes within the Church. Kjølbye-Biddle suggests that they refer to penitential funerary ritual, picking up the theme of 'sackcloth and ashes'.[110] This is plausible given both their date and their distribution, if we accept the hypothesis that funerary liturgy could directly affect the making of the grave. They first appear a generation or so after Benedict of Aniane had confirmed the practice of singing the seven Penitential Psalms at the death-bed as part of his regulation of Carolingian ritual, part of a movement designed to encourage the living to identify with the dying and the dead.[111] If the connexion between penance and charcoal burial is valid, it suggests that the ninth-century English Church was receptive to the Carolingian innovations at many levels.

Charcoal and ash embody a complex symbolic association of penitence and purity. We have seen how ash functions within the rites for the sick and dying, and it was a central part of the ceremonies of Ash Wednesday, as Ælfric dramatizes in his homily for that day. He stresses the contrast between the 'clean ashes' (*clæne axan* 17) on the heads of the penitent and the dust to which they will moulder (*manna lichaman þe for-molsniað to duste* 28), beseeching his congregation to go to church to be ashed: *nu do we þis lytle on ures lenctenes anginne þæt we streowiað axan uppan ure heafda to geswutulunge þæt we sculon ure synna behreowsian* (now let us do this, at least, at the beginning of our Lent, that we strew ashes on our heads to signify that we ought to repent of our sins).[112] This is followed by the tale of a foolish man who refused ashes, announcing his intention of 'taking pleasure' with his wife instead (*sæde þæt he wolde his wifes brucan*), only to die shortly afterwards, running himself through with his own spear. *He wearð ða bebyrged and him læg onuppan fela byrðena eorðan binnan seofon nihton þæs ðe he forsoc þa feawa axan* (He was buried then, and a great burden of earth lay upon him within seven days of him refusing that small amount of ash), Ælfric concludes.[113] He contrasts the light ash and the heavy burden of the soil, representing absolution and sin, as well as the clean ash with the dirt both of the earth and of the human body, particularly the sexually active human body. Ash Wednesday prayers habitually cite Christ's words, that he would rather have penance than death from a sinner (*dixisti penitentiam te malle peccatorem quam mortem*), and this reiterated phrase may also have served to connect the ideas of penitential ash and salvific burial: there is *meritum in puluerem*, the rite asserts.[114]

From its early ninth-century beginnings, charcoal burial spreads widely and has been seen as broadly diagnostic of late Anglo-Saxon burial practice, but it is much commoner at the larger churches. At some minster sites, such as Exeter and Winchester, nearly fifty per cent of the excavated burials use charcoal, and

---

[110] Kjølbye-Biddle, 'Dispersal or Concentration', pp. 228–33.
[111] Paxton, *Christianizing Death*, p. 140.
[112] *LS* I, XII, pp. 262–4, lines 37–40.
[113] *LS* I, XII, p. 264, lines 56–8.
[114] D. H. Turner, *The Claudius Pontificals*, HBS 97 (London, 1971), pp. 84–5.

Biddle draws attention to the thickness of the charcoal layer at the latter site.[115] At St Oswald's, Gloucester, thirty four charcoal burials were found. Twenty-one per cent of the Anglo-Saxon burials here overall were charcoal burials, but this rises to forty-two per cent in the area north of the church, perhaps the higher status area; Heighway also points out that thirty-three of the total of thirty-four charcoal burials were close to the church.[116] In contrast, only one such burial was found at each of the urban parish churches of St Helen on the Walls, York, and St Nicholas in the Shambles, London.[117] However, St Mark's, Lincoln, shows that this is not necessarily typical of urban sites: the excavated area here produced eight charcoal burials from mid-tenth- to mid-eleventh-century levels. They were in association with a timber building (possibly a church), seven of them congregating together with an outlier about six metres to the south of the others. Mid-eleventh- to mid-twelfth-century levels at the same site provided another two, both on the site of the recently demolished timber building.[118] However these ten burials represent only around eight per cent of the total excavated at St Mark's. This is a smaller percentage than is found at many minsters but more than at most urban parish churches, and it suggests again that we need to look for a local rather than a national explanation for the practices carried out at each cemetery.

How much charcoal is necessary to define a charcoal burial? Certainly more than was found at Addingham, a rural cemetery but possibly associated with a base of the archbishop of York, where six graves produced 'flecks' of charcoal.[119] Despite complete excavation of the churchyard, Raunds had no full-scale charcoal burials at all, although 'pieces' of charcoal were present in four per cent of the graves.[120] St Peter's, Barton-on-Humber, like St Helen's, York, and St Nicholas, London, had only one, in a prominent position to the south of the door.[121] At some sites, therefore, charcoal is considered appropriate for many funerals, at others for none, at still others for a tiny minority of the graves. In some ways this last category is the most problematic, since if charcoal symbolizes a widely desired rite we might expect to see it equally widely popular at sites where it was known at all. Could it sometimes have been reserved for those who were thought to be in need of particular help, who had failed for whatever reason to die *mid gedefenesse*, with decency?

Not all charcoal burials are the same. At St Mark's, Lincoln, all the bodies seem to have been in coffins, laid on a thin charcoal bed, with more charcoal then inserted between the coffin and the sides of the grave.[122] At Exeter, around three-quarters of the charcoal burials had coffins, as was also the case at St

[115] M. Biddle, 'Excavations at Winchester, 1963–3, Second Interim Report', *Antiquaries Journal* 44 (1964), pp. 188–219, 211.
[116] Heighway, *Golden Minster*, p. 202.
[117] Henderson, 'Exeter'; M. Carver, *Underneath English Towns: Interpreting Urban Archaeology* (London, 1987), p. 95; White, *St Nicholas Shambles*, p. 25.
[118] Gilmour and Stocker, *St Mark's Church and Cemetery*, pp. 16 and 20.
[119] Adams, 'Pre-Conquest Cemetery at Addingham', pp. 179–84.
[120] *Raunds*, p. 37.
[121] Rodwell and Rodwell, 'St Peter's Church, Barton on Humber', p. 301.
[122] Gilmour and Stocker, *St Mark's Church and Cemetery*, pp. 15–20.

Guthlac's, Hereford. At the latter site a juvenile in a coffin had been put in the grave, the gap between the coffin and the sides of the grave was then filled with charcoal, charcoal mixed with clay had been packed down over the coffin lid, and finally a layer of charcoal mixed with grain covered the whole grave-cut.[123] This burial was carbon-dated to *c.* 890–1030, and is the single most complex charcoal burial from the sites under consideration here; the combined symbolic potential of clay, grain and ash suggests that layers of meaning were being created. At Winchester, a few graves contained 'bright yellow sand', and in one this was mixed with charcoal.[124]

There seem to be five broad categories of charcoal burial: uncoffined, charcoal burial with stone head-supports, coffined burial with charcoal outside the coffin, coffined burial with charcoal inside the coffin, and charcoal mixed with other substances. It is likely that this complexity represents overlapping and intersecting local variation, rather than a nationally applicable grammar, and given the many generations during which the practice endures its meaning probably changes over time. The penitential associations of the practice are convincing, but this idea raises more questions than it answers. A penitential function elides into a protective one. The rite for consecrating a church in the tenth-century Claudius Pontifical I says that consecrated ashes may be scattered *pro redemptione peccatorum, corporis sanitatem et animae tutelam* (for the redemption of sinners, the health of the body and the protection of the soul). The ashes are then mixed with salt and water: *ut ubicumque fuerit aspersa per inuocationem sancti tui nominis omnis infestatio inmundi spiritus abiciatur. terrorque uenenosi serpentis procul pellatur* (so that wherever they have been scattered, through the invocation of your holy name, any infestation of an unclean spirit may be cast out, and the terror of the poisonous serpent be driven far away).[125] The perception of the corpse as singularly vulnerable to the attack of worms or serpents, explored in detail in the following chapter, may have added to the appeal of adding consecrated ash to the grave-cut. Despite the attraction of such comprehensive psychic and physical defences, at no time do all the burials from a particular cemetery appear to use charcoal, and this suggests that complex processes of choice and intentionality are at work. At St Mark's, Lincoln, all ten charcoal burials are close together, and Gilmour and Stocker suggest that they overlap the period of change from the hypothesized timber church to the new stone one in the middle of the eleventh century.[126] This looks like a good candidate for the involvement of a gild or other association of people linked by burial. If the explanation for charcoal burial lies in the penance-oriented anxieties of those involved in making the grave, and if this practice has as close a link with the

[123] C. G. Henderson and P. Bidwell, 'The Saxon Minster at Exeter', in S. M. Pearce (ed.), *The Early Church in Western Britain and Ireland* (Oxford, 1982), BAR British Series 102, pp. 145–75, 155; Shoesmith, *Castle Green*, pp. 27–8.
[124] Biddle, 'Excavations at Winchester, Seventh Interim Report', p. 322.
[125] H. M. J. Banting (ed.), *Two Anglo-Saxon Pontificals (the Egbert and Sidney Sussex Pontificals)*, HBS 104 (1989), p. 41; Turner, *The Claudius Pontificals*, pp. 45–6.
[126] Gilmour and Stocker, *St Mark's Church and Cemetery*, p. 92.

ordines as has been postulated here and elsewhere, then we might envision clerical involvement, at least at the planning level.[127] The apparent connexion with minster sites may be real, rather than simply reflecting the greater number of burials, since the disparities are so great at most sites. This tells us nothing about the identity of those buried in this way, as so many of the old minsters retained exclusive burial rights, but it may tell us something about the wider community's access to and interest in complex ritual.

Burials with stones

The distribution pattern of charcoal burials is quite different from that of burials containing stones. This clumsy phrase disguises what Boddington, speaking only of the small and short-lived churchyard at Raunds, calls 'an almost bewildering display of different grave arrangements', present in around half of Raunds's three hundred and sixty-three graves.[128] The absence of charcoal burial here certainly suggests that different social factors are operating, and these factors are unlikely to be governed by cost, as neither practice is intrinsically expensive. The stones from Raunds may have been found in the digging of the grave, or brought from quarries adjoining the site.[129] In these graves, at Raunds and elsewhere, stones may be found under the head, either side of the head, by the feet and along the body, lining the whole grave, over or under the body, as single stones or in clusters. At Barton, one grave had a loom-weight propping the head, and altogether stones were found in over a dozen burials, coffined and uncoffined, either beneath the skull or to either side of it.[130] Of the hundred and twenty mid-tenth- to early twelfth-century burials from St Mark's, Lincoln, one had a limestone rubble floor to the grave-cut, and another had a cist burial in which limestone slabs were mortared to form 'a close approximation to a stone coffin', complete with four slabs mortared in place for a lid.[131] These were the only two graves from our period to be constructed in stone, and it is notable that no burial from St Mark's was found to have stones at the head, although only a small part of the cemetery was excavated. Likewise, only one pillow-stone was found at Exeter, adding to the picture of local communities having distinct models of appropriate funerary activity.[132] Many of the graves from the north-east bailey of Norwich Castle had much more chalk in the fill than is to be found in the surrounding soil, and Ayers suggests that they may originally have been provided with a capping of chalk, and that some graves may in addition have contained dense, crushed chalk at the head or feet.[133] The people in charge of burial at Norwich, like Raunds, were

---

[127] Thompson, 'Constructing Salvation', pp. 238–40.
[128] *Raunds*, p. 69.
[129] G. Cadman and M. Audouy, 'Recent Excavations on Saxon and Medieval Quarries in Raunds, Northamptonshire', in D. Parsons (ed.), *Stone: Quarrying and Building in England AD 43–1525* (Chichester, 1990), pp. 187–206, 193–4.
[130] Rodwell and Rodwell, 'St Peter's Church, Barton on Humber', p. 301.
[131] Gilmour and Stocker, *St Mark's Church and Cemetery*, pp. 16 and 20.
[132] Henderson and Bidwell, 'The Saxon Minster at Exeter', p. 155.
[133] Ayers, *Excavations within the North-East Bailey of Norwich Castle*, p. 19.

using materials at hand to redefine the graves they were constructing. These graves, while disparate, are united in the way they protect the body, or parts of the body such as the head and torso, from the soil, by using an enduring and inorganic material. Unlike charcoal burial, the majority of these require no preparation in advance, and no bringing of extraneous material to the churchyard. Like charcoal burial, though, they demarcate the grave; while this was invisible at surface level it would nonetheless be a message to future grave-diggers that a body lay here, perhaps in the hope that it would be left alone, or that the grave-diggers would re-use the grave with respect.

Another quality shared by many charcoal burials and burials with stones is that they require a series of activities connected with the actual deposition of the body. Stones are placed at the head end of the burial, the body is lowered into position, then more stones may be laid around the head, or the head and the torso. At Raunds clay was also packed around some of the bodies, and in some graves the stones supported a wooden cover, placed over the corpse before the grave was filled. Did this happen in silence? English *ordines* do not mention any ritual activity concerned with the fabric of the grave, although they record the deposition of the body and the recital of prayers. Sicard quotes several continental rites with rubrics that highlight different moments of the burial; although none of these has a direct Anglo-Saxon connexion they illustrate yet again the scope for liturgical creativity. The late eleventh-century rite from St Stephen's, Caen, specifies that the grave-cut is to be purified before and after the corpse is placed with it: *Hic spargatur aqua in sepulcro et illud a sacerdote incensetur. Deinde sine mora deponatur corpus et ipsum aqua aspergetur deinceps thurificetur* (Here water is to be sprinkled in the grave and it [the grave] is incensed by the priest. Then without delay the corpse is deposited and it may be sprinkled with water and then incensed). The tenth- to eleventh-century Bobbio Ritual suggests that the priest may be reciting prayers during the filling of the grave: *sacerdos uero usque quo finiatur humandi officium orationes decantet* (assuredly in succession the priest should keep singing prayers until the end of the burial service).[134] These texts point to spaces within the recorded English rites that could have been filled by priest, gild-members, community or kin, local custom intersecting with the Latin prayers.

Although stones may be found in any part of the grave, the commonest arrangements are around the head, or the head and torso, and this may suggest that these parts of the body, identified with breathing and the senses, were seen as the seat of identity. In some cases other body parts came in for special treatment. At Raunds particular care had been taken in the graves of two young men (5311 and 5074), both of whom had leg problems: for the former an arrangement of stones had been placed around the leg in question, and in the latter case three stones supported the damaged knee from beneath.[135] This, together with the inclusive attitude to the burial of lepers, suggests that when a disabled body is

---

[134] Sicard, *Liturgie de la mort*, p. 223.
[135] *Raunds*, p. 42.

treated differently in death, we may want to postulate reasons other than the disability. At Ripon a young man with a deformed spine was found near an otherwise isolated multiple burial, and we should be open to the possibility that he was apparently excluded from consecrated burial for criminal behaviour rather than because of his affliction.[136] The tending of these disabled men from Raunds may also suggest the ultimate fusion of the medical and the spiritual, a popular reinterpretation of Ælfric's patristically derived insistence that the body damaged in life will be healed at the resurrection, *þeah ðe he ær wære lama on his life, ac his lima beoð him ealle ansunde* (even if he were formerly lame when alive, yet his limbs will be all healthy for him).[137] Whereas the charcoal burials work towards the ultimate salvation of body and soul, the burials with stones seem more concerned for the interim comfort and safety of the corpse. The persistent hints that some kind of life continued in the grave may provide a context for these practices; Cross draws attention to two English translations of Caesarius of Arles's homily *De Elemosina*, in which a rich man's corpse admonishes the living from the tomb. Both translators insert emphatic reminders that dead bones cannot really speak, and Irvine wonders whether Caesarius's original text was 'too easily misunderstood' for an English audience.[138]

Coffins

There is nothing uniquely late Anglo-Saxon about the use of coffins, but coffins with elaborate fittings appear more frequently in the later period. There has been some debate about whether some of these, particularly those with locks, represent coffins or 're-used domestic chests', but little discussion of the possible meaning of these various practices. This is in contradistinction to the discovery of a clinker-built object, whether coffin or bier, in one of the graves at York Minster, whose possible connexion with either the cart or the boat burials of contemporary conversion-period Denmark has been much discussed. These coffins are mysterious and intriguing objects, nonetheless, and they show just as much as variety as the other categories under discussion here.

There were 'elaborately scrolled iron fittings' on some of the coffins found in graves at the Old and New Minsters at Winchester.[139] At St Oswald's, Gloucester, one coffin appeared to have been charred, and the woman inside, buried probably in the early eleventh century, had been buried with stones around the head as well as a boar's tusk by her shoulder (an object identified as amuletic when found

---

[136] R. A. Hall and M. Whyman, 'Settlement and Monasticism at Ripon, North Yorkshire, from the 7th to the 11th Centuries AD', *Medieval Archaeology* 40 (1996), pp. 62–150, 123–4.

[137] *Supp.* I, XI, p. 432, lines 322–4.

[138] Caesarius simply writes *Clamat ad te*, but, as Cross notes, the English adapters of his text add phrases such as *Ðus cleopedon þa ban to us gif hie sprecan meahton of þare byrgenne* (Vercelli XIII), *þonne, leofe men, þeah þe ðe deade ban of þare burignes specon ne magon* (Bodley 343). Cross, '"The Dry Bones Speak"-Theme'; Scragg, *Vercelli Homilies* XIII, p. 235, lines 33–4; S. Irvine, *Old English Homilies from MS Bodley 343*, EETS OS 302 (London, 1993), VII, p. 185.

[139] Biddle, 'Excavations at Winchester, Third Interim Report', pp. 256–8.

in furnished-period graves, and usually, as here, accompanying women).[140] Other St Oswald's coffins had iron brackets which appeared to be decorative rather than functional, and some of the surviving nails were so long that they suggested pieces of wooden grave furniture rather than simple coffins.[141] There were virtually no nails found at Barton, but here the coffins themselves survived, made entirely of wood, very plain and so flimsy that they might be interpreted as grave-liners rather than a box sturdy enough to carry a corpse.[142] Rounds similarly turned up no evidence for nails or coffin fittings, although several graves produce evidence for timber coffins and five sarcophagi were found, four fragmentary and one, massive, tapering and anthropomorphic, close to the church door and probably associated with the building of the first tiny church in the tenth century.[143]

The cemetery underlying York Minster produced five coffins with 'splendid' iron fittings, two of which definitely had locks, out of a total of one hundred and nine excavated burials.[144] Kjølbye-Biddle suggests an early to mid-ninth-century date for the earliest of these, a woman buried in an oak chest with lock, hinges and metal fittings, and she adduces tenth-century Scandinavian parallels for the re-use of domestic chests as coffins, as well as the chest/coffin with a lock from grave 74 at Winchester.[145] Burial 79 was the burial of someone in early adolescence, found with a mid-ninth-century coin and a piece of gold thread. Burial 81 was in a lock-less but elaborately strapped container, of which Kjølbye-Biddle concludes 'this could be a simple chest elaborated for secondary use as a coffin, or an unusual coffin rather laboriously strapped together'. At Rounds there was evidence both for coffins and for wooden planks laid either above or below the arrangements of stones covering the body.[146] It is evident that in many cases people used what came to hand to construct a special space for the corpse, but if, as Kjølbye-Biddle argues, the clinker-built object from the York Minster site carried symbolic weight, then it is worth considering whether the chests with locks may have done the same. The decorative strapping is also interesting. Locks presuppose keys, and a coffin in the grave with only the lid visible, embellished with iron strapping and hinges, would have looked very like a door leading down into ground. The young man in grave 1074 at Ripon was buried in a chest with lock and key, and keys found separately in graves in Ripon and Thwing have been interpreted as intentional deposits rather than casual losses.[147] Certainly at later periods doors carried significant burdens of iconography: the ironwork at Stillingflect a little south of York still displays high-medieval wrought-ironwork showing Adam and Eve and the serpent, and Noah's Ark, and at least one

---

[140] A. Meaney, *Anglo-Saxon Amulets and Curing Stones*, BAR British Series 96 (Oxford, 1981), pp. 131–47.
[141] Heighway, *Golden Minster*, pp. 202–16.
[142] Rodwell and Rodwell, 'St Peter's Church, Barton on Humber', p. 301.
[143] *Rounds*, pp. 42–5.
[144] Kjølbye-Biddle in Carver, *Excavations at York Minster*, p. 518.
[145] *Ibid.*, pp. 491–3.
[146] *Rounds*, pp. 40–2.
[147] Hall and Whyman, 'Settlement and Monasticism at Ripon', pp. 86 and 110.

Scandinavian church door uses the same technique to illustrate Sigur∂r's fight with the dragon.[118] Even without a narrative programme, a door may be a resonant object in itself, as the imagery associated with the *hostiarius* suggests.

Grave-markers: industrial production?

The variety of shape, size and image found in ninth- to eleventh-century funerary sculpture is such that generalization is impossible, from region to region, from church to church, and even within one cemetery. Monuments may be upright crosses, recumbent slabs or hogbacks, they may stand alone or have head- and foot-stones, they may have abstract, plant, animal or human ornament, they may be inscribed in Latin or English, in the roman or runic alphabets, their carving may be symbolic, iconic, narrative or decorative. Some churches, such as St Mark's, Lincoln, or Lythe (N. Yorkshire) produce numerous stones, others only one or two. The excavation at St Peter's, Barton-on-Humber, found none. They are overwhelmingly associated with churches, and are often the earliest evidence for ritual activity on a site. Few crosses or slabs, and no hogbacks, have been found over graves, although the presumption is that most of these stones are funerary, rather than primarily memorial or devotional. From the late ninth century gravestones, crosses and other sculpture become much more common and overall much larger. Bailey estimates that five times as many churches have ninth- to eleventh-century sculpture as have seventh- to ninth-century pieces.[149] This is particularly noticeable in the north and east of England, and it is tempting to correlate it with the Danish-led settlement of the 860s and 870s, and the Hiberno-Norse incursions after 918. A multi-causal explanatory model should not be ruled out, however. Three early tenth-century stones from North Lincolnshire were probably exported from York, and Everson and Stocker suggest this indicates 'Viking-age' and 'Hiberno-Norse' influence.[150] But for much of this time, particularly after the decisive battle of *Brunanburh* in 937, West Saxon kings were York's overlords, if only from a distance. More importantly the archbishops of York maintained their presence in the city, and one of these North Lincolnshire stones, Holton-le-Clay, is in a style closely associated with stones from what was probably York Minster's lay cemetery.[151] Some of the Yorkshire stones are discussed in Chapter Five as part of a wider discussion of worm, snake and dragon funerary iconography; these stones are mentioned here as a reminder that English and Scandinavian, ecclesiastical, mercantile and aristocratic ideas and influences are likely to have travelled together along the same vectors.

---

[148] E. Ploss, *Siegfried-Sigurd, der Drachen-Kämpfer* (Köln, 1966), Tafel 23.

[149] Bailey, 'The Chronology of Viking-Age Sculpture in Northumbria'.

[150] Everson and Stocker, *Lincolnshire*, p. 81.

[151] C. Norton, 'The Anglo-Saxon Cathedral at York and the Topography of Anglian York', *JBAA* 151 (1988), pp. 1–42; J. Lang, 'Continuity and Innovation in Anglo-Scandinavian Sculpture: A Study of the Metropolitan School at York', in Lang (ed.) *Anglo-Saxon and Viking Age Sculpture*, pp. 145–72.

The discussion in the present chapter concentrates on two connected groups from the East Midlands which contradict many of the broad generalizations outlined above. The mid-Kesteven group and the Fenland group overlap in the tenth and eleventh centuries, although the mid-Kesteven group may be slightly earlier. Both groups are strikingly internally homogeneous, and this very homo-geneity is fascinating, attesting to centralized production on a near-industrial scale, and suggesting a regional monumental culture at odds with the local idiosyncrasies of the graves.

Everson and Stocker have identified forty-seven mid-Kesteven stones, found in Nottinghamshire, Leicestershire and Derbyshire as well as Lincolnshire, and they draw attention to their uniformity of design and stone type.[152] Whenever enough of the slab survives to be sure of the overall design, it has a double-ended cross embedded in panels of interlace. The stones are very thick, almost square in section, and have interlace panels down the long sides. Fifteen have a small bull's head motif centrally placed on the side panels, organically connected to the interlace, and these cluster in the heartland of the distribution area south and south-west of Lincoln. We might want to read this as a mason's signature, or a mark of kinship or affinity, or as a symbol of power, possibly punning on the meanings of *feoh* (cattle/wealth). Everson and Stocker link them to the so-called 'Trent Valley hogbacks', calling the mid-Kesteven stones 'hog-back-like', and there are clear typological similarities between these two groups. However, taken on their own, the Trent Valley stones are not very like hogbacks, and the mid-Kesteven group, with their flat tops and straight sides, do not resemble hogbacks at all. If we concede the connexion, and the priority of the Trent Valley stones, then masons or patrons must at some point have taken the decision radically to reinvent these monuments. Their shape and dimensions suggest rather that these stones, up to two meters in length, were intended to resemble rectangular chest-coffins like those from York, reconstructed as flat-topped and straight-sided on the basis of their metal fittings. If so, the standardized carving of cross and interlace may be intended to reproduce the pall cloaking the coffin, although there is no giveaway clue as there is with the pre-Viking-Age slab from Kirkdale (N. Yorkshire) with its rows of tassels carved along the sides.[153] An undated Bury St Edmunds will authorizes the spending of five ore for the coffin (*þruþ*) and twenty-one pence for the pall (*hoferbredles*), suggesting that the burial furniture of the Anglo-Danish gentry could be elaborate.[154] The mid-Kesteven package, including the crosses, the standardized iconography and the evocation of the coffin and pall, all points to ecclesiastical management. With the Newent Stone Book we saw one way for funerary ritual to be made permanent in the private

[152] Everson and Stocker, *Lincolnshire*, p. 44.
[153] P. Rahtz and L. Watts, 'Three Ages of Conversion at Kirkdale, North Yorkshire', in Carver, *Cross Goes North*, pp. 289–309, p. 307.
[154] Robertson, *Anglo-Saxon Charters* VIII, pp. 253 and 501–2. Robertson notes the presence of Scandinavian terms such as mark and ore, *ærflæ* (arval) for the funeral feast, and the mention of a second funeral feast paralleled in Sweden and Norway but otherwise unknown in England.

environment of the grave; the gentry of the East Midlands chose a more public way of displaying a similar message.

There are no complete extant examples of the mid-Kesteven school, and the Fenland school has not been much better served by time.[155] The only stone to be found *in situ* in Raunds was a full-length slab broken into several pieces, carved with a central spine linking three crosses, the spaces between the crosses filled with interlace panels. It is a characteristic example of this group, of which sixty-four have been identified to date, scattered through Lincolnshire, Cambridgeshire, East Anglia and the East Midlands, with two outliers in Bedfordshire and one in London.[156] Most of these are ascribed to the eleventh century, though a tenth-century date is possible at Raunds.[157] Fox classifies them primarily according to whether the interlace is also within the body of the cross, whether the central spine is relief or incised, and whether the spine terminates in a cross, a U, a V or a ring.[158] Examples were found sealed by early Norman layers at Peterborough Cathedral and Cambridge Castle, and in both cases the original context seems to have been a churchyard. This gives us a reliable *terminus ante quem*, but there is no similarly trustworthy evidence for the beginning of the style, and no reason to assume that they could not have been in use at Peterborough before it was reformed as a Benedictine house under Æthelwold in 970.[159] Again, the consistency of the iconography suggests either that it was being overseen centrally, or the artists were responding to a uniform and severe taste.[160] The variety with the central spine and terminal Us or Vs looks like an attempt to reproduce a coped Roman sarcophagus lid in two dimensions, and here we may see the kind of direct influence from Roman burial practices hypothesized by Cramp, or mediated by the re-use of Roman sarcophagi as saints' shrines, or by earlier coped stones which also looked back to antique sarcophagi.[161] The bishop of Lindsey may have controlled local production of sculpture after the middle of the tenth century; similarly the ruins of Roman York may have been administered as an archiepiscopal asset.[162] The quarries at Barnack are the likeliest source for the Fenland stones;[163] could their iconography as well as their production have been controlled by an ecclesiastical authority?

[155] C. Fox, 'Anglo-Saxon Monumental Sculpture in the Cambridge District', *Proceedings of the Cambridge Antiquarian Society* 17 (1920–1), pp. 15–45, 19–20.

[156] Everson and Stocker, *Lincolnshire*, p. 47; D. Tweddle *et al.*, *South-East England*, CASSS IV (Oxford, 1995), p. 83.

[157] Cramp, 'The Monumental Stone', p. 107.

[158] Fox, 'Anglo-Saxon Monumental Sculpture', pp. 15–45.

[159] Tweddle *et al.*, *South-East England*, p. 83.

[160] Fox, 'Anglo-Saxon Monumental Sculpture', p. 28.

[161] Cramp, 'The Monumental Stone', p. 103; R. E. Routh, 'A Corpus of the Pre-Conquest Carved Stones of Derbyshire', *Archaeological Journal* 94 (1937), pp. 1–42.

[162] D. Stocker, 'Monuments and Merchants: Irregularities in the Distribution of Stone Sculpture in Lincolnshire and Yorkshire in the Tenth Century', in Hadley and Richards, *Cultures in Contact*, pp. 179–212, 196; D. Stocker and P. Everson, 'Rubbish Recycled: A Study of the Re-use of Stone in Lincolnshire', in Parsons, *Stone*, pp. 84–5.

[163] Tweddle *et al.*, *South-East England*, pp. 11–12.

The keys of the kingdom

While most of the Fenland stones play minor variations on a theme, there is one whose iconography is more inventive, Cambridge Castle 1 (Plate 3). One of the U-shaped terminals of its central spine contains a motif which, Fox argues, represents 'the Keys of the Kingdom and the Cross in one', and he associates it with the iconography of St Peter's keys on fols 4r and 56v of the Benedictional of Æthelwold, an identification which is supported by Deshman.[164]

It also resembles the keys held by Peter in the eleventh-century relief carving from Daglingworth in Gloucestershire. Peter as *Ianitor Caeli*, holding the keys of heaven, is a powerful and multivalent image, one whom we have already encountered in the Abbotsbury gild statutes, authorizing absolution in the *uisitatio infirmorum* in Laud 482 and underpinning the rite for confirming the *hostiarius*. Peter is one of the most complex figures in the New Testament, but while many different elements of his life and cult serve as devotional focuses, his keeping of the keys is the aspect on which most people chose to concentrate.[165] Matthew 16 is the only authority for the bestowing of the keys (*traditio clavium*), when Christ singles Simon (Peter) out for special treatment, in response to his statement of faith, *Tu es Christus Filius Dei vivi* (Thou art the Christ, the Son of the living God). Christ replies by calling him 'the rock on which the Church will be built', and goes on to promise that the Church will prevail over the gates of hell (*portae inferi*), while Peter is given the keys of heaven (*claves regni caelorum*) and the power to bind and loose in heaven and on earth. This passage prompted considerable debate over how many keys Christ meant, and which doors they were to open and close. The mention of the *portae inferi* could imply that the gates of hell are also at Peter's command, and some anonymous homilies, including Vercelli XV, explore this idea, as we will see in Chapter Six.[166] Matthew 16 is capable of being read on multiple symbolic and literal levels; Bede identifies the keys of heaven as embodying the knowledge to understand the hearts of men and the power to grant and refuse entrance.[167] He reads *portae inferi* as vulnerability to worldly temptation: a house built on a rock will not have doors of this kind. In Bedan terms, then, the Cambridge Castle gravestone is invoking *scientia*, *potentia* and the Cross. The very material of which the slab is made may be punning on the name of Peter (*super hanc petram aedificabo ecclesiam meam*): as we saw with the *becun*-stones, Anglo-Saxon funerary monuments were capable of great linguistic and symbolic creativity.

---

[164] Fox, 'Anglo-Saxon Monumental Sculpture', pp. 32–3 and plate 3; R. Deshman, *The Benedictional of Æthelwold*, Studies in Manuscript Illumination 9 (Princeton, 1995), p. 76, n. 120.

[165] Higgitt, 'The Iconography of St Peter'; Clayton, *The Cult of the Virgin Mary in Anglo-Saxon England*; V. Ortenberg, *The English Church and the Continent in the Tenth and Eleventh Centuries*; S. De Gregorio, 'Ælfric, *Gedwyld* and Vernacular Hagiography: Sanctity and Spirituality in the Old English Lives of SS Peter and Paul', in D. Scragg (ed.), *Ælfric's Lives of Canonised Popes*, Old English Newsletter, Subsidia 30 (Kalamazoo, 2001), pp. 75–98.

[166] M. Clayton, 'Delivering the Damned: A Motif in Old English Prose', *Medium Aevum* 55 (1986), pp. 92–102.

[167] Bede, *Homiliae in Natale Beatorum Apostolorum Petri et Pauli*, PL 94, col. 222.

Plate 3: The gravestone from Cambridge Castle (I), present whereabouts unknown. Illustration: V. Thompson, after C. Fox. This grave-slab has a symbol at the wider end which represents the cross of Christ and the keys of St Peter, suggesting that the Last Judgement and entrance to the gates of heaven were being invoked by the stone's designer.

This grave-slab was probably made in the middle of the eleventh century, but Peter's ubiquity from the very beginning of the spread of Roman Christianity in England suggests that over time his cult had put down deep and wide-reaching roots, which resulted in various kinds of growth. The key-imagery on this grave-cover, like the locks on some coffins, suggests that the grave may be read as a doorway. The stone that covers Christ's grave is described as *ostia monumenti* (the door of the monument) in Mark 15:46, and the Gospels are full of door imagery, most notably in John 10:9, where Christ says *ego sum ostium per me si quis introierit saluabitur* (I am the door, and anyone who enters through me will be saved). Wulfstan claims that the performance of penance opens the door of heaven: *doð dædbote eowra synna 7 eow sona wyrð heofona rices duru raðe untyned* (do penance for your sins and at once the door of heaven will be swiftly opened to you), the opposite of Vercelli IX's use of *betyned* to describe the shutting down of the body and the closing of the damned into hell. The twelfth-century fragmentary *Soul and Body* poem from Worcester twice describes the corpse as destined to live in the *durelease huse*, and the version of the poem quoted in Bodley 343 has a chilling passage where the soul threatens, *Dureleas is þet hus and dearc is wiðinnen. ðær þu bist feste bidytt and deað hefð þa cæge* (Doorless is that house and it is dark inside. There you will be closely confined, and death holds the key).[168] The poet does not pause to resolve the paradox of how a house with no door can still have a key, but goes on to assert that *nefst þu nenne freond, þe þe wylle faren to, ðæt efre wule lokien, hu þe þat hus the likie, ðæt efre undon ðe wule ða dure* (you have no friend who will come to see you, who will ever look to see how you like your house, that will ever undo the door for you).[169] The Cambridge Castle gravestone denies this grim and lonely prospect, asserting that the corpse does have friends; it takes issue with the idea of the 'doorless house', and appoints an alternative key-holder in the person of Peter. Peter is associated with the dead in so many ways in Anglo-Saxon literary and visual imagery that it seems he may have been perceived as their particular guardian. When the Blickling homilist retells the episode in which a would-be disciple asks Christ for permission to bury his father (Matthew 8:22 and Luke 9:60), the dutiful son is identified as Peter: *hu Drihten cwæþ to Petre, þa he bæd þæt he moste faran 7 his fæder bebyrgen* (how the Lord spoke to Peter, when he asked that he might go and bury his father).[170] No scriptural or exegetical explanation is given for this, and perhaps the Anglo-Saxon homilist simply took it for granted that Peter was the disciple most likely to express concern for the dead.

---

[168] *Soul and Body* fragment from Bodley 343, fol. 170r: Buchholz, *Die Fragmente*, p. 11.
[169] *Ibid.*, lines 18–20.
[170] Morris, *Blickling Homilies* II, p. 23, lines 152–4.

5

The Gravestone, the Grave and the *Wyrm*

Many Anglo-Saxon texts and images attest to a heightened awareness that the body, living and dead, is threatened with being eaten at every stage of its existence before the Last Judgement, after which the damned body will continue to be devoured in perpetuity. These threats may come from creatures of the air (eagles and ravens), creatures that walk on earth's surface (wolves), and creatures that slither and crawl on or beneath the soil, and it is the last of these, the *wyrm*, that is most continually linked to the condition of both body and soul, before and after Judgement. *Wyrm* is the generic Anglo-Saxon word used to describe the dragon of *Beowulf*, the *smeawyrmas* that invade the living body in the leechbooks, and the corpse-devouring *moldwyrmas* of the *Soul and Body* poems, as well as other creatures, some of which appear, at first at least, to have little in common.

Wyrm is such a broad category that, used loosely, it risks becoming meaningless: it includes scorpions and spiders as well as dragons, snakes, maggots, lice and fleas. Neville calls the Anglo-Saxons 'imprecise' in their use of *wyrm*, and she draws attention to Isidore of Seville's broad use of *serpens* and *vermis*, implying that Anglo-Saxon 'imprecision' has its origin in the learned tradition.[1] But this fails to take into account the ubiquity of these creatures in Anglo-Saxon culture. *Wyrmas* partake of some common qualities with which a Linnaean system of classification fails to cope, including poisonousness, an intimate relationship with human flesh, a taste for the same, an uncanny way of moving (*creopende*), the ability to disappear underground and a closeness to the dead. Three or four of these are enough to qualify a creature as one of the *wyrmcynn*, and with these in mind, we can examine the various *wyrmas* as they appear in written sources, and see whether the same varieties are represented iconographically, in memorial and funerary carvings particularly.

The meaning of early medieval animal art is much debated.[2] Distinguishing between the ornamental and the significant, the traditional and the innovative, the indigenous and the alien can be a thankless task, based often on intuition as much as any other criterion. It is assumed here that early medieval animal art is likely to be meaningful, representing the outcome of a series of stylistic and symbolic choices on the part of patron and artist. Those meanings are bound to change depending on the nature and style of the animal, the medium and type

---

[1]   Neville, *Representations of the Natural World*, p. 108, n. 88.
[2]   N. Wicker, 'The Scandinavian Narrative Styles in Response to Christian and Mediterranean Narrative Art', in Carver, *Cross Goes North*, pp. 531–50, 538–9; G. Speake, *Anglo-Saxon Animal Art and Its Germanic Background* (Oxford, 1980), pp. 85–92.

of object on which the image appears, its intended audience, and the period at which it is made. Decorating something with abstract imagery makes it culturally articulate, but decorating it with plants, animals or human beings brings it to life, investing it with some of the force of the living things depicted. The stones of the East Midlands schools we examined in the last chapter fall into the former category; it may be significant that they appear to be later, more regulated, more uniform and much less lively than the stones considered here.

Wyrm imagery is ubiquitous; it is also continuously reinvented. The crosses, slabs, hogbacks and endstones that constituted the grave-furniture of later Anglo-Saxon churchyards carry an extraordinary variety of symbols and stories involving *wyrmas*. The second half of the current chapter considers a selection of these from the north and east of England; they draw on a pool of ideas from a range of North Sea cultures, all of whom were in contact and whose artistic styles influenced each other, literally chasing each other's tails in some cases. Causation and correlation are hard to disentangle in all this.[3] Would the English and Irish churches have reinvented and elaborated their existing traditions of monumental sculpture without Scandinavian input of any kind, either artistic or political? Although *wyrmas*, graves and gravestones remain the primary focuses, discussing them gives us the opportunity for a wider exploration of cultural disruption and continuity and the role of the Church in these parts of the country, an essential background to understanding death and burial.

The wyrm *in written sources*

Indigenous Germanic traditions about the underworld as 'the dark dwelling of corpses and serpents' merge with Christian imagery of hell as the home of the serpent of Eden, associated with the dragon and basilisk upon which Christ tramples.[4] However, it is doubtful whether all *wyrmas* evoke damnation, or even the potential of damnation.[5] Recognition of the multivalency of the serpent, in particular, has a long history in Christian exegesis. It is among the examples chosen by Augustine to illustrate the complexity of biblical imagery: *Ita serpens in bono est: 'Estote astuti ut serpentes', in malo autem: 'serpens Euam seduxit in astutia sua'*. Elsewhere in the same text he recommends getting to know the behaviour of real serpents as a way of decoding the layers of their positive symbolic meanings, referring to snakes shedding their skins as well as their habit of inducing enemies to attack their body rather than their head. The first of these symbolizes the Christian shedding sin and the second represents martyrdom, in which the body rather than the head (faith) is lost.[6] He also links the serpent with

3 F. Henry, 'The Effects of the Viking Invasions on Irish Art', *Proceedings of the International Congress on Celtic Studies 1959* (Dublin, 1962), pp. 61–72; F. Klingender, *Animals in Art and Thought to the End of the Middle Ages* (London, 1971), pp. 138–9; B. Sawyer, *The Viking-Age Rune-Stones* (Oxford, 2000), p. 10.
4 H. R. Ellis Davidson, *Gods and Myths of Northern Europe* (Harmondsworth, 1964), p. 162.
5 Lang, *Northern Yorkshire*, pp. 49–50.
6 Thus the serpent is good in 'Be as wise as serpents', but bad in 'the serpent seduced Eve in its

human corpses, playing with the imagery from Genesis 3:14 and 19 where both serpent and man are sentenced by God, the former to eat dust and the latter to come from and return to dust (*terra*, *puluis*), and suggesting that the struggle between humanity and serpentkind is the *Leitmotif* of the fallen universe.[7]

Positive serpent imagery was well known in Anglo-Saxon England. The Rule of Chrodegang draws on Matthew 10:16, advising that *ðam ærcediacone 7 þam prauost gebyrað þæt hi beon swa snottre swa næddran 7 swa milde swa culfran* (it befits the archdeacon and the provost that they be as wise as adders and as mild as doves).[8] The *Regularis Concordia* specifies that on Maundy Thursday, Good Friday and Easter Saturday, a staff shaped like a serpent with a candle fixed in its mouth is to be carried in procession, referring to John 3:14 where Christ on the Cross is compared to the brazen serpent of Moses.[9] Some of the many sculptural images of men holding snakes could embody Christ's promise of immunity to poison and the ability to handle snakes unharmed (Mark 16:17–18), verses which inspire Æthelwold of Winchester to recover after the dastardly secular canons whom he had expelled from the Old Minster attempted to poison him.[10] Two pieces of goldsmith's work from *c.* 800, both now in the Ashmolean Museum, Oxford, also attest to the serpent's multivalency. The Windsor pommel is decorated with snakes consuming each other's tail, while a massive gold finger ring includes double-headed snakes among its ornamental repertoire. Both pieces also have filigree and granule decoration suggesting an inhabited vine-scroll pattern, where birds and animals symbolize the faithful feeding on Christ, the true vine. If so the snakes are playing the part of Christian souls, with the artists employing eucharistic iconography that may be paralleled in earlier sculpture from northern and western Britain.[11]

Kitzinger argues that, while early medieval artists and audience took an aesthetic delight in zoomorphic interlace, intertwining creatures could also serve an apotropaic function, and they sometimes occur with protective inscriptions.[12] 'Apotropaic' is a loose term, however; *wyrmas* represented many different kinds of threat and we might look for an equally wide range of protective measures. One of these threats is the comparatively prosaic one of being bitten by an adder, Britain's only native venomous snake, and Speake hypothesizes that snakes on

cunning'. Augustine, *De Doctrina Christiana*, ed. and trans. R. P. H. Green (Oxford, 1995), II, 60 pp. 82–4 and III, 80, p. 166.

[7] Augustine, *Exposition on Psalm 104*, *PL* 37, col. 1386.

[8] A. S. Napier, *The Old English Version of the Rule of Chrodegang together with the Latin Original* (London, 1916), p. 17.

[9] Symons, *Regularis Concordia*, p. 39.

[10] Lapidge and Winterbottom, *Life of St Æþelwold*, ch. 19, p. 34; Mark 16:17–18 is explicitly rejected by Ælfric as relevant to contemporary life in his *Ascension Day* Homily: *CH* I, pp. 345–53.

[11] D. A. Hinton, *A Catalogue of the Anglo-Saxon Ornamental Metalwork 700–1100 in the Department of Antiquities, Ashmolean Museum* (Oxford, 1974), pp. 63–7; D. MacLean, 'Snake Bosses and Redemption at Iona and in Pictland', in R. M. Spearman and J. Higgitt, *The Age of Migrating Ideas: Early Medieval Art in Northern Britain and Ireland* (Stroud, 1993), pp. 245–53.

[12] E. Kitzinger, 'Icons and Interlace: Form and Function in Early Insular Art', in Spearman and Higgitt, *Age of Migrating Ideas*, pp. 3–15.

jewellery may have protected against snakebite. Meaney shows how the account of *nædderwyrt* in the Old English *Herbarium* reveals its Mediterranean origin through its description of a range of exotic poisonous snakes that would not have been encountered locally, but it is clear that the people of Anglo-Saxon England believed they were endangered by many different kinds of *wyrmas*, and this recipe to make oneself *trum wið eall næddercyn* must have been appealing.[13] The *Herbarium* also passes on classically derived information about the herb called *dracentse* which is good for *ealra nædrena slite* (the bite of all snakes), it comes from dragon's blood and its root resembles a dragon's head.[14] This suggests a readiness to accept the principle of fighting like with like, using the virtues of the more powerful dragon to defeat the adder. One of the manuscripts of *Solomon and Saturn* calls the Paternoster *wyrma wlenco* (the pride of *wyrmas*, 82), implying that the prayer is such a treasure that *wyrmas* (dragons, perhaps) would want to guard it.[15] This is echoed in the Cotton *Maxims*: *Draca sceal on hlæwe, frod, frætwum wlanc* (It is the dragon's nature to inhabit the burial mound, wise, proud in treasure, 26), and well-omened dragons occur in the dream prognostics in Tiberius A iii: *gif he þince þæt he dracan geseo, god þæt biþ* (fol. 38v). Positive references thus cluster around the snake/serpent subcategory of *wyrm*; there are a few references of this kind to dragons, but none to maggots, earthworms or parasites. *Wyrmas* are not uniform, some are better than others, there are tensions within the group and one variety may be deployed to defeat another.

It is assumed here that all these creatures were understood as equally real and equally symbolic: *wyrmas* of every variety were useful conceptual tools.[16] Cavill's discussion of the monstrous creatures in the Cotton *Maxims* shows how the gnomic poems provide an interpretative structure by which new knowledge can be assimilated to existing models.[17] The Anglo-Saxons may not have encountered dragons, but they lived with an awareness of the possibility of encountering dragons, and they would have had the cultural equipment to make sense of them, had such an encounter taken place. The dragon in *Beowulf* inhabits an ambiguous moral space: he is powerful and he may be inimical, but he is not diabolical.[18] If the poet had wanted to make explicit the apocalyptic theme some critics have detected, he could have equated the dragon with the devil, just as he clarifies Grendel's descent from Cain.[19] Ælfric acknowledges the reality of these creatures,

[13] Meaney, *Anglo-Saxon Amulets and Curing Stones*, p. 51; M. A. D'Aronco and M. L. Cameron, *The Old English Illustrated Pharmacopoeia* (Copenhagen, 1998), pp. 49–83; Speake, *Anglo-Saxon Animal Art*, p. 85; Bonser, *Medical Background to Anglo-Saxon England*, p. 283.
[14] Cockayne, *Leechdoms* I, pp. 106–9.
[15] Menner, *Poetical Dialogues of Solomon and Saturn*, p. 84.
[16] P. Gravestock, 'Did Imaginary Animals Exist?', in D. Hassig (ed.), *The Mark of the Beast: The Medieval Bestiary in Art, Life and Literature* (New York and London, 1999), pp. 119–35.
[17] Cavill, *Maxims in Old English Poetry*, p. 181.
[18] J. R. R. Tolkien, 'Beowulf: The Monsters and the Critics', Sir Israel Gollancz Memorial Lecture 1936 (London, 1971, reprinted from *The Proceedings of the British Academy* 22), pp. 23–4.
[19] M. Green, 'Man, Time and Apocalypse in *The Wanderer, The Seafarer* and *Beowulf* JEGP 74 (1975), pp. 502–18; A. Brown, 'The Firedrake in *Beowulf*', *Neophilologus* 64 (1980), pp. 439–60.

including the *wyrmcynn*, *hyrned nædder* and *micel draca* among fierce desert creatures, together with wolves and lions.[20]

Wyrmas might also be more intimate companions. Analysis of human faecal material from ninth- to eleventh-century levels in York suggests that the city's residents had chronic if tolerable infestations of intestinal parasites, including mawworm (*Ascaris*) and whipworm (*Trichuris*).[21] This is reflected in the contemporary medical literature, although the recipes scattered liberally throughout the leechbooks associate *wyrmas* not only with nematodes but also with many other kinds of affliction.[22] This is not unique to Anglo-Saxon England; in her study of Spanish peasant communities in the 1970s, Cátedra was struck by the connexions drawn between worms, disease and the evil eye.[23] Nor is the association between *wyrmas* and disease limited to vernacular texts: in the *Life of King Edward* a woman with infected glands is cured when Edward causes pus, blood and *uermes* to emerge from holes in her face and throat (*a diversis foraminibus uermes cum sanie et sanguine egrediuntur*), suggesting that animate and inanimate matter were closely associated, or even that the *wyrmas* themselves were considered a disease.[24] This may have been a more powerful conviction in the vernacular than the Latinate tradition, however. There is a group of cognate words (noun *worms, wyrms*, adjective *gewyrms, wyrmsig*, verb *wyrmsan*), found in the leechbooks and glossing Latin words such as *lues, purulentus* and *putredo*, which suggests that these morbid substances and processes were thought of as having an intrinsically vermicular nature, and very few descriptions of the decaying corpse separate catabolic decay from the presence of *wyrmas*. Vercelli IV repeatedly associates the idea of being food for *wyrmas* with *geolstor* (pus or decaying matter).[25]

In none of the texts cited so far, not even the *Life of King Edward*, are the *wyrmas* or the associated diseases connected to the moral condition of the sufferer. There are some exceptions, however: we saw in the last chapter how Herod was punished for putting his faith in physicians rather than penitence. Earlier in this narrative, Ælfric provides a clinical description of the symptoms of Herod's *unasecgendlic* (indescribable) disease, which combines the experience of the diseased but living body, the corpse and the damned soul. It may be 'indescribable' but this does not deter Ælfric from conflating his sources to provide a detailed picture:

[20] *CH* I, VI, p. 230, lines 178–82.
[21] A. K. G. Jones, 'A Human Coprolite from 6–8 Pavement', in A. R. Hall *et al.*, *Environment and Living Conditions at Two Anglo-Scandinavian Sites* (London, 1983), pp. 225–9.
[22] 'There is hardly a symptom, from toothache to fits, that is not at one time or another ascribed to worms, in A.S. literature': Grattan and Singer, *Anglo-Saxon Magic and Medicine*, p. 99 n. 4.
[23] M. Cátedra, *This World, Other Worlds: Sickness, Suicide, Death, and the Afterlife among the Vaqueiros de Alzada of Spain* (Chicago, 1992), pp. 69–74.
[24] Barlow, *Life of King Edward*, p. 92.
[25] *Ne sie he næfre wyrma mete, ne to grimmum geolstre mote wyrðan*, line 126; *ðu eorðan lamb ⁊ dust ⁊ wyrma gifel, ⁊ þu wambscyldig fætels ⁊ gealstor ⁊ fulness ⁊ hræw*, lines 208–9; *hwi noldest ðu niman þara wyrma mete, ⁊ forlæten me fram þam fulan geolstre*, lines 248–9. Scragg, *Vercelli Homilies*, pp. 95–8.

he eal innan samod forswæled wæs and toborsten . . . Wæterseocnesse hine ofereode beneoðan þam gyrdle to ðan swiðe þæt his gesceapu maðan weollon, and stincende attor singallice of ðam toswollenum fotum fleow.[26]

he was all swollen together inside and bursting . . . Dropsy overran him under the girdle to the extent that his genitals swarmed with maggots, and stinking poison flowed incessantly from his swollen feet.

Ælfric is precise here about the creatures with which Herod was afflicted; he uses the unusual word *maða* (maggots), thus giving an exact picture of Herod's body bloated, stinking, liquescing and swarming with maggots. Ælfric also makes it explicit that Herod is having a foretaste of all the pains (*hwilcum suslum*) of hell, foremost among which is the attack by *wyrmas*. These subsets of the *wyrmcynn* are a powerful weapon in the homilist's repertoire, drawn on to intensify the horror of damnation.

The aggressive wyrm

It may be easier to see what Anglo-Saxon *wyrmas* are by looking at a part they do *not* play. In early modern religious writing, the worm is very often a metaphor for humility, something which has its ultimate source in biblical texts such as Psalm 21:7, 'I am a worm and not a man', where the psalmist presents himself as a figure of contempt, weak, vulnerable, grovelling in the dust.[27] To the Anglo-Saxons, *wyrmas* may be connected with humiliation: it is degrading to be associated with and devoured by the *wyrmas* of the grave. But the creatures themselves are not humble or impotent, and people do not identify themselves with them. Although Psalm 21 is translated into English (*ic eom wyrm and nales mon*) the metaphor of the humble *wyrm* is almost completely ignored by Anglo-Saxon writers. Overwhelmingly, their *wyrmas* are dangerous, mysterious and hungry.

At times *wyrmas* find themselves in company with carrion birds and wolves: *ðu wyrma gecow ⁊ wulfa geslit ⁊ fugle geter* (you thing chewed by *wyrmas* and bitten by wolves and torn by birds), the damned soul flings at its body in Vercelli IV.[28] The *wyrm* is thus associated with predators as well as scavengers, and in some ways it is the most implacable. By burying the corpse one attempts to protect it from the other beasts, but not from the *wyrm*, who hovers on the edge of the group of animals and birds frequently characterized as 'the beasts of battle', the wolf, raven and eagle, neither a full member of the club nor wholly excluded. In his discussion of the poetry where wolf, raven and eagle are linked to battles, Griffith suggests that the theme had its origins in 'a particularly morbid and macabre observation of real events'. The connexion to 'real events' is surely right, but Griffith implicitly disconnects poetry from continuing lived experience, thus underestimating its power. Late Anglo-Saxon England was full of wolves, ravens,

---

[26] *CH* I, V, p. 221, lines 125–34; *CH Comm.*, pp. 43–4.
[27] Pers. comm. Sheila Wright.
[28] Scragg, *Vercelli Homilies* IV, p. 100, lines 265–6.

eagles and battles, and these threats were part of ordinary life, neither 'morbid' nor 'macabre'. He goes on to argue that through repetition the image of birds and animals devouring human remains became 'formulaic' and 'fixed', implying that it thereby lost its power to distress.[29] However, the wider theme of the devouring of the human body is not confined to the 'beasts of battle motif'; it is found in so many different contexts that it is likely to express a source of ever-present anxiety, and in homilies, canon lawcodes, images and verse, we see the result of long struggles to make sense of an inherently hostile environment. Ravens take pleasure in the damned corpse in *Soul and Body*, they feast on the hanged man in *The Fortunes of Men*, Noah's raven pecks at the eyes of a severed head in London, BL Cotton Claudius B iv (fol. 15r). This last is a detail which has no scriptural support, and the severed head affixed to the front of the Ark is an apparently unique motif (Plate 4). When Ælfric wanted a striking image for greedy priests, the raven came to mind: *Sume preostas fægniað þonne men forðfarað, 7 gegaderiað hy to þam lice, swa swa grædige hremmas þær þær hy hold geseoð, on holte oþþe felda* (Some priests rejoice when men die, and they gather about the body, just like greedy ravens when they see a corpse in holt or field).[30] All these creatures were a necessary part of thinking about death, in battle and elsewhere, an image of unbridled and inappropriate appetite, but also part of everyday life, needing acknowledgement in a society that lived very close to the food chain.

The breakdown of the body after death is almost always expressed entirely in terms of being eaten by *wyrmas* or other animals, with the internally generated processes of decay apparently causing much less interest. Similarly, bodies in art may be shown in the process of being cut up or eaten but they are never shown rotting, and the repertoire of Anglo-Saxon artists does not include skulls or other human bones, not even Adam's skull at the foot of the Cross. The Newent Stone Book, with its stylized corpse in a coffin or sarcophagus, is as close as they come. An interesting iconographic omission, given that it is so present in the written sources, is the depiction of the dead body riddled with maggots, and in this Anglo-Saxon artists are very different from the artists of the later Middle Ages. It may be that there are early depictions of the threatened cadaver, but the artistic conventions are so different that they have not been identified.

The soul and body *Poems*

The image of the devouring *wyrm* is also prominent in *Soul and Body*.[31] Although the poem survives in both the Vercelli and the Exeter books, the two versions are not identical. Both describe the soul returning to address the body after death, but Exeter (E) deals only with the damned while Vercelli (V) follows this with a description of the saved (incomplete due to a missing leaf). It is impossible

---

[29] M. S. Griffith, 'Convention and Originality in the Old English "Beasts of Battle" Typescene', *ASE* 22 (1992), pp. 179–99, 184.

[30] *Councils*, p. 295.

[31] D. Moffat (ed. and trans.), *The Old English* Soul and Body (Woodbridge, 1990).

Plate 4: Noah's raven pecking a human head (London, British Library, MS Cotton Claudius B iv, fol. 15r). By permission of the British Library. There is no scriptural justification for this image, although there are later stories explaining that the raven failed to return to the Ark because it had found a corpse to eat. The naturalism of the image suggests the artist may have been drawing on personal observation.

to prove which version is earlier, but Moffat is convincing when he argues for the saved soul passage 'being a later, less inspired addition, probably not by the same poet'.[32] Despite its 'lesser inspiration', the additional passage on the blessed soul renders V much more complex, introducing the troubling idea that virtuous bodies also decay.[33]

The events in the poem common to E and V are set in the interim between death and the Last Judgement, with the damned soul compelled to return to its body every seventh night (9–14). It harangues the body for eighty-five lines, followed by a description of the body decaying and being devoured by *wyrmas*. The 'damned soul' poem is bracketed by short statements pointing out the universal applicability of its moral; in this, it resembles other poems designed to turn one's thoughts towards eternity, such as Cynewulf's *Fates of the Apostles* (Vercelli fols 52v–54r). The framing sentences and the structural resemblance to other poems support the argument that the 'damned soul' section originally stood alone.

The soul's journey here is not strictly one of separation from the body, as it loops continuously between *hellegrund* (the ground of hell) and the grave, echoing an idea in the 'Sunday Letter' homilies, that some of the souls in torment have a break from Saturday evening till dawn on Monday.[34] Wright cites a Latin text from CCCC, MS 279, which claims that after death the soul visits the place where it died, its grave, its birthplace and the site of its baptism, and that it returns to the grave every Sunday.[35] These suggest a widespread belief that the soul, periodically at least, could be closely linked to the body. Furthermore, the physical decay of the body is correlated to the moral decay of the soul. This is implicit in the soul's harangue when it insults the body, calling it *eorþan fylnes* (foulness of earth, 18a), *wyrma gifl* (food for *wyrmas*, 22b) and *wyrmum to wiste* (feast for *wyrmas*, 25a); it becomes explicit in the narrative passage describing the onslaught of the *wyrmas*:

> *Gifer hatte se wyrm þam þe geaflas beoð nædle scearpran. Se geneþeð to ærest ealra on þam eorðscræfe, he þa tungan totyhð ond þa toþas þurhsmyhð ond þa eagan þurhiteð ufon þæt heafod ond to ætwelan oþrum gerymeð, wyrmum to wiste.*[36]

> Gifer (Greed) is the name of the *wyrm* whose teeth are sharper than a needle. He is the first of all to venture into the grave; he tears the tongue and batters through the teeth and eats through the eyes into the head and makes room for the others at the abundant banquet, the feast for *wyrmas*.

The vividly personified Gifer (capitalized in E but not in V) is a very different creature from the *maðas* that infested Herod. His sharp teeth identify him as much with earthly and hellish serpents as with maggots, as he leads his criminal band

---

[32] Moffat, Soul and Body, p. 44.

[33] Quoted here from Moffat, with the damned soul section taken from E and the saved soul from V.

[34] Napier XLIII: *hellware . . . gif heo æfre fulluhtes onfangen hæfdon*, p. 211; Napier XLIV: *þa þa beoþ on witincgstowan, gef hi mid ænigan þingan Crist gegladodan*, p. 219; R. Priebsch, 'The Chief Sources of Some Anglo-Saxon Homilies', *Otia Merseiana* I (1899), pp. 129–47.

[35] Wright, *The Irish Tradition*, p. 258.

[36] Lines 116–22a.

(*hloþum*, 112a) to their reward, as they despoil (*reafiað*, 111a) the corpse. *Gifer* is an appropriate instrument of punishment for a body which had been *wiste wlonc* (proud at banquets, 39a), depriving the soul of its spiritual food, and is now itself *wyrmum to wiste*, its reversed position in the food chain reinforcing the message that being eaten by *wyrmas* is a manifestation of sin. Gifer and his cohorts are also described as *moldwyrmas* (71a), a word unique to this poem. A *moldwyrm* not only lives in the soil, it also devours organic material including human flesh and transforms it into soil. It is thus analogous to death itself, which has transformed the body into *eorðan fylnes* and *lames gelicnes* (image of clay, 19a).

The soul concludes by wishing that the body had been created a bird, a fish, an ox, a *wilddeor* (wild creature) or one of the *wyrmcynna*, rather than human and immortal (75–85). There is a logic to this list, moving from creatures of the air to creatures of the water, then to domesticated and herbivorous animals (the ox) and wild, probably carnivorous animals (the 'worst wild creature of the waste' should be the wolf), before concluding with creatures below earth's surface. Moffat translates *wyrmcynna* as 'dragonkind', but this passage is embedded in references to the *wyrmas* in the grave and Gifer and his legions of *reþe wyrmas* (fierce *wyrmas*, 111b) are probably 'the worst of *wyrm*-kind'. Better to be one of the *wyrmas* devouring human flesh than the damned flesh they devour.

The eating of the damned body is described in notably aggressive language. The narrative passage quoted above has that emphatic rhyme *totyhð... þurhsmyhð*, the soul observes *ond þec sculon moldwyrmas monige ceowan, seonuwan beslitan* (and many earth-*wyrmas* must chew you, slit the sinews, 71–2) and the narrator develops this in self-consciously gruesome detail:

> Biþ þæt heafod tohliden, honda toleoþode, geaflas toginene, goman toslitene, seonwe beoð asogene, sweora bicowen [fingras tohrorene: V only]. Rib reafiað reþe wyrmas, drincað hloþum hra heolfres þurstige.[37]

> The head is cracked open, the hands are dismembered, the jaws yawn, the gums are slit, the sinews are sucked, the neck chewed through, [the fingers shattered]. Cruel *wyrmas* plunder the ribs, in gangs they drink the corpse, thirsty for blood.

This battery of verbs and past participles conjures up the corpse swarming with *wyrmas* whose purposeful and varied activities are in contrast to the helplessness of *geomor gast* (mournful soul, 107a) and the corpse: *Ligeð dust þær hit wæs ne mæg him ondsware ænig secgan* (The dust lies where it was and cannot give him any answer, 104b–105). The relation of the body to the soul presents some challenges of interpretation, and again Godden's model of the *mod* embedded in the body is appropriate, although this is not among the texts he discusses.[38] The soul before death appears helpless, trapped in flesh (*flæsce bifongen*, 34a). The

---

[37] Lines 108–12.
[38] Godden, 'Anglo-Saxons on the Mind'; Moffat, Soul and Body, pp. 18–19 and 39–40; A. J. Frantzen, 'The Body in *Soul and Body I*', *Chaucer Review* 17 (1982), pp. 76–88; B. P. Kurtz, 'Gifer the Worm: An Essay towards the History of an Idea', *University of California Publications in English* 2/2 (1929), pp. 235–61.

body in life was entirely ignorant of the soul or Christ's sacrifice (27–30); although he had been baptized (85), he never took communion (41–2). Now the tables are turned, and the soul has a voice while the body is silenced, *dumb ond deaf* (64a). But if the body is entirely insensible the soul's return would be pointless, and the poet offers a pragmatic explanation for the body's failure to respond: *Bið seo tunge totogen on tyn healfe hungregum to hroþor; forþon heo ne mæg horsclice wordum wrixlan wið þone wergan gæst.*[39] The poem thus suggests, like so many other texts, that the body is silenced and immobilized but conscious.[40] There is no reference to the body experiencing pain, but this is also the case when the living body is damaged in battle in Anglo-Saxon poetry, and the assertion in *The Seafarer* that the corpse cannot feel pain (*ne sar gefelan*, 95) may be intended to counter a belief that it could.[41]

This implication of awareness in the dead and buried body is reinforced by the Vercelli section on the blessed soul, who has come to comfort the body during the tribulations of burial: *Forþan me a langaþ, leofost manna, on minum hige hearde þæs þe ic þe on þyssum hynðum wat wyrmum to wiste* (Therefore it distresses me continuously, most beloved of men, hard in my mind, that I know you to be in this humiliating state, a feast for *wyrmas*).[42] The soul advises the body not to sorrow (157), implying necessarily that the body is capable of sorrowing. The saved body, the soul's dearest friend (*wine leofesta*, 135), is clearly suffering in its *laðlic legerbed* (vile grave, 156), and there are two references to the *wyrmas*. But it is in a *legerbed*, a word whose positive connotations we explored in Chapter Four, and, in contrast to the almost gleeful cascade of descriptive language in the first part, here the *wyrmas* only *gretað* the body, an ambiguous verb which could mean 'attack', or no more than 'touch' or 'approach'. Frantzen, arguing that V is a unified composition, suggests that the poet 'could not disguise the inevitable truth that the good body too was decaying'.[43] But the poet could easily have denied that good bodies rot, as Ælfric does in his lives of Edmund and Æthelthryth.[44] There was nothing to stop him employing the language of saintly incorruption and omitting the *wyrmas* altogether. In Vercelli IV, the good soul at Doomsday asks to rejoin his body, adding *ne sie he næfre wyrma mete* (may he never be food for *wyrmas*), a locution that suggests the body is intact and has not been devoured in the grave.[45]

The saved soul passage in V is not a continuation of the poem on the damned soul. Rather, it is taking issue with it, expounding a radically different theology

---

[39] The tongue is torn into ten pieces as a pleasure for the hungry ones; this is why it cannot readily bandy words with the condemned soul. Lines 113–15.

[40] In contrast, a late fourteenth-century soul and body poem shows the corpse indignant, articulate and, indeed, mobile (*þe hed heued up . . .*): W. Linow (ed.), *þe Desputisoun bitwen þe Bodi and þe Sowle* (Erlangen and Leipzig, 1889), p. 75.

[41] I am grateful to Alice Cowen of the Centre for Medieval Studies, University of York, for sharing insights from her doctoral research into the Anglo-Saxon vocabulary of violence and pain.

[42] V, lines 153–5a.

[43] Frantzen, 'The Body in *Soul and Body I*', p. 83.

[44] *LS* I, XX, p. 439, lines 107–12; *LS* II, XXXII, pp. 327–8, lines 184–8.

[45] Scragg, *Vercelli Homilies* IV, p. 95, line 126.

of the corpse. The first section was written by someone who identified decay with individual sin, the second by someone who saw it as a side-effect of the Fall. The second echoes some of the language of the first, picking up the phrase *wyrmum to wiste* and matching *eorðfæt* (earth-vessel, 8a) with *lamfæt* (loam-vessel, 131a), but the effect is to neutralize the violent language characterizing the first part. The poem's message becomes more reassuring: 'Don't worry, beloved friend,' says the saved soul, 'you can be eaten by *wyrmas* in a loathsome grave, and nonetheless be saved.' In this reading, the Vercelli poem embodies the thoughts and arguments of several different people. There is the poet of the 'damned soul' poem, fascinated by the details of decay and convinced that such a terrible fate can only represent punishment. There is the poet of the 'saved soul' continuation, with his defiant response and reinterpretation, asserting the inevitability, even the irrelevance, of decay. Finally, there are the scribes of the Vercelli manuscript and at least one lost antecedent, who chose to keep these texts together despite their incompatibility, allowing us to catch a glimpse of a heated debate. The Vercelli compiler was also fascinated by the minutiae of death, burial and judgement and it is not surprising to find the more complex version of the poem here. The two parts of *Soul and Body* are a poetic parallel to the graves in late Anglo-Saxon cemeteries, showing the coexistence of different theories about decay and salvation.

Images of the wyrm

Turning from *wyrmas* in graves to *wyrmas* on gravestones, even more variety is apparent. Although there has been much recent speculation about the inspiration and technique of the sculptors of these images, the subject goes almost unmentioned in primary sources. Critical attention has focused on the stones from the north and east with human figures, but in many cases human figures are accompanied by *wyrm*-like creatures, and in many others the creatures stand alone. Can the *wyrm*-theories expressed in literature be used to shed light on some of these stones?

In *The Wanderer*, the speaker describes his own exile, the loss of his lord and friends, and the decay of the entire world. The speaker laments,

> *Eala beorht bune, eala byrnwiga, eala þeodnes þrym. Hu seo þrag gewat, genap under nihthelm swa heo no wære. Stondeð nu on laste leofre duguþe weal wundrum heah wyrmlicum fah. Eorlas fornomon asca þryþe, wæpen wælgifre, wyrd seo mære.*[46]

> Alas, the bright cup, alas the mail-clad warrior, alas the glory of the lord. That time is passed away, taken under night's helmet as if it had never been. There stands now, in the place of the beloved band of warriors, a wall high/deep with wonders [or 'wondrously high/deep'], adorned with the bodies of *wyrmas* [(or '*wyrm*-like [things]')]. The power of the spears, slaughter-greedy weapons, mighty fate, took the men away.

The speaker in *The Wanderer* once prized beautiful possessions and human relationships, but now he sees their heart-breaking unreliability, and he puts his

---

[46] Lines 94–100.

faith in God as his foundation. Not only the kinsman and the lord but the weapons, the treasure and the hall have all passed away, leaving in their stead only this mysterious wall associated with *wyrmas* and *wundor* (wonder), a couplet best interpreted as a description of graves and their monuments.[47] As in the riddles collected elsewhere in the Exeter Book, the reference to *wundor* here alerts the reader to approaching mysteries. The wall is *heah*, both high and deep, simultaneously standing above ground and drawing the onlooker's attention down into the grave. It stands in the footsteps of the men of the *duguþ*, literally replacing them, and the poet's use of the collective noun, *duguþ*, suggests that the wall may be a group of monuments. It is patterned (*fah*) with *wyrmlicum* (*wyrm*-bodies), just like so many of the grave-markers, some of which were once coated with gesso and brightly painted. An obvious visual correlative for the poem is an upright cross-shaft such as Middleton 2 (N. Yorkshire), with its lavishly accoutred warrior on one broad face and contorted beast on the other (Plate 5). To contemplate first one face and then the other is to re-enact the words of the poem: the *wyrm*-wall literally stands in the place of the warrior. In making this association with Middleton no claims are being staked about the origin of *The Wanderer*. Many stones from many places could be described as *wyrmlicum fah*.

The Wanderer reveals an overlap between the imaginative worlds of poems and gravestones. It gives us a poetic reading of the function of a gravestone: something more permanent than a human being, an aristocratic accessory, more enduring than goblets, armour and weapons, but still part of this transitory life. The *weal wundrum heah* bears no comparison with the *fæstnung* (foundation) provided by God at the end of the poem, although the same verb, *stondan*, describes both. *Wyrmlic* is a very rare and complicated word, occurring only here and in a confessional prayer, and the poet of *The Wanderer* may be punning on '*wyrm*-bodies' and '*wyrm*-like [things]', using it to signal the semantic range of *wyrm* and reminding his audience that, whether one is listening to or reading a poem, or contemplating a gravestone, one should be alive to the multiple meanings the word *wyrm* contains.[48]

Up to this point we have focused on the smaller end of the scale, the intestinal parasites of the leechbooks, the blow-fly maggots and sharp-toothed *moldwyrmas* of *Soul and Body* and Ælfric's sermon for the Nativity of the Holy Innocents. At the other end of the scale are the dragons killed by Beowulf and Sigurðr, great beasts that guard treasure and, in *Beowulf* and the Cotton *Maxims*, inhabit ancient barrows. We are not given many clues about their appearance: the *Beowulf* dragon shows that a creature may have wings and still be a *wyrm*, and some kinds of *wyrmas* (notably the arachnids) have legs. There are obvious dangers in applying the information derived from many different kinds of texts, whose intent

---

[47] I had developed and published a preliminary version of this argument before encountering Richard Bailey's suggestion along the same lines: *England's Earliest Sculptors*, p. 108; V. Thompson, 'Memory, Salvation and Ambiguity: A Consideration of Some Anglo-Scandinavian Grave-Stones from York', in H. Williams (ed.), *Archaeologies of Remembrance: Death and Memory in Past Societies* (New York, 2003), pp. 215–26.

[48] The prayer is in BL Royal 2 B v, fol. 190v and Tiberius A iii fol. 47r.

Plate 5: The ring-headed cross with warrior and dragon imagery from St Andrew's Church, Middleton (N. Yorkshire). Illustration: A. Pluskowski. This tenth-century cross shaft sets up an opposition between the warrior with his range of weapons and the dragon entangled in his own body, both within the framework of the cross. The iconography of this sculpture can be read as both secular and spiritual.

is nowhere to specify the anatomy of the *wyrm*, to the iconographic repertoire. Each image must be interrogated separately, and its qualifications for being a *wyrm* evaluated. Even with this proviso, there are probably as many kinds of *wyrm* in the visual repertoire as there are in the verbal, and only a sample can be discussed here.

This variety is clear in the stones from Yorkshire alone.[49] There are the winged beasts on slabs from the Minster and the sites of several of York's parish churches (St Olave, St Denys, St Mary Bishophill Junior), coupled in one example with interlace that terminates in animal heads. St Mary Bishophill Junior also provides an upright shaft with so-called 'exploded plant-scroll' undulating over one broad surface, and an interlace panel and a life-like snake on the other. Another stone from the Minster shows a man fighting two dragons, one of which is closely paralleled on a Crucifixion scene from St Mary Castlegate. Looking a little further afield, there are the Jelling-style dragons from Middleton in the Vale of Pickering, the naked men among snakes at Masham and Thornton Steward in Wensleydale, the dragon-headed end-beasts on hogbacks from the coast at Lythe, Easington and Barmston, the neatly coiled snakes at Crathorne, Melsonby and Forcett. Almost every kind of *wyrm* in written sources has its monumental parallel, and the Crathorne stone supports the idea that there is a structural grammar underpinning the images, with its life-like snake coiled on an upper panel and a winged dragon lower down on the same face.

The present discussion concentrates on a few stones and groups of stones from Yorkshire, counterbalancing the textual bias towards southern and western centres. Contextualizing these stones is deeply problematic. It is often assumed that the practice of Christianity had been seriously damaged by the Viking settlements in the north and east of England from the 860s and 870s onwards, particularly among the land-owning classes. In Chapter Two we noted Kilbride's complaint that the mechanics of Christianization had not been dissected sufficiently closely, but one could apply his criticisms with equal force to the reverse process. What pressure, applied at what level, for how long, does it take to detach a people from Christian buildings, hierarchy, calendar, saints, prayers and ceremonies? Answering these questions is hindered by ignorance of the extent to which Christianity had become discursive among the Northumbrian population, by the unknowable ratio of non-Christians to Christians, and by the lack of evidence for anyone actively trying to eradicate Christian practices or to replace them with a different belief system.[50] Dumville draws attention to the lack of surviving documents from early Anglo-Saxon Northumbria, arguing that 'that very absence speaks volumes for the nature of institutional discontinuity in the Anglo-Scandinavian period'.[51] Yet the archbishopric appears to function

---

[49] All examples are illustrated in J. Lang, *York and Eastern Yorkshire*, CASSS III, and *Northern Yorkshire*, CASSS VI.

[50] N. Lund, 'The Settlers: Where Do We Get Them From – And Do We Need Them?', in Bekker-Nielsen *et al.*, *Proceedings of the Eighth Viking Congress*, pp. 147–71.

[51] D. Dumville, 'Textual Archaeology and Northumbrian History subsequent to Bede', in D. M. Metcalf (ed.), *Coinage in Ninth-Century Northumbria*, BAR British Series 180 (1987), pp. 43–55, 52.

throughout, and when Archbishop Wulfhere removed from York to Addingham between 867 and 873 it may have been to escape warring Northumbrian factions as much as the Vikings.[52] The years immediately after 1066 may have been as devastating for the Northumbrian Church as the 860s and 870s, and the lack of surviving evidence need not be ascribed to a single event.[53] Kirby reviews the evidence for the Northumbrian State and Church prior to the 860s to 870s and concludes that we must not be misled by the poor documentary record nor the kingdom's subsequent collapse into thinking it was significantly less sophisticated than the other English kingdoms.[54]

The place of the stones with their various *wyrm* images in all this depends on how we read them. Are they the assertion of status by incoming Scandinavians with little understanding of Christianity, but who had seen and liked English and Irish monastic sculpture? Or do they manifest Christian ideas, as the eighth and earlier ninth century crosses did, but now erected on new sites and carrying evolving iconography? With the arrival of the Vikings Northumbria fractured along its old fault line of the Tees valley, reverting to what had been the separate polities of Bernicia in the north and Deira in the south. Bailey stresses the homogeneity of the pre-Viking sculpture, implying a common tradition based around the Northumbrian bishoprics of York, Hexham, Lindisfarne and Whithorn and contrasts it with the variety visible in the tenth-century stones of Deira, as well as the way that Bernicia, marked by the continuity of the House of Bamburgh and the community of St Cuthbert, retained the earlier traditions.[55] Does this suggest that the Deiran church was no longer behind the production of sculpture, or that they were commissioning different artists in new idioms? The conquerors of Deira quickly came to an accommodation with both the archbishop of York and the community of St Cuthbert, and the latter is said to have been behind the choice of Guthred as Deiran king in *c*. 883. When Guthfrith of York (possibly the same person) died in 895, he was buried in York Minster. Christian iconography appears soon afterwards on the York coinage of Sigfrid and Cnut, and the Danes accepted Alfred's nephew Æthelwold as king in 900. Despite attacks from West Saxon armies and the arrival in York of the Hiberno-Norse in the early decades of the tenth century, this is a story of continuity as much as disruption, although it is hard to see what this meant for church, congregation, faith or burial at a local level. These carved stones are our most direct source about Northumbrian religion across the period from around 800 to 950, embodying a long process of development and negotiation within the church and its response to the external stresses of civil war, invasion and associated regime changes. In order to understand what they mean both as funerary or memorial markers, and as part of the

---

52 R. Bailey, *Viking Age Sculpture* (London, 1980), pp. 40–2.
53 Abrams, 'Conversion and Assimilation', pp. 141–2.
54 Kirby, 'Northumbria in the Ninth Century', in D. M. Metcalf (ed.), *Coinage in Ninth-Century Northumbria*, pp. 11–25, 14–16.
55 J. Lang, 'Survival and Revival in Insular Art, Some Principles', in C. Karkov, R. T. Farrell and M. Ryan (eds), *The Insular Tradition* (New York, 1997), pp. 63–77, 73; Bailey, 'Chronology of Viking Age Sculpture in Northumbria'.

iconography of the *wyrm*, this broader picture must be taken into account. Referring to these stones as 'Anglo-Scandinavian' or 'Hiberno-Norse' disguises their complex references to earlier Northumbrian, Mercian and even Roman traditions. Such labels also imply an exclusive link between a mode of material culture and an ethnic category imposed by modern historians, which need not correspond to the complex and fluid nature of social groupings.[56] The signalling of ethnicity may not have been among the intentions of the patrons and sculptors of these stones, and even if it were, ethnicity can be a question of allegiance. If the rebellious West Saxon ætheling Æthelwold had died in York, rather than at the Battle of the Holme in 903, what kind of monument might have been raised over *his* grave?

Middleton: armed against the devil

The Middleton 2 cross-shaft, with its iconography of warrior and *wyrm*, comes from a church in the Vale of Pickering just south of the North York Moors, an area in which many parish churches preserve ninth- to eleventh-century sculpture.[57] This landscape of small parishes, some pre-dating the arrival of the Scandinavians, others newly established in the tenth century, indicates that any hiatus in pastoral care resulting from the change of regime in the 860s and 870s must have been slight.[58] Of thirty-five parishes in this part of Ryedale, twenty-nine had churches before 1100, and Faull argues that much of the grouping of farms and estates into parishes in Yorkshire was taking place at this time, with estates being rearranged and new churches founded.[59] Middleton is close to the postulated superior church at Pickering, and there is a prominent pre-Viking Age cross-head built into the west face of Middleton's early eleventh-century tower, suggesting either that an earlier church stood on the site or that the cross had been brought from elsewhere. Abrams draws attention to recent work on iconic re-use of Swedish rune-stones, built prominently into churches, which may represent powerful local families asserting their connexion with the new building.[60]

Middleton 2 is the most complete stone, but there are other fragmentary ones, very similar although apparently less well armed, which Bailey has shown come from the same 'warrior' template.[61] Middleton 2's stylized human figure (universally interpreted as male) wears a pointed hat or helmet and a belt-knife and is surrounded by axe, spear, shield and sword. Two balls, one above each shoulder, have been interpreted as the finials of the back of his chair.[62] He does not hold any

[56] S. Lucy, *The Anglo-Saxon Way of Death* (Stroud, 2000), pp. 174–86.
[57] Kirkdale, Kirkbymoorside, Sinnington, Middleton, Pickering and Ellerburn. Lang, *York and Eastern Yorkshire*, pp. 40–2.
[58] Hadley, *Northern Danelaw*, pp. 288–9.
[59] R. Morris, *Churches in the Landscape* (London, 1989), p. 144; M. Faull, 'Late Anglo-Saxon Settlement Patterns in Yorkshire', in Faull (ed.), *Studies in Late Anglo-Saxon Settlement*, pp. 129–42, 131.
[60] Abrams, 'The Conversion of Scandinavia', p. 120.
[61] R. Bailey, *Viking Age Sculpture*, pp. 247–9.
[62] Lang, 'Late Pre-Conquest Crosses in Ryedale', p. 18.

of his weapons but is empty-handed, and the weapons appear to float as if in free-fall around him. On the reverse is a dragon that shows signs of Scandinavian influence, bound in tendrils emerging from its body to lock legs, torso and jaws. The shaft is topped by a ring-headed cross. Although there is no inscription, it is usually seen as commemorative, and probably as marking a burial.

It was suggested above that the poet of *The Wanderer* was signalling the multiple meanings that these stones could encode. A symbolic object may intentionally transmit different messages to different audiences, and appeal on many levels;[63] such an object would have been extremely useful in tenth-century Yorkshire, in a Church which must to a great extent have been a missionary Church, even though its activities leave almost no documentary record. Other than the few references to the baptism of kings and other leaders cited above, there are no references to the process of conversion of pagans in the Anglo-Scandinavian polities, or indeed to the maintenance of Christianity among the indigenous inhabitants, although the evidence of the stones, both iconographically and in their association with churches, suggests that Christianity was maintained in some form.[64] As Urbańczyk points out, Christianity is not socially acquired but learnt, not only in the 'conversion' generation but continuously, and its practice is predicated on the sacraments, dependent in turn on the presence of priests and access to a bishop.[65] Wulfstan of York, addressing the clergy of his diocese, visualizes every priest as a missionary: did the tenth-century archbishops do the same?[66] If so, this would provide one possible explanation of why there are no narratives of heroic West Saxon missionaries setting off to bring the faith to the Danes.

This is speculation; the stones are silent and there is no contemporary evidence that specifies whether lay or clerical hands and minds were behind the production of these stones.[67] The numerous ring-headed crosses, of which Middleton is one, have been connected to the Hiberno-Norse expansion into the north of England of the first half of the tenth century. While it is impossible to know the precise religious affiliation of any of their carvers or patrons, it should be stressed that this sculpture was inspired by Irish and English Christian traditions, erected in sites that were to become churchyards (and perhaps sometimes already were), and popular among people who found the cross an appropriate form on which to express their ideas. Middleton 2 is above all a Christian symbol. Although Lang suggests that the Middleton cross-heads 'may have been regarded simply as the conventional terminal for a standing shaft' and that 'the eye is held not so much by the cross as by the illustrative panel', the warrior and the dragon vanish if the cross is viewed in silhouette, their presence contained within and subordinated to

[63] C. Hicks, *Animals in Early Medieval Art* (Edinburgh, 1993), pp. 8–9.
[64] Hadley, *Northern Danelaw*, p. 310.
[65] P. Urbańczyk, 'Christianisation of Early Medieval Societies: An Anthropological Perspective', in Crawford, *Conversion and Christianity*, pp. 129–33; Abrams, 'Conversion and Assimilation', p. 139.
[66] Wulfstan, Canons of Edgar 16: *ꝥ riht is þæt preosta gehwylc Cristendom geornlice lære ꝥ ælcne hæþendom mid ealle adwæsce. Councils*, pp. 312–20.
[67] Cramp, *Studies in Anglo-Saxon Sculpture*, p. 148.

the cross, the embodiment of Christ.[68] The cross-head, measured from top to bottom, is almost exactly the same height as the shaft that supports it. The warrior has come in for most modern critical attention because he is a more unusual survival than the cross, but would contemporaries necessarily have had the same priorities? It is interesting that the warrior is not brandishing or even grasping any of his kit, he is armed but neither aggressive or even active. The weapons represented on this stone might simply refer to its marking the grave of a man of warrior status, or they might have a more symbolic level of meaning. The metaphor of the weapons of faith is widespread, drawn from biblical sources such as Exodus 15:3 (*Dominus quasi vir pugnator*, The Lord is a man of war), Psalm 34:2 (*Adprehende arma et scutum et exurge in adiutiorum mihi*, Take arms and shield and rise to help me) or the extended metaphor of Ephesians 6. The last of these texts is an enduringly influential exposition of the weaponry of the spiritual warrior, the *lorica iustitiae*, *scutum fidei*, *galea salutis* and *gladium spiritus* (breastplate of justice, shield of faith, helmet of deliverance and sword of the spirit). This is cited by Ælfric and developed by Wulfstan, who adds that priests are to put aside worldly weapons and *mid gastlican wæpan campian wið deofol*.[69] In an Ash Wednesday homily from CCCC 190, this theme becomes *Nimað earnostlice rihtwissnisse byrnan and soðre hælo helm and þæs halgangastes sweord, þæt is godes word* (Earnestly take the mailcoat of righteousness and the helmet of true salvation and the sword of the Holy Ghost, that is God's word). In the frontispiece to the New Minster *Liber Vitae* of 1031, Cnut is shown with his right hand supporting a gold altar cross and his left hand on the hilt of his sword, indicating that at least one newly arrived Danish immigrant got the message.

The warrior and the dragon occupy identical panels on either broad face of the cross-shaft, suggesting a dialogue or opposition. If the warrior is armed with the weapons of faith, then the dragon could refer to the devil of Revelation 20:2. To suggest this reading is not to deny the possibility of others, it merely asserts one plausible contemporary response. The soul, defended against the dragon-devil, within the protection of the cross, in life, at death and at Doomsday: this is an interpretation of Middleton 2 that might occur to a priest or biblically minded layman contemplating the stone. The warrior may also be an incarnation of the *lorica* (breastplate) genre of prayer, in which protection for every part of the body is separately invoked.[70] The *lorica* has strong Irish associations, a textual analogue to the ring-headed cross with which Middleton 2 is surmounted.[71] It is also notable that the warrior's arm-pits and the spaces between his neck and shoulders have been drilled out in exaggerated circles; this may simply be a

---

[68] Lang, 'Late Pre-Conquest Sculptures in Ryedale', p. 20.

[69] Ælfric's Letter to Wulfstan (2a); Wulfstan adds: 'fight against the devil with spiritual weapons'. Only in CCCC 201, Whitelock, Brett and Brook, p. 299.

[70] For example 'Lorica of Loding' with vernacular gloss: A. B. Kuypers (ed.), *The Prayer Book of Aedeluald the Bishop, Commonly Called the Book of Cerne* (Cambridge, 1902), pp. 85–8; 'Lorica of Gildas', Grattan and Singer, *Anglo-Saxon Magic and Medicine*, pp. 130–46 (BL Harley 585), is glossed in English and refers to God as *helm hælo* and *byrne*.

[71] Wright, *The Irish Tradition*, p. 99.

construction technique, but it also draws attention to the shape of the warrior's body as an echo of the drilled-out cross above him.

Compared to the theological complexities expressed on Northumbrian crosses of earlier centuries, the interpretation suggested above is extremely simple. However, this makes sense in the light of the very different audience that is being envisaged. The inhabitants of tenth-century Middleton might have found it hard to respond to the iconographic programmes of the eighth-century crosses from Ruthwell or Rothbury, lacking the training to unlock their complex liturgical and scriptural references.[72] The crosses associated with their own Church were transmitting simpler messages to an audience arguably illiterate in both Latin and the vernacular, untutored in the hymns and psalms of the offices, an audience some of whom might be the children of converts or even newly baptized themselves. The messages were also being transmitted in a contemporary idiom: the panoply wielded by the Middleton 2 warrior was a familiar one and the imagery simultaneously refers to both the spiritual and the social identity of the (presumably locally wealthy and powerful) man above whose grave it may have stood. Here is a man who can look after himself very well, in life and death.

There are many stones with warriors on from the north of England and their iconographies vary widely, suggesting that they do not always mean the same thing. The mid-ninth-century stone from St Mary Bishophill Junior in York shows that there was an earlier tradition of such imagery: two laymen, one with a horn and the other with a sword, stand on one broad face, while the narrow faces display plant-scroll and a ribbon beast. Secular human figures and perhaps also secular patronage were part of local monumental culture before Northumbria's fall to the Viking armies, challenging the idea that either the iconography or the social context of the Middleton stones was a new development.[73] Alcuin's dissatisfaction with the behaviour of Archbishop Eanbald in 801 suggests that the latter's archdiocese may already have been receptive to lay ideas; Alcuin complains that Eanbald has 'landed possessions', he has been 'harbouring the king's enemies', coveting the wealth of others and has too great 'a number of thegns in his retinue'.[74]

Middleton also needs to be compared to the Nunburnholme stone from the Yorkshire Wolds, on which a seated man, with sword and helmet or possibly halo, appears (in the cross's original arrangement) on a panel above a very similar figure, also seated and holding a rectangular object, probably a book, identical to that held by the Christ Child elsewhere on the same stone. A visual analogy is being drawn here between the two men's accessories. Ælfric's pastoral letters reiterate the common idea of a priest's books as his spiritual weapons, an image that also circulated in the *Capitula* of Theodulf, which describes *rædinga haligra*

[72] J. Hawkes, 'The Rothbury Cross: An Iconographic Bricolage', *Gesta* 35/1 (1996), pp. 77–94; J. Hawkes, 'Anglo-Saxon Sculpture: Questions of Context', in J. Hawkes and S. Mills (eds), *Northumbria's Golden Age* (Stroud, 1999), pp. 204–15.

[73] Lang, *York and Eastern Yorkshire*, p. 84; R. Cramp, 'The Anglian Tradition in the Ninth Century', in Lang, *Anglo-Saxon and Viking Age Sculpture*, pp. 1–32, 10.

[74] *EHD* I, p. 797.

boca as *þa wæpena* with which the devil is defeated.[75] Cockayne prints a charm/ prayer from CCCC, MS 41 invoking the protection of the *godspellboc* in terms of armour and weapons: *Mattheus helm Marcus byrne leoht lifes rof Locos min swurd scearp and scirecg scyld Iohannes wuldre gewlitegod* (Matthew be my helmet, Mark my mail-coat, shining, protector of life, Luke my sword, sharp and bright-edged, John my shield, brightened with glory).[76] The gospels are invoked here as protection against *þa laþan se me lyfes eht* (the foe that hunts my life), and we might also connect this to the imagery of the Newent Stone Book. Like the serpent, the armed warrior is an image whose complexity Augustine explores in *De Doctrina Christiana*, showing how the symbolism of shield and breast-plate shift according to context.[77] The warrior and his terrible foe at Middleton refer to secular power and protection, certainly, but that need not prevent them from also embodying more subtle concepts. Hines speaks of Anglo-Scandinavian culture as 'consciously articulated at the highest social and most sophisticated artistic level, not simply the confusion of cultures in contact': the people who made and viewed these stones were doubtless capable of reading much denser symbolic messages than those postulated here.[78]

Masham: naked before God

A very different *wyrm*-related message is proclaimed by a broadly contempo-rary stone originally from Masham in Wensleydale, sixty kilometres west of Middleton (Plate 6). Masham is well known for its exceptional late eighth- to early ninth-century carved column and may have been a very important church, although its status in the later Anglo-Saxon period is unknown.[79] The surviving section of the tenth-century shaft has similar scenes on its two broad faces, on both of which there is a stylized naked or nearly naked man, surrounded by approaching snakes, his arms raised apparently in prayer and his penis exposed, and Lang suggests that stones from nearby Coverham, Spennithorne and Thornton Steward are by the same artist.[80] He entertains, without whole-heartedly endorsing, the idea that Masham and the fragmentary piece from North Otterington might represent the torments of the damned in hell, as does the much earlier and grander Rothbury Cross, which, as Hawkes argues, depicts 'the serpents and monsters that constantly attack the genitals and devour the deformed souls of the Damned', in a manner reminiscent of the fate of Herod.[81]

75 *He sceal habban eac þa wæpna to þam gastlicum weorce, ær þan þe he beo gehadod, þæt synd þa halgan bec: saltere ⁊ pistolboc, godspellboc ⁊ mæsseboc, sangbec ⁊ handboc, gerim ⁊ passionalem, penitentialem ⁊ rædingboc. Councils*, pp. 206–7; Sauer, *Theodulfi Capitula*, p. 309.
76 Cockayne, *Leechdoms* I, p. 390.
77 Augustine, *De Doctrina Christiana* III, 82–3, p. 169.
78 Hines, 'Scandinavian English: A Creole in Context', p. 417.
79 Lang, *Northern Yorkshire*, p. 171; Hadley, *Northern Danelaw*, pp. 133 and 257.
80 Lang, *Northern Yorkshire*, pp. 49–50, 83 (Coverham 1), 172 (Masham 3), 198 (Spennithorne 1), 210 (Thornton Steward 2).
81 *Ibid.*, p. 186; Hawkes, 'Rothbury Cross', p. 90.

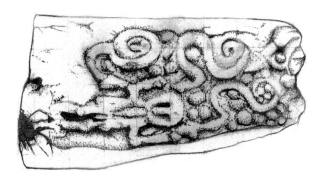

Plate 6: The cross-shaft from St Mary's Church, Masham (N. Yorkshire), present whereabouts unknown. Illustration: A. Pluskowski. The unusual nudity of these figures, surrounded by serpents, evokes the dead person facing the Last Judgement 'naked but for his good deeds'.

153

It may be that, at Masham at least, no conventional Christian story is being illustrated, but what these stones do represent is the work of a man with a great interest in *wyrmas*. Unsophisticated artistic technique could express complex ideas, as Bailey shows in his discussion of the stone from Minnigaff (Dumfriesshire).[82] Any interpretation of the Masham Stone has to take into account its fragmentary nature, but it is unusual to have such similar figural scenes on both broad faces of a shaft, presumably a cross-shaft since it tapers, although no part of the head remains. The only immediately noticeable difference between the two scenes is that the figure on face A has small round stumps for hands, while the figure on face B either has his four fingers spread or is holding something comb-like in his right hand (his left hand has disappeared where the stone has been re-dressed).[83] It is also unusual to have men with exposed genitalia in pre-Conquest art of any medium.[84] Naked men and snakes are again found in conjunction on the stone from Thornton Steward, although here the different faces have very different scenes, with a contorted naked man and three figures (only heads surviving) on one face, and a naked man with a snake on the other.[85] All this suggests that, while the carver had no great technical skill, he did have a strong and consistent idiom and project.

In his discussion of the Masham Stone, Lang says that 'the snakes are associated with and in proximity to the humans, they do not attack them, nor do they entangle themselves . . . it is possible that the snakes are simply decorative fillers'. The evidence for the significance of the imaginative role played by *wyrmas* adduced so far in this chapter demonstrates the inherent improbability of this last comment. On this stone they may not 'attack' or 'entangle' the naked praying figures, but they do approach them closely, nuzzling the men's hands and elbow, threading and coiling their way through a multitude of pellets. Whereas on the Rothbury Cross the serpents direct their attack against the exposed genitalia, they do not do so at Masham, which supports the idea that these are not souls suffering in hell. The Rothbury Cross is a didactic and contemplative monument rather than a funerary one, a context in which images of the damned are much more appropriate.

The nakedness of the Masham figures gives them an air of vulnerability, with only their arms upraised in prayer to defend them. Discussing the North Otterington fragment, Lang cites *Christ and Satan, hwilum nacode men winnað ymb wyrmas* (sometimes naked men strive with *wyrmas*, 131) from Satan's speech describing hell.[86] Bailey uses the same line to explain the scene of a bound man

---

[82] R. Bailey, 'Ambiguous Birds and Beasts: Three Sculptural Puzzles in South-West Scotland', Fourth Whithorn Lecture (Whithorn, 1995: no page numbering).

[83] Cf. the combing gesture depicted on the seventh-century Frankish Niederdollendorf stone: E. James, *The Franks* (Oxford, 1988), pp. 142–3.

[84] H. Cowdrey, 'Towards an Interpretation of the Bayeux Tapestry', in R. Gameson (ed.), *The Study of the Bayeux Tapestry* (Woodbridge, 1997), pp. 93–110, 98.

[85] Thornton Steward 2: Lang, *Northern Yorkshire*, p. 210.

[86] Lang, *Northern Yorkshire*, p. 186.

among serpents from Great Clifton (Cumbria).[87] However, this use in *Christ and Satan* is a near-unique reference to the combination of hell, nudity and *wyrmas*, and if we concede the value of using texts preserved in southern manuscripts to gloss northern sculpture, then it is worth looking to see what Anglo-Saxon *nacodnesse* looks like.

Most references are to nudity in the context of death and coming judgement, describing the newly dead soul going forth naked but for its sins.[88] Ælfric's *Assumptio Iohannis* combines this with the idea that we were born naked, that common motif in confessional formulae, and tells the story of John the Baptist raising a man from the dead. John commands the mourners to *unwindan þæs cnihtes lic*, in an obvious parallel with the confessional and penitential motif of the raising of Lazarus where the shroud symbolizes sin and the baring of the body represents absolution. The idea of going naked to Doomsday blends into the commonest context in which nakedness is discussed, 'clothing the naked' as one of the seven corporal acts of mercy for which Christ congratulates the saved. In parallel, He excoriates the sinners for their neglect, identifying Himself among the poor and naked whom they have failed to clothe (Matthew 25:42–3), thus associating nudity with poverty, charity and the presence of Christ in every human being.[89] This is a common scene both in Ælfric's work and the anonymous homilies, and it is also regularly cited in prescriptive texts such as the Benedictine Rule and the *Capitula* of Theodulf, suggesting that where the Southumbrian church was concerned it might be encountered in almost any environment. These themes are blended in the anonymous addition to one of Ælfric's supplementary homilies:

> swa þam menn dyde þe wurde færinga nacod beforan eallum folce, 7 nyste þonne mid hwam he his sceamigendlican bewruge: swa him byð on Domesdæg[90]

> just as the man does who suddenly finds himself naked in front of everybody, and has no idea with what he might hide his blushes: that is what it will be like for him on Doomsday.

This passage sets up a telling juxtaposition of the body embarrassed by nakedness and the much more deeply shamed soul. Although the idea of shame at Doomsday is common, no other writer connects fear of Judgement with the everyday anxiety of being seen naked in public. The cumulative evidence, positive and negative, suggests that nudity carried an aura of profound shame and vulnerability; this was partly, no doubt, owing to the Judaeo-Christian tradition, but the texts imply that this was a deeply felt anxiety, not only one acquired from books or sermons.

The nudity of the Masham figures thus intersects with a complex of ideas about shame, poverty, charity, vulnerability, death and burial. These naked and endangered figures could represent the interim state of either soul or body, but the round

---

87 Bailey, *Viking Age Sculpture*, p. 140; R. Bailey and R. Cramp, *Cumberland, Westmorland and Lancashire North-of-the-Sands*, CASSS II, p. 111.
88 For example *CH* I, IV, p. 210, lines 125–6; *CH* I, XXXVIII, p. 513, lines 184–5.
89 *Supp.* I, XI, p. 440, line 442.
90 *Supp.* II, XXVII, p. 779, lines 117–20.

pellets through which the *wyrmas* move are reminiscent of the *greot 7 molde 7 wyrmas* of the grave in Vercelli IX, and the evidence for burial practices with penitential associations suggests that we are to identify the Masham figures with the corpse. Their failure to attack the men echoes the behaviour of the *wyrmas* in the 'saved soul' part of *Soul and Body*: like them, the Masham *wyrmas gretað* the bodies rather than devouring them. Texts and sculpture alike explore the idea of the human being defenceless and vulnerable after death. If this stone is a grave-marker, it is making a plea for intercessory prayer on behalf on the man buried here, appealing directly to the sense of shared humanity and the emotional and religious sensibilities of the onlooker. The Masham Stone may thus fill the gap left by the apparent absence of early medieval depictions of the *wyrm*-menaced corpse, and work in an analogous, though unrelated, way to the cadaver tombs of the fourteenth and fifteenth centuries.

The contrast between the men represented on the Middleton and Masham Stones is extraordinary, the former a one-man-band of early medieval weaponry, the latter naked and defenceless. But the messages they encode are closer than they appear at first, since both draw on widespread ideas about the meaning of the clothed and naked human body, based on authoritative Christian tradition and indigenous custom. Masham in particular is, in its own way, as radical a theological statement as the Gosforth Cross, which juxtaposes images of the doom of pagan gods with the Crucifixion. Masham confronts contemporary anxieties head on, tapping into a rich seam of fear about public shame and nakedness and exploiting it to generate both compassion and contrition in the viewer.

The York Metropolitan School: draca sceal on hlæwe, frod, frætwum wlanc

The next stones under consideration come from the site of York Minster and some of York's smaller churches. The Minster stones are from the cemetery underlying the foundations of York's cathedral, which was moved to its current site by Archbishop Thomas of Bayeux in the later eleventh century. These Norman foundations cut diagonally across the ruins of the Roman military headquarters building and an Anglo-Scandinavian cemetery which lay within the space of the former courtyard of the *principia*; this cemetery was aligned to the north-east–south-west Roman grid system, rather than east–west. Norton argues that this cemetery represents lay burials to the south of the pre-Conquest cathedral, which was also on the Roman lay-out, and that the standing parish church of St Michael-le-Belfry, which adjoins the burial ground, had its origins in a cemetery chapel dedicated to the archangel.[91] This may be the cemetery where Guthfrith was buried on his death in 895.[92] The pre-Conquest cathedral has not yet been located, and its precise relationship to this cemetery is unknown, but it is likely that there was a close association and the Minster priests would have been responsible for the funerals of those buried here. When the Normans remodelled

---

[91] Norton, 'The Anglo-Saxon Cathedral at York'.
[92] Campbell, *Chronicle of Æthelweard*, p. 51; *EHD* I, p. 261.

this area, they broke up some of the gravestones for re-use as building rubble, while the southern part of the cemetery was cobbled over, with several carved grave slabs preserved *in situ* above their burials.

However, this was not the first time some of these stones had been re-used. Although the layer preserved by the Norman cobbling was early to mid-eleventh century, many of the stones were late ninth- to early tenth-century in design. It was clear that they had been re-used rather than simply retained as some of the graves were also marked at the head and foot by smaller upright stones which had been cut down from other early slabs. The York site thus preserves evidence from two different phases of the cemetery's life, the early tenth century when York was the headquarters of an independent Anglo-Scandinavian statelet, and a century or more later, when the cathedral was associated with committed men like Wulfstan II (1002–23) and Ealdred (1060–9), after York had been assimilated by the expansionist West Saxon kingdom to the south.

The stones from York Minster fall into several groups, the largest and finest of which is the one which Lang collectively ascribes to the York Metropolitan School. Lang defined the criteria and numbered the stones belonging to this group, which also includes stones or fragments from several of the city's parish churches, and his numbering is followed here. These stones are much more accomplished in design and execution than the Yorkshire stones considered so far, suggesting that the carvers' patrons were on a social and cultural par with their approximate contemporaries who commissioned the gravestones with stylized foliage from Æthelflæd's church of St Oswald in Gloucester.

Nearly all of these stones are slabs rather than shafts, and they are mostly massive, with York Minster (YM) 35 the longest at 188 cm in length; the exception where size is concerned is the stone from All Saints' Pavement, which is complete but only 85 cm long. Many may have had their dimensions dictated by the sources of the stone, as they are mostly Roman-quarried ashlar blocks, with one or two probably re-cut sarcophagus lids, and one (YM 37) originally a Roman half-column. None of the York Metropolitan School stones carries any inscription, nor is there any smooth surface for a painted text, and the inference is that they only ever conveyed an iconographic message, unlike the stone from St Maurice, Winchester, on which runic lettering was cut and then painted.[93] The decorative elements on the stones are laid out in a variety of ways, with the design divided into two panels on some stones (All Saints' Pavement, probably St Denys 1), and four panels on others (YM 35, 37, 38, 39 and St Olave 1a), while some are too truncated or fragmentary to conclude definitively about the original layout (YM 36, 40, St Mary Bishophill Junior). All but one of the York Metropolitan School stones (YM 39) share the motif of the 'York winged beast', a winged and maned biped with antecedents in pre-Viking Age English sculpture. This is particularly clear on YM 38 (Plate 7). Several of the stones are so similar that it seems certain that they come from not only the same workshop but the same

---

[93] B. Kjølbye-Biddle and R. Page, 'A Scandinavian Rune-Stone from Winchester', *Antiquaries Journal* 55 (1975), pp. 389–94.

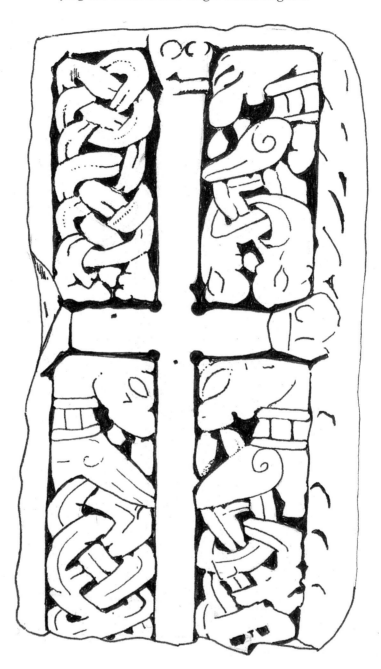

Plate 7: York Metropolitan School, York Minster 38 (Yorkshire Museum, York). Drawing: V. Thompson. This is one grave-slab of a group of about a dozen similar stones, nearly all from York and probably from the same workshop, active around 900. Their use of elaborate animal imagery and the ambiguity of their invocation of the cross may shed light on the complexities of belief in Anglo-Danish York.

template and even the same hand. York in the late ninth and early tenth centuries was a fast-growing mercantile centre, with its own kings, situated in a web of trade routes that stretched west to Chester and Dublin and north-east to Scandinavia and beyond, as far as Byzantium. It was certainly the largest and possibly the only city in Yorkshire.[94] New churches were being founded, presumably by local grandees under the aegis of the archbishops, and York's stone workshops could have been patronized by clients from the political, merchant and ecclesiastical elites, if indeed it is possible to differentiate between these classes in any meaningful way. A crowded, multi-cultural city full of competing interests is likely to have been a violent and edgy place, and both Church and State authorities may have found keeping the peace a challenge. However, this task of integration must have been made easier because, for all their differences, the various different groups in York's society shared a huge percentage of their broader cultural and symbolic language, and a wide repertoire of animal art was part of that common inheritance.[95]

Just as the armed warrior embraces both secular and spiritual interpretations, so does the dragon, and in this environment it may have seemed a particularly appropriate motif for a grave. In a discussion of imagery on Swedish runestones, which are also rich in dragons, Lager suggests a parallel with the densely packed, riddling images of *kenningar*, where the audience is challenged to solve apparent contradictions and word-games in order to reach the deeper meaning they conceal.[96] This is an interpretative mode which had long been familiar in England; Webster defines 'a fondness for visual riddles [which] goes back into pagan Germanic culture . . . [and] a fascination with learned verbal games – word play, encryption, the complexities of orthography and of parallel scripts' as fundamental to Anglo-Saxon Christianity.[97] This way of thinking was not a learned import but an ingrained way of understanding the world and reinventing it through art, common at some level to several of the cultures of north-western Europe.

The York winged beasts are not the only defining characteristic of the York Metropolitan School workshop. As noted above, all the larger stones are divided into either two or four panels, arrangements that result in considerable challenges of interpretation. Discussing the four-panelled stones, Lang notes that the 'minster crosses appear more like borders than Christian symbols', but does not further explore the problems which this kind of ambiguity could cause.[98] Where the dividing borders meet the edge of the stone they terminate in a stylized inward-facing head consisting of eyes and muzzle. YM 39 has four beast-inhabited panels, separated length-wise by a long spine, but the upper and lower sections of the stone are separated not by a straight cross-bar (as in e.g. YM 38)

[94] Faull, 'Late Anglo-Saxon Settlement Patterns', pp. 129–42, 137.
[95] Hicks, *Animals in Early Medieval Art*, pp. 195–210.
[96] L. Lager, 'Art as a Reflection of Religious Change: The Process of Christianization as Shown in the Ornamentation on Runestones', in Pluskowski, *Early Medieval Religion*, pp. 117–32.
[97] L. Webster, 'The Iconographic Programme of the Franks Casket', in Hawkes and Mills, *Northumbria's Golden Age*, p. 227–8.
[98] Lang, *York and Eastern Yorkshire*, p. 39.

but by curling lateral limbs which terminate in animals heads, one full-face, the other profile. If the four-panelled stones are crosses, this implies that the patrons of YM 39, All Saints' Pavement and St Denys 1 chose to reject a cross-based design.[99] This is entirely plausible, given the complexity of symbolism (swords, hammers, ravens, crosses, hands, the name of St Peter) which appears on York's coinage at the time, mirroring the rapid reversals of regime the city was experiencing, and hinting at the richness of its culture, now largely invisible to our eyes.[100] If the four-panelled stones are intended not as crosses but as borders with animal-head terminals, they look so like crosses that they would be sending out contradictory messages. In the end, it is impossible to be dogmatic about whether the four-panel designs embody crosses or not. The stones must remain ambiguous and open-ended, and perhaps that is how their designers planned them. An onlooker who wanted to see a cross would see one; a patron who wanted a cross could commission a stone like Clifford St 1, in which the cross is emphasized with interlace and a central boss. In some ways, the York Metropolitan School stones are theologically neutral, their decoration drawing on secular rather than ecclesiastical wells of inspiration. What *is* clear is that, crosses or not, the York winged beasts, as well as the associated beast chains, animal-head interlace and terminals, had a wide appeal.

No two of these stones are exactly identical, though YM 35 and 37 appear only to differ in details of their interlace. This could suggest that motifs were added at random, but, given the quality of the carving and the sophistication of the postulated clientele, it seems more likely that each stone represents the outcome of a unique and complex negotiation between craftsman and client. It is also worth reiterating at this point that we do not see these stones as their first owners saw them, and the addition of plaster and paint would make them even more various than they do now. This mixture of similarity and difference also suggests an underlying grammar to the ornament; perhaps, even without inscriptions, each stone successfully identified the individual buried there to its intended audience. It might also mean that there were links of kinship or affinity between the people commemorated by York Metropolitan School stones, beyond their simply shopping in the same masons' yard.

These designs are likely to have been drawn up in consultations between craftsmen and patrons and possibly priests, drawing on an already familiar, complex iconography of fierce, winged long-bodied beasts that also existed in other materials, such as woven or embroidered textiles, carved wood or tooled leather.[101] Although the combination of motifs on each stone was unique to that *stone*, the combination might already have existed in these other media and have

[99]   None of the definitely *two*-panel stones comes from the Minster site, and the Minster site is the only one that be confidently associated with a church as early as *c.* 900. At the parish churches, the Anglo-Scandinavian sculpture is usually the earliest evidence for ritual activity on the site. While it is probable that all these stones marked Christian burial, the precise form of that Christianity may have had different nuances in newer, smaller, perhaps proprietary churches.

[100]   R. Hall, *Viking Age York* (London, 1984), pp. 17–19.

[101]   The Otley beast which Lang sees as ancestral to the York winged beasts is probably based on a design from an imported textile. Lang, *York and Eastern Yorkshire*, p. 35.

had an established meaning, perhaps referring to a particular individual: the innovation comes in the idea that this was a suitable form for a grave-slab, itself a medium in the process of being reinvented. Earlier stones from the Minster carry simple crosses, but the York Metropolitan School stones either resist being read simply as cross-slabs or reject that reading outright, which suggests that the York winged beasts may have had a different apotropaic function, although one that, like the cross, was acceptable in a church-associated graveyard.

As we have seen, dragons need not be evil. Rather, in native tradition, they are powerful creatures who live in burial mounds and guard treasure. Transferred onto the York Metropolitan School stones, they move their powers across with them, so they now live on a grave and guard the treasure of salvation, rather than the transient, corrupting riches of silver and gold. Like the Paternoster in *Solomon and Saturn* (Chapter Two above), the bodies and souls of the people buried beneath these stones could also be described as *wyrma wlenco* (the pride of *wyrmas*). There is no impassable doctrinal barrier here. If snake motifs on jewellery might embody a charm to forestall snake-bite, and the herbs *nædderwyrt* and *dracentse* could heal someone of adder-bite, the York Metropolitan School gravestones could represent an analogous attempt to harness the unstable, tricky but immensely powerful *draca* to defend the corpse, against threat in general, or specifically against the menace it would encounter from *moldwyrmas*, on the same principle of fighting like with like.

These stones had a long history as Roman ashlar by the time they were re-used by the craftsmen of the York Metropolitan School and this in itself may have added to their attraction.[102] They were recarved and installed in the city's churchyards around 900 and were presumably *in situ* for some time. It is unknown when the stones from the small churches were removed, but at the Minster it was within a hundred to a hundred and fifty years. This is very like St Oswald's, Gloucester, where we saw that within a century of their installation the stones were broken up for building rubble. Other analogies, nearer to York, are the churches of Hovingham in the Vale of Mowbray and St Gregory's Minster, Kirkdale, on the edge of the Vale of Pickering, both of which have earlier carvings re-used in eleventh-century walls. In both of these cases there is prominent recycling both of tenth-century crosses and earlier pieces: Hovingham, like Middleton, has a pre-Viking Age equal-armed cross built into the west face of its tower, and the exquisitely carved tomb/shrines from Kirkdale, now inside the church, were originally reset either side of the west door.[103]

However, the Minster gravestones were not re-used casually as building rubble nor employed iconically, set into walls.[104] They were re-used in their original role as gravestones. Their plaster and paint would by this point be faded, and their re-use might have involved re-plastering, re-painting. In some cases (YM 30 and 31), more than one stone was re-used to construct the new memorial, cut down to

[102] T. Eaton, *Plundering the Past: Roman Stonework in Medieval Britain* (Stroud, 2000), pp. 75–9.
[103] Taylor and Taylor, *Anglo-Saxon Architecture*, Hovingham, I, pp. 326–8, Kirkdale, I, pp. 357–61; Rahtz and Watts, 'Three Ages of Conversion', p. 307.
[104] Stocker and Everson, 'Rubbish Recycled', pp. 84 and 93.

provide upright head- and foot-stones at each end of the recumbent slab. In other cases (YM 32 and 33) new end-stones appear to have been carved, and the iconography of the beast continues to evolve. YM 33 depicts two entwined beasts confronting each other and raising their forelegs to acknowledge what Lang describes as 'a small vertical figure with the incised features of a human face; no limbs are visible', who is held between them. The beasts are descended from an earlier aesthetic: they are closely related to those on a ninth-century pinhead from the site of St Mary's Abbey, but in changing medium, role and platform they necessarily change their meaning.[105] The little figure descends in some sense from the inward-facing beast-head border-ends of the earlier stones, but he has not only relocated, he has also become human rather than animal. This is a small difference in terms of the carving, the only major change being that he now has a nose rather than a muzzle, but it is a very large difference where the iconography of a Christian gravestone is concerned: he is now a creature with an immortal soul. A mid-tenth to early eleventh-century onlooker who was familiar with contemporary burial practice could have interpreted this as a representation of the body buried here, shrouded but with the face revealed, flanked by guardian beasts.

As with the Gloucester stones, we must ask whether the re-use at York Minster represents a slighting of the original inhabitants of these graves and, as with Gloucester, a definitive answer is impossible. All that we can do is consider various possibilities. If each unique combination of motifs had originally referred to a particular individual, one might argue that the memory of that person had faded away with the paint and plaster over the generations, with the stone reverting to neutral, and in this context we might note Effros's observation of Merovingian cemeteries that 'once successive generations could no longer distinguish the tombs of their ancestors, they lost much of the impetus for commemorating them or for caring for their burial plots'.[106] Conversely, a particular stone's appeal might have been *enhanced* by its connexion to a specific person, with the new user or their kin becoming in some sense their heir. The recycling of the stones could have been part of a redefinition of the city's elite, associated perhaps with the rearrangement of the kingdom and Cnut's creation of the earldom of Northumbria. Earl Siward was buried in the church of St Olave which he had founded at some point between 1030 and 1055, and the York Metropolitan School stone found near St Olave shows signs of re-use along the same lines as the stones in the Minster cemetery, where his followers might have been buried. It seems unlikely that the stones were recycled merely because eleventh-century York had no one able to carve in stone, since the Minster and other York churches such as St Mary Bishophill Senior furnish a few examples of eleventh-century gravestones, although nothing like as many as there are surviving from the late ninth to tenth centuries, nor in the quantities of the mid-Kesteven or Fenland schools discussed in Chapter Four. The only solid ground shared by all the theories proposed here is that the imagery carried by these stones

---

[105] Illustrated in R. Cramp, *Anglian and Viking York*, Borthwick Papers 33 (York, 1967), frontispiece.
[106] Effros, *Caring for Body and Soul*, p. 133.

was clearly as attractive to some people in the eleventh century as it had been a century or more earlier, though whether that attraction lay in the stones' aesthetic appeal, their nature as expensive objects, their elite associations or in the protective power of the *wyrmas* it is now impossible to say.

Sigurðr and Weland: the Smith and the wyrm

One of the *in situ* slabs from the York Minster site is carved with scenes from the tale of Sigurðr, and there are several other examples from across the north of England.[107] There are also several stones with images of another Germanic hero, Weland the smith. All these have been much discussed, but there are several reasons for considering them here. Sigurðr's story has a place in any account of *wyrmas*, and the function of the Sigurðr (and Weland) stones as specifically funerary artefacts needs consideration. If we are reading this sculpture overall as the product of the Northumbrian church, the 'Viking' character of these stones may also require re-evaluation. Both heroes have been proposed as possible analogues to Christ, and a new argument is adduced here which strengthens this reading.

The York Minster stone (YM 34) shows a swordsman flanked by *wyrmas* along one long side. The badly weathered flat surface shows Sigurðr roasting and tasting the dragon's heart, with the decapitated body of Reginn, and the horse Grani. There are no English narratives from this period that tell the story represented here. In *Beowulf*, Sigemund rather than Sigurðr is implied as the dragon-slayer, although Mitchell and Robinson argue that the *Beowulf* poet could be referring to Sigurðr without naming him.[108] Thirteenth-century Icelandic manuscripts record the stories of Fáfnir, the dragon whom Sigurðr kills, by which time Fáfnir is seen as a shape-shifter; according to *Skáldskaparmál* he is one of three sons of a farmer, who kills his father, steals the wergild the gods have paid for killing one of his brothers, and flees to the wilderness to transform himself into a dragon and brood over the gold.[109] The remaining brother, the dwarf Reginn, who is a smith, adopts Sigurðr and incites him to kill Fáfnir, which he achieves by waiting in a ditch he has dug and piercing Fáfnir from below with his sword. In the poem *Fáfnismal* Fáfnir has a long riddling and prophetic conversation with Sigurðr as he lies dying.[110] Reginn has told Sigurðr to roast the dragon's heart but not to eat it. As it cooks Sigurðr burns his thumb; he sucks the burn and tastes the dragon's heart blood, allowing him to understand the language of the birds, who tell him that Reginn plans to betray him, and he cuts off Reginn's head. While the story is likely to have evolved in the three hundred years that separate the English and Icelandic sources, the essentials of the encounter with Fáfnir appear common to both traditions, and for the sake of simplicity the dragon-slayer will be called

---

[107] J. Lang, 'Sigurd and Weland in Pre-Conquest Carving from Northern England', *Yorkshire Archaeological Journal* 48 (1976), pp. 83–94.

[108] B. Mitchell and F. C. Robinson, *Beowulf: An Edition* (Oxford, 1998). p. 77.

[109] J. Young, *The Prose Edda* (London, 1954), pp. 110–12.

[110] L. M. Hollander, *The Poetic Edda* (Austin, 1962), pp. 223–32.

Sigurðr here.[111] In *Beowulf* the dragon (who like Sigurðr is unnamed) is described as both *draca* and *wyrm*.[112]

The corpus of stones which depicts the other culture-hero, Weland, may usefully be discussed together with the Sigurðr stones, although Weland is primarily associated with images of birds and flight rather than dragons, and the images identified with him on sculpture all show him flying. According to the Old Norse poem, *Völundarkviða*, Völundr (Weland) was able to escape captivity, despite being hamstrung, through flight.[113] The Exeter Book poem *Deor* refers both to Weland's captivity and to his rape and impregnation of Beaduhild, the daughter of the king who had captured him.[114] This latter scene is also represented on the front of the late seventh/early eighth-century Franks Casket, which may be Northumbrian. Here it forms part of a series of contrasting stories, drawn from the Gospels, Roman history (Romulus and Remus, the sack of Jerusalem) and indigenous legend, with the scenes commenting on each other and drawing parallels and contrasts.[115] The Franks Casket is a demanding object, requiring literacy in two scripts (roman and runic, with variations on the latter on the different panels), two languages (Latin and English), two verse forms (alliterative and hexameter), and three narrative traditions (indigenous, Roman and biblical). The Weland scene is the only one on the entire casket with no caption, and its audience could presumably be expected to recognize a familiar story from the elements of the smithy, the man with bent legs holding a head in his tongs, the decapitated bodies, the woman, and the man catching birds.[116] Weland is presented as an exemplum of skill, wisdom and endurance in *Deor*, *Beowulf*, *Waldere* and Alfred's translation of Boethius's *Consolatio Philosophiae*, which may represent a long process of reinventing him as a type of Christian hero.[117]

In *Deor*, the section on Weland begins *Welund him be wurman wræces cunnade* (Weland among *wyrmas* endured torments/exile, 1). This line has been seen as problematic, primarily because there are no *wyrmas* in the extant Weland stories, and most editors and translators have preferred to emend it or simply ignore it. However, Cox brings together a wide range of evidence that associates serpentine imagery with smithcraft.[118] It is also possible that variants of the Weland story once circulated which have been entirely lost. A now-elusive but once well-known tradition that linked Weland with *wyrm*-images would provide

[111] J. Lang, 'Sigurd and Weland', pp. 83–94; R. Frank, 'Skaldic Verse and the Date of Beowulf', in *The Dating of Beowulf*, ed. Colin Chase (Toronto, 1981), pp. 123–39.

[112] *Beowulf*, lines 892b, 886b, 891a, 897b.

[113] U. Dronke, *The Poetic Edda. II, The Mythological Poems* (Oxford, 1997), pp. 242–328. McKinnell suggests that the poem may have been composed in Yorkshire between *c.* 900 and *c.* 1050. J. McKinnell, 'The Context of *Völundarkviða*', *Saga-Book of the Viking Society* 23 (1990), pp. 1–27.

[114] Bailey, *Viking Age Sculpture*, p. 103.

[115] Webster, 'The Iconographic Programme of the Franks Casket', pp. 229–30; L. Webster, 'Stylistic Aspects of the Franks Casket', in Farrell, *The Vikings*, pp. 20–31.

[116] Dronke, *The Poetic Edda. II*, pp. 270–2.

[117] K. S. Kiernan, '*Deor*: The Consolations of an Anglo-Saxon Boethius', *NM* 79 (1978), pp. 333–41; E. Coatsworth and M. Pinder, *The Art of the Anglo-Saxon Goldsmith* (Woodbridge, 2002), p. 187.

[118] R. Cox, 'Snake Rings in *Deor* and *Völundarkviða*', *Leeds Studies in English*, New Series 22 (1991), pp. 1–20.

a context for the appearance of the winged Weland motif on stones like the fragmentary hogback from Bedale which has Weland on one long side and 'very Anglian' *wyrmas* on the other.[119]

This remains hypothetical, however. What is clear, is that although later sources present Sigurðr and Weland as part of huge story cycles, containing numerous *dramatis personae*, there is very little to show that other scenes from these stories, either involving these two heroes or any other characters, formed part of the Anglo-Scandinavian artistic repertoire.[120] The only such evidence come from a very different environment, the Old Minster, Winchester, where a section of carved stone frieze may show part of the story of Sigemund, Sigurðr's father. This, Biddle argues, could have been part of a narrative cycle analogous to the Bayeux tapestry, and was possibly part of the decoration of Old Minster under Cnut (1016–42).[121] Though the Winchester carving was not part of a tomb, it probably stood very close to the graves of several of the West-Saxon kings, as well as that of Cnut himself. But the scenes which fascinated Northumbrians in a funerary context were those connected with Sigurðr's dragon-fight and his moment of revelation when he tastes the dragon's blood, and Weland's escape in his flying apparatus.[122] Why were these two heroes, and these particular scenes, of such interest? Weland in his flying machine could be seen as a type of the Resurrection or Ascension of Christ; when he has a female figure in his grasp he may be seen as liberating a soul.[123] It has been suggested that an image of Sigurðr on a gravestone makes claims that the person buried there was a hero in the same league, or that Sigurðr is an Anglo-Scandinavian equivalent of St Michael, while Stocker argues that these scenes show 'the acceptance of the Christian god into the pagan pantheon'.[124] If Norton is right in seeing the York church of St Michael-le-Belfry as originating in a pre-Conquest funerary chapel, then the Minster Sigurðr stone lay in its shadow. Byock argues that Michael and Sigurðr (whom he calls 'not quite a saint') can be seen as figures who battle the forces of chaos, and he regards the frequent positioning of Sigurðr images on the portals of Norwegian stave-churches as a protective symbol.[125] The variety of readings supplied by different scholars is a testimony to the richness of these stories and the number of interpretations they invite.

These stones refer to common Germanic heroic tradition, but it is very unlikely that they were produced as a concession to paganism, and this is underlined by their obsessive reiteration of two episodes in the lives of two particular heroes.

[119] Dronke, *Poetic Edda. II*, pp. 280–5; Lang, *Northern Yorkshire*, pp. 61–2.
[120] Lang, 'Sigurd and Weland', p. 94.
[121] M. Biddle, 'Excavations at Winchester 1965, Fourth Interim Report', *Antiquaries Journal* 46 (1966), pp. 308–32, 329–32.
[122] Bailey, *Viking Age Sculpture*, p. 117.
[123] Dronke, *Poetic Edda. II*, pp. 280–5.
[124] Bailey, *Viking Age Sculpture*, pp. 124–5; D. Stocker, 'Monuments and Merchants: Irregularities in the Distribution of Stone Sculpture in Lincolnshire and Yorkshire in the Tenth Century', in Hadley and Richards, *Cultures in Contact*, pp 179–212, 194.
[125] J. L. Byock, 'Sigurðr Fáfnisbani: An Eddic Hero Carved in Norwegian Stave Churches', in T. Paroli (ed.), *Poetry in the Scandinavian Middle Ages* (Spoleto, 1990), pp. 619–28, 626.

Sigurðr is the foster-son of a smith, Weland is *the* legendary smith. Bradley, pursuing an unconnected line of enquiry, has looked at the lexical range for the word *smiþ* and the traditions and practices surrounding smiths in Old English literature, with the aim of establishing why Christ is referred to as a *smiþ* or a *smiþes sunu*, in, for example, the gloss to Matthew 13:55 in CCCC, MS 140 (*Witodlice þes ys smiþes sunu*), and again in Mark 6:3 (*Hu nys þys se smið, Marian sunu*). [126] He shows that the biblical descriptions of Joseph's profession refer to him only as an artisan, and that early scholars in the Western Church, including Isidore, Bede and Benedict of Aniane, assume this refers to metal-working rather than wood-working. He also demonstrates conclusively that Anglo-Saxon legal and poetic texts, translations and glosses universally characterize the *smiþ* as a metal-worker, sometimes explicitly differentiating him from the carpenter. Bradley raises the idea that this re-reading might lead to the identification of previously unrecognized images of St Joseph. He does not suggest that this might also lead to a re-interpretation of already recognized images of smiths and their foster-sons, such as Weland and Sigurðr. However, if they share this quality with Christ, it reinforces the case for reading the English references to Sigurðr and Weland as types of Christ as well as heroes from familiar Germanic legends.

The Sigurðr stone from York Minster was found above a grave (burial 54) in a densely packed area of the cemetery; although no information is available about this particular grave-cut or skeleton the massive stone alone suggests considerable investment in the burial. [127] It had presumably been re-used, as stratigraphically it is associated with the York Metropolitan School stones discussed above, although it had no head- or foot-stones. One of the dragons on the long side is virtually identical with a dragon to the side of the cross on a crucifixion scene from St Mary Castlegate, one of York's newly founded small churches, and this cross, in a mixture of Anglian, Irish and Anglo-Scandinavian styles, may well be by the same hand as the Minster stone. [128] This, like the Sigurðr stone's use and possible re-use within the Minster-connected cemetery, indicates that a heroic scene on a gravestone has no implications for syncretism or assertive paganism, either on the part of the craftsman or the person whose grave it marks. The evidence of *Beowulf*, *Deor*, *Waldere*, Alfred's translation of Boethius, and the Franks Casket is that both Sigurðr and Weland were figures who were so well known in the Anglo-Saxon tradition that their stories could be conveyed by hint and allusion. Given this, we might query whether the impetus to create monuments carrying these stories need have come from Scandinavians at all. The decision could have been made by the personnel of a Church already familiar with these stories, who appreciated their usefulness as vehicles for conveying important ideas. The Franks Casket suggests that this mode of communication had a long and

[126] J. Bradley, 'St Joseph's Trade and Old English *Smiþ*', *Leeds Studies in English*, New Series 22 (1991), pp. 21–42.; R. Liuzza, *The Old English Version of the Gospels*, EETS OS 304 (1994).

[127] Carver (ed.), *Excavations at York Minster* I, pt 1, pp. 75–92.

[128] Lang, *York and Eastern Yorkshire*, p. 97; L. P. Wenham *et al.*, *St Mary Bishophill Junior and St Mary Castlegate* (London, 1987), pp. 161–3.

respectable pedigree within the Northumbrian Church; the Gosforth Cross, with its intimate knowledge of pagan mythology, may, as Cramp says, 'reflect a radical theological approach which would otherwise never have been suspected in Viking-age Cumbria' or it may represent part of a vibrant and long-lasting tradition with very early Anglian roots, almost all evidence for which has vanished.[129]

Other Sigurðr imagery comes from Kirby Hill, a church which has produced a sizable corpus of sculpture. This includes a late eighth-/early ninth-century impost with close parallels from nearby Ripon, suggesting that, despite the Scandinavian toponym, there was an important earlier church on the site, and there are also up to eleven pieces of ninth- to tenth-century sculpture. Ripon, too, of course, has also produced a stone with Sigurðr imagery. Two of Kirby Hill's stones are relevant to the present discussion, nos. 2 and 9; the latter has been lost, but a drawing survives.[130] Kirby Hill 2 is built into the church wall and only one face is visible; this shows part of a Crucifixion scene above, which would have continued on to the lost cross-head, and below the decapitated head of Reginn, Sigurðr cooking Fáfnir's heart, and possibly Fáfnir's body below. The drawing of Kirby Hill 9 shows a horse (Grani?) on one face and the dragon's body pierced by a sword on another. The churches of York Minster, Ripon and Kirby Hill produce Sigurðr imagery in a context that suggests continuity, of monumentality at least, across the supposed watershed of the Scandinavian incursions. Another stone that buttresses this reading comes is the Nunburnholme cross-shaft, where the late Anglian cross was recarved with several scenes, including the armed and possibly haloed warrior and the book-carrying priest referred to above, a Madonna and Child, a possible Crucifixion, and what Lang reads as Sigurðr and Reginn, all by a single artist, and in a mixture of Anglian and Anglo-Scandinavian modes.[131] The proposed Sigurðr scene has been superimposed on an only slightly earlier carving of a priest celebrating mass, providing a narrative commentary on the more explicit eucharistic imagery. The recutting of this stone is in itself fascinating, suggesting that monuments could be seen as the locus of debate rather a unilateral assertion of meaning.

Of course, Sigurðr and Weland imagery is found outside the sphere of influence of the Northumbrian church, in both Man and Scandinavia, and the earliest Scandinavian stone, from Gotland, predates all the carvings we have looked at here, with the exception of the Franks Casket. But these two widely understood stories have a particular meaning and function in the context of ninth- to eleventh-century Northumbria. The images appear primarily on stones interpreted as cross-shafts, and at Nunburnholme they are part of a particularly sophisticated iconographic programme, a trend also visible at Leeds and Halton (Lancashire).[132] Rather than an imposition on Christianity by pagan incomers, they are more likely to be produced within the Church, by a secular clergy to

---

[129] Cramp, *Cumberland, Westmorland and Lancashire North-of-the-Sands*, p. 102.
[130] Lang, *Northern Yorkshire*, pp. 130 and 133.
[131] Lang, *York and Eastern Yorkshire*, pp. 189–93.
[132] W. G. Collingwood, *Northumbrian Crosses of the Pre-Norman Age* (London, 1927), pp. 159–63.

whom they were already familiar narratives and motifs, who may have either revived or continued the tradition of using them to mediate the meaning of another *smiþes sunu*, Christ. Byock, discussing the Scandinavian incarnations of the story, suggests that by 'late Viking times', the story had already detached itself from the realm of myth and become associated with heroic history.[133] Sigurðr tasting the dragon's blood is another way of presenting Christ 'tasting death' (a biblical idiom which is found in *Dream of the Rood*, line 101; Vercelli homily IV, p. 93, line 66; Vercelli homily XVII, p. 281, line 17), defeating the devil and returning with greater power than before. Weland's flight from captivity conflates images of the Resurrection and the Ascension, whereby Christ escapes the fetters of mortality. Both these images are supremely appropriate in a funerary context, as both emphasize Christ's central promise, that death is not the end for those who put their faith in the cross.

The hammer-head cross-slab from Kilmorie (Galloway), within the former diocese of Whithorn, is another radical theological statement, incorporating the iconography of the smith into a complex Christian programme. The crucified Christ is on one upper face; immediately below Him there is a man with two birds on his right and smith's tools on his left. He holds his hands together before him. Christ has open eyes and His feet are apart, He is standing before rather than nailed to the cross. The other face has a cross-head on which is carved a chalice from which plant-scroll emerges above; below, within the outline of the cross-shaft, there is a mass of writhing serpents. Bailey sees this as a funerary monument and explores the eucharistic, baptismal and resurrection iconography of the cross. He also stresses its 'symbolic ambition' and the otherwise unsuspected presence of sophisticated theological thinking in tenth-century Galloway, while claiming that the 'problem about the identity of the figure with the birds' is 'beyond the scope of this paper'.[134] Collingwood advises resisting the urge to see him as either Sigurðr or Weland.[135] However, despite these wise *caveats*, in the light of the arguments explored above perhaps we can read him as both Sigurðr and Weland, with the artist choosing to emphasize the iconographic elements, the birds and the tools, common to both stories, and to make their symbolism explicit by subordinating them to the living Christ. The figure of Christ on the upper part of one face corresponds to the eucharistic imagery of the chalice on the other; if the same principle of correspondence governs the lower half of the stone then a parallel is being drawn between the Sigurðr/Weland figure and the serpents. The combination of human and animal symbols of transformation and rebirth suggests that both sides of the stone represent an invitation to cast off the old self of sin and enter a new life.

---

[133] Byock, 'Sigurðr Fáfnisbani', p. 624.
[134] Bailey, 'Ambiguous Birds and Beasts' (no page-numbering).
[135] Collingwood, *Northumbrian Crosses*, p. 92.

Wyrmas *and transformation*

Wyrmas, big, small, good and bad, embody many ideas, but they meet around themes of transformation, providing interpretative frameworks for making sense of fundamental experiences of change, growth and decay. It was asserted above that positive meanings cluster around the snake/dragon group rather than the smaller and perhaps less heroic kinds of *wyrm*, but there is one important exception. Ælfric explores miraculous metamorphic qualities in his account of the silkworm, a passage which pulls together a wide range of resonant images and has no identifiable direct source. [136] Ælfric was clearly fascinated and delighted by the symbolic potential of these little creatures. His account sounds as if he has taken Augustine's advice and used personal observation to understand the exemplary symbolism inherent in their behaviour, *is full swutol bysen on ðisum syllicum wyrmum* (there is a clear example in these wonderful worms), he says, and he speaks of their rebirth in spring sunshine as something he has himself witnessed, *swa swa we oft gesawon* (as we have often seen). He summarizes their life-cycle and their ability to create *godweb* by their *syllicum cræfte* (is he punning here on *syllic* 'wonderful' and *seoluc* 'silk'?), marvelling that they can be reduced *deade to duste* over the winter, then laid in *leadenum dihsen* (in lead dishes) to be reborn in spring, *ælc dust to wyrme swa swa hi ær wæron* (each [speck of] dust to a worm, just as they were before). They reappear *ealle hwite* (all white) just as God raises the dust of human bodies to radiance and eternal life.

The *wyrmcynn* embody and enable many different kinds of transformation connected with literal and spiritual death, burial and rebirth. The serpent shedding its skin is a model for the Christian shedding his carapace of sin. Tasting the dragon's blood leads to hidden knowledge, and the biblical serpent is an archetype of wisdom. The *moldwyrm* devours and reduces the complex human body back to the *lam* and *eorþ* from which it was originally formed. The silkworms not only make silk *mid wundorlicum cræfte*, they body forth God's promise of resurrection. But these creatures, 'deep with wonders', are not easily reduced to formulae, and Anglo-Saxon artists and writers were open to the full range of meanings the *wyrmas* represent.

---

[136]   *CH* I, Appendix B, pp. 533–4; *CH Comm.*, pp. 134–5.

6

Judgement on Earth and in Heaven

In an influential passage of his *Moralia in Job*, Gregory the Great draws together relevant biblical texts to construct a Doomsday narrative. He identifies four groups of people: the very good and bad, who will not come to judgement, and the ordinarily good and bad, who will be called to God's tribunal.[1] Gregory's fourfold schema of ultimate human destinies is a useful one against which to measure the complexity of burial practice in later Anglo-Saxon England and to assess its purpose. He first deals with those to be judged and damned, associating them with the dismissal of those who have failed to recognize Christ in the poor (Matthew 25:41–3). He then moves on to consider bad people who do not even merit judgement, having lived entirely outside the law of Christ (Psalm 1:5, John 3:18 and Romans 2:12). They will rise again but only to go directly to hell since they either rejected or had no access to the *sacramenta fidei*. He then discusses those who are judged and saved, to whom Christ speaks in Matthew 25:34–5, welcoming them into His Father's kingdom. The last group are the saints, and Gregory connects them with Christ's promise in Matthew 19:28 to those who give up everything in His name, that they shall sit upon thrones and be judges with Him. In this brief analysis, Gregory rounds up many of the biblical texts central to the understanding of the court-room aspect of the Last Judgement, and his fourfold structure was picked up by early medieval English and Irish writers, although modified by Ælfric, who imagined the heathens also coming to judgement but meeting an automatic verdict of damnation.[2] This powerful vision of judgement provides a blueprint for the secular judicial system and the management of dying and dead bodies in this world as well. Despite the number of texts denying that human beings can predict the fate of the soul, written and archaeological evidence alike chart attempts not only to predict but to engineer both salvation and damnation through the location and structure of graves. The institutions of Anglo-Saxon society and contemporary visions of the afterlife reflexively structure each other, both explicitly, as the eschatological growlings of Wulfstan's lawcodes attest, and more subtly, in the treatment of the corpse and the placing of burials. The boundaries between the jurisdiction of the reeve and

---

[1] *PL* 76, cols 78–380. This is picked up by Isidore (*PL* 83, cols 596–7) and both are drawn on by Julian of Toledo in his *Prognosticon*, a major influence on Ælfric: Raynes, 'MS Boulogne-sur-Mer 63 and Ælfric'. We have already looked at Gregory's other defining work on death and judgement, the *Dialogues*.

[2] *CH* I, XXVII, p. 406, lines 176–92; F. M. Biggs, 'The Fourfold Division of Souls: The Old English 'Christ III' and the Insular Homiletic Tradition', *Traditio* 45 (1989), pp. 35–51.

ealdorman on the one hand, and the priest and bishop on the other, were unclear to many at the time. Studying the bodies and graves of the anathematized and the executed, as well as those of the saints and the great mass of people who fall into neither extreme, reveals an interlocking network of ideas about sex, violence, masculinity, integrity and death.

Place of burial

We need to look at charters, canon law, secular legislation, homilies and burials to see what decisions about burial were available, and who was making them. In some cases the categories were established by priests, as we see in an escha-tological homily in Oxford, Bodl. Hatton, MS 115, from the second half of the eleventh century. This contains a passage on the sins which render sinners' corpses so foul that they are no longer fit to be buried among their community.[3] It comes soon after the beginning of the homily, which is addressed to an audience of priests, and it follows an expanded list of the eight capital sins and a resumé of the seven pains of hell, with a reminder that there is neither confession nor absolution in hell. The preacher then turns his attention to some very specific sins, in a passage which merits quoting in full:

> *7 se preost se þe hæbbe nunnan oð his ende, oððe læwde man se þe hæbbe cyfese ofer his æwe, oððe hwa him to gesybne man hæbbe oð his endedæg, syn hi eall amansumode of ealra heofonwara haligdome 7 eorþwarena. Ne gesinge þær nan man nane mæssan þær he inne syn, ne husl ne gehalgodne hlaf ne sylle, ne hi man ne byrge binnan gehalgodan mynstre, ne furþum to hæþenum pytte ne bere, ac drage butan cyste butan hi geswicon.*

> And the priest who keeps a nun until his death, or the layman who keeps a mistress outside his marital vow, or one who maintains an incestuous relationship until his death, let them all be anathematized by the holiness of all heaven-dwellers and dwellers on earth. Let no mass be sung in their presence, let them not be given the eucharist or consecrated bread, nor let them be buried in a hallowed minster, nor even be carried to the heathen pit, but dragged without a coffin, unless they desist.

The sins are all sexual, but the list does not include all sexual sins. There is no anathema here of a priest with a sexual partner who is not herself pledged to chastity, for example, nor does the text say that the nun or the mistress is to forfeit decent burial. This is not a blanket condemnation of sexual irregularity but a subset containing the extremes of unacceptable sexual behaviour, placing the responsibility for this behaviour squarely on the shoulders of the male partner. It is his body which is so corrupted by his inappropriate lust that he is outcast by both heaven and earth, and the *eorþware* who reject him appear to include both the living and those already buried in hallowed ground.

The anathema is equally specific. Not only is the sinner excluded from the eucharistic community in life, he is also deprived of a *gehalgod* burial, consigned

---

[3] Printed in Scragg, *Vercelli Homilies*, pp. 159–83. Hatton 115 is a later eleventh-century MS and the homily draws on several sources but Scragg notes that 'it also preserves some unique early readings', p. xxxi.

instead to the *hæþen pytt*, to which he is not be carried in a coffin but dragged. The homily's author thus has three different models of burial in mind, the first of which has all the appropriate ritual, what the author of the prayer against sudden death would term burial *mid gedefenesse* (with decency), and this involves the body being incorporated into the company of the faithful departed, in the consecrated ground belonging to a *gehalgod mynster*. The second model involves exclusion from churchyard burial but still has a degree of dignity, with the corpse carried in or on a *cyst*. The third is one of utter degradation, with the anathematized corpse dragged uncoffined (*drage butan cyste*) to the grave. In many ways, the second of these is the most thought-provoking, as there is very little other textual evidence for the idea that one could be buried with any decency outside the churchyard, although the archaeological data supports the idea of excluded but coffined burials.[4] One complex question raised by this passage is the purpose of exclusion from the churchyard: is this an instrument of social humiliation, or is it an attempt to bring about the damnation of the person thus treated? While each is plausible, a close reading of the texts on exclusion and execution suggests the latter.

Hatton 115 is only one of very many references to the concept of separate consecrated and heathen burial grounds in later Anglo-Saxon England, although it is one of the more subtle. This field has been greatly illuminated in recent years by the researches of Gittos and Reynolds, who have respectively demonstrated the probable tenth-century origins of English rituals for churchyard consecration, and the ubiquity of specialized execution cemeteries.[5] Gittos suggests that the consecration rite may have developed in England independently of, and perhaps earlier than, its Frankish and Roman parallels.[6] Her work is a salutary reminder of the innovatory nature of the practices under consideration here, and provokes the questions of how quickly the concept and the ritual of churchyard consecration spread across England, and whether bishops retroactively consecrated existing burial grounds, or if the rite only came into play when a new graveyard was established. This in turn invites us to consider that priests would still have overseen burials in technically unhallowed ground in those areas where no episcopally consecrated cemetery was yet available. It is also possible that long-established minster churchyards may never have been formally consecrated, and perhaps they were understood instead to have been hallowed by association with the generations of liturgical activity they had witnessed. Reynolds's work on the landscape of justice reveals a dramatic ritual environment in which criminals' severed heads and hanged bodies were exhibited in association with ancient earthworks and important boundaries, then buried in a disorderly way, often prone, with hands tied, randomly oriented, in conscious opposition to the ideal constructed in texts like Laud 482. He brings together documentary and

---

[4] For example at Sutton Hoo. A. Reynolds, 'Anglo-Saxon Law in the Landscape: An Archaeological Study of the Old English Judicial System', unpublished Ph.D. thesis (University of London, 1999), pp. 164–5; Ogbourne St Andrew, pers. comm. S. Semple and A. Reynolds.

[5] Gittos, 'Creating the Sacred'.

[6] C. Treffort, *L'Église carolingienne et la mort* (Lyon, 1996), pp. 141–2.

archaeological evidence to show that the *hæþen byrgels* so common in charter bounds refer primarily to the graves of these outcasts, and argues that each hundred had such a site, often combining place of execution and 'heathen' cemetery.[7] There would thus have been very many such places, only a few kilometres apart and sometimes intervisible, peppering the late Anglo-Saxon landscape.

These tensions between holy and unholy places structure each other, and before examining the pictures that different texts draw of excluded burial we should look briefly at that ideal of bounded and consecrated ground. Rites for consecrating cemeteries, like those for churches, could only be performed by bishops, and they are preserved in several Anglo-Saxon pontificals. Gittos draws attention to the stability of the prayers in this rite across the different Anglo-Saxon pontificals, arguing for it being already established by the time it is first preserved in later tenth-century manuscripts.[8] The Claudius I rite is typical; it focuses on cleansing the ground, expelling evil spirits and creating a space in which the corpses may rest quietly until revived by the angel's trumpet. The people whose bodies are to be buried within this space are designated as God's *famuli* and *sancti*, those who have received the *baptismi gratiam* and persevered *in fide catholica usque ad uitae terminum* (in the catholic faith until the end of life), but they are not perfect, they are still hoping for merciful remission of their sins. The rite identifies the cemetery with the land purchased for burial by Abraham and God's promise to the people of Israel of their own land *in aeuo durantem*, which, together with the request that those commended for burial should rest *in hoc cimiterio* until the end of time, constructs an ideal image of the virtuous dead as the lawful tenants of this piece of land, who have the right not to be disturbed.[9] But permanent tenancy of the grave was already unlikely by the time these rites are first recorded. The rites only create the fiction of an inviolable resting-place, but it was a fiction whose importance may have outweighed reality for many people.

Surprisingly, perhaps, the earliest surviving reference to exclusion from consecrated ground comes not from a strictly ecclesiastical text but from the second lawcode issued by Athelstan (924–39), which specifies that the swearer of any false oath (*manað*) is never to be considered oath-worthy again, *ne binnon nanum gehalgode lictune ne licge, þeah he forðfore* (nor lie in any hallowed corpse-enclosure, should he die) unless his bishop testifies to his completed penance.[10] This code differs in several ways from the eleventh-century Hatton 115 homily quoted above. It focuses on perjury rather than sexual behaviour, it excludes the culprit from the community of the oath-worthy rather than the

---

[7] Reynolds, *Later Anglo-Saxon England*, pp. 99–111; Reynolds, 'Burials, Boundaries and Charters'.
[8] Gittos, 'Anglo-Saxon Rites', in Lucy and Reynolds, *Burial in Early Medieval England and Wales*, p. 201.
[9] D. H. Turner (ed.), *The Claudius Pontificals*, HBS 97 (London, 1971), pp. 60–1; Banting, *Two Anglo-Saxon Pontificals*, pp. 57–9.
[10] He is never to lie within a consecrated corpse-enclosure, if he die, unless he has the testimony of the bishop, to whose diocese he belongs, that he has made such amends as his confessor prescribed to him. II Athelstan (Grately), Liebermann, *Gesetze* I, p. 164.

congregation, and, whereas Hatton 115 lets the sinful off if they desist (*geswicon*), II Athelstan specifies that such a man is only to be reprieved if his bishop confirms that penance has been imposed by his confessor and that the guilty man has carried it out. (Incidentally, this is another early, but entirely casual reference to *scrift*, further supporting Meens's argument that confession is rarely referred to because it was so common.)[11] It specifies that the oath-breaker is not to lie in a 'hallowed corpse-enclosure' but unlike Hatton 115 it does not give particulars of what his fate is to be instead. Paradoxically, the eleventh-century homily preserves what may be an older expression, referring to burial in a 'hallowed minster', whereas II Athelstan's use of *gehalgod lictun* refers very specifically to a sacred bounded space designed primarily for burial. If this is an episcopally consecrated cemetery it is probably the earliest surviving such reference in Europe, although the possibility remains that the lawcode's compiler may have been thinking of churchyards made holy by liturgical association rather than formal consecration.[12] The lawcode and the homily share many assumptions, but there is also much they do not share, and these cannot easily be divided into lay and Church concerns.

Athelstan shows a readiness to use the Church as a means of regulating behaviour, and he put his codes together in close consultation with his churchmen. In the twelfth-century Latin recension of II Athelstan in *Quadripartitus*, the code concludes with the statement that it was drawn up with the advice of the archbishop of Canterbury.[13] Wulfhelm of Canterbury (926–41) is also mentioned at the beginning of I and III Athelstan, and the last clause in VI Athelstan refers to a message being sent to inform him of legislative revision.[14] Ecclesiastical and secular law weave in and out of each other elsewhere, in Alfred's reliance on Mosaic texts, for example, and as the tenth century progressed definitions of sin and crime tended to converge.[15] However, the *punishments* for sin and crime do not and cannot map precisely on to each other, since their goals are different. Canon law is directed towards individual salvation whereas secular law is concerned with controlling the community. III Edgar (Andover) 5:1–2 states that the shire-court is to be held twice a year, and that it is to be overseen by both the bishop and the ealdorman ⁊ *þær ægðer tæcean ge Godes riht ge woruldriht* (and there prescribe both God's law and secular law), a sanguine statement which wallpapers over the different world-views of clergy and laity.[16] Barlow argues that these legal systems 'were not in rivalry but were regarded as complementary', but this cannot always have been the case. This clash of ideologies is most apparent where the death penalty is concerned, since the laymen are concentrating on

---

[11] Meens, 'The Frequency and Nature of Early Medieval Penance', p. 53.

[12] Blair, *The Church in Anglo-Saxon England*, ch. 8.

[13] Liebermann, *Gesetze* I, p. 167.

[14] Liebermann, *Gesetze* I: I Athelstan, p. 146; III Athelstan p. 170; VI Athelstan, pp. 182–3.

[15] F. Barlow, *The Norman Conquest and Beyond* (London, 1983), p. 6; Wormald, *The Making of English Law*, pp. 449; K. O'Keeffe, 'Body and Law in Late Anglo-Saxon England', *ASE* 27 (1998), 209–32, 222.

[16] Liebermann, *Gesetze* I, p. 202. Wormald suggests that the shire-court at this period is a new institution: P. Wormald, *Legal Culture in the Early Medieval West* (London, 1999), pp. 284–5.

putting an end to crime in a very permanent and visible way, both excising the criminal like a tumour from the body of society and deterring others from committing crime, while the clergy's aim should have been to bring the sinner to repentance.[17]

A survey of the sins and crimes expected to prevent burial in consecrated ground is instructive. After II Athelstan, the next references come in I Edmund (939–46), which was drawn up in London with Oda of Canterbury, Wulfstan I of York and *manega oðre biscopas*, and it has a strong ecclesiastical focus.[18] Its first clause introduces the concept of sexual sin, so prominent a century later in Hatton 115, into the debate for the first time, announcing that both men and woman in holy orders are to set an example and keep their chastity *be heora hade*, in keeping with their vows. Should they fail, then they are to incur the penalty prescribed by the canons, *þæt hi þolian worldæhta 7 gehalgodre legerstowe, buton hi gebetan* (that they forfeit all their possessions and consecrated burial, unless they repent).[19] This is a much broader category of sexual misconduct than in Hatton 115, explicitly covering anyone in orders, male and female, who fails to keep the vow of chastity, no matter whom he or she chooses as a partner. It is also misleading, since earlier collections of canon law have no references to the use of burial location as a penalty, although Wulfstan II of York, at least, was happy to insert such clauses into older collections, as we shall see. The fourth clause of the same code goes on to add that this fate also awaits those who have sex with nuns (laymen presumably, since the ordained have been comprehensively dealt with), homicides (*manslaga*) and adulterers (*æwbrice*).

The penalty next occurs in I Æthelred (Woodstock), 4–4.1, as a punishment for recidivist oath-breakers who resist arrest by the king's reeve: *Gif he þonne borh næbbe, slea mon hine 7 on ful lecge* (if he has no surety, let him be slain and lie in foulness).[20] Here for the first time the death penalty and exclusion from consecrated ground coincide explicitly in the lawcodes, although the context sounds more as if the man is to be cut down than formally executed. This is also the earliest passage to specify the destination of the unacceptable corpse. *Ful* may refer to literal filth, or to guilt, and it is ambiguous as to whether the man who has been killed is simply to lie in a foul place (such as a ditch?), or whether he is to have a marginally more formal burial among the graves of other people deemed as unacceptable as himself. *Quadripartitus* translates *in ful lecge* as *in dampnatis inhumetur*, which shows that twelfth-century readers assumed it meant the latter.[21] Here, then, there may have been an overt attempt to bring about the damnation of the executed man through the location of his grave and the company he will be keeping until Doomsday.

---

[17] Barlow, *The English Church, 1000–1066*, p. 266.
[18] Wormald points out the connexions of I Edmund to the 'Constitutions' of Archbishop Oda but the latter does not use burial location as a penalty. *The Making of English Law*, p. 310
[19] Liebermann, *Gesetze* I, p. 184.
[20] *Ibid.* I, p. 220.
[21] This recurs in II Cnut 33.1. *Ibid.* I, pp. 336–7.

Æthelred's later lawcodes show a great concern with the death penalty, but there are no further explicit references to the concept of consecrated ground. There is however the thought-provoking clause in III Æthelred, 7–7.1, which reveals that people otherwise unspecified in these texts had unconsecrated burial forced upon them:

> *And gif hwa þeof clænsian wylle, lecge an C to wedde, healf landrican 7 healf cinges gerefan binnan port, 7 gange to þrimfealdne ordale. Gif he clæne beo æt þam ordale, nime upp his mæg; gif he þonne ful beo, licge þar he læg, 7 gilde an C.*[22]

> And if anyone should wish to redeem a thief, let him pledge 100, half to the land-owner and half to the king's reeve within the town, and go to the three-fold ordeal. If he be clean/innocent at the ordeal, let him take up his kinsman; if he be foul/guilty, let him lie where he lay, and forfeit the 100.

This provides a mechanism for retroactively redeeming wrongly convicted thieves, their innocence proved not on their own bodies but on the bodies of proxies, their kinsmen (*mæg*), who are prepared for the dead man's sake to submit to the three-fold ordeal and risk a heavy financial penalty. The exonerated man's body could then be exhumed, presumably to be reinterred in consecrated ground, or if the kinsman failed the ordeal by being *ful* he would remain where he was, the 'foulness' of the guilt echoing the 'foulness' of the oath-breaker's burial in I Æthelred. It seems that excluded burial could prove unbearable for the kin of the condemned man, and that new rituals had to be devised for those who were desperate to prove their relative's innocence, or at least to have him reinterred and given the slightest chance of salvation. Another important motive fuelling this process was no doubt concern for the family's good name, but the echoes of the language of salvation and damnation in *ful* and *clæne* suggest that heavenly as well earthly reputations were at stake. The clause also implies an inbuilt awareness that the authorities could execute the innocent.

S 886 (995) also shows that the authorities expected thieves and their associates to be denied consecrated burial. This text records the theft of a bridle by a servant, leading to a fight between his masters and the bridle's owners. Two of the thief's supporters had been killed, and they should have been denied Christian burial but Æthelwig, the reeve of Buckingham, had illegally allowed the burials to go ahead. Æthelwig had been charged with this offence, but was later pardoned.[23] The role of the reeve in this story shows the extent to which this punishment could be administered by lay officials, an interpenetration of secular and clerical authority which has its counterpart in the Church's administration of the ordeal. These texts make it clear that thieves could be, and were, excluded from churchyards, and yet theft is not among the crimes which explicitly incur the penalty in the lawcodes. III Æthelred does not specify where thieves are to be buried, it merely assumes that they will have been buried somewhere their kinsmen find distressing. This may suggest a long-standing norm of burying thieves and other executed criminals in a separate site; when the references to

---

[22] III Æthelred, 7–7.1. *Ibid.* I, p. 230.
[23] J. Kemble, *Codex Diplomaticus Aevi Saxonici* (London, 1839–48), p. 1289.

exclusion begin to appear in the lawcodes from the reign of Athelstan onwards, this represents not a new invention but an elaboration of existing practice, with additional categories of sinner and criminal now thought appropriate for this treatment.

Wulfstan II of York was responsible for writing Æthelred's later lawcodes. Although he is deeply concerned with the death penalty, he avoids the subject of excluded burial here, but returns to it in the lawcodes he compiled for Cnut, however, which stress that no one may be buried in consecrated ground without true belief and that this is also to apply to oath-breakers. The phrase *in fulan lecge* from I Æthelred is reiterated in II Cnut, and its layers of meaning are illuminated by the Latin translations, which variously render it as *cum dampnatis, in loco latronum* and *inmundo*, 'among the damned', 'in the place of the thieves', and 'dirty'.[24]

Wulfstan also takes great interest in the question of consecrated burial in the so-called 'Canons of Edgar' (1005–8) which survive in three eleventh-century manuscripts and make use of Ælfric's pastoral letters, which draw in turn on a wide body of canon law.[25] Wulfstan's reworkings of canon law reveal a fascination with the problem posed by every kind of burial, and he is ready to rewrite his sources to insert references to *clæne* burial where he thinks it appropriate. The 'Canons of Edgar' are addressed to priests with the aim of establishing acceptable standards of behaviour and ministry, and they are informative about Wulfstan's concerns regarding the dignity of Christian burial. The canons he collects and translates include one which forbids dogs, horses and particularly pigs from entering the *cyrictune* (26), one asserting the idea, also found in V and VI Æthelred, that a priest who lives a chaste and non-violent life will be entitled to the rights of a thegn in life and in death (68a: *ge on life, ge on legere*),[26] another expressing concern that anyone buried within the church itself must be established as exceptionally virtuous (29), and one enjoining priests to bury people appropriately without allowing *ænig unnytt* (any frivolity) around the body (67).

In the 'Canons of Edgar', Wulfstan interprets the meaning of churchyard burial differently from any other surviving Anglo-Saxon writer. His clause on access to consecrated burial reads:

> [22] 7 riht is þæt ælc man leornige þæt he cunne pater noster 7 credan, be ðam ðe he wille on gehalgodum legere licgan oððe husles wyrðe beon; forðam he ne bið wel Cristen þe þæt geleornian nele.[27]

---

[24] I Cnut 22.5 *Forþam he nah æfter forðsiðe Cristenra manna gemanan ne on gehalgedan restan oððe her on life husles beon wyrþe.* Liebermann, *Gesetze* I, p. 304, II Cnut 33 *And gif hwylc man si, þe eallum folce ungetrywe, fare þæs cincges gerefa to, 7 gebringan hine under borge, þæt hine man to rihte læde þam ðe him on spræcan.* 33.1 *And gif he þone borh næbbe, slea hine man 7 on fulan lecge. Ibid.* I, pp. 336–7.

[25] *Councils*, pp. 313–18.

[26] V Æthelred 9–9.1, Liebermann, *Gesetze* I, p. 240, repeated in VI Æthelred 5–5.3, Liebermann, *Gesetze* I, p. 248.

[27] *Councils*, p. 322.

[22] And it is right that everyone learn so that he understand Pater Noster and Creed, in so far as he wishes to lie in a consecrated grave or be entitled to communion; because he is not really a Christian who refuses to learn them.

Whereas earlier (and later) prescriptive texts threaten exclusion from consecrated burial as a punishment for immoral, anti-social and illegal behaviour, here the situation is reversed. One has to *earn* churchyard burial, not by social rank but by both knowing *and understanding* (*leornige þæt he cunne*) Creed and Paternoster. His use of *willan* and *nellan* repositions people who do not know these key texts as wilfully imperfect Christians who are actively refusing to share in community in life and death. Wulfstan is compiling an authoritative text for the clergy of his archdiocese, and, Fowler argues, 'hardly one of the ideas is strictly his own', yet his source, the *Capitula* of Theodulf, does not mention burial in this context.[28] Wulfstan's attempt to redefine the language of consecrated burial does not seem to have taken root: the *Northumbrian Priests' Law* (like I Edmund a century earlier) firmly associates exclusion with sexual misconduct, linking it to those who die in incestuous relationships (both blood and spiritual) and to nuns and their lovers, and in the latter case it is clear that both the man and the woman (*ge he ge heo*) are to be punished. It also clarifies the purpose of the punishment as an attempt to bring about damnation: the sinners are to forfeit both *clæne legere* and *Godes mildse* (God's mercy).[29]

Looking at the whole range of references to these practices over around a hundred and thirty years, from Athelstan to the *Northumbrian Priests' Law* and the Hatton 115 homily, a wide range of problematic behaviour emerges. It includes general and specific sexual misdemeanours by both ordained and lay, failure to know the basics of the faith, oath-breaking and homicide. The penalty appears also to have applied to thieves, but this fails to make the official record in so many words. Exclusion appears to have been particularly connected, in the minds of the lawcodes' compilers, with the breaking of promises, the clerical or monastic *had*, the layman's *að* or *wedd*, the marital *æw* and perhaps, for those who refuse to be *wel Cristen*, the baptismal vows made on their behalf. Magennis draws attention to 'the particular enormity of treachery in a world whose secular institutions are based so firmly on personal ties and whose idea of society is focused so centrally on values of mutual obligation'.[30] Ecclesiastical institutions were founded on the same principles, and this horror at the fracture of social bonds extended to the dead body as well as the living one.

The variety of available burial locations and styles is extremely complex. Those pleasing to God may be buried inside a church, although according to the *Capitula* of Theodulf their graves should be dug deep, and the church floor re-laid so evenly that there should be no sign of the grave.[31] We may question whether this was always strictly followed, given the unweathered nature of some

28 Fowler, *Wulfstan's Canons of Edgar*, p. xxxiv; Sauer, *Theodulfi Capitula*, cap. XXII, pp. 332–3.
29 *Councils*, pp. 465–6.
30 H. Magennis, *Images of Community in Old English Poetry*, CSASE 18 (Cambridge, 1996), p. 22.
31 *oððe hig feor on eorðan bedelfe oððe oferwege, ⁊ þære cyrcean flor emlice ⁊ gerysenlice gewyrce, þæt þær nan byrgen gesyne ne sy.* Sauer, *Theodulfi Capitula*, pp. 314–15.

of the surviving grave-markers, but on the whole very few Anglo-Saxon burials are found within churches. Those who are merely acceptable members of the eucharistic community are buried *on gehalgodum legere* (in hallowed resting-place), presumably outside, and here the sculptural evidence clearly shows that people could have highly visible monuments. Some of these funerals, even when supervised by priests, are attended by *unnytt* (frivolity) disapproved of by the Church. There are those who are excluded from hallowed ground but who still have some kind of formal funeral, and finally those who have both an excluded and degraded burial, a category which may include sexual wrongdoers as well as the condemned oath-breakers and executed thieves. Finally, the corpses of the executed may be found innocent, exhumed and reburied, presumably with some attendant ceremony of reincorporation into the body of the faithful. These are texts which are at odds with the message of many of the homilies, that death and burial are the same for everyone. Both messages are true.

Thus the simple contrast of consecrated and unconsecrated burial which the lawcodes attempt to construct collapses on closer reading of the evidence. Burial practice in later Anglo-Saxon England formed a spectrum, with many possible nuances of location, furnishing, monumentality, ritual and personnel, depending on social, legal and spiritual standing, local custom, and proximity to a church, and the range of options was very different in 850 from what it was to be by 1050. In Chapter Three, we looked at the idea that Church ritual could develop in response to external pressure, with new areas of liturgical focus and elaboration offering themselves as the Church extended its influence and presence in the lives of the ordinary laity. Consecrated burial may fall into this category; it is certainly suggestive that it first presents itself as a negative, something to be denied to certain types of sinners, some time before it appears to be on offer to the fair-to-middling Christian. A possible profile of development might be that, in the Middle Saxon period, most of the population was buried in field cemeteries, with Christian funeral rites but no major ceremonial actually at the grave. The exceptions to this were the churchmen and women and the lay elite, who were buried in minsters, and the executed criminals, who were buried in the cemeteries Reynolds has identified. From around 900, several different trends combined to change the *status quo*. The Church became much more closely involved in the administration of the law, with the result that the boundaries of sin and crime were gradually redrawn. The references to exclusion in II Athelstan and I Edmund are simply that, they exclude the body of the oath-breaker or homicide from the *gehalgod lictun* or *legerstow* but they do not yet specify where it is to go instead. This may reflect an early tenth-century landscape in which place of burial and salvation were not necessarily linked, where cemeteries either formally con-secrated or holy by long association with churches were still comparatively rare and only for the privileged. As such places became more common with the appearance of many more small local churches with graveyards, many sinners who had died of natural causes while still under sentence of excommunication were now rerouted to the humiliating (and possibly damning) environment of the execution cemetery, the *ful* place first recorded in I Æthelred. The 'neutral' field cemeteries may have begun to fall out of favour partly because, since they were not associated with a church, they came to have an uneasy aura of exclusion about them. Thus, one impetus for the development of a formal consecration ceremony may have been the sinister associations of the State-administered burial zones for the condemned and anathematized, resulting in increasing lay demand for churchyard burial.

The next section of this chapter looks at the death penalty, including the involvement of Wulfhelm and Oda of Canterbury, Theodred of London and Wulfstan I of York in the legislative process of the first half of the tenth century. We should perhaps also look to their generation of archbishops and bishops for the origins of the English tradition of consecrating cemeteries. Another factor in the rite's development may have been the desire of the next generation, the mid-tenth-century archbishops and bishops, usually appointed out of monasteries, to extend control over the smaller churches.[32] This could have been a particularly useful regulating device in the east of the country where local secular clergy and lords had been asserting their desire to bury in local churches.[33] These trends can only have been gratifying to the kings since exclusion was another powerful weapon to add to the battery already contained in the lawcodes, and, if Æthelwig of Buckingham is typical, the power to exclude certain corpses from hallowed ground was wielded by the royal, not the ecclesiastical, representatives in the regions.

Throwing away God's handiwork: the Church and the death penalty

We have already caught a glimpse of the complexity of the lawcodes' attitudes to thieves, their executions and burials. Capital punishment comes and goes from the lawcodes, and clearly not everything made it into the written law. But there are other texts with which to supplement the lawcodes, paramount among which, again, are the pastoral letters written by Ælfric for his contemporaries and superiors, particularly Wulfstan, archbishop of York.

Ælfric and Wulfstan had very different attitudes to the death penalty. Ælfric writes as one who is anxious about the moral status of the men sitting in judgement: his primary concern is that priests should have no involvement in the judicial process because of the harm it caused them. Wulfstan drew up pro-grammes of legislation in which the death penalty is imposed, for both Æthelred II (978–1016) and Cnut (1016–42): *his* concern is that the death sentence should not be applied lightly, and his anxieties centre on the soul of the condemned man. It may be that this difference in focus is no more than a symptom of the genres in which the two men were writing, with Ælfric epitomizing canon law and Wulfstan working within the existing framework of secular law. However, the cumulative evidence suggests otherwise. The kind of project on which Ælfric was engaged here, bringing texts together and translating them, is always a creative process,

---

[32] D. Knowles, *The Monastic Order in England* (Cambridge, 1966), Appendix 4 (monastic bishops 960–1066), pp. 697–701.

[33] Everson and Stocker, *Lincolnshire*, pp. 76–9.

and it has long been recognized that Wulfstan's lawcodes bear his unmistakable stamp. It is possible that we see here a clash of idealism and pragmatism in the works of two men who took this subject very seriously, a clash that may have coloured their personal relationship. In order to explore this further, it needs to be set in the context of the extant evidence for the administration of the death penalty.

Prior to the tenth century, execution is rarely specified as an automatic punishment.[34] From the reign of Athelstan (924–39), however, lawcodes prescribe death for a wide range of crimes. The heavy application of the death penalty thus coincides with the first appearance of exclusion from consecrated ground, although the two punishments apply to different crimes, theft and perjury respectively. II Athelstan imposes execution automatically on anyone over the age of twelve who steals goods worth more than eight pence.[35] VI Athelstan, drawn up in association with the peace-guild of the bishops and reeves of London, initially reiterates the death penalty for thieves over twelve, although the value of the stolen goods is now raised to over a shilling.

Although Athelstan's lawcodes were compiled with Wulfhelm of Canterbury, any problem the archbishop may have had with the idea of capital punishment leaves no trace in the surviving texts.[36] The only evidence that the theory of the death penalty was debated at this period comes at the end of VI Athelstan, in a coda which records Athelstan reconsidering the harshness of his laws and raising the age of culpability to fifteen, because the existing situation seemed too cruel, and too many young men were being killed:

> *se cyng cwæð nu eft æt Witlanbyrig to his witan 7 het cyðan þam arcebiscope be þeodrede biscop, þæt him to hreowlic þuhte, þæt man swa geongne man cweald oððe eft for swa lytlan, swa he geaxod hæfde, þæt man gehwær dyde.*[37]

> The king has now spoken again to his councillors at Whittlebury, and has sent word to the archbishop (i.e. Wulfhelm) by Bishop Theodred that it seemed too cruel to him that a man should be killed so young, or for so small an offence, as he had learnt was being done everywhere.

This clause describes the king revising legislation which he had earlier drawn up with the archbishop's approval, and the Whittlebury meeting was the only one of Athelstan's recorded councils at which Wulfhelm was not present.

The lawcodes use neither a consistent nor a detailed vocabulary to describe how criminals were to die. II Athelstan 1–1.2 says that *man ne sparige nænne þeof* (no thief is to be spared) and 2.1 says that lordless fugitives are to be cut down like thieves (*hine lecge for ðeof*), both of which sound more as if a man has

---

[34] Individual cases can be decided by the king, who can demand the wergild or sell the criminal into slavery abroad (Wihtred, 26 and cf. 28; Ine, 6, 12), or the death penalty can be commuted to financial compensation if the accused reaches sanctuary (Ine, 5). Only an Englishman condemned to penal slavery who then absconds is to be hanged without the possibility of commuting the penalty (Ine, 24), presumably because after this all other sanctions have been exhausted.

[35] The death penalty is also in force for witchcraft (6) and resisting arrest (20.6). V Athelstan also prescribes death for anyone who shelters men who have unlawfully returned from exile.

[36] Wormald, *The Making of English Law*, pp. 299–300.

[37] Liebermann, *Gesetze* I, pp. 182–3.

the right to kill a criminal whom he encounters than the result of due legal process. In contrast, clause 4 (treachery) of the same code reads *he beo his feores scyldig* (be he guilty of his life) as does 6 (witchcraft), which sounds like a court-imposed sentence rather than a lynch mob. VI Æthelstan 1.3 introduces a new phrase with *þæt hine man slea* (that he be struck), and since this comes after being proven guilty at the three-fold ordeal it is presumably a State-sponsored execution, although it also says that anyone who defends a thief may be cut down (*lecge*) with him. III Edmund, which is only preserved in *Quadripartitus*, says that the leader of a band of slaves who steal is to be taken and killed or hanged (*occidatur uel suspendatur*), which may differentiate between those who are struck down in the act and those who are brought to trial, or between two forms of the death penalty (decapitation and hanging?).[38] IV Edgar concludes a long series of clauses about a man whose cattle-trading habits prove untrustworthy with *sy he þeof 7 þolige heafdes*, which could refer to decapitation or simply capital punishment.[39] Modern legal language depends on precision, but these phrases in the lawcodes suggest a conscious degree of ambiguity. Perhaps they are intentionally expressed in language precise enough to make it clear that the king commands that the thief is to die, but vague enough to respect regional custom and allow a local court to decide exactly how.[40] If this is so, there may be a change in the reign of Æthelred. His early codes reiterate language we have already heard, but III Æthelred goes into precise detail about a thief who fails at the ordeal: *Gif he þonne ful beo, slea man hine, þæt him forberste se sweora.*[41] 'Strike him so that his neck breaks' leaves little room for manoeuvre.

V Æthelred (1008) is completely different from any of its predecessors. This is the first code written by Wulfstan, and its concern for English souls and the bodies they inhabit is evident from the opening clauses, which encourage faith and the rejection of *ælcne hæþendom*, before banning the selling of Christians overseas and executing them for petty crimes. He urges *þæt man Cristene men for ealles to lytlum to deaðe ne fordeme* (Christian men not be condemned to death for little things) since 'God's handiwork and the bargain he made at such at a price' should not be thrown away, instead life-sparing (*friðlice*) punishments are to be thought up, *folce to þearfe* (for the people's good).[42] As O'Keeffe notes, this represents a profoundly different understanding of the purpose of punishment, though it is questionable whether it represents a cultural shift, as she argues, or whether it is the result of one particularly conscientious churchman's meditation on the operation of a Christian legal system.[43] Wulfstan returns to this idea and develops it in VI Æthelred 10–10.3, repeating the phrases quoted above and going on to say that every crime should be judged carefully and a fitting punishment prescribed. The language of the law-courts is here completely absorbed into the

---

[38] *Ibid.* I, p. 191.
[39] *Ibid.* I, p. 212.
[40] J. C. Holt, *Colonial England, 1066–1215* (London, 1997), pp. 20–4.
[41] Liebermann, *Gesetze* I, p. 230.
[42] V Æthelred 3. *Ibid.* I, p. 238.
[43] O'Keeffe, 'Body and Law in Late Anglo-Saxon England', pp. 209–32.

language of the confessional, comparable to those passages in Laud 482 where penance for theft depends on the value of the item stolen. Wulfstan concludes with a wholly characteristic idea, the embedding of justice within the terms of the Paternoster: *7 geþence swyþe georne se þe oþrum deme, hwæs he sylf gyrne, þonne he þus cweðe; 'Et dimitte nobis debita nostra' et reliqua* (and let everyone who judges other people think of what he himself yearns for, when he says thus 'and forgive us our trespasses' and so on). This gentle attitude is borne out by the sparse references to the death penalty in V Æthelred and VI Æthelred. It appears in V Æthelred 28–30, where those who desert the army when the king is present, or come into the king's presence when excommunicated, are to *plihte him sylfum 7 ealre his are* (forfeit himself and all his goods), while those plot against the king's life are *feores scyldig* (guilty of life), although there is mention of the possibility of both wergild and ordeal. In VI Æthelred the phrase in the first two instances has been modified still further to *plihte his are* and *plihte heora are 7 eallon heora æhtan*, although *feores scyldig* survives for the third. Wulfstan thus suggests the possibility of the death penalty, not its automatic imposition, and for only a small range of very serious crimes compared to the 'bloody code' of Athelstan.

In his lawcodes for Cnut Wulfstan's attitude to the death penalty follows very similar lines, expressing concern for the souls of the sinners. In the ecclesiastical code I Cnut death appears as a penalty for breaking royal or ecclesiastical sanctuary (*þolige landes 7 lifes*, 2.1), and in its secular counterpart, II Cnut, it is mentioned in connexion with witchcraft and prostitution (*on earde forfaren hig mid ealle*, 4a) and theft (*to timan forweorðan*, 4.2), as well as plotting against the king (*si he his feores scyldig*, 57) but in every case he provides the opportunity for repentance and redemption. His concern does not stop with this attempt at preemptive legislation, since he also tries to safeguard the well-being of the souls of condemned prisoners, maintaining that 'if a man condemned to death require confession, it is never to be refused him' (*gif deaðscyldig man scriftspæce gyrne, ne wyrne him man næfre*, 44), as well as trying to ban executions on Sundays (45). The language of confession and penance permeates both I and II Cnut to a greater extent than any other of Wulfstan's legislative programmes.

He may also have tried to keep criminals out of the hands of the secular authorities entirely, and to encourage a system instead by which contrition, confession, penance and absolution, administered by priests and bishops, replaced secular courts. In the prologue to the so-called 'Laws of Edward and Guthrum', Wulfstan describes the late ninth- and early tenth-century kings decreeing that secular law (*woruld bote*) is only to be used on recalcitrant people who refuse to submit to ecclesiastical penance and the *bisceopa dihte* (bishops' instructions).[44] This is anachronistic in the era around 900 for which he is claiming it; it may have seemed a little more plausible to Wulfstan for his own time, a century later. His longing to bring about an environment which facilitated salvation can be seen again in his addition to Ælfric's instructions that if a priest die in a brawl or a

---

[44] Liebermann, *Gesetze* I, p. 128

battle, no mass may be sung or prayers said, although he may nonetheless be buried. Wulfstan modifies this, adding that it should be a quarrel *þe he silfe geworhte* (which he incited himself) and specifying the nature of the burial: *on clænan legere, 7 lætan swa siððan eal to Godes dome* (in a clean grave, and leave the rest to God's judgement).[45] Wulfstan says that life-sparing punishments are for 'the benefit of the people' (*folce to þearfe*) without specifying whom he has in mind. His philosophy overall suggests that this phrase should be interpreted as widely as possible: his *folc* includes the criminals, the people who set up the gallows and tighten the nooses, the kings, bishops, ealdormen and reeves who sit in judgement, and the community at large. Wulfstan's guiding principle here, as with his redefinition of the criteria structuring Christian burial, was that no soul should be despaired of. Whether his ideals filtered through into the secular courts is harder to say.

'Who set you as a judge over thieves and robbers?': Ælfric on execution

Although Athelstan's lawcodes give no hint that Wulfhelm of Canterbury had any qualms about execution, we should not construct a picture of the pre-Benedictine Reform episcopate as uncritical supporters of the death penalty. One complicating figure is Theodred, bishop of London (*c.* 920 – *c.* 950), the king's messenger to the archbishop in the passage quoted above from VI Athelstan which raises the age of culpability to fifteen. That it was Theodred who may have brought the harshness of the law to Athelstan's attention is suggested by the bishop's reappearance in a cameo role in a miracle story in Abbo's *Passio Sancti Edmundi*, which was translated into Old English by Ælfric a generation later. Both Abbo's and Ælfric's versions include the story of how Theodred ordered the hanging of eight thieves who had attempted to rob St Edmund's shrine. He belatedly realized that this had been an inappropriate response for a man in holy orders, and he is described as repenting his *reðne dom* (cruel judgement) for the rest of his life. We do not know when in Theodred's long episcopate these two events occurred, but taken together they suggest that he was deeply involved in both the administration and the development of the law.

While VI Athelstan is a plea for mercy for young thieves, Ælfric's priority (following Abbo) in telling this story is to warn priests not to be involved in secular judgements. He finishes the anecdote by drawing on canon law to support the idea that bishops and priests should keep their hands clean: *hit ne gebyraþ þam þe beoð gecorene Gode to þegngenne þæt hi geþwærlæcan sceolon on æniges mannes deaðe* (it does not benefit those who are chosen for serving God that they should concur in the death of any man). This is in marked contrast to Wulfstan's concern with the soul of the man in the dock. His experience both of the Church and of the law would have been very different from that of Ælfric.[46]

---

[45] Only in CCCC 201, Ælfric's First Old English Letter for Wulfstan, 189, *Councils*, p. 297, addition in Wulfstan's own hand.

[46] J. Wilcox, 'The Wolf on Shepherds: Wulfstan, Bishops, and the Context of the *Sermo Lupi ad Anglos*', in Szarmach, *Old English Prose*, pp. 395–418.

First as bishop of London and then as bishop of Worcester and archbishop of York, he is likely to have overseen the shire-court twice a year for nearly thirty years.[47] Wulfstan clearly saw his role as one of moderator; in his treatise *Episcopus* he stresses the bishops' function as peace-makers when working with secular judges. His secular lawcodes are a different matter, reflecting the exigencies of his situation as a politician and legislator working with lay authorities, in which he cannot avoid the imposition of the death penalty altogether. What he can and does do, is to suggest alternative punishments such as mutilation, fines, confiscation of property, imprisonment and penal slavery.

Ælfric was moving in a mental world defined by texts as much as by experience, and where he was concerned textual authority was paramount and did not admit of compromise. By comparison, Wulfstan was in an invidious position, caught between incompatible secular and clerical standards of behaviour and trying to mediate between them. A glimpse of some irreconcilable clashes between cultures (and perhaps between these two churchmen) emerges in Ælfric's first Pastoral Letter to Wulfstan, written around 1006, in both Latin and English. In this letter, Ælfric forbids priests to carry weapons, to fight in battle or brawl, to work as reeves, or to frequent taverns and get drunk. This seems at first to be a somewhat random list of inappropriate lay activities, but there may be an underlying logic, the possibility of involvement in violent death. Drunkenness and death in brawls are linked together in the Exeter Book poem *The Fortunes of Men* (48–50): one leads to the other. A reeve is also likely to encounter violent death; Ælfric might have in mind legislation like VI Athelstan, the *friðgegyld* (peace-gild) agreement of the bishops and reeves of London, on what to do when faced with a defiant kindred who protect a thief. This text does not distinguish between behaviour appropriate for reeves and for bishops when it describes the requirement to recruit as many men as 'we think appropriate to intimidate the guilty' before going in pursuit of a thief *7 we ridan ealle to 7 urne teonan wrecan 7 þone þeof lecgean 7 þa þe him mid feohtan 7 standan* (and we are all to ride thither and avenge our injury and kill the thief and those who fight with him and support him).[48]

Ælfric's concern about the involvement of churchmen in the deaths of murderers and thieves may also imply that this was a topical issue in the tenth and eleventh centuries. The evidence of surviving writs reveals the ever-greater involvement of local land-owners in legal proceedings. From the 950s, royal writs begin to include phrases referring to the right to profit from the administration of justice. These rights include jurisdiction (*sake and soke*) and, first recorded in the reign of Cnut, *infangenþeof*, the specific right to try a thief arrested on one's property. Since the hanging of a thief was accompanied by the confiscation of his possessions, involvement in the death penalty was potentially a highly profitable exercise. As soon as rights of *sake and soke* and *infangenþeof* appear, they are given to ecclesiastical land-owners; the first reference to *sake and soke*, in 956, is

[47] Liebermann, *Gesetze* I, pp. 200–5.
[48] *Ibid.* I, pp. 173–83.

in connexion with a land-grant to the archbishop of York, and the earliest appearance of *infangenþeof*, in 1020, records Cnut giving the archbishop of Canterbury comprehensive judicial and financial rights over wrongdoers throughout his estates.[49] To the mind of an anxious reformer such as Ælfric, there is infinite potential for corruption here. At first sight, estate administration seems an odd companion to the other obviously violent behaviours he cites, but if priests are not only acting as reeves (bad enough in itself) but increasingly finding themselves sitting in judgement and administering harsh penal codes, then this grouping makes more sense. His concern about violent death becomes explicit in his conclusion to this section of the Letter to Wulfstan, which also reiterates his primary anxiety, the state of the priest's 'gentle innocence':

> *We ne moton beon ymbe mannes deað. þeah he manslaga beo oþþe morðfremmende oþþe mycel þeofman . . . tæcean þa læwedan men him lif oþþe dead, þæt we ne forleosan þa liþan unscæþþignysse, we, þe furþon ne moton ænne fugel acwellan.*[50]

> We may not be involved in the death of any man. Even if he commits manslaughter or murder, or is a great thief . . . let the laymen offer him life or death, so that we may not lose our gentle innocence, we who may not kill so much as a bird.

Unlike Wulfstan, Ælfric does not question the validity of the existence of the death penalty. In his terms, condemning a man to death is just as appropriate an action for the lay authorities as it is an inappropriate one for the religious.

He returns to the subject in the second Latin letter for Wulfstan, and here he may be personally critical of the archbishop. He starts by warning that priests are not to be judges and condemn thieves and robbers, citing Christ's own words from Luke 2:13–14, where Christ refuses to adjudicate in a contested inheritance, and he goes on

> et tu estimas te posse sine culpa de furibus aut latronibus iudicare? Caue, ne forte dicatur tibi a Christo: Quis te constituit iudicem furum aut latronum? Nam Christus, mittens discipulos ad praedicandum, dixit eis: Ite, ecce ego mitto uos sicut agnos inter lupos.

> and you think yourself capable without fault of judging thieves and robbers? Beware, lest Christ say to you 'Who set you as a judge over thieves and robbers?' For Christ, sending his disciples to preach, told them 'Go, behold, I send you as lambs among wolves' (Luke 10:3).

There are complex acts of ventriloquism going on here. Ælfric wrote his Pastoral Letters in the first person but not in his own voice; he writes as if his correspondent is speaking, with the idea that the bishop or archbishop receiving the letter will be conveying it to the priests or bishops of the diocese.[51] It is interesting therefore that in this passage he uses the second person singular rather than plural, and that he should draw on Luke 10:3 as his text, describing ideal bishops as lambs among wolves. Ælfric expands on the simile, defining lamb-like innocence, drawing on 2 Timothy 2:3 as authority for the argument that those fighting for God (*militans deo*) should not be involved in secular affairs, and condemning

---

[49] F. E. Harmer, *Anglo-Saxon Writs* (2nd edn, Stamford, 1989), pp. 73–9 and 183–4.
[50] *Councils*, pp. 299–300.
[51] Hill, 'Ælfric, Authorial Identity and the Changing Text', pp. 183–8.

judges and executioners: *Qui uero iudex aut occisor latronum est, non potest inter agnos innocentes computari* (truly, a judge and executioner of thieves cannot be counted among the innocent lambs). Thieves should be endured as part of worldly tribulation, and he regrets that contemporary bishops are failing to do so: *Sed ualde dolendum est in his diebus tanta neglegentia est in sacerdotibus et episcopis, qui . . . non audent de iustitia loqui, quia iustitiam nec faciaŋt nec diligunt* (But it is greatly to be regretted these days that there is so much negligence among priests and bishops who . . . should not dare to speak of justice, because they neither love justice nor deliver it).[52] The concepts and sentiments in Ælfric's letter have impeccable authority, and are appropriate for Wulfstan to preach to his subordinates. But were they meant to strike home? A few years later Wulfstan is on the record as calling himself Lupus, and Ælfric may be playing on this, accusing him of being insufficiently lamb-like. The picture painted here of modern (*his diebus*, a phrase which appears twice), worldly bishops, sitting in judgement over thieves and condemning them to death, may be Ælfric's harsh verdict on the compromises of Wulfstan, a man deeply involved in the world, who used the Christian understanding of capital punishment in his attempt to moderate the ruthlessness of the lay authorities, and to further the creation of what Wormald terms a 'Holy Society'.[53]

Reactions to the executed body

In III Æthelred, quoted above, we saw the provisions that take into account the grief and anger of the family of a executed thief, prepared to put their own bodies in the front line and endure the pain and potential public ignomiy of the ordeal. Other texts also register powerful responses to capital punishment. The archetypal executed body in Anglo-Saxon England was that of Christ Himself, and there are many retellings of His trial, sentencing and death. In Vercelli Homily I and a group of associated homilies the comparatively restrained *crucifige crucifige* of the biblical crowd becomes *Ho hin man raðe, he is deaþe scyldig* (hang Him swiftly, He is guilty of death), echoing the language of the lawcodes and suggesting a dramatic process by which Christ's Passion is assimilated to the imagery of contemporary capital punishment.[54]

These narratives are further complicated by the presence of the two common thieves crucified with Christ, one of whose souls is saved in the last moments of his life through his recognition of Christ as the Son of God. In the didactic text 'Twelve ways to forgiveness', copied in two versions in Laud 482, the good thief is acknowledged as the archetypal martyr. He was also a devotional focus, and a prayer for the hour of None identifies the person praying with the thief on the cross.[55] The supplicant describes Christ as hanging on the gallows, and recounts

---

[52] B. Fehr, *Die Hirtenbriefe Ælfrics in altenglischer und lateinischer Fassung* (Hamburg, 1914), Letter 3, pp. 66–7.
[53] P. Wormald, *Legal Culture*, pp. 225–46.
[54] Scragg, *Vercelli Homilies* I, p. 30, lines 164–5.
[55] Muir, *A Pre-Conquest English Prayer-Book*, p. 139.

the story of *þone scaþan . . . þe on þe gelyfde* (the criminal . . . who believed in You), whom Christ took with Him into paradise. It concludes with a reference to confession (*Ic þe eadmodlice mine synna andette*) and a request to be treated like the thief: *þat ic mote æfter minre forþfore neorxnawonges gatu agan* (that I may after my death attain the gate of paradise). By employing words like *galgan, ahangen, scaþan* and *hangadest* the prayer dissolves the distinction between crucifixion and the contemporary practice of execution by hanging, as do many other texts including *The Dream of the Rood*, also in the Vercelli Codex. Anglo-Saxon churchmen (and perhaps also laymen), when faced with the question of contemporary capital punishment, must have been reminded of the Passion by prayers like this. They may also have considered the idea that a man may be condemned by the State and still, like the thief, be saved, or even, like Christ, be innocent. Underlying this there is also the difficult question, so frequently repeated by Wulfstan, of whether it is appropriate for an earthly power to end even a guilty human life when God incarnate had purchased that life at so great a cost.

Christ's body is far from being the only executed and displayed corpse in Anglo-Saxon writing. There are several narrative texts which explore this idea, including the *Legend of the Seven Sleepers*, the Exeter Book poem *The Fortunes of Men* and the *De Obsessione Dunelmi*. These are very different texts, the first an English adaptation of a legend that was also widely popular in its Latin recension, the second a vernacular gnomic poem, and the third a post-Conquest Latin account of some Durham estates. However, all show an interest in what it means to exhibit bodies which have undergone a violent death, and each presents them in complex and perhaps unexpected ways.

The Seven Sleepers: *execution and affective narrative*

The *Legend of the Seven Sleepers* tells the story of seven Christians of Ephesus who flee to a cave when Christianity was still illegal and fall asleep there, only to awake hundreds of years later to find their forbidden faith is now the official religion. The story survives in eleventh-century manuscripts that are primarily Ælfrician in content, although this particular text is not by Ælfric, and Magennis argues that while it is a product of someone educated in the atmosphere of the Benedictine Reform, it does not derive from the Winchester circle associated with Æthelwold.[56] Both the Latin and English versions in circulation in Anglo-Saxon England use strikingly affective language, and the English is particularly concerned with emotion and motivation, to an extent not commonly found in Anglo-Saxon writing.[57] The author's vision seems to be informed by the contemporary landscape of capital punishment, turned to a didactic purpose.

Before the seven sleepers escape to the cave, there is a vivid account of the torture and execution of the Ephesian Christians by the emperor. Those who will

---

[56] H. Magennis (ed.), *The Anonymous Old English Legend of the Seven Sleepers*, Durham Medieval Texts, no. 7 (Durham, 1994).

[57] H. Magennis, 'The Anonymous Old English *Legend of the Seven Sleepers* and Its Latin Source', *Leeds Studies in English*, n.s. 22 (1992), pp. 43–56.

not submit are killed and their bodies are put on display: *þa heafodleasne man hengc on ða portweallas, and man sette heora heafda swilce oðra ðeofa buton portweallas on þam heafodstoccum* (the headless bodies were hanged on the town-walls, and the heads were set like so many thieves outside the town-walls on head-stakes).[58] Although in outline this is very close to the Latin parallel printed by Magennis, the Anglo-Saxon writer has altered the picture slightly, specifying that it is the *headless* bodies which are hung from the walls, that the heads are displayed on head-stakes outside the walls, suggesting something more technical than the *lignum* of the Latin version, and he inserts the idea that the Christians are being treated 'as if they were so many thieves'. *Heafod-stoccas* is a term which crops up in charter bounds, and Reynolds has demonstrated the probability that they were used for precisely this purpose. At the Old Dairy Cottage site two kilometres north of Winchester an execution cemetery was excavated in which seventy-eight per cent of the bodies had been decapitated; the site of the excavation corresponds with three adjoining sets of charter bounds which mention 'head-stakes' at this spot.[59] The charter bounds with landmarks such as *þam heafod stoccan* (the head-stakes) include early tenth-century grants from Eadwig to the nuns of Wilton and Æthelstan to Holy Trinity.[60] Like the grants of *sake and soke* and *infangenþeof*, this suggests that executed and displayed corpses could be part of the landscape of ecclesiastical estates as well as lay ones.

This impression of contemporary applicability is strengthened by the English adaptor's rewriting of the responses to the displayed bodies, both from the citizens and from the carrion birds. Where the latter are concerned, the Latin text refers only to *uolucres caeli* (birds of the air), but the English specifies them as scavengers and 'birds of battle': *hrocas and hremmas and feala cynna fugelas* (rooks and ravens and many kinds of bird). In the Latin they take the martyrs' flesh *in ore suo* (in their mouth), while in English it is more precisely *heora blodigon bilon* (their bloody bills). Both texts refer to the birds eating the soft internal organs (*carnes . . . et uiscera* and *flæsc . . . ðearmas and inneweard*), but only the English writer includes the detail that the birds also *þara haligra martyra eagum ut ahaccedon* (pecked out the eyes of the holy martyrs), and then flew into the city, presumably bringing the eyes with them. This increased attention to detail is matched by his reworking of the reactions of the onlookers. As Magennis notes, he picks up the idea that parents and children betrayed each other from fear, but he makes this into a much more complex relationship, and extends the definition of kinship to include siblings:

And ða magas beheoldon hu heora magas þrowodon and on portweallon to wafersyne hangodon; se broðor beheold his swuster on wite, and seo swuster beheold hire broðor on yrmðe.[61]

58 Magennis, *Seven Sleepers*, p. 35 and Appendix p. 74.
59 Reynolds, 'Anglo-Saxon Law in the Landscape', pp. 130 and 163.
60 *Ibid.*, pp. 175–7.
61 Magennis, *Seven Sleepers*, p. 36.

And kin beheld their kin suffering and hanging from the walls; the brother saw his sister in torment, and the sister saw her brother in agony.

The Latin writer refers to the spectacle of the hanging bodies in a rhetorical question (*Quis ergo luctus fuit huic maior . . . ?*), but he does not personalize them as someone's family in the way the English writer does, nor does he offer his audience the chance to view the bodies through the eyes of their siblings.

Magennis points out that, as well as a hagiographical treatment of the seven sleepers, the story also has a specific doctrinal purpose, to emphasize the literal truth of the resurrection of the body, prefigured in the way that the seven sleepers rise from death. He suggests that this message is 'proportionately less emphasized in the Old English than in other versions', but we should rather understand the writer to be achieving the same end through narrative and symbol rather than explicit didacticism.[62] The awakening of the seven sleepers prefigures the aesthetics of the resurrection, with their faces blooming *swilce rose and lilie*, and this is spelled out by the bishop's message to the emperor, in which he writes *us se towearde ærist ealra manna nu gecyðed open tacna, and Godes halige martyras syndon arisene* (the forthcoming general resurrection is now declared to us in a clear sign, and God's holy martyrs have risen). But the sleepers are not the first 'holy martyrs' we have met in this text, and we may assume that the others, first decapitated and displayed by the State then shredded and digested by carrion birds, will also be resurrected in similarly flower-like bodies. Magennis claims that the details of the mutilated bodies 'have been added by the Old English writer with unÆlfrician enthusiasm', but the author had a serious doctrinal intent, conveyed through affective language and the evoking of compassion and horror, rather than a schoolboy gleefulness in gory detail.[63] His text resonates with the passage from III Æthelred on the reburying of thieves' bodies, showing again an awareness of the relative nature of judgements of guilt and innocence.

The Fortunes of Men: *judgement left to God*

The same complex attitude underpins the representation of the hanged man in *The Fortunes of Men*, an Exeter Book poem which catalogues various untimely deaths as part of a series of events that might occur throughout life. We have already looked at this poem's attitude to knowledge of the future in contrast to the prognostics; its attitude to the hanged man and the other corpses it describes suggest that it also engages in vigorous debate with authoritative versions of the body's significance. The subject of the poem is the different kinds of lives that men may lead, the talents they may display and the deaths they may encounter. Raw suggests that its main theme is 'man's helplessness', but that is only part of the poet's intent, and not the final message the reader is meant to internalize.[64]

---

[62] *Ibid.*, p. 21.
[63] H. Magennis, 'Style and Method in the Old English Version of the Legend of the Seven Sleepers', *English Studies* 66 (1985), pp. 285–95.
[64] B. Raw, *The Art and Background of Old English Poetry* (London, 1978), p. 73.

The poem's very structure highlights the poet's interest in the relationship between life and death. It begins with a description of a couple having a child and bringing him up lovingly, unaware of the potential dangers in store (1–9). It then moves on to its list of death and disaster (10–57), before continuing with a range of the skills and pleasures available to human beings (58–92) and closing with praise of God's artistry and an invitation to give thanks (93–8). The theme of death is thus emphasized in two ways, first in that it takes up nearly half the poem (forty-seven lines out of ninety-eight) and second in that the catalogue of death is positioned counter-intuitively, immediately following a description of birth and followed in turn by the account of different ways of life. This ingenious playing with expectation means that the poet's main theme, that death can happen at any time, is built into the overarching structure as well as being visible on the small scale in his anecdotes of the different forms that death may take.

There are many different deaths listed in *The Fortunes of Men:* being eaten by a wolf; killed by famine, or by bad weather, or by a spear; dying in battle; falling from a tree, being burned, being hanged; alcoholism and provoking a fatal quarrel in the mead hall. Isaacs and Swenson have separately argued that these deaths have liminal, even shamanic, associations, but there is no need to situate them outside normal expectation.[65] On the contrary the poet is intentionally bringing all of these terrifying fates into the realm of ordinary life. They are juxtaposed with an account of a man who overcomes misfortunes in youth *mid godes meahtum* (through God's power) to live a long and prosperous life surrounded by his family (58–63), but we do not learn how he dies. The poet then lists morally neutral though God-given talents, including skill at board-games, scholarship, gold-smithing, falconry, music and story-telling, none of which connects with (or precludes) any of the fates mentioned earlier. These juxtapositions challenge the audience to work out the connexions between the different elements of the poem, but this is something of a trick question: the riddle's solution is that there is no connexion.

The poem opens with the arrival of a child, also *mid godes meahtum*,[66] focusing on the child's bodily rather than its spiritual life, on the physicality and energy of *geongan leomu* and *liffæstan leoþu* (young limbs, and lively joints). The parents seem like little gods in charge of their creation: *Fergaþ swa ond feþað fæder ond modor, giefaþ and gierwaþ* (So they ferry him and feed him, father and mother, guide him and garb him, lines 11–12a), until this illusion of omnipotence is demolished: *God ana wat hwæt him weaxendum winter bringað* (God alone knows what the winters will bring him as he grows up! lines 12b–13). The poet opens up a range of terrifying potential fates for these cherished children, still focusing on their physicality rather than their spirituality. The first death is being devoured by a wolf: the child has moved from being fed to becoming food itself. The second is *hungor*, again a poignant contrast to the care given by the parents.

---

65 N. D. Isaacs, 'Up a Tree: To See *The Fates of Men*', in Nicholson and Frese, *Anglo-Saxon Poetry*, pp. 363–75, 366; K. Swenson, 'Death Appropriated in *The Fates of Men*', *Studies in Philology* 88 (1991), pp. 123–39, 127.

66 *Fortunes of Men*, lines 1–3a.

Later on, the hanged man also becomes food for the black raven, who *nimeþ heafodsyne*, steals his eyes. All the deaths listed are brutal and sudden; the poet has no interest in the slow processes of disease, in death in or after childbirth, or in old age. Even starvation is a thief: *Sumne sceal hungor ahiþan* (Hunger shall steal one, 15a). Nor are his corpses shown in prolonged decay. Instead, they fall apart or are dissected in dramatic ways, an instructive contrast to the slow fade-out depicted in Vercelli IX, and the antithesis of a death *mid gedefenesse*. These scattered, burnt or devoured bodies are also the opposite of the ideal constructed in the grave through the use of stones, charcoal and coffins. The moment of separation when soul and body part company is mentioned three times, but the destination of these souls is unknown – their deaths are never placed in a context of heavenly judgement.[67] Only two of the poet's dead men are judged at all, the hanged man and the drunkard. *Bið him werig noma* (his name shall be cursed), the poet says of the first. *Noma* does not alliterate, and the poet could have equally well chosen *sawl* or *gast*; the choice of *noma* suggests that this man has been condemned by his fellows, not damned by God. Of the second, the poet says that men will tell tales of his drunkenness and refers to him as a *sylfcwale* (suicide). Reputation is the focus in both these cases, not salvation.

Living and dying in this poem are not part of the same plot: they are linked by 'and' rather than 'because'. God plays the role of a Boethian Providence rather than a personal Lord who has entered historical time: *Swa wrætlice weoroda nergend geond middangeard monna cræftas sceop and scyrede and gesceapo ferede æghwylcum on eorþan eormencynnes* (So with art the Saviour of the hosts throughout the world shaped the skills of men, and appointed and guided the fate of every member of mankind on earth, lines 93–8). Christ is not mentioned, nor are heaven and hell. Nonetheless, this work was produced, reproduced and preserved in a Christian context, pursuing a radical, even transgressive, line of thought when compared to the hagiographic or judicial mainstream. The poet resists the theory that someone's way of dying tells you about the state of their soul, and he implies the converse, that even people who have been cast out by the community, exiled, reviled or executed, have a chance for salvation. The most spiritual image in the whole poem (*sawlhord*, treasure of the soul, 34b) is applied to the body of the hanged man, and we are given no idea whether this man is guilty or innocent, or for what crime he has been condemned. *The Fortunes of Men* is also a sustained plea against complacency, reminding the reader that anything that can happen, can happen to you. Raw's reading, that the poem is about helplessness, is only true in a limited sense.[68] One cannot govern the shape death takes, but one can live in continual awareness of the imminent possibility of violent, unanticipated and undeserved death, giving thanks to God for the mercies he prescribes (*þæs þe he fore his miltsum monnum scrifeð*, 98).

---

[67] *sawle bireafod, fealleþ on foldan, feorð biþ on siþe*, lines 25b–26; *biþ his life scæcen*, line 39b; *þær him lifgedal lungre weorðeð*, line 45.

[68] Raw, *Art and Background of Old English Poetry*, p. 73.

De Obsessione Dunelmi: *the bodies of the enemy*

These texts discuss the bodies of the martyr and the criminal: the final category of displayed body under consideration is that of the enemy killed in battle. *De Obsessione Dunelmi* is a brief Latin narrative of eleventh-century Northumbrian politics, written at the end of that century, and in its account of the display of enemy heads it highlights many problematic and contradictory elements in the understanding of the meaning of these corpses and their display. The story starts with the description of the siege of Durham by the Scots from which it takes its modern title.[69] King Malcolm and the Scottish army, having devastated Northumbria, laid siege to Durham, probably in 1006.[70] Bishop Ealdhun of Durham had married his daughter to Uhtred, son of the earl of Northumbria, and Uhtred came to his father-in-law's aid, massacring the Scottish host, decapitating them and transporting the heads to Durham for exhibition on the city walls:

> Interfectorum uero capita, elegantiora crinibus, sicut tunc temporibus mos erat, perplexis, fecit Dunelmum transportari, eaque a quatuor mulieribus perlota per circuitum murorum in stipitibus praefigi; mulieribus autem quae ea lauerant mercedem dederant vaccas singulis singulas.[71]

> The heads of the slain, made more presentable with their hair combed, as was the custom in those days, he had transported to Durham, and they were washed by four women and fixed on stakes around the circuit of the walls; the women who had previously washed them were each rewarded with a single cow.

The author of *De Obsessione Dunelmi* does not tell us whether Bishop Ealdhun was complicit in this triumphalism but there is no hint in the narrative that Uhtred set up his trophies around the walls outside the cathedral in the face of his episcopal father-in-law's protests, and the author of *De Obsessione* (himself either secular canon or Benedictine monk of Durham) recounts the detail without criticism. The bodies of the dead Scots are translated from the raw violence of the battlefield to formal display on the walls of Durham by an elaborate ritual 'as was then the custom'. The way the story is told suggests that these are details added for local and historic colour. We do not know Uhtred's motives in paying for the washing and combing of the severed heads, but the dead Scots should not necessarily be seen in the same light as executed thieves or murderers, and there may be a measure here of respect for the dead fallen in battle. Whatever the process represents, it makes it clear, as with Abbo's story of Bishop Theodred, that corpses resulting from violent death, on the battlefield or the gallows, were potent symbols, subject to a quasi-dramatic exhibition. This is also clear from the excavated execution cemeteries which are almost invariably sited on elevated locations, in association with earlier barrows or earthworks and near routeways, all of which suggests the creation of a theatre of execution.[72]

---

[69] C. J. Morris, *Marriage and Murder in Eleventh-Century Northumbria: A Study of the 'De Obsessione Dunelmi'*, Borthwick Paper 82 (York, 1992).
[70] Fletcher, *Bloodfeud*, pp. 52–6.
[71] Arnold, *Symeonis Monachi Opera Omnia* I, p. 216.
[72] Reynolds, *Later Anglo-Saxon England*, pp. 103–10.

That such display was a deep-rooted tradition is suggested by the fate of the seventh-century king Oswald, who similarly had his head displayed on a stake after his death in battle.[73] As we saw in Chapter One, Oswald was eventually the subject of a cult in several different sites, including Durham, Bamburgh and Æthelflæd's mausoleum in Gloucester. Oswald's transformation from battle-trophy to relic exemplifies the way that that most potent symbol, a human head on a stake, shifts between meanings. Ealdhun, as bishop of Durham, was the guardian of Oswald's head at the same time as he was complicit in displaying the heads of the Scots. Like Theodred, Ealdhun transgresses the ideals of priestly behaviour transmitted by Ælfric: bishops were supposed to dissociate themselves from criminal bodies, but contact with saints' bodies was a defining episcopal activity.[74]

The same blurring of meaning occurs with the tending of enemy's corpses and saintly corpses, visible in Ælfric's *passio* of St Edmund. The thieves, after all, are not the only significant bodies in this story. After Edmund is translated from his original shrine to the new church at Bury St Edmund's, a widow, Oswyn, lived *æt þæs halgan byrgene* (at the saint's grave) and had the job of trimming the saint's hair and nails every year and keeping them in a shrine as relics on the altar.[75] Like the women of Durham, Oswyn seems to have a quasi-official function in tending to the dead body; part of her curiously intimate job is to generate an apparently never-ending supply of relics from the saint's incorrupt corpse.

These texts construct a three-way opposition, between the laymen who kill enemies in battle and execute criminals, the churchmen who canonize and translate the corpses of the saints, and the women mediating between the living and dead, whose job involves caring equally for both the vilified and the vener-ated. There are exceptions to this model: as well as the transgressive bishops, there is the Winchester monk Edwin, whose desire to groom St Cuthbert leads him to disobey the direct orders of his abbot and travel to Durham, where he is allowed to wash, comb, trim and reclothe the body, and take the old clothes away with him.[76] These bodies, the Scots, Edmund, Cuthbert, are all unusual, but they may represent the extreme end of ordinary practice, the washing, tending and reclothing of the body before burial, and outside monasteries this is likely to have been women's work. Perhaps this is where the *wrecche wif* of the fragmentary Worcester *Soul and Body* comes in, not as a burial specialist exactly but as the kind of layer-out who lasted in many English communities into very recent times. The people whose bodies are excluded from this tending are the criminals; Reynolds notes the extreme carelessness with which they were buried as well as the evidence that they were clothed, suggesting that this represents an intentional inversion of a meaningful and widespread norm. In Chapter Two, we looked

---

[73] *LS* II, XXVI, p. 137, line 166 and p. 143, line 260.

[74] M. Lapidge, 'Æthelwold as Scholar and Teacher', in B. Yorke (ed.), *Bishop Æthelwold: His Career and Influence* (Woodbridge, 1988), pp. 89–117, 113.

[75] *LS* II, XXXII, pp. 189–94.

[76] Harmer, *Writs*, pp. 387–95 and pp. 401–3: the letter itself is probably a twelfth-century concoction, but the anecdote may well record an early eleventh-century event.

briefly at the 'Quinity' illustration from Ælfwine's Prayerbook and noted its demarcation of the sacred and profane. This picture could also be seen as an embodiment of the ideals of tenth- and eleventh-century justice, Christ the Judge on His bench among His counsellors and kin, at the centre of the charmed circle, while the rejected, chained, defeated and damned are literally expelled to the periphery, to the marginal *cwealm-stowas* and the *hæþen pytte*.

The last judgement

We have seen how the Doomsday categories of souls suggested by Gregory's *Moralia in Job* underlie many of the Church- and State-imposed sentences of death and excluded burial, and how Church and State authorities could manipulate the resulting landscape to generate assumptions about the fates of individuals, whether by moving Oswald's relics to a new tomb, or burying the bodies of adulterers and oath-breakers *in ful* with their hanged or decapitated companions. We have also seen how the texts preserved in Laud 482 model the confessional encounter and Last Judgement on each other, and how Archbishop Wulfstan attempted to theorize the secular legal system in terms of the discourse of confession and the Lord's Prayer. A variety of sources has stressed the intimacy of the encounter with Christ at Doomsday, particularly again the passages anthologized in Laud 482 which emphasize the supporting role of the priest in testifying on his parishioner's behalf. This has its inverse in the Sodbury lawsuit, which invites us to imagine the souls of Eastmund and Eanbald, themselves priests, accusing their descendants of theft *beforan Godes heahsetle æt þam miclan dome* (before God's high seat at the great judgement). The idea of intimacy is also stressed in the Masham Stone and the associated nexus of ideas centred on nudity, which can simultaneously signify innocence and shame. Again and again, these texts stress the significant eschatological experience as the end of time rather than the moment of death. While we have not yet looked directly at any Doomsday narratives or images in detail, other than Vercelli IX, many of the sources so far have contributed to this composite yet consistent picture.

In her recent study of the Anglo-Saxon visualization of the interim paradise, Kabir draws attention to the variety of ways in which this might be represented in vernacular literature. She contests Gatch's assertions about the coherency of Ælfric's beliefs about paradise, while demonstrating the richness of vernacular writings 'freed from pressures to conform or elucidate doctrine'.[77] Visions of the Last Judgement participate in a similarly creative enterprise, focusing variously on the reunion of body and soul, the presence of various intercessors, the audience of all intelligent creation and the face-to-face encounter with Christ. Grundy shows how Ælfric's eschatological thinking depends primarily on Augustine, enriched by ideas from Gregory's *Dialogues*, the *Prognosticon Futuri Saeculi* of Julian of Toledo, and Bede's Visions of Fursey and Dryhthelm, but clearly there

---

[77] Kabir, *Paradise, Death and Doomsday*, pp. 73–6 and 57–65. For a similar reading of Old English legends of the Fall see V. Thompson, 'The Understanding of Death', pp. 38–60.

were many other traditions in circulation.[78] The theme is ubiquitous, both in detailed treatment and as a deep structural element underlying many other narratives and documents.

Vercelli Homily IV: love story and courtroom drama

Vercelli IV, which has no identifiable source, conjures up a vast court with a trial in progress. The narratorial viewpoint pans around the crowds of men, angels and demons who have come to hear the soul accused (*þæt hie þæt gestal gehyrað*) before focusing on Christ instructing His angelic messengers to invite the good soul home to heaven. Although parts of the homily appear in several other manuscripts, this Doomsday vision is unique to Vercelli IV. Scragg expresses surprise that this should be the case as he finds it more 'aesthetically appealing' than the 'relatively unremarkable' passages that were to enter the canon.[79] But Vercelli IV sails close to the wind in its treatment of the soul–body relationship, and this might explain why the scene is unique.

After the soul has heard the angels' invitation to come into *þinum huse*, the story abruptly changes key, as the soul replies with an apparent *non sequitur*:

> *Ic gesio hwær min lichama stent on midre þisse menigo. Lætaþ hine to me. Ne sie he næfre wyrma mete, ne to grimmum geolstre mote wyrðan. He swanc for me, 7 ic gefeah on him.*[80]

> I see where my soul stands in the midst of this crowd. Let him come to me. Never let him be food for worms, nor become foul putrid matter. He worked for me and I rejoiced in him.

This is a startling moment, comic both in that it plays with the audience's expectation, as the soul's outburst diverts the course of the narrative envisaged by Christ and the angels, and in that it refocuses the story on the erotically informed reunion of blessed body and soul. The sense that this is a love story comes partly from the soul's grammatically feminine and the body's masculine gender, but also from details such as the soul looking at the body *swiðe bliðum eagum* (with such happy eyes) and telling it *Ic gefeo in þe* (I rejoice in thee), and the soul becoming the intercessor for the body. Immediately before the soul's speech quoted above, the angels address the soul with *we ðe lædað to ðam þe þu ær lufodest* (we are taking you to the one whom you loved before). There has been no mention of the body yet, and the presumptive referent of *ðam* in this sentence is Christ. The body seems about to be left behind when the soul spots it in the crowd, and this sense that the body could potentially be abandoned is reinforced by the soul's then being given a long speech to Christ, asking that the body may come too, and pleading its virtues:

---

[78] L. Grundy, *Books and Grace: Ælfric and Theology*, King's College London Medieval Studies VI (Exeter, 1991), p. 213 and ch. 4, *passim*.

[79] Scragg, *Vercelli Homilies*, p. 88.

[80] *Ibid.*, p. 115, lines 124–7.

Drihten, ne todæl ðu me 7 minne lichoman. . . . Dryhten hælend, ic bidde ðe eaðmodre stefne 7 mildre þæt þu ne læte minne lichoman on forlor lædan þa he swiðost swanc for me on þinum naman. Ne læt hine, dryhten, swa gedrehtne.[81]

Lord, do not separate me and my body . . . Lord saviour, I beseech You with humble and meek voice that You do not let my body go to destruction when it worked so hard for me in Your name. Do not let it, Lord, be thus oppressed.

The idea that Christ might save the soul but reject the body is theologically dubious, to say the least, and perhaps explains why none of the manuscripts which share other passages with Vercelli IV chose to repeat this scene. As it turns out, the body is not rejected, and the risk of a heretical rejection of the material world as inherently corrupt has been averted, but the possibility has been raised that Christ could have decided otherwise.

The reunion of body and soul is described in richly sensuous language, with the audience invited directly to participate (*men þa leofestan, utan geþencan . . .*) in visualizing the soul speaking to the body *glædlice . . . wynsumlice . . . fægre . . . mildlice* (happily . . . joyfully . . . beautifully . . . gently) as the two blend into one in a complex development of images. The body shimmers through *manigfealdum bleon* (many changes of appearance), first regaining the look of an ordinary human being (*medmicles mannes hiwe*), then of the loveliest one (*fægerestan mannes hiwe*); taking on the beauty of lilies and roses, then metals and jewels (*golde 7 seolfre 7 swa þam deorwyrðestan gymcynne 7 eorcnanstanum*), and finally heavenly bodies (*he glitenað swa steorra, 7 lyht swa mone, 7 beorhtaþ swa sunna þonne hio biorhtust bið scinende*), upon which Christ (*se hælend*) invites them into heaven. This is an informative aesthetic hierarchy to set against the lawcodes' proscriptions of worship of pagan gods (understood euhemeristically as falsely venerated humans), plants, stones and the moon, stars and sun. The pagans worship these things: the Christians, through worship of their Creator, partake of and transcend their beauty. In Vercelli IX, discussed in Chapter Two, we saw one way of conveying the joys of salvation; here Vercelli IV provides another, as aesthetically, even erotically, appealing although very different in content.

If the reunion of good soul and body resembles a love story, the reunion of evil soul and body may be compared to a domestic row of epic proportions, in which, as in *Soul and Body*, the body appears as the helpless recipient of the soul's abuse: *þu eorðan lamb 7 dust 7 wyrma gifel, 7 þu wambscyldiga fætels 7 gealstor 7 fulnes 7 hræw . . . a me þuhte þæt wyt wæron to lange ætgædere* (Oh, you thing of earth and clay and dust and worm-feast, and you belly guilty vessel and pus and foulness and corpse . . . I always thought we were together too long).[82] The soul turns from haranguing the body to apostrophizing death (*La ðu deað . . . Eala ðu deað*) for over sixty lines, using the speech to sum up the body's sins in terms of corporal acts of mercy left undone. Death is bitterly reproached for not taking the *treowleasan flæsc* (faithless flesh) earlier. Finally the soul turns back

[81] *Ibid.*, pp. 95–6, lines 136–44.
[82] *Ibid.* IV, p. 98.

to the body, and in an extraordinary speech, piling noun upon noun, it ascribes itself twenty-five different qualities, an anthology conflating other authors' definitions of soul with those of mind and life-force, before concluding *Eall þæt þu wære, ic was þis eall on þe 7 siðþan ic ana wæs of ðe, eall þis þe losode* (all that you were, I was all this in you, and when I was separate from you, all this was lost to you).[83] This rhetoric defeats itself, as the soul's harangue is predicated on the idea that in life it had been the powerless prisoner of the hell-bent body, and yet, had it really provided the body's thoughts and motive power, it would logically have been able to control the body's behaviour. This internal contradiction informs other turns of phrase in the same speech, where the soul, having asserted *ic wæs þin lufu* (I was your love) goes on to say *eall þæt þu lufodest, eall þæt ic feode* (all that you loved, I hated). It would therefore be unwise to accept this portrait as a reliable depiction of the Anglo-Saxon understanding of the soul: it is a *damned* soul speaking, after all. The homilist is deploying a coherent ironic mode, setting up the bad soul as the mouth-piece of inconsistency and challenging the audience to question its reliability.

Attention then turns to the body, *ðæt deade flæsc* (that dead flesh), who during this whole speech has been sweating ugly drops of foul perspiration (*swiðe laðlicum swæte*). In tandem, evil body and soul begin to change. They become like ugly men, then grow pale and bruised, alternating between pallor and darkness (*collsweart*) in images that could easily apply to the changing colours of a newly dead corpse, but they are very much alive, they are both terrified (*butu swiðe forhte*) and they tremble (*bifigiende*). At this point a new character enters the script, the devil, who appeals to the judge to be given *min agen* (my own), cheerfully taking the credit for teaching body and soul their evil ways (*ic hie lærde hiora unriht*), his use of the third person plural undermining the soul's earlier claims to passive victimhood. Finally we hear the voice of Christ. Whereas the good person perceived Him as *se hælend* (the saviour), the bad one does not even see Him, only hearing *se cyninges stefn* (the king's voice), commanding the soul to re-enter the *forlorene* body: *ða gyt ætsomne syngodon, gyt eac ætsomne sweltan* (since you sinned together, you shall die together). Christ's voice thus seals the verdict on soul as well as body: they are equally culpable.

'Porter of the gates of hell': St Peter and the last judgement

In Vercelli IV, Christ's is the only voice of authority at Doomsday.[84] In contrast, two other homilies incorporate a more complex cast, with Mary, Michael and Peter successfully interceding for condemned souls (Vercelli XV, CCCC, MS 41/303). Clayton notes their problematic theology, explicitly condemned by Ælfric, and concludes that no single source can be identified for the theme,

---

[83] The soul claims responsibility for conception, gestation, spirit, beauty, joy, speech, smell, breath, sight, hearing, gladness, glory, thought, fairness, love, stability, faith, movement, ability to walk, support, memory, sport, rejoicing, laughter and mirth.

[84] Scragg, *Vercelli Homilies*, p. 89.

although it 'was a relatively well-known one in Anglo-Saxon England'.[85] She also argues that the Virgin was the most important intercessor. However, these narratives have another prominent character in Peter, who is not only the final intercessor, but also the protagonist of the following scene of locking the damned into hell. Whereas Clayton's interest in these homilies lies primarily in establishing their textual interrelationships and possible sources, they may also be read for their literary value, their guiding of audience response, their possible institutional origins and their relationship with other Anglo-Saxon cultural fields.

The more complex of the two versions of the intercession story comes in Vercelli XV, where it takes up sixty lines, placing the events before judgement; the shorter account, in CCCC 41/303, places it even more challengingly *after* judgement. Vercelli XV begins with Mary seeing *þone earmigan heap 7 þone sarigan 7 þone dreorigan* (the pitiful and sorry and mournful crowd) of souls about to be damned; she weeps and falls at Christ's feet, reminding Him that He was once a child in her womb and begging Him not to let so many *þines handgeweorces* (of your handiwork) fall into the devil's clutches. He gives her a third of a redeemable subset of the sinners, but there are still many *sarig 7 dreorig*, wishing that they had never been born. It is now Michael's turn to approach Christ. Like Mary, he weeps, unlike her he crawls (*crypð mid handum 7 fotum*); he too receives a third of the sinners. These two vignettes, similar in structure, set up an expectation that the third will follow the same pattern, but in fact it is very different. Whereas with Mary and Michael the focus has been on their outward behaviour as they approach Christ, with Peter it is on his emotions. He is described in exactly the terms previously applied twice to the sinners, *swiðe sarig 7 swiðe dreorig* (so sorry and so mournful), he sheds *miclan sarigan tearum* (many sorry tears) and he falls at Christ's feet explicitly *mid myclum eadmedum* (with much humility), which with the other two intercessors we had been left to infer from their actions. This interest in Peter's inner state constructs him as a more complex figure than the others, and his identification with the sinners suggests that we are being prompted to supply the story of his own triple denial of Christ and subsequent forgiveness. This is also inferred from the phrasing of the intercessory appeals: Mary and Michael both make it clear from the start that they are begging on other people's behalf (*ne forlæte ðu næfre . . .* ; *nu ic ðe bidde . . . þæt ðu næfre forlæte . . .*) whereas Peter's speech begins ambiguously *Ic bidde þe . . . ðæt ðu me forgife* (I ask you You . . . that You grant/forgive me) before clarifying that he is asking favours not for himself but for the sinners. Peter is himself more approachable because he understands sin and repentance from within.

Peter then appeals to Christ, citing Matthew 16 and claiming the keys to both hell and heaven in so many words, *ðu me sealdest 7 me geuðest heofona rices cægan 7 eac helle wita* (You gave me the keys of heaven and also of hell torment), and He gives Peter a third of the sinners. Christ then invites the blessed into heaven while devils drive the damned to hell, accompanied by Peter: *se halga*

---

85   Clayton, 'Delivering the Damned', p. 101.

Petrus gæð mid 7 bereð helle cægan on handa (the holy Peter goes too and carries hell's key in his hands). The homilist encourages his audience (*Eala, broðor mine*) to imagine the sorry cries, groans and gnashing of teeth as the damned are herded into hell. Peter then locks the wretched souls into eternal torment (*ecan cwylmnesse*), before turning away and throwing the key behind him:

> *7 he þonne weorpeð ða cearfullan cæge ofer bæc in on þa helle. ðis he deð for ðam þe he ne mæg locian on ðæt mycle sar . . . Eala, broðor mine, hu mycel 7 hu hlude bið se cnyll þonne seo cæge fealleð in ða helle.*[86]

> and he then throws that key full of care over his back into hell. He does this because he cannot look at all that sorrow . . . alas, my brothers, how great and how loud is the knell as the key falls in hell.

The homilist adds a cautionary note that the damned souls and the devils *ne ðurfan . . . wenan* (need not expect) that they will ever again have respite, and finishes with a brief vision of God with his entourage of angels, apostles and blessed entering heaven for an eternity of glory.

On the evidence of imperfect Latinity evinced by the earlier part of Vercelli XV (a translation of the *Apocalypse of Thomas*), Scragg ascribes the homily to an environment of 'intellectual impoverishment'.[87] From a different perspective, one that does not privilege Latinity above all other accomplishments, the homily could equally be read as indicative of intellectual freedom. This last passage draws on a variety of techniques to create the affectivity which has been noted here so often as a distinguishing feature of the homilies collected in Vercelli. We are addressed directly, invited to listen to and learn from the experience of the damned souls. We are also privileged to understand Peter's feelings and motives as he locks the gates of hell, to feel the weight of 'the key full of care', to share his distress as he turns away from the doors of hell, unable to look at the sorrow and pain. The passage underlines this internal conflict with the echo of *beluceð* and *locian*: Peter locks but cannot look. The same effect is used powerfully in the last line quoted above, with the triple echo of *cnyll . . . fealleð . . . helle*, itself reproducing the sound of the key as it crashes to the ground. That this is intentional is shown by the equivalent line in the much shorter version printed by Assmann, which stresses the universal resonance of the crash with a fourfold consonance: *Hlud bið se cnyl ofer ealle eorðan ðonne seo cæg fealleð innan helle* (Loud is the *knell* over *all* earth when the key *falls* in *hell*).[88] A few lines earlier, this homilist has lamented that the devil sends *slæpnesse 7 . . . slæwð, þæt we ne magon þone beorhtne beacn þære bellan gehyran* (sleepiness and . . . sloth, so that we do not hear the bell's bright beacon). As we saw with the songs in Vercelli IX, Anglo-Saxon preachers used their sound effects to good purpose, and these two similar-sounding yet utterly different knells are the aural poles between which human destiny lies.

Assmann XIV does not include the Doomsday intercession, only the scene of

---

[86] Lines 194–9, p. 261.
[87] Scragg, *Vercelli Homilies*, p. 252.
[88] Assmann XIV, pp. 164–9, 168–9.

St Peter locking the door; it also assures its audience that no man need believe that anyone can release him from hell unless he repent before his death, which suggests that the omission of the intercession scene was intentional. As Clayton points out, Ælfric also has problems specifically with the vision propounded in CCCC 41/303 that anyone may be saved *æfter þam dome* (after the Judgement).[89] Ælfric ascribes this idea to *gedwolmen* (heretics), about whom he goes into some detail. Their heresy and lies (*gedwyld . . . leasunge*) arise from their desire to lie in their fleshly lusts (*on heora flæslicum lustum symle licgan woldon*), they are *fulan* (foul), *manful* (evil) and *arleas* (merciless), and when they die in their sins, neither Mary nor any other saint will lead them into the 'clean house' of heaven. Ælfric is setting up a by now familiar antithesis of *clæn* and *ful*, the former quality associated with the blessed dead and the latter with sexual activity, appropriate in the context of a homily for the feast of a virgin saint. The *gedwolmen* here are likely to be secular canons, whom Ælfric detests as much for their uxoriousness as their unorthodox theology, arguing elsewhere that priests who *licgað nu on heora lustum* (lie now in their lusts) will never sing the heavenly song.[90]

We thus have four different readings of the role of Peter and other saints at Judgement. In the Corpus version, the end is not the end: intercession can happen even after Christ has said *Discedite* (Go) to the damned. This is what Ælfric explicitly finds objectionable, and perhaps also the authors of Vercelli XV and Assmann XIV, since the former sets the intercession before judgement and warns that the damned 'need not believe' in respite, and the latter both omits the intercession and denies it is possible in similar terms to Vercelli.

Ælfric does not mention the tradition constructing Peter as the keeper of the keys of hell. As we saw in Chapter Four, Bede does not link the *portae inferi* of Matthew 16 to keys of any kind, or even explicitly to Peter. In contrast, the authors of Vercelli XV, Assmann XIV and the Corpus homily take it for granted that Peter has been given keys to both eschatological portals and feel no need to explain Peter's role here, suggesting it was widely recognized. To have four surviving texts reworking the idea of intercession at judgement suggests that it was a subject of considerable debate, with rival theories being propounded in a way that Ælfric found unforgivable: *Ne hopige nan man to þyssere leasunge* (Let no one put faith in these lies). As we shall see from a different kind of source, St Peter's role as gate-keeper of hell may also have been contested. If Peter is imagined as *Ianitor Inferi* as well as *Ianitor Caeli* he becomes implicitly a much darker and more difficult figure.

Peter, intercession and the priesthood.

Images of Peter and ideals of priesthood converge in one of Anglo-Saxon England's best-known pictures, covering fols 6v and 7r of the New Minster *Liber Vitae* (Plate 8). This is usually referred to as a Last Judgement but, as Johnson

---

89 Clayton, 'Delivering the Damned', p. 92; *CH* II, XXXIX, p. 333, lines 184–9; *CH Comm.*, pp. 654–61.
90 Assmann II, pp. 13–23, line 19.

Plate 8: St Peter embodying intercessory prayer (London, British Library, Stowe 944, fols 6v–7r). By permission of the British Library. This much-reproduced drawing of 1031 shows the struggle for the human soul in the middle register, with its ultimate fates of either salvation (above) or damnation (below). It encapsulates many of the frequently reiterated themes of devotional literature addressed to St Peter in its unparalleled representation of the saint's keys as a weapon. The drawing comes from the same New Minster Winchester as the Quinity (Plate 1) and shows an equally inventive iconographical approach.

has recently pointed out, it is no such thing.[91] He argues that instead it should be read as a vision of the interim judgement that occurs at death, but the picture works more coherently if seen as a many-layered exploration of intercessory prayer. Judgement plays an important part in this, but it is not what we are being shown: rather the image focuses on two moments, the present as experienced by the person contemplating the picture, now, before death, and the fates in prospect for the saved and damned, after the end of time.

The images in the New Minster *Liber Vitae* were made for a very small audience, and we know who they were: the community of New Minster, Winchester, consisting of seventeen priests, eleven deacons and nine *pueri* in 1031, when the manuscript was made.[92] The New Minster monks were thus all priests, or intending to become priests, and would have used this book during the mass. It is worth noting that the group of unhaloed blessed in the top left-hand corner is led by a deacon, that one of the clerics looking on in the middle register is a priest, and the soul over whom Peter and the devil struggle is a *puer*, thus providing models for all the different members of the New Minster community.

The *Liber Vitae* is an intensely New Minster manuscript. It contains a history of the house's foundation (although the role of the secular canons in its early decades is down-played) as well as the long lists of benefactors and those with whom it is in confraternity. Visually, it also asserts the house's particular identity. The previous folio (6r) contains the image of Cnut and Emma presenting a cross to New Minster, and Parker has suggested that this scene, with monks in the arcaded choir below, king, queen and high altar in the middle register, and Christ flanked by Mary and Peter above, represents the New Minster church, with images of Christ, Mary and Peter in the apse.[93] This dedication image also intentionally echoes the lavish New Minster foundation charter of the later tenth century, which shows Edgar flanked by Mary and Peter with Christ above.[94] The Charter embodies the New Minster's lands and buildings, the *Liber Vitae* embodies its personnel and their *bedrædenne* (confraternity of prayer). The books lying side by side would together have epitomized the entire community, past and present. It has also been suggested that Ælfwine, dean then abbot of the New Minster, was the artist both of his prayerbook (containing images of St Peter and the Crucifixion as well as the Quinity) and of the *Liber Vitae* drawings.[95] Compared to most Anglo-Saxon art we know an extraordinary amount about the context of this picture, and this knowledge helps to resolve its meaning.

The picture divides into three registers. At the top, the widest, stretching across both folios, the blessed advance from the left as Peter beckons them into heaven, where four figures are already adoring Christ. This represents events after the Last

---

[91] D. F. Johnson, 'A Scene of Post-Mortem Judgement in the New Minster *Liber Vitae*', *Old English Newsletter* 34:1 (Fall, 2000), pp. 24–30.

[92] Keynes, *New Minster* Liber Vitae, p. 91.

[93] E. Parker, 'The Gift of the Cross in the New Minster *Liber Vitae*', in E. Sears and T. K. Thomas (eds), *Reading Medieval Images: The Art Historian and the Object* (Michigan, 2002), pp. 177–86, 178.

[94] F. Wormald, 'Late Anglo-Saxon Art. Some Questions and Suggestions', in M. Meiss (ed.), *Studies in Western Art* I (Princeton, 1963), pp. 19–26

[95] Keynes, *New Minster* Liber Vitae, p. 68; Günzel, *Ælfwine's Prayerbook*, p. 8.

Judgement, when the saved are admitted into Christ's presence, the direct contact represented by the horn of oil in Christ's left hand. In the middle register a priest and a bishop look on from the left, while on the right a struggle takes place between Peter and a devil for a boy's soul. In the bottom register (on fol. 7r only), an angel locks the door of hell on the damned. In this picture, Christ has been reduced to a tiny background figure and Peter is promoted as the means of access to salvation. But he is not the doorkeeper of hell, and the emphasis on the angel in that role takes on new significance in the light of Vercelli XV, Assmann XIV and the Corpus homily discussed above.

There are several points about this picture which suggest it needs to be read as an essay on Peter and priesthood. In the top left-hand corner an unhaloed group of blessed wait for an angel to usher them forward, and their leader is a deacon, who appears to be escorting the souls in his care. But this is not the only figure with whom the New Minster community are being invited to identify, and there are many ways into this picture. The figure of the boy over whom Peter and the devil fight is a vulnerable soul reliant on Peter's intervention: again a suitable figure with whom to identify. The watching clerics in the middle register provide a bridge between onlooker and participant; they are haloed but in contemporary dress, unlike the classically dressed and haoled group of blessed above them.

Oakeshott suggests, and Higgitt supports, the hypothesis that one of the sources for this picture was the triumphal arch mosaic in St Prassede in Rome, which shares the unusual iconography of Peter standing with his keys at the already open gate of the heavenly city.[96] This is one of the three mosaics installed by Pope Paschal (817–24) which include a representation of the pope himself in an intercessory role among the people close to Christ or the Virgin, strengthening the argument that the *Liber Vitae* image is primarily about intercession if the mosaic is indeed a model. The two clerics here watch Peter battling for the soul, and following their gaze we are invited to follow their example and identify him as the spiritual as well as the literal centre of the picture, and as our own spiritual champion.

Finally, the New Minster monk/priest looking at this picture might identify with Peter. Priests are themselves intercessors, Peter is the archetype of priesthood, and his powers to bind and loose were passed on to all his heirs. Ælfric, himself a New Minster graduate, follows Bede in arguing that *ðone ylcan anweald hæfð se ælmihtiga getiðod biscopum 7 halgum mæssepreostum* (the Almighty has granted the same power to bishops and holy mass-priests), although, as Godden points out, he particularly stresses that Peter is the only way to heaven: *nan man ne cymð into godes rice buton se halga Petrus him geopenige se infær* (no man comes to God's kingdom unless St Peter opens the entrance for him).[97] As we saw in the confessional prayer in Laud 482's *uisitatio*, the priest is explicitly addressed as an intercessor, and in one of the commonest formulas for

---

[96] W. Oakeshott, *The Mosaics of Rome from the Third to the Fourteenth Centuries* (London, 1967); J. Higgitt, 'The Iconography of St Peter'.

[97] *CH* I, XXVI, p. 391, lines 90–1 and 80–1; *CH Comm.*, p. 214.

absolution, which is also found translated into English, the priest speaks with Peter's voice: *Absoluo te uice beati Petri apostoli apostolorum principis, cui dominus potestatem ligandi atque soluendi dedi.*[98] In Laud 482 this comes at the end of the *uisitatio*, in Lanalet it is part of the *absolutio penititentis*, while in the late eleventh-century *agenda mortuorum* from St Stephen's, Caen, it is spoken over the body in the grave.

Paradoxically, the hypothesis that the St Prassede mosaic lurks behind this picture indicates how innovatory its imagery really is. The boldness and originality of late Anglo-Saxon artists have been much remarked, and Carver, in his comparative study of the Utrecht and Harley Psalters, argues for the importance of the details of the artefacts they depicted.[99] The most distinctive artefacts in this picture are the keys of heaven and hell, which are rendered prominent in several ways. Heaven's key appears twice, and in the middle register is being used as a weapon, an unparalleled image. Hell's key also appears twice: the angel simultaneously locks the door and brandishes the key at the devils and the damned. There is no narrative requirement to show it twice, and this suggests that the artist wanted to stress both the locking of hell's gate and the physical appearance of hell's key, which is stylistically very different from Peter's.

Peter's keys are a shifting symbolic field, and one of particular interest to eleventh-century Christendom as the Orthodox and Roman worlds drew further and further apart. One trend, visible at least from the days of Pope Paschal, had been to show the keys terminating in the letters E and R (presumably for *Ecclesia Romana*) but, other than in a psalter from the reign of Athelstan (London, BL Cotton Galba A xviii, fol. 2v), this does not seem to have been picked up by the English Church. Instead, the insular tradition early developed an iconography of Peter with massive keys, terminating in geometric patterns, exemplified not only by the New Minster *Liber Vitae*'s three images, but also on the gravestone from Cambridge Castle (discussed in Chapter Four) and the iconic relief carving of Peter from Daglingworth (Gloucestershire), showing that this imagery was not confined to pages of manuscripts only available to a small and specialist audience. In the late tenth-century Benedictional of Æthelwold, Peter is shown in six separate images, twice with no keys, twice with small keys, and twice with large keys, exemplifying the way that they carry different meanings dependent on their setting. Peter's keys really require a book-length study of their own, but this brief survey is enough to contextualize the New Minster *Liber Vitae* and to show that a major theological point is being made. The keys of heaven and hell are not the same, nor are they carried by the same person. The New Minster *Liber Vitae* image is thus a polemic, fighting against the construction of Peter as hell's gatekeeper, just as Ælfric explicitly takes issue with intercession after judgement, and as the Cambridge Castle gravestone contests the idea of the doorless house

---

[98] M. Forster, 'Die altenglischen Texte der Parisier Nationalbibliothek', *Englische Studien* 62 (1927–8), pp. 113–31.

[99] M. Carver, 'Contemporary Artefacts Illustrated in Late Saxon Manuscripts', *Archaeologia* 108 (1986), pp. 117–45, 120.

where death holds the key.

Time works on many levels in this picture, just as it does in the Quinity miniature. The top and bottom registers show the beginning of the eternal experiences of joy and pain, potential futures either of which might yet be realized as the fate of the person contemplating the book. This may be why the human soul in the middle register is shown as a young boy, to stress its potential rather than actual qualities and to show there is still room for growth. In contrast, the damned man and woman (the only woman in the scene, and in this quite unlike the St Prassede mosaics) next to him are clearly adults. The middle register thus shows a different kind of moment, continual rather than eternal, the struggle over the human soul taking place in linear time. This is not a judgement scene: Peter has deployed his key to good effect but the devil has not yet relinquished his grip on the boy's wrist and the fight could still go either way. The scene in the middle register is happening here and now, an external representation of the invisible battle happening within the soul of the onlooker. It invites us to follow the boy's example and devote ourselves to the heroic, salvific powers of Peter.

The New Minster *Liber Vitae* is thus an image of continual potential. In this, it echoes the certainty of the rubrics of Laud 482, that it is never too late to repent. This certainty also underpins texts as various as the prayer which focuses on the good thief crucified with Christ, and Wulfstan's insistence in II Cnut 44 that a condemned man must be allowed to see a confessor. St Peter, a figure who has occurred in many different contexts and media over the course of this book, exemplifies the complexities inherent in any attempt to make sense of death within a Catholic, Christian universe. The evidence surveyed here (not merely the New Minster *Liber Vitae* but texts and objects as disparate as homilies, prayers and gild statutes, the Cambridge Castle grave-marker and perhaps even keys in graves) suggests that St Peter was a particular devotional focus at times when people contemplated their own mortality. Both as an archetype of the forgiven sinner and as the keeper of heaven's keys, Peter appears in so many different contexts that it is hard to believe that interest in him was confined to elite groups such as the circle of Æthelflæd of Mercia, or the monks of New Minster. Perhaps, in texts such as the Abbotsbury gild statutes, we catch a glimpse of a truly popular cult.

Conclusion

Late Anglo-Saxon ideas about dying and death formed a coherent system, albeit one in which the many constituent parts were often in tension or conflict. Ideas about the sacred, neutral and profane, the body and its boundaries, sexuality, the living, dying and dead, the present life in linear time and the future life beyond time, all of these worked continuously to structure each other, and affected social and cultural experience at every level. This study has integrated different kinds of source and methodology to demonstrate this underlying coherence, it has oscillated between the experiences of an individual woman in Chapter One and, in Chapter Two, an overview of the whole country and period. Chapter Three's case study of a single liturgical and penitential manuscript shows how one cathedral community, Worcester in the mid-eleventh century, sought to establish an impressively high standard of pastoral care for the sick and dying. Chapter Four looked at the vulnerable microcosm of the healthy, sick and dying body, and how protection was invoked for it in ways other than the liturgical. Chapter Five looked at one threat in particular, the *wyrm*, and how paradoxically this embodiment of decay and damnation could also be invoked as a guardian and a symbol of faith in resurrection. Chapter Six showed how excommunication and execution, the instruments of punishment wielded by Church and State, were profoundly informed by an awareness of the Last Judgement. Over the course of this book, it has become apparent that the dead were omnipresent in the late Anglo-Saxon landscape, whether enshrined in churches, buried in churchyards, consigned to the old field cemeteries, hanging from gallows or beheaded on stakes, or among the outcasts in the liminal barrow fields. They were also ubiquitous in the imagination of the living, appearing unexpectedly in dreams, consciously evoked through the workings of memory and the prompting of texts, anniversaries and tombstones, and engaged with through liturgy and prayer as well as less acceptable rituals. The bodies of the dead might be desirable, like Oswald and Cuthbert, frightening and disgusting, like the decaying corpse so often evoked in the homilies, or objects of pity and care. The places of the dead were places of power and knowledge. There were strong local traditions informing burial practice and commemoration, and these could be very different between communities, although the overwhelming majority of burials and monuments, country-wide, express belief in a Christian understanding of body, soul and resurrection.

At the beginning of this book, it was suggested that Anglo-Saxon sources lead towards general rather than individual conclusions. This remains true at the end:

we have few other anecdotes of named individuals to set against the tale of Æthelwig of Buckingham, arrested for allowing the wrong kind of people to be buried in a churchyard. But this does not mean that the surviving sources present a unified, general narrative. As we have seen, the debate over dying and death and the afterlife was a battleground where different ideas were passionately contested, and this comes through in sculpture and manuscript illustrations, homilies and poetry, the structure of graves and the wording of lawcodes. If these debates leave such prominent fossil traces, they must have been heated at the time.

To write the history of Anglo-Saxon death and burial using only the *ordines* would lead to the conclusion that everyone died with decency, embedded in ritual, while to write it from the penitentials would lead to the reverse conclusion, that everyone was liable to be murdered by a priest, or overlain by their mother in bed. To write such a history from the Chronicles would result in a lop-sided vision of battles and the deaths of kings, as would an over-reliance on *Beowulf*, while to use only *The Wanderer* and the other elegiac poems would stress transience and loss to the exclusion of all else. Relying only on pastoral letters would lead to an argument that the coffin, grave and monument were inconsequential, while an argument based only on archaeology would have to conclude that the material culture of burial was vitally important. This brief survey has shown that all these, and more, have to be considered. Each source is telling its own truth, and only by looking at each of them, on its own terms, and then in combination, will we ever get closer to this vivid and complex culture, most of whose greatest monuments are lost irretrievably.

Bibliography

MANUSCRIPTS

London, BL Cotton Tiberius A iii
London, BL Cotton Titus D xxvi
London, BL Cotton Titus D xxvii
London, BL Royal 2 B v
London, BL Stowe 944
Oxford, Bodl. Laud Miscellaneous 482

PRINTED PRIMARY SOURCES

Æthelweard, *The Chronicle of Æthelweard*, ed. A. Campbell (London, 1962)

Æthelwulf, *De Abbatibus*, ed. A. Campbell (Oxford, 1967)

Arnold, T. (ed.), *Symeonis Monachi Opera Omnia*, Vol. I (London, 1882)

Asser, *Life of King Alfred*, ed. W. H. Stevenson (Oxford, reprinted 1991)

Assmann, B. (ed.), *Angelsächsische Homilien und Heiligenleben*, reprinted with a supplementary introduction by P. Clemoes (Darmstadt, 1964)

Augustine, *De Doctrina Christiana*, ed. and trans. R. P. H. Green (Oxford, 1995)

Banting, H. M. J. (ed.), *Two Anglo-Saxon Pontificals (the Egbert and Sidney Sussex Pontificals)*, HBS 104 (1989)

Bately, J. (ed.), *The Anglo-Saxon Chronicle, A Collaborative Edition, Volume 3, MS. A* (Cambridge, 1986)

Bede, *Ecclesiastical History of the English People*, ed. B. Colgrave and R. A. B. Mynors (Oxford, 1969)

—— *Opera Homiletica*, ed. D. Hurst, CCSL 122 (1955)

——, *Homiliae*, PL 94

Bethurum, D. (ed.), *The Homilies of Wulfstan* (Oxford, 1957)

Boehmer, H. *et al.* (eds), *Texte und Forschungen zur englischen Kulturgeschichte* (Halle, 1921)

Buchholz, R. (ed.), *Die Fragmente der Reden der Seele an den Leichnam*, Erlanger Beiträge zur Englischen Philologie 6 (Erlangen and Leipzig, 1890)

Campbell, A. (ed.), *The Battle of Brunanburh* (London, 1938)

Clark, C. (ed.), *The Peterborough Chronicle 1070–1154* (2nd edn, Oxford, 1970)

Clemoes, P. (ed.), *Ælfric's Catholic Homilies; The First Series, Text*, EETS SS 17 (Oxford, 1997)

Cockayne, O. (ed.), *Leechdoms, Wortcunning and Starcraft of Early England*, 3 vols, RS 35 (London, 1864–6)

Colgrave, B. (ed.), *Felix's Life of Guthlac* (Cambridge, 1956)

—— (ed.), *Two Lives of St Cuthbert* (Cambridge, 1985)

Cubbin, G. P. (ed.), *The Anglo-Saxon Chronicle, A Collaborative Edition, Volume 6: MS D* (Cambridge, 1996)

Darlington, R. R. (ed.), *The* Vita Wulfstani *of William of Malmesbury* (London, 1928)

——, P. McGurk and J. Bray (eds), *The Chronicle of John of Worcester: Volume II, The Annals from 450–1066* (Oxford, 1995)

D'Aronco, M. A., and M. L. Cameron (eds), *The Old English Illustrated Pharmacopoeia* (Copenhagen, 1998)

Davril, A. (ed.), *The Winchcombe Sacramentary*, HBS 109 (1995)

Dobbie, E., *Anglo-Saxon Poetic Records VI: The Anglo-Saxon Minor Poems* (New York, 1942)

—— *Anglo-Saxon Poetic Records IV: Beowulf and Judith* (New York, 1953)

Doble, G. H. (ed.), *Pontificale Lanaletense*, HBS 74 (1937)

Dronke, U. (ed.), *The Poetic Edda. II, The Mythological Poems* (Oxford, 1997)

Fehr, B. (ed.), *Die Hirtenbriefe Ælfrics in altenglischer und lateinischer Fassung.* (Hamburg, 1914)

—— 'Altenglische Ritualtexte für Krankenbesuch, heilige Ölung und Begräbnis', in H. Boehmer (ed.) *Texte und Forschungen zur englischen Kulturgeschichte* (Halle, 1921), pp. 20–67

Forster, M., 'Die altenglischen Texte der Parisier Nationalbibliothek', *Englische Studien* 62 (1927–8), pp. 113–31.

Fowler, R. (ed.), *Wulfstan's Canons of Edgar*, EETS OS 226 (Oxford, 1972)

Garmonsway, G. N. (ed.), *Ælfric's Colloquy* (London, 1939)

Gordon, I. (ed.), *The Seafarer* (Manchester, 1979)

Gregory the Great, *Dialogues*, PL 77

Günzel, B. (ed.), *Ælfwine's Prayerbook: London, British Library, Cotton Titus D. xxvi + xxvii*, HBS 108 (London, 1993)

Harmer, F. E. (ed.), *Select English Historical Documents of the Ninth and Tenth Centuries,* (Cambridge, 1914)

—— (ed.), *Anglo-Saxon Writs* (2nd edn, Stamford, 1989)

Hecht, H. (ed.), *Bischofs Werferth von Worcester, Übersetzung der Dialoge Gregors des Grossen* (Leipzig, 1900)

Hollander, L. M. (trans.), *The Poetic Edda* (Austin, 1962)

Irvine, S. (ed.), *Old English Homilies from MS Bodley 343* EETS OS 302 (London, 1993)

Isidore of Seville, *Etymologiae, PL* 82

Jost, K. (ed.), *Die 'Institutes of Polity, Civil and Ecclesiastical'* (Bern, 1959)

Julian of Toledo, *Prognosticon Futuri Saeculi*, PL 96, cols 461–523.

Kemble, J. (ed.), *Codex Diplomaticus Aevi Saxonici*, 6 vols (London, 1839–48)

Keynes, S. (ed.), *The* Liber Vitae *of the New Minster and Hyde Abbey Winchester, British Library Stowe 944, together with leaves from British Library Cotton Vespasian A viii and British Library Cotton Titus D xxvii.*, EEMF 26 (Copenhagen, 1996)

Krapp, G. P., *Anglo-Saxon Poetic Records I: The Junius Manuscript* (New York, 1931)

—— *Anglo-Saxon Poetic Records II: The Vercelli Book* (New York, 1932)

—— and E. Dobbie, *Anglo-Saxon Poetic Records III: The Exeter Book* (New York, 1936)

Kuypers, A. B. (ed.), *The Prayer Book of Aedeluald the Bishop, Commonly Called the Book of Cerne* (Cambridge, 1902)

Lapidge, M., and M. Winterbottom (eds), *Wulfstan of Winchester: The Life of St Æ_elwold* (Oxford, 1991)

—— and P. S. Baker (eds), *Byrhtferth's Enchiridion*, EETS SS 15 (1995)

210

Liebermann, F. (ed.), *Die Gesetze der Angelsachsen*, 3 vols (Halle, 1903)

Linow, W. (ed.), *_e Desputisoun bitwen _e Bodi and _e Sowle* (Erlangen and Leipzig, 1889)

Liuzza, R. (ed.), *The Old English Version of the Gospels* EETS OS 304 (1994)

McCann, J. (ed.), *The Rule of St Benedict* (London, 1976)

McNeill, J. T., and H. Gamer (eds), *Medieval Handbooks of Penance: A Translation of the Principal Libri Poenitentiales* (reprinted New York, 1990)

Menner, R. J. (ed.), *The Poetical Dialogues of Solomon and Saturn* (New York, 1941)

Mitchell, B., and F. C. Robinson (eds), *Beowulf: An Edition* (Oxford, 1998)

Moffat, D. (ed.), *The Soul's Address to the Body: The Worcester Fragment* (East Lansing, 1987)

—— (ed. and trans.), *The Old English* Soul and Body (Woodbridge, 1990)

Morris, R. (ed.), *The Blickling Homilies of the Tenth Century*, EETS OS 58/63/73 (London, 1880)

Napier, A. S. (ed.), *Wulfstan: Sammlung der ihm zugeschriebenen Homilien nebst Untersuchungen über ihre Echtheit* (Zürich, 1967)

—— (ed.), *The Old English Version of the Rule of Chrodegang together with the Latin Original* (London, 1916)

—— and W. H. Stevenson (eds), *The Crawford Collection of Early Charters and Documents* (Oxford, 1895)

O'Donovan, J. (ed.), *Annals of Ireland* (Dublin, 1860)

O'Keeffe, K. (ed.), *The Anglo-Saxon Chronicle: A Collaborative Edition; Volume 5: MS C* (Cambridge, 2001)

Pope, J. C. (ed.), *Homilies of Ælfric, A Supplementary Series*, 2 vols. EETS 259 & 260 (Oxford, 1967/1968)

Raith, J. (ed.), *Die altenglische Version des Halitgar'schen Bussbuches* (Hamburg, 1933)

Robertson, A. J. (ed.), *Anglo-Saxon Charters* (Cambridge, 1939)

Robinson, F. C., and E. G. Stanley (eds), *Old English Verse Texts from Many Sources: A Comprehensive Collection*, EEMF 23 (Copenhagen, 1991)

Sauer, H. (ed.), *Theodulfi Capitula in England* (Munich, 1978)

Sawyer, P., *Anglo-Saxon Charters: An Annotated List and Bibliography*, Royal Historical Society Guides and Handbooks 8 (London, 1968)

Scragg, D. G. (ed.), *The Vercelli Homilies and Related Texts*, EETS OS 300 (Oxford, 1992)

Skeat, W. (ed.), *Ælfric's Lives of Saints Volume I*, EETS OS 76 and 82 (reprinted as one volume, Oxford, 1966)

Spindler, R. (ed.), *Das altenglische Bussbuch* (Leipzig, 1934)

Symons, T. (ed.), *Regularis Concordia: The Monastic Agreement* (London, 1953)

Taylor. S. (ed.), *The Anglo-Saxon Chronicle: A Collaborative Edition. Volume 4: MS B* (Cambridge, 1983)

Turner, D. H. (ed.), *The Claudius Pontificals*, HBS 97 (London, 1971)

Whitelock, D. (ed.), *Anglo-Saxon Wills* (Cambridge, 1930)

—— (ed.), *English Historical Documents, Volume I, c. 500–1042* (London, 1968)

—— (ed.), *The Will of Æthelgifu: A Tenth Century Anglo-Saxon Manuscript* (Oxford, 1968)

——, M. Brett and C. N. L. Brooke (eds), *Councils and Synods of Great Britain with Other Documents Relating to the English Church. Volume I. Part 1, 871–1066; Part 2, 1066–1204* (Oxford, 1981)

William of Malmesbury, *De Gestis Pontificum Anglorum*, ed. N. Hamilton, RS 52 (London, 1870)

—— *De Gestis Regum Anglorum,* 2 vols, ed. W. Stubbs, RS 90 (London, 1887 and 1889)

Wilson, H. A. (ed.), *The Missal of Robert of Jumièges,* HBS 11 (London, 1896)

Young, J. (trans.), *The Prose Edda* (London, 1954)

SECONDARY SOURCES

Abels, R., *Alfred the Great: War, Kingship and Culture in Anglo-Saxon England* (London and New York, 1998)

Abrams, L., 'History and Archaeology: The Conversion of Scandinavia', in B. Crawford (ed.), *Conversion and Christianity in the North Sea World* (St Andrews, 1998), pp. 109–28

——'Conversion and Assimilation', in D. Hadley and J. D. Richards (eds), *Cultures in Contact: Scandinavian Settlement in England in the Ninth and Tenth Centuries* (Turnhout, 2000), pp. 135–54

—— 'The Conversion of the Danelaw', in J. Graham-Campbell *et al.* (eds), *Vikings and the Danelaw: Select Papers from the Proceedings of the Thirteenth Viking Congress* (Oxford, 2001), pp. 31–44.

Abulafia, D. (ed.), *Church and City, 1000–1500: Essays in Honour of Christopher Brooke* (Cambridge, 1992)

Abusabib, M., *African Art: An Aesthetic Inquiry* (Uppsala, 1995)

Adams, M., 'Excavation of a Pre-Conquest Cemetery at Addingham, West Yorkshire', *Medieval Archaeology* 40 (1996), pp. 151–91

Ayers, B., *Excavations within the North-East Bailey of Norwich Castle, 1979,* East Anglian Archaeology 28 (1985)

Backhouse, J., *et al., The Golden Age of Anglo-Saxon Art* (London, 1984)

Bailey, M., 'Ælfwynn, Second Lady of the Mercians', in N. Higham, and D. H. Hill (eds), *Edward the Elder, 899–924* (London, 2001), pp. 112–27

Bailey, R., 'The Chronology of Viking Age Sculpture in Northumbria', in J. Lang (ed.), *Anglo-Saxon and Viking Age Sculpture and Its Context,* BAR British Series 49 (1978), pp. 173–203

—— *Viking Age Sculpture* (London, 1980)

—— 'Ambiguous Birds and Beasts: Three Sculptural Puzzles in South-West Scotland', Fourth Whithorn Lecture (Whithorn, 1995)

—— *England's Earliest Sculptors* (Toronto, 1996)

—— and R. Cramp, *Corpus of Anglo-Saxon Stone Sculpture II, Cumberland, Westmorland and Lancashire North-of-the-Sands* (Oxford, 1988)

Barasch, M., *Gestures of Despair in Medieval and Early Renaissance Art* (New York, 1976)

Barlow, F., *The English Church, 1000–1066* (2nd ed. London, 1979)

—— *The Norman Conquest and Beyond* (London, 1983)

Barrow, J., 'Urban Cemetery Location in the High Middle Ages', in S. Bassett (ed.), *Death in Towns: Urban Responses to the Dying and the Dead, 100–1100* (Leicester, 1992), pp. 78–100

Barrow, J., 'Survival and Mutation: Ecclesiastical Institutions in the Danelaw in the Ninth and Tenth Centuries', in Hadley and Richards, *Cultures in Contact,* pp. 155–76

Bassett, S. (ed.), *Death in Towns: Urban Responses to the Dying and the Dead, 100–1100* (Leicester, 1992)

Bekker-Nielsen, H. *et al., Proceedings of the Eighth Viking Congress* (Odense, 1981)

Biggs, F. M., 'The Fourfold Division of Souls: The Old English "Christ III" and the Insular Homiletic Tradition', *Traditio* 45 (1989), pp. 35–51

Biddle, M., 'Excavations at Winchester, 1963–3, Second Interim Report', *Antiquaries Journal* 44 (1964), pp. 188–219

—— 'Excavations at Winchester 1964, Third Interim Report', *Antiquaries Journal* 45 (1965), pp. 230–64

—— 'Excavations at Winchester 1965, Fourth Interim Report', *Antiquaries Journal* 46 (1966), pp. 308–32

—— 'Excavations at Winchester 1966, Fifth Interim Report', *Antiquaries Journal* 47 (1967), pp. 251–79

—— 'Excavations at Winchester 1968, Seventh Interim Report', *Antiquaries Journal* 49 (1969), pp. 297–329

—— and B. Kjølbye-Biddle, 'Repton and the "Great Heathen Army", 873–4', in Graham-Campbell, *Vikings and the Danelaw*, pp. 45–96

Biller, P., and A. J. Minnis (eds), *Handling Sin: Confession in the Middle Ages* (Woodbridge, 1998)

Binski, P., *Medieval Death: Ritual and Representation* (London, 1996)

Blackburn, M., 'Expansion and Control: Aspects of Anglo-Scandinavian Minting South of the Humber', in Graham-Campbell, *Vikings and the Danelaw*, pp. 125–42

—— and D. Dumville (eds), *Kings, Currency and Alliances: History and Coinage of Southern England in the Ninth Century* (Woodbridge, 1998)

Blair, J., 'Secular Minster Churches in Domesday Book', in P. Sawyer (ed.), *Domesday Book: A Reassessment* (London, 1985), pp. 104–42

Blair, J. (ed.) *Minsters and Parish Churches: The Local Church in Transition, 950–1200* (Oxford, 1988)

—— 'Minster Churches in the Landscape', in D. Hooke (ed.), *Anglo-Saxon Settlements* (Oxford, 1988), pp. 35–58

—— *The Church in Anglo-Saxon England* (Oxford, forthcoming)

—— and R. Sharpe (eds), *Pastoral Care before the Parish* (Leicester, 1992)

Bocock, R., *Ritual in Industrial Society* (London, 1974)

Boddington, A., *Raunds Furnells: The Anglo-Saxon Church and Churchyard*, English Heritage Archaeological Report 7 (London, 1996)

Bonner, G., D. Rollason and C. Stancliffe (eds), *St Cuthbert, His Cult and Community to AD 1200* (Woodbridge, 1989)

Bonser, W., *The Medical Background of Anglo-Saxon England* (London, 1963)

Bradley, J., 'St Joseph's Trade and Old English *Smi_*', *Leeds Studies in English*, n.s. 22 (1991), pp. 21–42

Brandon, S., *The Judgment of the Dead: An Historical and Comparative Study of the Idea of Post-Mortem Judgment in the Major Religions* (London, 1967)

Brody, S. N., *The Disease of the Soul: Leprosy in Medieval Literature* (Ithaca, NY, and London, 1974)

Brooks, N., and C. Cubitt (eds), *St Oswald of Worcester: Life and Influence* (London and New York, 1996)

Brown, A., 'The Firedrake in *Beowulf*', *Neophilologus* 64 (1980), pp. 439–60

Brown, C. G., *The Death of Christian Britain: Understanding Secularisation, 1800–2000* (London and New York, 2001)

Brown, G., 'The Carolingian Renaissance', in R. McKitterick (ed.), *Carolingian Culture: Emulation and Innovation* (Cambridge, 1994), pp. 1–51

Bullough, D., 'Burial, Community and Belief', in P. Wormald *et al.* (eds), *Ideal and Reality in Frankish and Anglo-Saxon Society* (Oxford, 1983), pp. 177–201

Burnell, S., and E. James, 'The Archaeology of Conversion of the Continent: Some Observations and Comparisons with Anglo-Saxon England', in R. Gameson (ed.), *St Augustine and the Conversion of England* (Stroud, 1999), pp. 83–106

Byock, J. L., 'Sigur_r Fáfnisbani: An Eddic Hero Carved in Norwegian Stave Churches', in T. Paroli (ed.), *Poetry in the Scandinavian Middle Ages* (Spoleto, 1990), pp. 619–28

Cadman, G., and M. Audouy, 'Recent Excavations on Saxon and Medieval Quarries in Raunds, Northamptonshire', in D. Parsons (ed.), *Stone: Quarrying and Building in England AD 43–1525* (Chichester, 1990), pp. 187–206

Cameron, M. L., *Anglo-Saxon Medicine*, CSASE 7 (Cambridge, 1993)

Campbell, J., 'England, *c*.991', in J. Cooper (ed.), *The Battle of Maldon: Fiction and Fact* (London, 1993), pp. 1–17

—— *The Anglo-Saxon State* (Hambledon & London, 2000)

Carver, M., 'Early Medieval Durham: The Archaeological Evidence', in N. Coldstream and P. Draper (eds), *Medieval Art and Architecture at Durham Cathedral* (London, 1980), pp. 11–19

—— *Underneath English Towns: Interpreting Urban Archaeology* (London, 1987)

—— (ed.), *Excavations at York Minster*, 2 vols (London, 1995)

—— 'Conversion and Politics on the Eastern Seaboard of Britain: Some Archaeological Indicators', in B. Crawford (ed.), *Conversion and Christianity in the North Sea World* (St Andrews, 1998), pp. 11–40

—— *Sutton Hoo: Burial Ground of Kings?* (London, 1998)

—— (ed.), *The Cross Goes North* (York, 2003)

Cátedra, M., *This World, Other Worlds: Sickness, Suicide, Death, and the Afterlife among the Vaqueiros de Alzada of Spain* (Chicago, 1992)

Cavill, P., *Maxims in Old English Poetry* (Woodbridge, 1999)

Cecil, R., 'An Insignificant Event? Literary and Anthropological Perspectives on Pregnancy Loss', in R. Cecil (ed.), *The Anthropology of Pregnancy Loss: Comparative Studies in Miscarriage, Stillbirth and Neo-Natal Death* (Oxford, 1996), pp. 1–14

—— (ed.), *The Anthropology of Pregnancy Loss: Comparative Studies in Miscarriage, Stillbirth and Neo-Natal Death* (Oxford, 1996)

Chase, C. (ed.), *The Dating of Beowulf* (Toronto, 1981)

Clayton, M., 'Delivering the Damned: A Motif in Old English Prose', *Medium Ævum* 55 (1986), pp. 92–102

—— *The Cult of the Virgin in Anglo-Saxon England* CSASE 2 (Cambridge, 1990)

—— 'Homiliaries and Preaching in Anglo-Saxon England', in P. Szarmach (ed.), *Old English Prose: Basic Readings* (New York and London, 2000), pp. 155–98

Clemoes, P., *Interactions of Thought and Language in Old English Poetry*, CSASE 12 (Cambridge, 1995)

—— and K. Hughes (eds), *England before the Conquest* (Cambridge, 1971)

Clercq, C. de, '*Ordines unctionis infirmi* des IXe et Xe siècles', *Ephemerides Liturgicae* 44 (1930), pp. 100–22

Coatsworth, E., and M. Pinder, *The Art of the Anglo-Saxon Goldsmith* (Woodbridge, 2002)

Cohen, A., *The Uta Codex: Art, Philosophy and Reform in Eleventh-Century Germany* (University Park, 2000)

Coldstream, N., and P. Draper (eds), *Medieval Art and Architecture at Durham Cathedral* (London, 1980)

Conde Guerri, E., *Los 'fossores' de Roma paleo-cristiana: estudio iconografico, epigrafico y social* Studi di Antichità Cristiana 33 (Vatican City, 1979)

Coonaert, E., 'Les Ghildes médiévales: (Ve–XIVe siècles): définitions, évolutions', *Revue historique* 199 (1948) pp. 22–55, 43

Cooper, J. (ed.), *The Battle of Maldon: Fiction and Fact* (London, 1993)

Corazza, V. (ed.), *Vercelli tra oriente ed occidente tra tarda antichità e medioevo* (Vercelli, 1997)

Cowdrey, H., 'Towards an Interpretation of the Bayeux Tapestry', in R. Gameson (ed.), *The Study of the Bayeux Tapestry* (Woodbridge, 1997), pp. 93–110

Cox, R., 'Snake Rings in *Deor* and *Völundarkvi_a*', *Leeds Studies in English*, n.s. 22 (1991), pp. 1–20

Cramp, R., *Anglian and Viking York*, Borthwick Papers 33 (York, 1967)

—— 'The Anglian Tradition in the Ninth Century', in J. Lang (ed.), *Anglo-Saxon and Viking Age Sculpture in Its Context*, pp. 1–32

—— 'The Viking Image', in R. T. Farrell (ed.), *The Vikings* (London, 1982), pp. 8–19

—— *Studies in Anglo-Saxon Sculpture* (London, 1992)

Crawford, B. (ed.), *Conversion and Christianity in the North Sea World* (St Andrews, 1998)

Crawford, S., *Childhood in Anglo-Saxon England* (Stroud, 1999)

Crick, J., 'Posthumous Obligation and Family Identity', in W. O. Frazer and A. Tyrrell (eds), *Social Identity in Early Medieval Britain* (Leicester, 2000), pp. 193–208

Cross, J. E., "'The Dry Bones Speak"-Theme in Old English Homilies', *JEGP* 57 (1956), pp. 434–9

—— 'The Literate Anglo-Saxon – On Sources and Dissemination', *Proceedings of the British Academy* 58 (1972), pp. 67–100

Crowe, C., 'Early Medieval Parish Formation in Dumfries and Galloway', in M. Carver (ed.), *The Cross Goes North* (York, 2003), pp. 195–206

Cubitt, C., *Anglo-Saxon Church Councils, c. 650- c. 850* (Leicester, 1995)

—— 'Monastic Memory and Identity in Early Anglo-Saxon England', in W. O. Frazer and A. Tyrrell (eds) *Social Identity in Early Medieval Britain* (Leicester, 2000), 253–76

Cumberledge, N., 'Reading Between the Lines: The Place of Mercia within an Expanding Wessex', *Midland History* XXVII (2002), pp. 1–15

Daley, B., *The Hope of the Early Church: A Handbook of Patristic Eschatology* (Cambridge, 1991)

Danforth, L., *The Death Rituals of Rural Greece* (Princeton, 1982)

Daniell, C., *Death and Burial in Medieval England* (London, 1997)

Davidson, H. R. E., *Gods and Myths of Northern Europe* (Harmondsworth, 1964)

De Gregorio, S., 'Ælfric, *Gedwyld* and Vernacular Hagiography: Sanctity and Spirituality in the Old English Lives of SS Peter and Paul', in D. Scragg (ed.), *Ælfric's Lives of Canonised Popes*, Old English Newsletter, *Subsidia* Vol. 30 (Michigan, 2001), pp. 75–98

Deshman, R., *The Benedictional of Æthelwold*, Studies in Manuscript Illumination 9 (Princeton, 1995)

Dickins, ?.,'The Day of Byrhtnoth's Death and Other Obits from a 12th-Century Ely Calendar', *Leeds Studies in English* 6 (1937), 14–24

Dickinson, T., and E. James (eds), *Death and Burial* (York, 1992)

Dolley, R. H. M. (ed.), *Anglo-Saxon Coins* (London, 1961)

—— and C. E. Blunt, 'The Coinage of Alfred the Great', in R. H. M. Dolley (ed.) *Anglo-Saxon Coins* (London, 1961), pp. 77–94

Dolley, M., 'The Palimpsest of Viking Settlement on Man', in H. Bekker-Nielsen *et al.*, *Proceedings of the Eighth Viking Congress* (Odense, 1981), pp. 173–81

Dumville, D., 'Textual Archaeology and Northumbrian History Subsequent to Bede', in D. M. Metcalf (ed.), *Coinage in Ninth-Century Northumbria*, BAR British Series 180 (1987), pp. 43–55

—— *Wessex and England from Alfred to Edgar: Six Essays on Political, Ecclesiastical and Cultural Revival* (Woodbridge, 1992)

—— *Liturgy and the Ecclesiastical History of Late Anglo-Saxon England* (Woodbridge, 1992)

Durkheim, É., *The Elementary Forms of the Religious Life* (New York, 1965)

Dunn, M., *The Emergence of Monasticism, From the Desert Fathers to the Early Middle Ages* (Oxford, 2000)

Eaton, T., *Plundering the Past: Roman Stonework in Medieval Britain* (Stroud, 2001)

Effros, B., *Caring for Body and Soul: Burial and the Afterlife in the Merovingian World* (University Park, 2002)

Eliade, M., *The Sacred and the Profane: The Nature of Religion* (New York, 1959)

Everson, P., and D. Stocker, *Corpus of Anglo-Saxon Stone Sculpture V: Lincolnshire* (Oxford, 1999)

—— 'The Straight and Narrow Way: Conversion of the Landscape in the Witham Valley', in Carver, *Cross Goes North*, pp. 271–88

Farrell, R. T. (ed.), *The Vikings* (London, 1982)

Faull, M. (ed.), *Studies in Late Anglo-Saxon Settlement* (Oxford, 1984)

Finberg, H. P. R. (ed.), *Scandinavian England: Collected Papers by F. T. Wainwright* (Chichester, 1975)

Fletcher, R., *Bloodfeud: Murder and Revenge in Anglo-Saxon England* (London, 2002)

Flint, V. I., *The Rise of Magic in Early Medieval Europe* (Oxford, 1991)

Fox, C., 'Anglo-Saxon Monumental Sculpture in the Cambridge District', *Proceedings of the Cambridge Antiquarian Society* 17 (1920–1), pp. 15–45

Fowler, R., 'An Old English Handbook for the Use of a Confessor', *Anglia* 83 (1965), pp. 1–34

Frank, R., 'Skaldic Verse and the Date of Beowulf', in C. Chase (ed.), *The Dating of Beowulf* (Toronto, 1981), pp. 123–39

Frantzen, A., 'The Body in *Soul and Body I*', *Chaucer Review* 17 (1982), pp. 76–88

—— 'The Tradition of Penitentials in Anglo-Saxon England', *ASE* 11 (1982), pp. 23–56

—— *King Alfred* (Boston, MA, 1986)

—— *Before the Closet: Same-Sex Love from Beowulf to Angels in America* (Chicago, 1998)

Frazer, W. O., and A. Tyrrell (eds), *Social Identity in Early Medieval Britain* (Leicester, 2000)

Gameson, R., 'Book Production at Worcester in the Tenth and Eleventh Centuries', in N. Brooks and C. Cubitt (eds), *St Oswald of Worcester: Life and Influence* (London and New York, 1996), pp. 194–243

—— 'The Origin, Art and Message of the Bayeux Tapestry', in R. Gameson (ed.), *The Study of the Bayeux Tapestry* (Woodbridge, 1997), pp. 157–211

—— (ed.), *The Study of the Bayeux Tapestry* (Woodbridge, 1997)

—— (ed.), *St Augustine and the Conversion of England* (Stroud, 1999)

Garrison, M., 'The Study of Emotion in Early Medieval History: Some Starting Points', *Early Medieval Europe* 10:2 (2001), pp. 243–50

Gatch, M. M., *Preaching and Theology in Anglo-Saxon England: Ælfric and Wulfstan* (Toronto, 1977)

Geake, H., 'The Control of Burial Practice in Anglo-Saxon England', in Carver, *Cross Goes North*, pp. 259–69

Geertz, C., *The Interpretation of Cultures* (New York, 1973)

Gem, R., 'Anglo-Saxon Architecture of the 10th and 11th Centuries', in J. Backhouse *et al.* (eds), *The Golden Age of Anglo-Saxon Art* (London, 1984), pp. 139–42

Gennep, A. van, *The Rites of Passage* (London, 1960)

Gilmour, B. J., and D. A. Stocker, *St Mark's Church and Cemetery* (Trust for Lincolnshire Archaeology, 1986)

Gittings, C., *Death, Burial and the Individual in Early Modern England* (London, 1984)

Gittos, H., 'Creating the Sacred: Anglo-Saxon Rites for Consecrating Cemeteries', in S. Lucy and A. Reynolds (eds), *Burial in Early Medieval England and Wales*, Society for Medieval Archaeology Monograph 18 (London, 2002), pp. 195–208

Gneuss, H., 'Liturgical Books in Anglo-Saxon England and their Old English Terminology', in M. Lapidge and H. Gneuss (eds), *Learning and Literature in Anglo-Saxon England* (Cambridge, 1985), pp. 91–142

—— 'Origin and Provenance of Anglo-Saxon Manuscripts: the case of Cotton Tiberius A iii', in P. R. Robinson and R. Zim, *Of the Making of Books: Medieval Manuscripts, their Scribes and Readers* (Aldershot, 1997), pp. 13–48

Godden, M., 'An Old English Penitential Motif', *ASE* 2 (1973), pp. 221–39

—— 'Old English Composite Homilies from Winchester', *ASE* 4 (1975), pp. 57–65

—— 'Ælfric and the Vernacular Prose Tradition', in P. Szarmach and B. Huppé (eds), *The Old English Homily and its Backgrounds* (New York, 1978), pp. 99–117

—— 'Anglo-Saxons on the Mind', in M. Lapidge and H. Gneuss (eds), *Learning and Literature in Anglo-Saxon England* (Cambridge, 1985), pp. 271–98

—— 'Ælfric's Saints' Lives and the Problem of Miracles', *Leeds Studies in English* n.s. 16 (1985), pp. 83–100

—— *Ælfric's Catholic Homilies: Introduction, Commentary and Glossary*, EETS SS 18 (Oxford, 2000)

Gottlieb, B., *The Family in the Western World, from the Black Death to the Industrial Revolution* (Oxford, 1993)

Graham, T., 'The Old English Liturgical Directions in Corpus Christi College, Cambridge, MS 422', *Anglia* 111 (1993), pp. 439–46

Graham-Campbell, J., 'Pagans and Christians', *History Today* (Oct. 1986), pp. 24–8

—— *Cultural Atlas of the Viking World* (Oxford, 1994)

—— 'Pagan Scandinavian Burial in the Central and Southern Danelaw', in Graham-Campbell *et al.*, *Vikings and the Danelaw*, pp. 105–24

—— *et al.* (eds), *Vikings and the Danelaw: Select Papers from the Proceedings of the Thirteenth Viking Congress* (Oxford, 2001)

Gräslund, A.-S., 'The Conversion of Scandinavia – A Sudden Event or a Gradual Process?', in A. Pluskowski (cd.), *Early Medieval Religion*, Archaeological Review from Cambridge 17:2 (2000), pp. 83–98

Grattan, J., and C. Singer, *Anglo-Saxon Magic and Medicine Illustrated Specially from the Semi-Pagan Text 'Lacnunga'* (Oxford, 1952)

Gravestock, P., 'Did Imaginary Animals Exist?', in D. Hassig (ed.), *The Mark of the Beast: The Medieval Bestiary in Art, Life and Literature* (New York and London, 1999), pp. 119–35

Green, M., 'Man, Time and Apocalypse in *The Wanderer*, *The Seafarer* and *Beowulf*', *JEGP* 74 (1975), pp. 502–18

Griffith, M. S., 'Convention and Originality in the Old English "Beasts of Battle", Typescene', *ASE* 22 (1992), pp. 179–99

Grundy, L., *Books and Grace: Ælfric and Theology*, King's College London Medieval Studies VI (Exeter, 1991)

Hadley, D., *The Northern Danelaw: Its Social Structure, c. 800–1100* (Leicester, 2000)

—— 'Burial Practices in Northern England in the Later Anglo-Saxon Period', in Lucy and Reynolds, *Burial in Early Medieval England and Wales*, pp. 209–28

—— and J. D. Richards (eds), *Cultures in Contact: Scandinavian Settlement in England in the Ninth and Tenth Centuries* (Turnhout, 2000)

Hall, A. R. *et al.*, *Environment and Living Conditions at Two Anglo-Scandinavian Sites* (London, 1983)

Hall, R., *Viking Age York* (London, 1984)

Hall, R. A., and M. Whyman, 'Settlement and Monasticism at Ripon, North Yorkshire, from the 7th to the 11th Centuries', *Medieval Archaeology* 40 (1996), pp. 62–150

Halsall, G., 'Burial, Ritual, and Merovingian Society', in J. Hill and M. Swan (eds), *The Community, the Family, and the Saint: Patterns of Power in Early Medieval Europe* (Turnhout, 1998), pp. 325–38

—— 'The Viking Presence in England? The Burial Evidence Reconsidered', in Hadley and Richards, *Cultures in Contact*, pp. 259–76

Hamilton, S., *The Practice of Penance, 900–1050* (Woodbridge, 2001)

Hare, M. J., 'The Two Anglo-Saxon Minsters of Gloucester' (Friends of Deerhurst Church, 1992)

Hardt, M., 'Royal Treasures and Representation in the Early Middle Ages', in W. Pohl and H. Reimitz, *Strategies of Distinction: The Construction of Ethnic Communities, 300–800* (Leiden, 1998), pp. 255–80

Haslam, J., 'The Towns of Wiltshire', in J. Haslam (ed.), *Anglo-Saxon Towns in Southern England* (Chichester, 1984), pp. 87–147

—— (ed.), *Anglo-Saxon Towns in Southern England* (Chichester, 1984)

Hassall, T. G., 'Excavations at Oxford 1972, Fifth Interim Report', *Oxoniensia* 38 (1973), pp. 268–98

Hassig, D. (ed.), *The Mark of the Beast: The Medieval Bestiary in Art, Life and Literature* (New York and London, 1999)

Hawkes, J., 'The Rothbury Cross: An Iconographic Bricolage', *Gesta* 35/1 (1996), pp. 77–94

—— 'Symbolic Lives: The Visual Evidence', in J. Hines (ed.), *The Anglo-Saxons: From the Migration Period to the Eighth Century* (Woodbridge, 1997), pp. 311–38

—— 'Anglo-Saxon Sculpture: Questions of Context', in Hawkes and Mills, *Northumbria's Golden Age*, pp. 204–15

—— 'Sacraments in Stone: The Mysteries of Christ in Anglo-Saxon Sculpture', in Carver, *Cross Goes North*, pp. 351–70

—— and S. Mills (eds), *Northumbria's Golden Age* (Stroud, 1999)

Heighway, C., 'Excavations at Gloucester, 4th Interim Report: St Oswald's Priory, Gloucester, 1975–6', *Antiquaries Journal* 58 (1978), pp. 103–32

—— 'Saxon Gloucester', in J. Haslam (ed.), *Anglo-Saxon Towns in Southern England* (Chichester, 1984), pp. 359–83

—— *The Golden Minster: The Anglo-Saxon Minster and Later Medieval Priory of St Oswald at Gloucester*, CBA Research Report 117 (York, 1999)

Henderson, C. G., 'Exeter', in J. Schofield *et al.* (eds), *Recent Archaeological Research in English Towns* (London, 1981), pp. 36–7

—— and P. Bidwell, 'The Saxon Minster at Exeter', in S. M. Pearce (ed.), *The Early Church in Western Britain and Ireland*, BAR British Series 102 (Oxford, 1982), pp. 145–75

Henry, F., 'The Effects of the Viking Invasions on Irish art', *Proceedings of the International Congress on Celtic Studies 1959* (Dublin, 1962), pp. 61–72

Hertz, R., 'A Contribution to the Study of the Collective Representation of Death', in R. and C. Needham, *Death and the Right Hand* (New York, 1960), pp. 27–86

Hicks, C. (ed.), *England in the Eleventh Century: Proceedings of the 1990 Harlaxton Symposium* (Stamford, 1992)

—— *Animals in Early Medieval Art* (Edinburgh, 1993)

Higgitt, J., 'The Iconography of St Peter in England, and St Cuthbert's Coffin', in G. Bonner, D. Rollason and C. Stancliffe (eds), *St Cuthbert, His Cult and Community to AD 1200* (Woodbridge, 1989), pp. 267–85

Higham, N. J., and D. H. Hill (eds), *Edward the Elder, 899–924* (London, 2001)

Hill, D., and R. Cowie, *Wics: The Early Medieval Trading Centres of Northern Europe* (Sheffield, 2001)

Hill, J., 'Monastic Reform and the Secular Church: Ælfric's Pastoral Letters in Context', in C. Hicks (ed.) *England in the Eleventh Century: Proceedings of the 1990 Harlaxton Symposium* (Stamford, 1992), pp. 103–18

—— 'Ælfric, Authorial Identity and the Changing Text', in D. G. Scragg and P. E. Szarmach (eds), *The Editing of Old English* (Cambridge, 1994), pp. 177–89

—— and M. Swan (eds), *The Community, the Family, and the Saint: Patterns of Power in Early Medieval Europe* (Turnhout, 1998)

Hillgarth, J. N., 'Popular Religion in Visigothic Spain', in E. James (ed.), *Visigothic Spain: New Approaches* (Oxford, 1980), pp. 3–60

Hines, J., 'Scandinavian English: A Creole in Context', in P. Ureland and G. Broderick (eds), *Language Contact in the British Isles* (Tübingen, 1991), pp. 403–27

—— (ed.), *The Anglo-Saxons: From the Migration Period to the Eighth Century* (Woodbridge, 1997)

—— and T. Malim (eds), *The Anglo-Saxon Cemetery at Edix Hill (Barrington A)*, CBA Research Report 112 (1998)

Hinton, D. A., *A Catalogue of the Anglo-Saxon Ornamental Metalwork 700–1100 in the Department of Antiquities, Ashmolean Museum* (Oxford, 1974)

Hohler, C., 'The Red Book of Darley', in H. Slott (ed.), *Nordisk kollokvium II: I. Latinsk liturgiforskning. 12–13 Maj 1972*, pp. 39–47

Holt, J. C., *Colonial England, 1066–1215* (London, 1997)

Hooke, D. (ed.), *Anglo-Saxon Settlements* (Oxford, 1988)

Hourihane, C. (ed.), *From Ireland Coming: Irish Art from the Early Christian to the Late Gothic Period and Its European Context* (Princeton, 2001)

Hughes, K., 'Evidence for Contacts between the Churches of the Irish and the English from the Synod of Whitby to the Viking Age', in P. Clemoes and K. Hughes (eds), *England before the Conquest* (Cambridge, 1971) pp. 49–67

Hunter Blair, P., 'Symeon's History of the Kings', *Archaeologia Aeliana* 16 (1939), pp. 87–100

Irvine, M., 'Anglo-Saxon Literary Theory Exemplified in Old English Poems: Interpreting the Cross in *The Dream of the Rood* and *Elene*', *Style* 20 (1986), pp. 157–81

Isaacs, N. D., 'Up a Tree: To See *The Fates of Men*', in L. E. Nicholson and D. W. Frese (eds), *Anglo-Saxon Poetry: Essays in Appreciation* (Notre Dame and London, 1975), pp. 363–75

Iversen, M., 'Mammen: A Princely Grave from 971 and a Craftsman's Hoard', in T. Dickinson and E. James (eds), *Death and Burial*, pp. 73–8

Ivison, E., 'Death and Burial at Medieval Corinth (*c.* 960–1400)', in T. Dickinson and E. James (eds), *Death and Burial*, pp. 117–21

James, E., *The Merovingian Archaeology of South-West Gaul*, BAR Supplementary Series 25, 2 vols (Oxford, 1977)

—— (ed.), *Visigothic Spain: New Approaches* (Oxford, 1980)

—— 'Burial and Status in the Early Medieval West', *TRHS*, 5th series 39 (1989), pp. 23–40

John, E., 'The World of Abbot Ælfric', in P. Wormald (ed.) *Ideal and Reality in Frankish and Anglo-Saxon Society* (Oxford, 1983), pp. 300–16

—— *Reassessing Anglo-Saxon England* (Manchester 1996)

Johnson, D. F., 'A Scene of Post-Mortem Judgement in the New Minster *Liber Vitae*', *Old English Newsletter* 34:1 (Fall, 2000), pp. 24–30

Jolly, K., *Popular Religion in Late Saxon England: Elf-Charms in Context* (Chapel Hill and London, 1996)

Jones, A. K. G., 'A Human Coprolite from 6–8 Pavement', in A. R. Hall *et al.*, *Environment and Living Conditions at Two Anglo-Scandinavian Sites* (London, 1983), pp. 225–9

Jong, M. de, 'Rethinking Early Medieval Christianity: A View from the Netherlands', *Early Medieval Europe* 7:3 (1998), pp. 261–76

Kabir, A., *Paradise, Death and Doomsday in Anglo-Saxon Literature*, CSASE 32 (Cambridge, 2001)

Kantorowicz, E. H., 'The Quinity of Winchester', *Art Bulletin* 29 (1947), pp. 73–85

Karkov, C., R. T. Farrell and M. Ryan (eds), *The Insular Tradition* (New York, 1997)

Keefer, S. L., 'Manuals', in R. Pfaff (ed.), *The Liturgical Books of Anglo-Saxon England*, Old English Newsletter Subsidia 23 (1995), pp. 99–109

Kemp, E. W., *Canonization and Authority in the Western Church* (Oxford, 1948)

Keynes, S., 'Crime and Punishment in the Reign of King Æthelred the Unready', in I. Wood and N. Lund (eds), *People and Places in Northern Europe, 500–1600* (Woodbridge, 1991), pp. 67–81

—— 'Cnut's Earls', in A. Rumble (ed.), *The Reign of Cnut, King of England, Denmark and Norway* (Leicester, 1994), pp. 43–88

—— 'King Alfred and the Mercians', in M. Blackburn and D. Dumville (eds), *Kings, Currency and Alliances; History and Coinage of Southern England in the Ninth Century* (Woodbridge, 1998), pp. 1–45

Kiernan, K. S., '*Deor*: The Consolations of an Anglo-Saxon Boethius', *NM* 79 (1978), pp. 333–41

Kilbride, W., 'Why I feel Cheated by the Term "Christianisation"', in A. Pluskowski (ed.), *Early Medieval Religion*, Archaeological Review from Cambridge 17:2 (2000), pp. 1–17

Kirby, D. P., 'Northumbria in the Ninth Century', in D. M. Metcalf (ed.), *Coinage in Ninth-Century Northumbria*, BAR British Series 180 (1987), pp. 11–25

Kitzinger, E., 'Icons and Interlace: Form and Function in Early Insular Art', in R. M. Spearman and J. Higgitt, *The Age of Migrating Ideas: Early Medieval Art in Northern Britain and Ireland* (Stroud, 1993), pp. 3–15

Kjølbye-Biddle, B., 'A Cathedral Cemetery: Problems in Excavation and Interpretation', *World Archaeology* 7 (1975), pp. 87–108

—— 'Dispersal or Concentration: The Disposal of the Winchester Dead over 2000 years', in Bassett, *Death in Towns*, pp. 210–47

—— and R. Page, 'A Scandinavian Rune-Stone from Winchester', *Antiquaries Journal* 55 (1975), pp. 389–94

Klingender, F., *Animals in Art and Thought to the End of the Middle Ages* (London, 1971)

Knowles, D., *The Monastic Order in England* (Cambridge, 1966)

Kurtz, B. P., 'Gifer the Worm: An Essay towards the History of an Idea', *University of California Publications in English* 2/2 (1929), pp. 235–61

Lager, L., 'Art as a Reflection of Religious Change: The Process of Christianization as Shown in the Ornamentation on Runestones', in A. Pluskowski (ed.), *Early Medieval Religion*, Archaeological Review from Cambridge 17:2 (2000), pp. 117–32

Lamb, R., 'Pictland, Northumbria and the Carolingian Empire', in B. Crawford (ed.), *Conversion and Christianity in the North Sea World* (St Andrews, 1998), pp. 41–56

Lang, J., 'Some Late Pre-Conquest Sculptures in Ryedale: A Reappraisal', *JBAA*, 3rd series 36 (1973), pp. 17–20

—— 'Sigurd and Weland in Pre-Conquest Carving from Northern England', *JBAA* 48 (1976), pp. 83–94

—— 'Continuity and Innovation in Anglo-Scandinavian Sculpture: A Study of the Metropolitan School at York', in J. Lang (ed.) *Anglo-Saxon and Viking Age Sculpture in Its Context*, BAR British Series 49 (Oxford, 1978), pp. 145–72

—— *Anglo-Saxon and Viking Age Sculpture in Its Context*, BAR British Series 49 (Oxford, 1978)

—— *Corpus of Anglo-Saxon Stone Sculpture III: York and Eastern Yorkshire* (Oxford, 1991)

—— 'Survival and Revival in Insular Art, Some Principles', in C. Karkov, R. T. Farrell and M. Ryan (eds), *The Insular Tradition* (New York, 1997), pp. 63–77

—— *Corpus of Anglo-Saxon Stone Sculpture VI: Northern Yorkshire* (Oxford, 2001)

Lapidge, M., 'Æthelwold as Scholar and Teacher', in B. Yorke (ed.), *Bishop Æthelwold: His Career and Influence* (Woodbridge, 1988), pp. 89–117

—— 'Ealdred of York and MS. Cotton Vitellius E. xii', in M. Lapidge, *Anglo-Latin Literature, 900–1066* (London 1993), pp. 453–67

—— *Anglo-Latin Literature, 900–1066* (London 1993)

—— and H. Gneuss (eds), *Learning and Literature in Anglo-Saxon England* (Cambridge, 1985)

Lees, C., *Tradition and Belief: Religious Writing in Late Anglo-Saxon England* (Minneapolis and London, 1999)

Le Goff, J., *The Birth of Purgatory* (Chicago, 1984)

Lendinara, P., *Anglo-Saxon Glosses and Glossaries* (Aldershot, 1999)

Lillie, E. L., and N. H. Petersen (eds), *Liturgy and the Arts in the Middle Ages* (Copenhagen, 1996)

Liuzza, R., 'Anglo-Saxon Prognostics in Context: A Survey and Handlist of Manuscripts', *ASE* 30 (2001), pp. 181–230

Loyn, H., 'Towns in Late Anglo-Saxon England: The Evidence and Some Possible Lines of Enquiry', in P. Clemoes and K. Hughes (eds), *England before the Conquest* (Cambridge, 1971), pp. 115–45

Lucy, S., *The Anglo-Saxon Way of Death* (Stroud, 2000)

—— and A. Reynolds (eds), *Burial in Early Medieval England and Wales*, Society for Medieval Archaeology Monograph 18 (London, 2002)

Lund, N., 'The Settlers: Where Do We Get Them From – And Do We Need Them?', in H. Bekker-Nielsen *et al. Proceedings of the Eighth Viking Congress* (Odense, 1981), pp. 147–71

Lynch, J., *Christianizing Kinship: Ritual Sponsorship in Anglo-Saxon England* (Ithaca, NY, and London, 1998)

Mac Lean, D., 'Snake Bosses and Redemption at Iona and in Pictland', in R. M. Spearman and J. Higgitt (eds), *The Age of Migrating Ideas: Early Medieval Art in Northern Britain and Ireland* (Stroud, 1993), pp. 245–53

Magennis, H., 'Style and Method in the Old English Version of the Legend of the Seven Sleepers', *English Studies* 66 (1985), pp. 285–95

—— 'The Anonymous Old English *Legend of the Seven Sleepers* and Its Latin Source', *Leeds Studies in English*, New Series XXII (1992), pp. 43–56

—— (ed.), *The Anonymous Old English Legend of the Seven Sleepers*, Durham Medieval Texts, no. 7 (Durham, 1994)

—— *Images of Community in Old English Poetry*, CSASE 18 (Cambridge, 1996)

McKinnell, J., 'Norse Mythology and Northumbria: A Response', in J. D. Niles and M. Amodio (eds), *Anglo-Scandinavian England: Norse–English Relations in the Period before the Conquest* (London, 1989), pp. 42–52

—— 'The Context of *Völundarkvi_a*', *Saga-Book of the Viking Society* 23 (1990), pp. 1–27

McKitterick, R., *The Frankish Church and the Carolingian Reform, 789–895* (London, 1977)

—— (ed.), *Carolingian Culture: Emulation and Innovation* (Cambridge, 1994)

McLaughlin, M., *Consorting with Saints: Prayer for the Dead in Early Medieval France* (Ithaca and London, 1994)

Meaney, A., *Anglo-Saxon Amulets and Curing Stones*, BAR British Series 96 (Oxford, 1981)

—— 'Ælfric and Idolatry', *Journal of Religious History* 13 (1984), pp. 119–35

—— 'Ælfric's Use of His Sources in His Homily on Auguries', *English Studies* 66 (1985), pp. 477–95

—— 'Variant Versions of Old English Medical Recipes and the Compilation of Bald's *Leechbook*', *ASE* 13 (1994), pp. 235–68

Meens, R., 'The Frequency and Nature of Early Medieval Penance', in P. Biller and A. J. Minnis (eds), *Handling Sin: Confession in the Middle Ages* (Woodbridge, 1998), pp. 35–61

Menuge, N. J. (ed.), *Medieval Women and the Law* (Woodbridge, 2000)

Metcalf, D. M. (ed.), *Coinage in Ninth-Century Northumbria*, BAR British Series 180 (Oxford, 1987)

Moore, R. I., *The Formation of a Persecuting Society: Power and Deviance in Western Europe, 950–1250* (Oxford, 1987)

—— *The Birth of Popular Heresy* (Toronto, 1995)

Morris, C. J., *Marriage and Murder in Eleventh-Century Northumbria: A Study of the 'De Obsessione Dunelmi'*, Borthwick Paper 82 (York, 1992)

Morris, R., *The Church in British Archaeology*, CBA Research Report 47 (London, 1983)

—— *Churches in the Landscape* (London, 1989)

Murray, A., 'Confession before 1215', *TRHS*, 6th series 3 (1993), pp. 51–83

—— 'Counselling in Medieval Confession', in P. Biller and A. J. Minnis (eds) *Handling Sin: Confession in the Middle Ages* (Woodbridge, 1998), pp. 63–78

Murray, C., *Rebirth and Afterlife: A Study of the Transmutation of Some Pagan Imagery in Early Christian Funerary Art*, BAR International Series 100 (Oxford, 1981)

Needham, R., and C. Needham, *Death and the Right Hand* (New York, 1960)

Nelson, J., 'Reconstructing a Royal Family: Reflections on Alfred, from Asser, Chapter 2', in I. Wood and N. Lund (eds), *People and Places in Northern Europe, 500–1600* (Woodbridge, 1991), pp. 47–66

Neville, J., *Representations of the Natural World in Old English Poetry* CSASE 27 (Cambridge, 1999)

Nicholson, L. E., and D. W. Frese (eds), *Anglo-Saxon Poetry: Essays in Appreciation* (Notre Dame and London, 1975)

Norton, C., 'The Anglo-Saxon Cathedral at York and the Topography of Anglian York', *JBAA* 151 (1998), pp. 1–42

Nöth, W., 'Semiotics of the Old English Charm', *Semiotica* 19 (1977), pp. 59–83

Ó Carragáin, E., 'Rome, Ruthwell, Vercelli: "The Dream of the Rood" and the Italian Connection', in V. Corazza (ed.), *Vercelli tra oriente ed occidente tra tarda antichità e medioevo* (Vercelli, 1997), pp. 59–100

O'Keeffe, K., *Visible Song: Transitional Literacy in Old English Verse*, CSASE 4 (Cambridge, 1990)

—— 'Body and Law in Late Anglo-Saxon England', *ASE* 27 (1998), 209–32

Opland, J., *Anglo-Saxon Oral Poetry: A Study of the Traditions* (New Haven, 1980)

Ortenberg, V., *The English Church and the Continent in the Tenth and Eleventh Centuries* (Oxford, 1992)

Orchard, A., 'Crying Wolf: Oral Style and the "Sermones Lupi"', *ASE* 21 (1992), pp. 239–64

Ottosen, K., 'Liturgy as a Theological Place: Possibilities and Limitations in Interpreting Liturgical Texts as Seen for Instance in the Office for the Dead', in E. L. Lillie and N. H. Petersen (eds), *Liturgy and the Arts in the Middle Ages* (Copenhagen, 1996), pp. 168–80

Owen, O., 'The Strange Beast that is the English Urnes Style', in Graham-Campbell, *Vikings and the Danelaw*, pp. 203–22

—— and M. Dalland, *Scar: A Viking Boat Burial on Sanday, Orkney* (East Linton, 1999)

Owen-Crocker, G., *The Four Funerals in Beowulf* (Manchester, 2000)

Pader, E.-J., *Symbolism, Social Relations and the Interpretation of Mortuary Remains*, BAR Supplementary Series 130 (Oxford, 1982)

Page, R. I., 'Old English Liturgical Rubrics in Corpus Christi College, Cambridge, MSS 422', *Anglia* 96 (1978), pp. 149–58

—— 'Anglo-Saxon Runes and Magic', in D. Parsons (ed.), *Runes and Runic Inscriptions: Collected Essays on Anglo-Saxon and Viking Runes* (Woodbridge, 1995), pp. 105–26

—— *An Introduction to English Runes* (2nd edn, Woodbridge, 1999)

Parker, E., 'The Gift of the Cross in the New Minster *Liber Vitae*', in E. Sears and T. K. Thomas (eds), *Reading Medieval Images: The Art Historian and the Object* (Michigan, 2002), pp. 177–86

Paroli, T. (ed.), *Poetry in the Scandinavian Middle Ages* (Spoleto, 1990)

Parsons, D. (ed.), *Tenth Century Studies: Essays in Commemoration of the Millennium of the Council of Winchester* (London, 1975)

—— (ed.), *Stone: Quarrying and Building in England AD 43–1525* (Chichester, 1990)

—— (ed.), *Runes and Runic Inscriptions: Collected Essays on Anglo-Saxon and Viking Runes* (Woodbridge, 1995)

Pasternack, C., 'Anonymous Polyphony and "The Wanderer's" textuality', *ASE* 20 (Cambridge, 1991), pp. 99–122

Paxton, F., *Christianizing Death: The Creation of a Ritual Process in Early Medieval Europe* (New York, 1990)

Pearce, S. M. (ed.), *The Early Church in Western Britain and Ireland*, BAR British Series 102 (Oxford, 1982)

Peters, E. (ed.), *Heresy and Authority in Medieval Europe* (London, 1980)

Pfaff, R. (ed.), *The Liturgical Books of Anglo-Saxon England*, Old English Newsletter Subsidia 23 (1995)

Ploss, E., *Siegfried-Sigurd, der Drachen-Kämpfer* (Köln, 1966)

Pluskowski, A. (ed.), *Early Medieval Religion*, Archaeological Review from Cambridge 17:2 (2000)

Pohl, W., and H. Reimitz, *Strategies of Distinction: The Construction of Ethnic Communities, 300–800* (Leiden, 1998)

Priebsch, R., 'The Chief Sources of Some Anglo-Saxon Homilies', *Otia Merseiana* 1 (1899), pp. 129–47

Rahtz, P., and L. Watts, 'Kirkdale Anglo-Saxon Minster', *Current Archaeology* 155 (December 1997), pp. 419–22

Raw, B., *The Art and Background of Old English Poetry* (London, 1978)

Raynes, E., 'MS Boulogne-sur-Mer 63 and Ælfric', *Medium Ævum* 26 (1957), pp. 65–73

Renoir, A., 'A Reading Context for *The Wife's Lament*', in L. E. Nicholson and D. W. Frese (eds), *Anglo-Saxon Poetry: Essays in Appreciation* (Notre Dame and London, 1975), pp. 224–41

Reynolds, A., 'Anglo-Saxon Law in the Landscape: An Archaeological Study of the Old English Judicial System', unpublished Ph.D. thesis (University of London, 1999)

—— *Later Anglo-Saxon England: Life and Landscape* (Stroud, 1999)

—— 'Avebury: A Late Saxon *Burh*?', *Antiquity* 75 (2001), pp. 29–30

—— 'Burials, Boundaries and Charters', in Lucy and Reynolds, *Burial in Early Medieval England and Wales*, pp. 171–94

Reynolds, S., *Kingdoms and Communities in Western Europe, 900–1300* (Oxford, 1984)

Richards, J. D., 'Cottam: An Anglo-Scandinavian Settlement on the Yorkshire Wolds', *Archaeological Journal* 156 (1999), pp. 1–111

—— 'Boundaries and Cult Centres: Viking Burial in Derbyshire', in Graham-Campbell, *Vikings and the Danelaw*, pp. 97–104

—— 'Pagans and Christians at a Frontier: Viking Burial in the Danelaw', in Carver, *Cross Goes North*, pp. 383–95

—— *et al*, 'The Viking Barrow Cemetery at Heath Wood, Ingleby, Derbyshire', *Medieval Archaeology* 39 (1995), pp. 1–50

Robinson, P. R., and R. Zim, *On the Making of Books: Medieval Manuscripts, Their Scribes and Readers* (Aldershot, 1997)

Rodwell, W., and K. Rodwell, 'Excavations at Rivenhall Church, Essex. Interim Report', *Antiquaries Journal* 53 (1973), pp. 219–31

Rodwell, W., and K. Rodwell, 'St Peter's Church, Barton on Humber: Excavation and Critical Study, 1978–81', *Antiquaries Journal* 62 (1982), pp. 283–315

Roesdahl, E., *Viking-Age Denmark* (London, 1982)

Rollason, D., *Saints and Relics in Anglo-Saxon England* (Leicester, 1989)

Rosenwein, B. H., *To Be the Neighbour of St Peter: The Social Meaning of Cluny's Property, 909–1049* (New York, 1989)

—— *Negotiating Space: Power, Restraint, and Privileges of Immunity in Early Medieval Europe* (Manchester, 1999)

Rosser, G., 'The Anglo-Saxon Gilds', in J. Blair (ed.) *Minsters and Parish Churches: The Local Church in Transition 950–1200*, Oxford University Committee for Archaeology: Monograph 17 (Oxford, 1988), pp. 31–4

—— 'The Cure of Souls in English Towns before 1000', in J. Blair and R. Sharpe (eds), *Pastoral Care before the Parish* (Leicester, 1992), pp. 267–84

Routh, R. E., 'A Corpus of the Pre-Conquest Carved Stones of Derbyshire', *Archaeological Journal* 94 (1937), pp. 1–42

Rowell, G., *The Liturgy of Christian Burial* (London, 1977)

Rubin, M., 'Religious Culture in Town and Country: Reflections on a Great Divide', in D. Abulafia (ed.), *Church and City, 1000–1500: Essays in Honour of Christopher Brooke* (Cambridge, 1992), pp. 3–22

Rubin, S., *Medieval English Medicine* (New York, 1974)

Rumble, A. (ed.), *The Reign of Cnut, King of England, Denmark and Norway* (Leicester, 1994)

Sawyer, B., *The Viking-Age Rune-Stones* (Oxford, 2000)

Sawyer, P., *Kings and Vikings: Scandinavia and Europe AD 700–1100* (London, 1982)

—— *Domesday Book: A Reassessment* (London, 1985)

—— *Anglo-Saxon Lincolnshire* (Lincoln, 1998)

—— and B. Sawyer, *Medieval Scandinavia: From Conversion to Reformation circa 800–1500* (Minneapolis, 1993)

Schapiro, M., 'The Image of the Disappearing Christ: The Ascension in English Art around the Year 1000', *Gazette des Beaux-Arts* 23 (1943), pp. 135–52

Schmidt, G. D., *The Iconography of the Mouth of Hell, Eighth-Century Britain to the Fifteenth Century* (London, 1995)

Schofield, J. *et al.* (eds), *Recent Archaeological Research in English Towns* (London, 1981)

Schreiter, R. J., *Constructing Local Theologies* (London, 1985)

Scragg, D. G., 'The Compilation of the Vercelli Book', *ASE* 2 (1973), pp. 189–207

—— (ed.), *Ælfric's Lives of Canonised Popes*, Old English Newsletter Subsidia 30 (Michigan, 2001)

—— and P. E. Szarmach (eds), *The Editing of Old English* (Cambridge, 1994)

Scull, C., 'Burials at Emporia in England', in D. Hill and R. Cowie, *Wics: The Early Medieval Trading Centres of Northern Europe* (Sheffield, 2001), pp. 67–74

Sears, E., and T. K. Thomas (eds), *Reading Medieval Images: The Art Historian and the Object* (Michigan, 2002)

Semple, S., 'A Fear of the Past: The Place of the Prehistoric Burial Mound in the Ideology of Middle and Later Anglo-Saxon England', *World Archaeology* 30:1 (1998), pp. 109–26

Shetelig, H., 'Ship-Burials at Kiloran Bay, Colonsay, Scotland', *Saga-Book* 5 (1906–7), pp. 172–4

Shoesmith, R., *Excavations at Castle Green, Hereford*, CBA Research Report 36 (London, 1980)

Sicard, D., *La Liturgie de la mort dans l'église latine des origines à la réforme carolingienne* (Munster, 1978)

Sidebottom, P. C., 'Schools of Anglo-Saxon Stone Sculpture in the North Midlands', unpublished Ph.D. thesis (University of Sheffield, 1994)

Slott, H. (ed.), *Nordisk kollokvium II: I. Latinsk liturgiforskning. 12–13 Maj 1972*

Smyth, A., *Scandinavian Kings in the British Isles, 850–80* (Oxford, 1977)

—— 'The Anglo-Saxon Chronicle: Questioning Old English History and Historians', *The Historian*, Spring 1996, pp. 2–7

Speake, G., *Anglo-Saxon Animal Art and Its Germanic Background* (Oxford, 1980)

Spearman, R. M., and J. Higgitt, *The Age of Migrating Ideas: Early Medieval Art in Northern Britain and Ireland* (Stroud, 1993)

Stafford, P., *Queens, Concubines and Dowagers: The King's Wife in the Early Middle Ages* (London, 1983)

—— *The East Midlands in the Early Middle Ages* (Leicester, 1985)

—— *Unification and Conquest: A Political and Social History of England in the Tenth and Eleventh Centuries* (London, 1989)

Stancliffe, C., 'Kings who Opted Out', in P. Wormald *et al.* (eds), *Ideal and Reality in Frankish and Anglo-Saxon Society* (Oxford, 1983), pp. 154–76

—— and E. Cambridge (eds), *Oswald: Northumbrian King to European Saint* (Stamford, 1995)

Stanley, E. G. (ed.), *Continuations and Beginnings: Studies in Old English Literature* (London, 1966)

—— 'The Judgement of the Damned', in M. Lapidge and H. Gneuss, *Learning and Literature in Anglo-Saxon England* (Cambridge, 1985), pp. 363–91

Stenton, F., *Anglo-Saxon England* (3rd edn, Oxford, 1971)

Stevenson, W. H., 'Yorkshire Surveys and Other Documents of the Eleventh Century in the York Gospels', *EHR* 27 (1912), pp. 1–25

Stocker, D., 'Monuments and Merchants: Irregularities in the Distribution of Stone Sculpture in Lincolnshire and Yorkshire in the Tenth Century', in Hadley and Richards, *Cultures in Contact*, pp. 179–212

—— and P. Everson, 'Rubbish Recycled: A Study of the Re-use of Stone in Lincolnshire', in D. Parsons (ed.), *Stone: Quarrying and Building in England AD 43–1525* (Chichester, 1990), pp. 83–101

Stone, L., *The Family, Sex and Marriage in England 1500–1800* (London, 1977)

Swan, M., and E. Treharne (eds), *Rewriting Old English in the Twelfth Century*, CSASE 30 (Cambridge, 2000)

Swenson, K., 'Death Appropriated in *The Fates of Men*', *Studies in Philology* 88 (1991), pp. 123–39

Symons, T., 'Regularis Concordia: History and Derivation', in D. Parsons (ed.) *Tenth Century Studies: Essays in Commemoration of the Millennium of the Council of Winchester* (London, 1975), pp. 37–59

Szarmach, P., 'The Vercelli Homilies: Style and Structure', in P. Szarmach and B. Huppé (eds), *The Old English Homily and Its Backgrounds* (New York, 1978), pp. 241–67

—— (ed.), *Vercelli Homilies IX–XXIII* (Toronto, 1981)

—— (ed.), *Old English Prose: Basic Readings* (New York and London, 2000)

—— and B. Huppé (eds), *The Old English Homily and Its Backgrounds* (New York, 1978)

Talbot Rice, D., *English Art, 871–1100* (Oxford, 1952)

Taylor, H. M., 'Repton Reconsidered: A Study in Structural Criticism', in P. Clemoes and K. Hughes (eds), *England before the Conquest* (Cambridge, 1971), pp. 351–90

—— and J. Taylor, *Anglo-Saxon Architecture* (Cambridge, 1965)

Temple, E., *Anglo-Saxon Manuscripts, 900–1066* (London, 1976)

Teresi, L., 'Mnemonic Transmission of Old English Texts in the Post-Conquest Period', in M. Swan and E. Treharne (eds), *Rewriting Old English in the Twelfth Century* CSASE 30 (Cambridge, 2000), pp. 98–116

Thacker, A., 'Chester and Gloucester: Early Ecclesiastical Organisation in Two Mercian Burhs', *Northern History*, XVIII (1982), pp. 199–211

—— 'Kings, Saints and Monasteries in Pre-Viking Mercia', *Midland History* 10 (1985), pp. 1–25

—— '*Membra Disjecta*: The Division of the Body and the Diffusion of the Cult', in C. Stancliffe and E. Cambridge (eds), *Oswald: Northumbrian King to European Saint* (Stamford, 1995), pp. 97–127

Thomas, K., *Religion and the Decline of Magic* (London, 1971)

Thompson, F. H. (ed.), *Studies in Medieval Sculpture* (London, 1983)

Thompson, V., 'Kingship-in-Death in the Bayeux Tapestry', *Reading Medieval Studies* 25 (1999), pp. 107–21.

—— 'Women, Power and Protection in Tenth and Eleventh Century England', in N. Menuge (ed.), *Medieval Women and the Law* (Woodbridge, 2000), pp. 1–18

—— 'The Understanding of Death in England from *c.* 850 to *c.* 1100', unpublished Ph.D. thesis (University of York, 2000)

—— 'Constructing Salvation: A Penitential and Homiletic Context for late Anglo-Saxon

Burial Practice', in Lucy and Reynolds, *Burial in Early Medieval England and Wales*, pp. 229–40

—— 'Memory, Salvation and Ambiguity: A Consideration of Some Anglo-Scandinavian Grave-Stones from York', in H. Williams (ed.), *Archaeologies of Remembrance: Death and Memory in Past Societies* (New York, 2003), pp. 215–26

Tolkien, J. R. R., 'Beowulf: The Monsters and the Critics', Sir Israel Gollancz Memorial Lecture 1936 (London, 1971, reprinted from *The Proceedings of the British Academy* 22)

Townend, M., 'Viking Age England as a Bilingual Society', in Hadley and Richards, *Cultures in Contact*, pp. 89–105

—— *Language and History in Viking Age England: Linguistic Relationships between Speakers of Old Norse and Old English* (Turnhout, 2002)

Treffort, C., *L'Église carolingienne et la mort* (Lyon, 1996)

Tristram, H. L. C., 'Stock Descriptions of Heaven and Hell in Old English Prose and Poetry', *NM* 79 (1978), pp. 102–13

Trumbower, J. A., *Rescue for the Dead: The Posthumous Salvation of Non-Christians in Early Christianity* (Oxford, 2001)

Turner, S., 'Making a Christian Landscape: Early Medieval Cornwall', in Carver, *Cross Goes North*, pp. 171–94

Turner, V., *The Ritual Process: Structure and Anti-Structure* (London, 1969)

Urbañczyk, P., 'Christianisation of Early Medieval Societies: An Anthropological Perspective', in B. Crawford (ed.), *Conversion and Christianity in the North Sea World* (St Andrews, 1998), pp. 129–33

Ureland, P., and G. Broderick (eds), *Language Contact in the British Isles* (Tübingen, 1991)

Verkerk, D. H., 'Pilgrimage *ad Limina Apostolorum* in Rome: Irish Crosses and Early Christian Sarcophagi', in C. Hourihane (ed.), *From Ireland Coming: Irish Art from the Early Christian to the Late Gothic Period and Its European Context* (Princeton, 2001), pp. 9–26

Wainwright, F. T., 'The Chronology of the "Mercian Register"', *English Historical Review* 60 (1945), pp. 385–92

—— 'Æthelflæd, Lady of the Mercians', in H. P. R. Finberg (ed.), *Scandinavian England: Collected Papers by F. T. Wainwright* (Chichester, 1975), pp. 305–24

Walton, P., *Textiles, Cordage and Raw Fibre from 16–22 Coppergate* (London, 1989)

Ward-Perkins, J. B., 'The Shrine of St Peter and Its Twelve Spiral Columns', *Journal of Roman Studies* 42 (1952), pp. 21–33

Webster, L., 'The Iconographic Programme of the Franks Casket', in J. Hawkes and S. Mills (eds), *Northumbria's Golden Age*, pp. 229–30

—— 'Stylistic Aspects of the Franks Casket', in R. T. Farrell (ed), *The Vikings* (London, 1982), pp. 20–31

Wenham, L. P. *et al.*, *St Mary Bishophill Junior and St Mary Castlegate* (London, 1987)

West, J., 'A Carved Slab Fragment from St Oswald's Priory, Gloucester', in F. H. Thompson (ed.), *Studies in Medieval Sculpture* (London, 1983), pp. 41–53

White, W., *The Cemetery of St Nicholas Shambles* (London, 1988)

Whitelock, D., 'The Prose of Alfred's Reign', in E. G. Stanley (ed.), *Continuations and Beginnings: Studies in Old English Literature* (London, 1966), pp. 67–103

Wicker, N., 'The Scandinavian Narrative Styles in Response to Christian and Mediterranean Narrative Art', in Carver, *Cross Goes North*, pp. 531–50

Wilcox, J., 'The Wolf on Shepherds: Wulfstan, Bishops, and the Context of the *Sermo Lupi ad Anglos*', in P. Szarmach, *Basic Readings in Old English Prose*, pp. 395–418

Williams, H. (ed.), *Archaeologies of Remembrance: Death and Memory in Past Societies* (New York, 2003)

Williams, J., 'A Review of Some Aspects of Late Saxon Urban Origins and Development', in M. Faull (ed.), *Studies in Late Anglo-Saxon Settlement* (Oxford, 1984), pp. 25–34

Wilson, D. M., *Anglo-Saxon Ornamental Metalwork 700–1100 in the British Museum* (London, 1964)

—— *Anglo-Saxon Art from the Seventh Century to the Norman Conquest* (London, 1984)

Wood, I., and N. Lund (eds), *People and Places in Northern Europe, 500–1600* (Woodbridge, 1991)

Wormald, P., 'Viking Studies: Whence and Whither?', in R. T. Farrell (ed.), *The Vikings* (London, 1982), pp. 128–53

—— *How Do We Know So Much about Anglo-Saxon Deerhurst?*, Deerhurst Lecture 1991 (Friends of Deerhurst Church, 1992)

—— *The Making of English Law: King Alfred to the Twelfth Century; Volume I, Legislation and its Limits* (Oxford, 1999)

—— *Legal Culture in the Early Medieval West* (London, 1999)

—— *et al.* (eds), *Ideal and Reality in Frankish and Anglo-Saxon Society* (Oxford, 1983)

Wrenn, C. L., *A Study of Old English Literature* (London, 1967)

Wright, C. D., *The Irish Tradition in Old English Literature* CSASE 6 (Cambridge, 1993)

Yorke, B. (ed.), *Bishop Æthelwold, His Career and Influence* (Woodbridge, 1988)

—— 'Anglo-Saxon Royal Burial: The Documentary Evidence', in T. Dickinson and E. James (eds), *Death and Burial*, pp. 41–6

Young, B. K., 'Merovingian Funeral Rites and the Evolution of Christianity: A Study in the Historical Interpretation of Archaeological Material', unpublished Ph.D. thesis (University of Pennsylvania, 1975)

Zarnecki, G., 'The Newent Funerary Tablet', *Transactions of the Bristol and Gloucester Archaeological Society* 72 (1953), pp. 49–55

Index

Anglo-Saxon Studies

DATE DUE

NN May12/16			
SEP 3./16			